FORESIGHT 2030:
CONVERSATIONS ABOUT THE DECADE AHEAD

Douglas S. Griffen

Foresight 2030: Conversations About The Decade Ahead
© 2021 Douglas S. Griffen

ISBN 978-0-578-31014-5

Book design and editing by Dee Dees
deedees44@hotmail.com

Book URL: www.foresight2030.info

Published by:
Advanced Strategy Center
Scottsdale, Arizona 85255

First Edition printed December 2021
V1.5.1 revised Summer 2023

Cover design by Ismail Derghal and 99Designs Process
smail.derghal@gmail.com
Icons used with permission of Flaticon
www.flaticon.com

Printed in the United States of America

PRAISE FOR THE FORESIGHT 2030 PROJECT

For over 30 years it has been my privilege to partner with Doug and his *Advanced Strategy Lab* to find the insight and foresight to guide the world's most influential brands, leaders, organizations and issues. How exciting and timely to apply all that experience and power to help leaders navigate the most challenging decade we will face. *Foresight 2030: Conversations About The Decade Ahead* is the pinnacle gift to tomorrow's thinkers, influencers and leaders from a rare talent at the pinnacle of a remarkable life. With all my heart, thank you Doug Griffen.
—*Dee Allsop, Managing Partner and CEO, Heart+Mind Strategies*

We spend so much time looking at the past—analyzing performance, watching metrics, researching what's happened before. The Foresight 2030 Project is a unique opportunity to explore the future, in a community of varied and engaged professionals in unique positions to see the trends that are coming, and to share their perspective about those trends. I found the whole experience engaging, thought-provoking and a refreshing shift from the work I do in the trenches every day. Well worth the time and I've gained some new ideas and perspectives as a result. Doug and his team are consummate professionals and their platform is a wonderful way to participate with others from across the country and the globe. I can't wait to participate again!
—*Susan Baier, Founder and 'Head Honcho' at the Audience Audit Agency*

The Foresight 2030 Project is an innovative, thoughtful way of looking into the future to gain a sense of what topics we are facing as a society. A diverse and important range of voices were included in this project, which I believe ensures we are seeing the full landscape and can better prepare for the challenges and opportunities that are most significant to us over the next decade. Doug is a thought leader and facilitator who understands how to elicit genuine insights in a deliberate and engaging way, and I'm very much looking forward to seeing what Doug has planned next!
—*Lauren Brown, Chief of Staff, ASU Foundation for a New American University (Arizona State University)*

Hindsight. That's the easy part. There are many media stars, looking omnipotent and making a fortune, taking chip shots at national leaders as a result of *hindsight*. Then there's *foresight*. Doug Griffen combines the alchemy of his research techniques with his incredible personal in-

III

teractive skills to draw out opinions and predictions from his intervie-wees. The result is *Foresight 2030*. What's the point of reading a book when you know how it's going to end? *Foresight 2030* drives us into the future with thought-provoking predictions that may change how you manage your life for the next decade.
—*Greg Giczi, President and General Manager, WNIT Center for Public Media (PBS)*

Foresight 2030 is an important book that provides a window into what are expected to be the most important and influential issues driving the next decade, in the USA and in the world as a whole. It is the first book that takes a meaningful and studied look at how this important and con-sequential decade will evolve. It is also a fascinating book, made espe-cially so through the use of the Advanced Strategy Lab approach, im-plemented by the impeccable facilitation skills of the book's author, Dou-glas Griffen. I've known and worked with Doug Griffen for almost 30 years and have found him to be one of the most thoughtful, creative and inspirational leaders I have worked with. Doug's idea, a monthly gather-ing of thought leaders to discuss issues of the day and the future, all ac-complished virtually, was typical Doug's "ahead of the curve" thinking. *Foresight 2030* is a culmination of Doug's learnings over the years, cou-pled with the input from the monthly panel of thought leaders. The book is an "easy read" on a complex set of issues, and is sure to be read and re-read as the decade progresses. Kudos to Doug for a truly inspired and inspirational project and book.
—*James J. Granger Sr., Retired CEO, Wirthlin Worldwide*

Foresight 2030 is a project that—simply put—meets the moment. At a critical juncture for our country, Doug has assembled a top-notch group of thought leaders to share their insights for the consequential decade ahead. The resulting analysis is deeply compelling. But what makes this book truly stand out is Doug's distinct, often humorous voice—a fore-telling of the future interwoven with the author's rich professional and life experience. Quite a read!
—*Scott F. Griffen, Deputy Director, The International Press Institute (Vienna, Austria)*

Firmly believing the future is ours to create stokes my enthusiasm for the Foresight 2030 Project, and I delighted in being able to have participated in many of the sessions. Combine that with multiple interesting collabora-tions with Doug over two decades and I'm confident his vision of tomor-row will be illuminating, eerily prescient and an enjoyable must read.
—*Sammy Papert, President, Wormhole Media Consultancy*

IV

This book is a prime example of Doug Griffen's unique skill at helping groups of smart people frame and prioritize big issues. As so many of us strain to understand the forces that will shape the next decade, we now have an important assist with this incisive picture of the most likely developments combined with collectively-prioritized ideas to help us work on ways to encourage the more positive outcomes.

—*Dave Richardson, Founding Partner, Artemis Strategy Group*

Doug Griffen has cracked the code in identifying the factors that will shape our world in the decade to come. Whether you are an optimist or a pessimist about our shared future, this book outlines the key issues that need to be addressed in order to create the better world that we all yearn for. I've trusted Doug and turned to the Advanced Strategy Lab as an invaluable tool for tapping into the hearts and minds of influential stakeholders for decades—it's never failed to reveal deep insights that have transformed the way leaders view their role and potential for impact in the world. This book is sure to become an invaluable resource as you set a course for the decade ahead.

—*Haley Rushing, Chief "Purposologist" at The Purpose Institute and co-author of "It's Not What You Sell, It's What You Stand For."*

Some people wish there was a crystal ball to see the future. *Foresight 2030* is as close to a crystal ball as we may get. This book offers insight and perspective on issues and opportunities looking at the next decade. The research and narrative that Doug Griffen presents create a roadmap for navigating uncertainty. This book is both a realistic and optimistic look at ways for business and community leaders to ramp up for the future.

—*Mark Stanton, President and CEO, Scottsdale Area Chamber of Commerce*

For Roland and all of our dogs—past, present and future. A genuine "Griff" and a beloved member of the Griff Squad. He reminded us of the simple pleasure of chasing a lizard all day with no particular need to catch. For that would only serve to stop the play on a long and joyful sunny day. God Bless.

DEDICATION AND THANKS

Where to begin. We'll start with the most important thanks—to that of the *Griff Squad*. That's my direct family—wife Janet, sons Scott, Jack and Sam, and daughter Betsy. Not only for their support and encouragement on the writing of the book, but for the role they played *in the book* as many times I reference them and our collective activities. Janet is the *Squad Leader* and has done such an important job of raising four outstanding and *very different* children who are all young adults now and serve as my personal *millennial focus group* for research. I am proud and gratified that I can still travel, play *life sports* and debate the decade ahead with all of them.

Early Griff Squad 2007 in Sundance, Utah:
Doug, Scott, Janet, Sam, Jack and Betsy

Next, my thanks to my two informal Foresight 2030 Project Advisors: James J. Granger, Sr., and my oldest son, Scott Griffen. I first met Jim in Washington, DC, in 1997 when he was CEO of Wirthlin Worldwide. He is also a *serious* baseball aficionado and unabashed Yankees fan. I share in the former, not the latter, and remind him often of the outcome of the 2001 World Series. Jim seemed to understand how important the timing of this project was for the country and was a great source of additional Foresighters and personal encouragement. Scott is a Yale graduate, has lived in Vienna, Austria, for over 10 years and is the Deputy Director of the International Press Institute. He provided a global perspective and is a talented journalist and writer. He provided important insight on strategy and timing for our various Foresight sessions. Interestingly, I introduced Scott to Jim on a trip we took to visit Washington, D.C., in

1998 when Scott was just 10 years old. *Just wanted the two advisors to get an early start on the project.*

My older brother Pete had a lot of time on his hands in 2020 as he opted to take a hiatus from his work until the vaccine rollout made it safe again. He was my dedicated *chapter reader* and my first point of review and participated in all 10 Foresight sessions. He resides in Sandy, Utah, and would call me the day after I sent him a chapter and give me five minutes of feedback on the chapter and then debate the topics for the next 90 minutes. We have debated politics on ski chairlifts for over 25 years. *Why stop now?*

In the middle of the project, as I was seriously wondering how I would ever find a way to publish the book once it was written, I noticed the name *Dee Dees* on a book that chronicled the adventures of Jerry Foster, a pioneering news helicopter pilot in Arizona who was the personal helicopter pilot for Barry Goldwater. I met Jerry at a book signing in Scottsdale and genuinely enjoyed the book and the Arizona history. Dee was his editor and is a talented historian and author in her own right. I tracked her down while she was on a two-month RV trip (a genuine nomad) across the country and convinced her to take on the project. I am deeply grateful for her editing expertise and moving me forward in the Amazon KDP technology and process.

My Advanced Strategy Lab process has used a number of different collaborative technologies over the past 25 years, including GroupSystems that I reference in my Prologue. Over the past 10 years I have been using the WIQ technology that is owned by Patricia Caporaso, who now resides in Prince Edward Island with her husband Alan Hilburg. My thanks to Patricia for her support on the platform. I will note that the *quid pro quo* on this project was my facilitation of strategic planning sessions for the PEI Music Festival, the PEI Nature Conservancy and the PEI Rowing Club. I feel like I should get a key to the City!

During the last nearly 20 years, and for all of our Foresight sessions, my primary project support has been in the form of Carl Lundblad, who manages much of the logistics of the sessions, runs the help desk, assists with real-time summaries and handles post-session documentation. He is now residing in Prescott, Arizona, but is nearly always on the end of the phone line and internet connection when we are conducting sessions. We have traveled the country together for our in-person sessions and set up countless laptops. We are always grateful to be back in Arizona at the end of trip. It is where our roots are. *Thank you Carl for all of the support.*

Author Griffen (left) and Lundblad. Cowboy Up!

In chapter 9, States as Brands, we shared five "Featured Foresights" from prominent Arizona leaders. My thanks to Don Henninger, Win Holden, John Little, Sandra Watson and Steve Zylstra for their views on Arizona in the decade ahead.

A special thanks to the Heart+Mind Strategies team that allowed us to field a set of specific questions in their Pulse survey in February, 2021. The questions went to 1001 Americans and gave us important validation and insights, many of which are covered in Chapter 12. My *co-author* of that same chapter 12, Maury Giles, is the Chief Growth Officer at the company, and we have been collaborating together on technology, process and topics for 25 years. I am deeply grateful for his work on chapter 12 and analysis of how 2020 affected American values.

And, so importantly, I thank the 121 Foresighters who joined us during the course of 2020/2021 on our 10 facilitated sessions. They are the real authors of this book and I am pleased to list them in the appendix at the end of the book. Some I had known for years, some I met as part of the journey of the sessions. *Thank you, Foresighters,* for sharing your expertise and your opinions.

Finally, I thank all of you as readers who are taking the time to review our work and consider the decade ahead. These are topics that matter and will influence all of our lives. The decade ahead is a *shared journey.* Thank you all for coming along.

TABLE OF CONTENTS

FOREWORD

Or Forward. *Always the best direction to go, is it not?*

This book is about looking forward. It's about the future and the decade ahead and how that decade will influence you and me and our families, this country and even the greater globe. It's a simple premise: this decade ahead—now through the end of 2029—may be the most consequential decade of our lives.

Bold talk from the author, wouldn't you say? Indeed I do say. Look, on one hand we have technology that is creating a new level of connection, freedom and personal knowledge. We have great medical advances in healthcare and disease prevention. We are moving to electric vehicles (EV) and more sustainable energy sources. Remote work is on the rise, we can live where we want and still have meaningful jobs and careers. The 4th Industrial Revolution and the Internet of Things promise to create new process automation and apply Artificial Intelligence (AI) against some of the most challenging problems we face. And commercial space travel may be just around the corner. *Beam me aboard, Scotty.*

And on the other hand. America has never been more divided. The technology we value so much is also creating a new level of *disinformation* via social media and hate groups. There is a wealth divide, a digital divide and a lack of access for many to the fundamentals of education, healthcare and housing. We are struggling with social equality and the basic idea that all lives matter. Our politics are polarizing and partisan. We ignore climate change and put our next generation at risk. And just try having a civil discussion around the Thanksgiving dinner table.

Strap on a seat belt, we are in for quite a ride this decade.

Whether you are a boomer like me, a millennial like my kids or a rising Gen Z member, this decade ahead matters. Being informed about what will influence the decade ahead matters. Mapping out your personal strategy and goals for the decade ahead matters. Being engaged in the issues, engaging in civil discourse and *making a difference* all matter. The confluence of the challenges we are looking at, along with the incredible opportunity for the decade ahead, is why I wrote this book. We have an *adventure* ahead of us—a journey to 2030.

So, first of all, thank you for picking up this book. Whether you bought a copy from Amazon, found one in a book store, borrowed one from a friend or family member, accessed it via Kindle, received one from me in the mail or *borrowed a copy from the front seat of my Jeep* (I keep a few spares with me at all times), I am delighted that you have joined me for a reflection on the future and the journey ahead for this decade.

But you are not just joining *me* on this reflection. You are joining a set of *Foresighters* I gathered in 2020/2021 via a series of digital sessions on critical topics. Ten sessions with an average of 40 participants in each session to explore everything from the future of work, technology and media, to the American Divide, a rethinking of education, the American Lifestyle and how a global pandemic may have shifted our values as Americans.

This is not meant to be a fast read. It's not a drive-by. It is designed to slow you down, reflect on where you are personally, and where we are collectively as a country, and consider the choices and influences ahead. Reflection is like an analog balance in this digital world. We are looking at a mosaic of issues in the decade ahead. Do you see the decade ahead as an optimist or as a pessimist? Are we just getting started, or is the sky is falling? Things will just happen as they happen, or perhaps *there is a puzzle to the pieces?*

So, in this foreword about the future, I wanted to give you some guidance about how to read this book to gain the full value and nuance about the topics, the structure of the 10 Foresight-based chapters and how they might elicit a level of reflection and insight on your part:

May I recommend a cold Tecate to get started.

Well, I will leave the beverage of choice to you, be it a good cup of coffee in the morning or an evening libation. But the first recommendation is: *read while relaxed*. A quiet setting. A table in the back yard, a park bench, a breakfast counter (one of my favorites), on a train ride, or even throw the book in your pack and read a chapter while resting after a good hike or bike. If you don't have enough quiet time in your life, *make some more*. It's one of the themes in the book; you'll catch that in the prologue and it carries through to the epilogue.

Next, and especially for chapters 2-11 that are based on the 10 Foresight sessions, put some time between each chapter. What's your take on the topic? How did you react to the conversation from our Foresighters? What did you think about on what might influence this topic in the decade ahead? Will the topic influence your life in the decade ahead? Did you agree with *anything* I had to say about the topic? Did you at least laugh a little along the way? (We strive to make this a little whimsical as well. I am 65 as I write this foreword and am entitled to *whim at will.)*

You will find it to be a personal journey as well. I hope that adds context and you get to know me a little along the way. *We all need to get to know each other a little better in the decade ahead.* Yet another theme of the book. Reflect on the people and things that matter to you. Wasn't 2020 itself a bit of a personal reawakening?

A Guided Tour of the Foresight 2030 Book
I do want to give you some sense of the structure of the Foresight chapters, as they follow a common approach. For the book, the prologue and epilogue are personal and reflective, no instruction needed. Chapter 1 sets the stage—it is where I was at the start of the decade and perhaps where we all were: excited about the decade ahead, ready to start the journey, unaware that our lives were about to be completely turned upside down. Unequipped and unprepared for what we had not considered.

Chapters 2-11 are the core of the book, what I had *intended to write about before the onset of a global pandemic.* I just write about them in 2020/2021 from the lens of the pandemic and a year that would reshape the decade in ways I had not imagined. Each of these core 10 chapters are based on a one-hour Foresight session—a digital conversation with anywhere from 30 to 50 people using an advanced collaboration technique that I call the *Advanced Strategy Lab,* which enables people to respond simultaneously and anonymously to a set of questions and assessments that I facilitate. I talk, they type. And man, did they ever type. Powerful responses and statements about America today and into the future. Imagine 50 people talking at the same time and being heard.

For the record, I have been facilitating these Advanced Strategy Lab sessions—in person as well as online—for over 25 years. It's what I do for a living. But I never imagined the level of interest, insight and *raw emotion* that I would get from these 10 sessions that looked at our next 10 years. And it wasn't that I just got this level of input from our Foresighters, it's that I know that *all of you* have just as strong emotion, insight and reaction to the topics. We all think about what's around the corner. We are all Foresighters at heart.

The Foresight chapters, while completely different in content, have somewhat the same flow as you read through the chapter:

- **Lyrics from a song to set the stage:** Now, keep in mind that I am 65 and was influenced by the end of the Sixties and Seventies for high school and college. You may or may not have any clue who *Buffalo Springfield* is, or *Jackson Browne,* or *The Doobie Brothers* or even *Alice Cooper.* But I chose the lyrics purposefully. If you know the song, replay it in your mind. If you don't, Google it (seriously) and listen to it. Don't be in a hurry...

the music from that era (God, I sound old), was part of our social fabric, it was a sound of our generation. It was influential.

- **Historical context for the topic:** Well, mostly historical with a mix of personal journey. As I was writing, I found it immensely useful (and interesting) to research the history of the issue—technology, the civil divide in America, the American Lifestyle, the development of mainstream media and social media. The context helps tell a story of how we got to where we were for that topic in 2020, and helped frame many of our Foresight questions. I hope you learned something in these early parts of the chapters; I always did.

- **Introducing a few of our Foresighters:** I always introduce some of our Foresighters in each chapter—just their words of who they are. I hope it helps you relate to the group for that particular session. They are, in many respects, just a set of average Americans who came together to share insights about the topic. It is *their voices* that really carry this book. It is *their conversations about the decade ahead* that really matter.

- **Selected questions and assessments:** For each session I wrote a specific *session guide* with a series of open-ended questions, assessments and short surveys. The participants did not see this guide ahead of time; they only knew the general topic. They were able to see each other's responses during the session, but all responses were anonymous. I share a couple of sample screen shots at the end of the Foreword.

A note on content. In each chapter I am sharing *selected* questions and a *sampling* of the responses. The transcript from each actual session would be 60-70 pages in length. The goal was to share a relevant set of the questions and responses that helped tell a story about the topic and its influence on the decade ahead. Often, I will add my own insights or conclusions about a certain question or set of responses. You may or may not agree with them, but I hope they are helpful in illuminating the impact of the topic on the future. Most important is what *you* think about the implication of the selected questions and responses.

- **Scenarios for the topic in the decade ahead:** To be honest, I kind of fell into this one in the first Foresight session where I wrote up a set of 20 hypothetical scenarios that might influence the decade ahead and then had participants assess the level of positive impact the scenario would have if it occurred and, also, the likelihood of the scenario occurring. The activity was really well received and I continued it through the remainder of the

4

sessions. This was my opportunity to test some thought leader-ship and ideas about the future. My only adjustment after the first session was to present about a dozen scenarios as opposed to 20. The full set of scenarios from the 10 chapters can be found in the appendix at the end of the book.

- **Five Foresights for the Future:** Towards the end of each chap-ter, I present five "Foresights for the Future" on the topic that rep-resent my assessment of the responses and their implication for the decade ahead. You know the disclaimer here...my book, my foresights. But they are based on a reflection of the input from the Foresighters, so I hope you will take the time to consider these and how they might align with your own views.

- **How the COVID pandemic impacted the topic:** At the end of each Foresight session, we included a question about how the pandemic was influencing or affecting the topic. How did the pandemic affect the future of work? The Presidential election? The American Lifestyle? In every case, not surprisingly, there was a profound impact. 2020 and the pandemic affected our views on nearly everything.

I also, very purposely, include a number of pictures/images along the way. Some are *historical* like the 1968 protests at the Chicago conven-tion (The Whole World is Watching); some are *hysterical* like Lady Bird Johnson (Technology) on the first "Zoom" call, circa 1964. I hope they give you a sense of the real context of some of our topics. Images are powerful. A picture is worth a thousand words. Check your smartphone photos right now. They're a record of your life.

Beyond the Foresighters: A Survey of 1000 Americans (Chapter 12)
Chapter 12 was a planned departure from the set of 10 preceding Fore-sight sessions. Our group size is a little bigger. It is based on quantitative survey polling conducted throughout 2020 and early 2021 where each survey was conducted with *a thousand Americans*. And it was statistically valid based on representation across age groups, political persuasion, geography, ethnicity and gender. "Side A" is written by me, and looks at a set of specific questions on the decade ahead that we added to the Feb-ruary 2021 survey. Quantifying the level of optimism for the decade, the impact of the January 2021 Inauguration, and a set of 15 influences about what might impact the decade ahead.

"Side B" of chapter 12 is written by my friend and colleague Maury Giles, a partner at Heart+Mind Strategies, where they look at how values influ-ence decisions. It is a fascinating look at how American values were impacted in 2020 and early 2021 by the global pandemic, the political divide and the economic downturn. I think you will find it to be a compelling read and an opportunity to reflect on how your own values and emotions were affected.

Afterword: Hindsight is 2020
My "bookend" to this Foreword is the *Afterword* section—written to pause and reflect on the unique impact that 2020 had to the start of this decade. We all need to do this, to really consider how significant 2020 was to America overall and our own individual lives. In the aftermath of disruption comes new opportunity and new choices. That's what the decade ahead will be all about—those *choices* we make as individuals, as families, as a country and as a globe.

The decade ahead. I hope you are looking forward to the journey. And I hope this book will help you think about the significance of this decade and how you will make it your best decade ever. And how we can make it the most consequential for America.

Now crack open that cold Tecate and get started!

Douglas S. Griffen
Author and Optimist
Foresight 2030: Conversations About The Decade Ahead

Screenshots from Advanced Strategy Lab Online Foresight Sessions:

TECHNOLOGY: What Makes You OPTIMISTIC About the Decade Ahead

Agenda Topic: Reflecting Forward

Instructions: Now, let's look ahead. We are here to consider the NEXT TEN YEARS. Now through December 31, 2029. What makes you OPTIMISTIC about the role of technology on decade ahead and how it might positively impact and influence us? (multiple responses)

Filters applied: 0 | New Filter |

Participation : 51/56 fully contributed

No.	Idea	Author
1.	Moving to Mars	ASC, B13
2.	Medical advancement	ASC, B78
3.	Electric vehicles and other technologies will decrease emissions	ASC, B08
4.	Looking forward to better connections	ASC, B104
5.	solutions to disease and	ASC, B53
6.	telemedicine	ASC, B11
7.	continued advancements in all fields including medical	ASC, B27
8.	entertainment avenues could be great. Virtual gaming, concerts etc	ASC, B26
9.	Medical advancements becoming more innovative and hopefully cheaper	ASC, B108
10.	information sharing	ASC, B43
11.	better medical care overall, and particularly in remote areas	ASC, B114
12.	medical research	ASC, B77

Instructions: Now, please assess each of the following factors/issues in terms of how significant you feel they are TODAY in influencing the level of division in America. Use a scale of 1-10 where a '1' means not at all important and a '10' means extremely important:

Select a Results Report

High/Low
Distribution
Range Graph
Avg. & Dev Graph

Filters applied: 0 | New Filter |

Show Results By: | ✔ By Criteria | Composite | Results for: ✔ Group Results | ▣ ▾

Participation : 31/59 contributed

HIGH/LOW REPORT

Rating Criteria: Level of Influence Today on Division

Rank	Idea	High	Low	Std. Dev.	Avg.	Participation Ratio
	Scale: 1 2 3 4 5 6 7 8 9 10					
1.	Trump Presidency	10	5	1.2	9.5	31/31
2.	Media overload/disinformation	10	5	1.5	8.8	31/31
3.	Lack of bipartisan politics	10	4	1.4	8.7	31/31
4.	Level of racism/social injustice	10	5	1.5	8.5	31/31
5.	Political/ideological views	10	3	1.5	8.5	31/31
6.	Handling of pandemic	10	3	1.6	8.4	31/31
7.	Social media influence	10	3	2.1	7.8	31/31
8.	Loss of institutional trust	10	3	2.0	7.7	31/31
9.	Sensationalizing everything	10	4	2.1	7.5	31/31
10.	Economic/wage gap	10	3	2.2	7.5	31/31
11.	Healthcare access/affordability	10	3	2.0	7.3	31/31
12.	Police brutality	10	2	1.9	7.0	31/31
13.	Attitudes towards immigration	10	3	1.6	6.9	31/31
14.	Gun control	10	1	2.1	6.4	31/31
15.	Climate change	10	1	2.5	6.1	31/31

7

PROLOGUE

January 28, 2006
10:00pm
The Corner Bar
Hotel Boulderado
Boulder, Colorado

It's been a good day. A *very good* day.

My friend Luis Solis and I skied Vail today. A superb day, plenty of snow. Good conditions, cold and crisp, but the sun poked through at times. Luis (at the time) was the CEO of GroupSystems, a company based in Broomfield. Luis had invited me up purportedly to talk about hiring me as a consulting advisor to GroupSystems or maybe to even acquire my company, the Advanced Strategy Center. Mostly, I think, Luis was just looking for someone to ski with.

I'm at the counter of the Corner Bar in the Hotel Boulderado. Love the place. The hotel first—a classic historical landmark that opened in 1909. One of those places that, when you walk in the doors, you are immediately in a time machine when the sights and sounds are from a simpler and more authentic era. Oh, and I love the Corner Bar as well. They say it is the locals' best watering hole, likely to become your "new home".

I'll settle for best local watering hole. I signal the bartender for another *Dog's Breath Ale.*

Now Vail, if you had never had the chance to ski it, is one of the premier ski locations in the country. Maybe in the world (just ask any local Vail skier). But I must tell you that there is just one area in Vail that I gravitate to when I ski there. I usually park at Lionshead, work my way over to Mid-Vail, grab a few warm-ups on Whistle Pig, Cappuccino and Christmas, then back up and left onto Timberline catwalk for a nice cruiser on Northwoods. Most of Vail catches the Northwoods Express lift for a return trip.

Luis and I, at my urging, veer off right onto the *little hard to see* Choker Cutoff. Which takes you to the Highline Runout and Chair 10. Before it had the fancy name of the *Highline Express,* it was simply Chair 10. A classic two-seater. Slow and steady, built for a toke and a joke on the way up and just enough time to recover your legs for my favorite run in all of Vail.

Blue Ox. One of those end-of-the-earth places where no one can find you unless you brought them along. There are no other runs to the skier's right as you come down Blue Ox. Just Forest Boundary. Wildlife Habitat. Wilderness. The End-of-the-Earth.

So we skied numerous laps on Blue Ox that day. A 50-yard warm-up from the top of the lift to the trail sign: *Highline* to the left, *Blue Ox* to the right. *"Let's go right, Louie-Louie,"* says I.

"We just went right, Griff," says he. *"Exactly. Feeling good, Luis!"* says I. *"Looking good Billy Ray!"* says he.

To this day, when I ski Vail, I go to ski Blue Ox. It's a throwback, another pleasant time machine to the simpler days. For Luis and I, the two-seater Chair 10 took 14 minutes to head back up the hill for the next lap. Now it is an express six-seater that takes half the time. The Vail Daily News called the new lift, "The Greatest Thing Ever" in a story run on January 7, 2008. Fake News! In the long run, it's not always about getting there faster. I'm not sure I have ever seen more than two people on the ultra-fast Highline Express 10 six-seater anyway. Sometimes the slow, quiet ride is best way to travel.

I glance at my watch: 10:30 p.m. The bartender was sure I was signaling the need for another *Dog's Breath.* I wasn't. I was watching the time for another reason. *I took the additional Dog's Breath anyway.*

I am writing some notes in my spiral binder. It goes with me just about everywhere. I start the day with it with some personal notes on a fresh page. *Always start the day on a clean, fresh page.* If it's a work day I add my priorities for the day. I rarely get them all done; it just makes me feel like I have made some progress if I can mark a few things off. *One step at a time, the journey is the goal.* And it's also where I launch new ideas/projects. Capturing an "aha" moment that might come to me at any time.

This Next Twenty-Five.

I've been working on this one for a while. September 9, 2005, was the "aha" moment. The publisher of the Phoenix Business Journal, Don Henninger, wanted to run a special edition for his 25th anniversary magazine and asked our Center (the Advanced Strategy Center, which I did *not* sell to Luis in Vail a few months later) to help with a special group brainstorming session with 25 "Leaders and Legends" in the Valley to understand the leaders that had the most impact of the last 25 years.

It was an impressive list. Eddie Basha, Karl Eller, Ira Fulton, John Junker, Jerry Colangelo and Ed Beauvais were a few notables on the list. We spent some two hours with our Advanced Strategy Lab with laptops and (you guessed it, GroupSystems software) to brainstorm and reflect on the last 25 years. My role in these group sessions was as the facilitator... keep things moving, make the software easy to navigate, help the group reach consensus on priorities.

And so we ended up with a list of 31 stories and accomplishments that were most significant to Phoenix and the metropolitan Valley over the last 25 years. *Heavy hitters.* They included the development of the Central Arizona Project, the building of the Palo Verde nuclear generating station, the attraction of the Mayo Clinic, the launch of America West Airlines, the Translational Genomics Research Institute (T-Gen), the arrival of Michael Crow at ASU (and he is still there!), the Fiesta Bowl football game and the overall sports impact of Jerry Colangelo (most notably the Phoenix Suns and Arizona Diamondbacks).

The special edition was published on November 11, 2005. And all I could think about was not the last 25 years, but the *next* 25 years. *This Next Twenty-Five.*

What would the next 25 years look like? Who would be the leaders? What would the stories be about? What if you could forecast *now* what it might be like *then?* I am thinking to myself, "You could be the next John Naisbitt!"

I am *so glad* I did not share this revelation with the bartender at the Corner Bar. I am quite sure it would have ended my string of Dog's Breath Ales.

But some of you will remember Naisbitt and his truly groundbreaking book in 1982 called *Megatrends: Ten New Directions Transforming Our Lives.* I was at IBM at the time at the San Jose facility where I was part of a program called the *Data Processing Executive Institute (DPEI).* We were hosting top IT executives (we called it DP at the time...) to look at the industry today (i.e., sell them IBM equipment) but also look at the *future.* I was hooked on the future and I was sure in 1982 that I would write a book someday on the future. *I think it is in one of my spiral binders.*

So, *This Next Twenty-Five.* It could be my attempt to look at the next 25 years for Phoenix. Maybe for Arizona. Maybe for the country...and *then it hit me.* This wasn't about the next twenty-five for Arizona or the USA or the Federation of Planets, this was about *my* next twenty-five years.

I looked at my watch again to confirm the coordinates in the Corner Bar. It was Saturday night, January 28, 2006. Now 11:00pm. In 60 minutes I would turn 50 years old. My book idea had morphed from Arizona's next twenty-five to a personal look at *my* next twenty-five. What if you could outline your life and priorities for the next twenty-five years? And *every year* identify 25 things you want to do/accomplish. To be clear, I am a year ahead of the movie *The Bucket List* but I am on the same wavelength.

Instead of a mid-life crisis, this was a mid-point correction. Surely this could be the best 25 years of my life. And it dawned on me that every day thousands of people turn 50. Why, this is their self-help book! *How to Keep Your Volkswagen Alive* no matter what shape it is in. Or the shape you are in, for that matter.

I was completing my list of 25 things for my first year of *This Next Twenty-Five*. I have never felt so *alive*. A time that many people dread (age 50) and I was *leaning in* with all of my fiber. The glass was way more than half-full. A spigot of ideas and opportunities had been turned on.

Speaking of glass, mine was empty. Pass me one final *Dog's Breath Ale*.

Beyond my initial list of 25 was one realization that would stay with me from that evening at the Corner Bar at Hotel Boulderado. I didn't know where the next twenty-five years would lead me, but I felt that I could maintain my fitness level, my mental acuity, my work passion, my writing passion and my sense of travel and discovery for the next twenty-five years. I might go straight downhill at age 75, but for the next 25 years I was confident about and committed to skiing, biking, swimming, tennis, golf and running. I had no intention (or financial means, as it turns out) of retiring at age 65. I was good for 10 years beyond that and I would stay engaged and vital in my work. And I would stay close to my family. Staying physically fit and mentally sharp, I was convinced, would enable me to have experiences for the next twenty-five that would be irreplaceable.

It's all about attitude.

Well, I never published *This Next Twenty-Five*, but I have lived up to the realization of how I could live the next twenty-five. And so, as I am about to hit 65, that night years ago at the Hotel Boulderado set the stage for *Foresight 2030: Conversations about the Decade Ahead*. It's pretty cool timing. In January of 2031 I will reach that next twenty-five. And we will be able to reflect on that last 10 that we envisioned in this book.

I hope in this decade ahead that you think about what matters to you. That you envision your life and your family and your friends as a slow and wonderful journey. That you find your Blue Ox trail and visit it often. And find that two-seater chairlift that takes a little more time than the high speed alternative.

Author Griffen and friend Luis Solis in Vail, January 28, 2006

CHAPTER 1: Smooth Sailing

Well, it's not far down to paradise, at least it's not for me
And if the wind is right you can sail away and find tranquility
Oh, the canvas can do miracles, just you wait and see…

--Christopher Cross, Sailing (1979)

January 1, 2020
West End, Tortola
British Virgin Islands

This is *definitely* one of those end-of-the-world places where no one can find you.

I feel an extraordinary sense of peace and calm. I am right where I want to be on January 1. This is it—the start of a new decade. And it's not just any decade or any year, this is 2020. It has a great nuance about it—2020 vision, hindsight is 2020. Incredibly symmetrical. I mean, I wasn't around for 1919 and I am quite sure I will miss 2121. Look, the America pop-duo of Zager and Evans took this out to 2525, but it was a bit apocalyptic (*…everything you think, do and say is in the pill you took today*).

I prefer my coffee. I am at Omar's Fusion Café at the Soper's Hole Wharf and Marina in West End, Tortola. Looking out over the water on a perfectly blue sky day. Breakfast is my favorite meal, a quiet table or counter, a good omelet and plenty of coffee. A newspaper to glance at (the real kind, printed) and my spiral notebook for notes and reflections.

Omar's Fusion Café, Soper's Hole

West End, Tortola, BVI

January 1, 2020. I am officially in my seventh decade (born 1956), but this is the decade I have been waiting for. I am going to *forecast* this decade. I am going to look ahead at the influences and implications of this particular decade as I think it will be one for the books. Or at least for my book.

Foresight 2030...it's got a certain ring to it. It's an obvious play on words, reversing the *Hindsight is 2020* adage. But this is a little more intricate. The idea is to use the first year of the decade as a lens to forecast the remainder of the decade. I just have a sense, as I reflect on slow stirring of a new day on the wharf, that we are in for an amazing ride this decade and 2020 will be my vantage point. Make that my *crow's nest*; after all, this is the Caribbean.

Reflecting on Decades

To be clear, there have been profound decades in the past. The Roaring Twenties—a period of economic prosperity with a distinctive cultural edge. So-called first-wave feminism, a rising stock market, jazz in full swing, consumerism with mass production of radios and washing machines (listen while you dry?). Crazy stunts. A black market in liquor. Some called it "The age of permanent prosperity." *Well, it looked good until the stock market crash of 1929*. Again, for the record, I wasn't part of that decade, but I must say it looked like a *damned good time.*

World War II and the 1940s was an extraordinary decade. It saw the "Greatest Generation" of those Americans who had grown up in the Great Depression but then were part of the effort to join allies and win the war effort. Tom Brokaw's book in 1988 popularized the term of *The Greatest Generation* and reflected about the men and women who did not fight or work on the home front for fame or recognition, but because *it was the right thing to do.* My mother and father were part of this generation: Barbara as a WAVE (Women's Auxiliary Volunteer Emergency Services) in the Navy decoding enemy messages in secret rooms in New York City—and an early advantage to her later double-crostics (advanced crossword) talents and dominance in family Scrabble games; Frank was a cadet in the Army at West Point and a flyer. He cracked up a plane on a training mission and was unable to see active duty, but returned to West Point to teach logistics to the other cadets after his graduation in 1943. They were the real deal.

Frank Griffen/Army West Point   *Barbara Griffen/Navy WAVE*

Barbara was interviewed many years after World War II in a book about Arizonans in the military, and she commented on that decade and that period in history:

"We thought it was necessary, we thought it was exciting and we thought it was our day. And it was a matter of times when everybody thought the world was good and we had to get this terrible war over with. We did what we thought was right. I think we are better people to have at least made the effort."

Spot on, Madre. What a different time and sentiment, contrasting to a 2020 that will start with a nation starkly divided on many fronts.

And that decade in the 1940s also saw the start of a new generation, of which I am a card-carrying AARP member: The Boomer Generation. Born between 1946 and 1964 and front-ended by the post-World War II baby boom. It's a big cohort still, with some 71.6 million Americans part

17

of the Boomer legion. They have been the dominant leadership force for decades and will still play a role in this new decade—but they will also be a transition force to a younger generation of leaders.

A Decade of Extraordinary Influence: The Sixties

The first decade, though, that I was really part of, was the *Sixties.* One word that brings up some of the most powerful images and powerful moments in our history. You think we are divided now? The Sixties were a confluence of so many influences. Start with sex, drugs, and rock and roll (why not?). As Wavy Gravy once famously said: "If you can *remember* the Sixties, then you really weren't there."

It was Kennedy and a young generation of hope with challenge to do new things. His speech at Rice University in 1962 created a sense of powerful optimism: "We choose to go to the moon...we choose to go to the moon in this decade and do the other things, not because they are easy, but because they are *hard.*" Just as the Greatest Generation understood the power of purpose, so did Kennedy. And that decade looked really good at the start. But it changed, and I remember the changes, *but I did not understand them.*

I watched a black and white TV with ships in the ocean and blurry images of the island of Cuba in October of 1962. I listened to news updates and watched my parents speaking softly away from us. I saw those ships turn around and everyone seemed to celebrate. *But I did not understand.*

I watched the news on November 22, 1963. It was a *Special Bulletin.* I was seven years old, but I knew that Special Bulletins were not good things. I remember walking out to pick up the newspaper on the front porch of my house in Phoenix, Arizona, the next morning. The Arizona Republic headline: MOURN TO THE WORLD: JFK DEAD. *And I did not understand.*

December 17, 1964. My father is driving to work in the morning and drops my oldest brother off to school. I am called into the Principal's office later that morning. My mother is there. It is quiet. Something is wrong. *Your father is dead.* A single car accident where he smashed into a telephone pole. *And I did not understand.*

1968. A busboy comforts a dying Robert Kennedy on a kitchen floor. Black men point towards where a shot was fired to kill Martin Luther King, Jr. *And I did not understand.*

I am headed into high school as a freshman at Central High in the summer of 1969. *The summer of 1969.* One year in one decade...Apollo 11

18

lands on the moon. Woodstock attracts 350,000 fans to a farm in New York. 250,000 protesters march on Washington against the Vietnam war. ARPANET, the predecessor to the Internet, sends the first electronic communications between locations. Sesame Street debuts on PBS. The first 747 jumbo jet takes off. The Concorde takes off on its first flight. The first Gap store opens. The Beatles record Abbey Road, their *final album.* Butch Cassidy and the Sundance Kid is released. The first artificial heart is transplanted. Richard Nixon takes office and proclaims in his inaugural address that, "Americans cannot learn from each other until we stop shouting at each other." *Really?*

WTF: I am 13 years old and just trying to understand what high school is all about.

I remember in the Fall of 1969 when there is a protest at lunch time at my school. There is loud music in the open grass area. There is *grass* in the open grass area. (Google that if you don't understand.) Someone has a bullhorn and is talking about *getting out.* The teachers are *freaking out.* Someone told me to support America and our troops and hands me a red, white and blue armband, and I put it on my arm and I write on it "Give 'em Hell." Am I supposed to choose sides? *And I do not understand.*

I did not understand any of these things because I did not have the life experiences to understand them. But I remember them. And I knew they were influencing me in some way. Influencing all of us. Because that is what decades do. They launch movements and generations. They signal transitions. They create optimism and despair, sometimes simultaneously.

The Foresight 2030 Project

So, at some point, I decided that the idea of chronicling a decade would be part of my purpose. To apply my life experiences and to listen to others about what might influence our next decade. I thought that 2000 and the decade through 2009 would be ideal. I mean, *the start of a new millennium.* I seriously consider the project, but really don't have a good mechanism to execute it. I think about *This Next Ten,* and even about *This Next Twenty-five,* and just remain curious about the future and its influences.

I am also an admitted optimist so I am looking for a *really good decade* to chronicle. The next Roaring Twenties or WWII Greatest Generation decade. I am wondering, though, if I am missing a good opportunity in 2000 because it was a great party on New Year's Eve and *everybody* has those "2000" glasses on.

At the end of that decade, it was clear that I had made the right choice not to chronicle that particular decade. I read the Time Magazine cover that was issued on December 7, 2009: *The Decade From Hell.* Now that would have been a poor choice for a young author. Time comments in the lead story:

Time cover—12/2009

"...it was the American Dream that was about to dim. Bookended by 9/11 at the start and a financial wipeout at the end. The first 10 years of this century will very likely go down as the most dispiriting and disillusioning decade Americans have lived through in the post-World War II era. We're still weeks ahead from the end of '09, but it's not too early to pass judgement. Call it the Decade from Hell, or the Reckoning, or the Decade of Broken Dreams, or the Lost Decade. Call it whatever you want—just give thanks that it is nearly over."

Shit. Call the suicide hotline for that writer. I was actually feeling pretty good before I picked up the magazine.

I waved off the project for the next decade. That Time episode was disturbing. Maybe we are on a downward spiral as a country and a globe. I don't want to take on 2010 through 2019, I feel like I am the editor of the Titanic's daily news flyer.

But something feels different as 2019 comes to a close. There are big issues on the horizon: recognition of climate change, the 4th Industrial Revolution, new medical advances, talk of commercial space flight, a real opportunity to advance equality in all dimensions, the rise of Gen Z and the implications of a generational leadership change from Boomers to Millennials.

And, two things I was looking forward to in 2020 to get things started: The Summer Olympics and the prospect of Trump getting voted out of office. At least I knew that one of those was a sure bet.

Right?

So in December of 2019 the game is on. *Foresight 2030: Conversations About The Decade Ahead.* I am committed and I have a good game plan. We'll do thought leadership sessions throughout the year on key topics

20

that could influence the decade ahead. Plenty to choose from—my spiral notebook from December 19, 2019, lists the starter set: the social impact of social media, next generation leadership, the future of technology, the future of work/life balance, America divided or united, trends in health/fitness and lifestyle, global calm or global conflict, the role of mainstream media (inform or influence), and how education and learning might change.

By the way, I am still at Omar's Fusion Café in West End, Tortola. But my mind was really wandering about the issue of decades and what this next decade might be all about. Reminds me about my English AP class in high school and watching *An Occurrence at Owl Creek Bridge*. Civil War and the guy is about be to be hanged off the bridge. The rope snaps taut and then breaks. For the next 30 minutes you see him hit the water, float away while troops pursue him. He sees and values things that he hadn't noticed before—the leaves on a tree, the sights and sounds of life, the appreciation of each and every moment of freedom. And then the rope snaps again, it was just a momentary reflection. He was still at the bridge. Hanging by the neck.

But the brief reflection was great!

Every great decade needs a great start. The remaining five days in Tortola were about as close to ideal as I could have imagined. Just the script I was looking for. Every day a full day, perfect sunrises to watch the boats and people slowly get ready for the day ahead. Soper's Hole is idyllic—still recovering from hurricane Irma in 2017, but regaining its true Caribbean look and feel. Blue skies, warm sun and gentle winds. Mornings at Smuggler's Cove, my favorite beach. Authentic. Good swims to recover from October 2019 knee surgery. Nigel's Beach Bar with cold Carib's. Two families and associated friends together all at the same end-of-the-world place where no one can find you. Evening dinners to reflect on the day and where we might set sail on the day ahead.

And sail we did. On Saturday, the 4th of January, we chartered a sailboat out of Road Town for the day. *A most perfect day.* A seasoned captain, a gracious charter-manager who rewarded us with rum punch and shrimp cocktails. Swimming and snorkeling in reefs and coves. Good winds on the way back—hoist the Jolly Roger! Perfectly quiet now. No need to talk, it's a ghost cat, Walter Mitty. Christopher Cross comes to mind again:

It's not far to never-never land, no reason to pretend
And if the wind is right you can find the joy of innocence again…
Just a dream and the wind to carry me
And soon I will be free

The crew—sailing out of Road Town   *A seasoned captain*

Reflecting on January 1

When we conducted our first Foresight 2020 session (see chapter 2), we asked people to reflect on January 1, 2020—where they were and their own optimism for the decade. There seemed to be a genuine vibe about the start of the decade. People were reflective, enjoying the opportunity to hit the pause button to consider the prospects of the future:

- "Hiking in the Superstitions with my children. Thinking about new opportunities for growth with my career, which will have a positive impact on my family life. Excitement for the year ahead, new home, fun vacations planned."
- "I was thinking that it would be a momentous time for me in that I was going to transition toward retirement and was thinking about my next phase of activity. I was also excited about the activities in my professional life and making good progress on implementing a bold strategic plan."
- "I was with my family in the mountains enjoying the fresh snow. Largely excited for the year ahead in terms of personal growth (family move, kids growing, etc.) and exciting projects on the horizon for our company."
- "On an airplane traveling internationally to a location I had never been; looking forward to the vacation and the year ahead."
- "New Year's Day in Park City. We skied Deer Valley. Life seemed normal, optimistic; we had our health, had just finished a great holiday with family. Plans for 2020 were in focus, with strong work, one retirement coming in our household and, in general, looking forward to the decade and optimistic about the year and what was to come."

These were powerful *analog* moments in a digital world. A rare time to slow down and reflect on what matters. Where were you on January 1, 2020, at the start of the decade? Were you optimistic about the future, about the decade ahead? In our first *Foresight* session we asked participants about whether, at start of the year, they were optimistic or pessimistic about the decade ahead:

Question: *Still reflecting on January 1, 2020: If you were to have forecast your view of the decade ahead THEN, would you say you were optimistic or pessimistic about the decade ahead?*

	Items	Times Selected
1.	**Optimistic about the decade ahead**	**87%**
2.	Pessimistic about the decade ahead	13%

This is not a fifty-fifty proposition. More than 85% were optimistic about the decade ahead. Why? Just because you were sitting on a beach with a *piña colada?* There was something else going on at the start of this decade that was influencing this optimism. We asked our first *Foresight* session participants to provide more context, more detail about their outlook:

- ✓ OPTIMISTIC: "Blessed with a prior decade and enthusiastic about the renewed start for family, friends, colleagues. Optimistic that our world would come together more than in recent years."
- ✓ OPTIMISTIC: "We have energy independence, ample food production, resources. Economy should continue to grow."
- ✓ OPTIMISTIC: "We have become a global planet and are learning the interconnectedness to, and interdependencies with, all people and the planet. We are all awakening to that and must learn to solve for that which is greater than my microcosm."
- ✓ OPTIMISTIC: "Change is good! Knowing what changes came in the last decade, the next one is going to be significant as well."
- ✓ OPTIMISTIC: "A new year always brings a sense of renewal and a time to start fresh; new ideas, new challenges, new adventures await."

Well now! That's what I am talking about. This *surely* will be the best decade of our lives! In fact, rather than a lengthy book project, this is starting to feel like an article will suffice.

I mean, what could go wrong?

Personal Outlook

And, if it is to be the best decade of our lives, then it would be appropriate to document what would make it so. In that spirit of optimism and reflection, and still with the quiet of my breakfast table over the water at West End, I considered the decade ahead and what would guide me to make it *my best decade ever.*

Happy to share:

1. **Achieve Personal Financial Security**: No debt, big equity, good savings for the future. (By the way, I am really glad I have many more years to work on this one...)
2. **Maintain my Health and Fitness**: It's part of who I am. 25+ ski days every year, 10+ triathlons in the summer. Lifestyle sports—mountain biking, tennis, swimming, hiking and running. Mind, body and soul. I am a George Sheehan disciple. Movement matters.
3. **Stay Connected to my Kids**: Four unique souls, so different and each so important. My goal is to have them strategically placed across the world in cool places so I can visit them often. Dad's guest room in each place. Truthfully, they are just fun to hang with. I play golf with them, swim Alcatraz with them, bike with them, hike with them, work with them, laugh with them. They are all Millennials, so they are like a built-in focus group for my work. *Oh no, Dad wants us to be on another one of his sessions!*
4. **Maintain my Facilitation Expertise**: My most profound mentor, Will Marré, once told me you have to be famous for something. Or at least pretty good at it. It's what I do for a living. I facilitate groups on issues that matter. CEOs, thought leaders, consumers. Mostly online, 25-50 people simultaneously. On more than one occasion I have been accused of sounding like an airline pilot. But I enjoy every minute of it.
5. **Be Part of a Purpose**: Find a cause that matters, something you believe in, that resonates. Local or global, but something where you can make a difference, make a *dent* in the future. I am a big believer in the role of purpose, whether for individuals or business. My friends at the Purpose Institute remind me that it was Aristotle who said: "Wherein your talents and the needs of the world intersect, therein lies your purpose."
6. **Write a Book**: Ah, this is a special club and some of you are already in. I admire anyone who has committed themselves to a subject and put it on paper, and had the good fortune to publish it. In 1981-1982 I wrote articles on running for the Los Gatos Times Observer. $25/article, every Thursday. The column was

entitled "In The Long Run". Part running, part philosophy. Pure joy, and I knew then I would write a book about the future.

7. **Continue to Explore**: I am a traveler at heart. Early days in Mexico, work and vacations in Europe, Latin America, Australia, Asia Pacific and the Caribbean. Walter Mitty has nothing on me. Over the next decade I will visit at least 10 new countries.

8. **Become More Compassionate**: Not my core strength, but one I value. I do subscribe to the Seuss doctrine of "a person's a person no matter how small." I am committed in the decade ahead to be more engaged, more observant, more connected. If you are a compassionate family, community, organization and country, you will be more inclusive.

9. **Choose Technology Wisely**: Strange one, huh? I spent 19 years in IBM at the start of my career. I use technology every day in my work. I pre-dated email, the internet, voicemail, texting and social media. I am, as many people can attest, an analog guy living in a digital world. I value technology and dedicate a chapter of this book on the future of technology and its value for the world in the decade ahead. I just prefer to write in my spiral notebook with a cold beverage or hot coffee.

10. **Maintain the Brotherly Circle**: I am always amazed and disheartened when people tell me that they do not stay close to their siblings. I understand all the reasons why that might be, but I don't get it. I have two brothers, both older (and wiser) than me. But I talk to them almost every day. I ski and play golf with Pete in Utah. I do triathlons with Bruce all over the western United States. I will stay connected through the decade. It's how we keep the circle intact.

Jeez, I need a shot of tequila. *Arriba, abajo, al centro, pa'dentro.* But look, if this is going to be a great decade, it cannot be a decade of chance. Take the time to put some principles around *your next ten* and where you want to be. It creates a framework for your decisions and priorities. If your organization has values, live them. If not, you are just going to feel like a pinball.

So, for me, January 1, 2020, was *smooth sailing.* It was the perfect start of the decade and I had a clear purpose ahead with the Foresight 2030 project. I would convene 10 thought leadership sessions with a set of wonderful and different people to gain their views on the decade ahead. Our goal is to look at what might most influence this decade. And to make some forecasts about what might happen. We might be right and we might be wrong. Maybe it will be a fifty-fifty proposition, but it will be a great journey. And 2020 will be a perfect lens from which we can forecast that journey.

Return to Reality

On the way back to Arizona from Tortola, I am still reflecting on my optimism for the decade ahead, but I note that already there are three events/occurrences that have caught my attention. It's still a little unclear what they mean, but it just seemed a little odd that all three came up at once:

✓ On January 3, the U.S. ordered the assassination of one of Iran's most senior military leaders, General Qassem Soleimani, via a drone. *Seriously? We are three days into the decade, people.* Iran is demanding revenge and people are genuinely concerned about the possibility of Iran and the U.S. going to war. I am not that excited about being in an airplane right now. As it turns out, Tehran makes all the wrong moves. They shoot down a Ukrainian airliner by mistake, which does not endear them to the world. Iran then launches a strike on U.S. bases in Iraq, but no Americans were killed. I hit you back, maybe not as hard, but I did hit you back. I think we collectively dodged a bullet on this one. A pretty uncomfortable way to start the year and a stark reminder that there are global realities ahead in the next decade and we must have clear policies and leadership.

✓ On a lighter note, but somewhat disturbing to those of us who are traditionalists in the sport, news is surfacing about a major cheating scandal in baseball involving the Houston Astros. Apparently, it has been an "open secret" for some time, which is a phrase that can move slightly ahead of "jumbo shrimp" in the oxymoron sweepstakes race. A camera in the Astro's home stadium relayed a feed of the catcher to a monitor situated in a recessed area where an Astros player was sitting near home plate. The player decoded the opposing team's catcher's signals and banged on a trash can to alert the hitter what the next pitch would be. *Now there is an elegant scheme.* But seriously, not a great look for America's pastime to send to young little leaguers.

✓ An outbreak of pneumonia cases was reported on December 31, 2019, in Wuhan, China. On January 1, 2020, the World Health Organization (WHO) set up an Incident Management Support Team to look into the outbreak. On January 5, the WHO issues a Disease Outbreak News Bulletin referencing the Huanan Seafood Market as a possible origin of the outbreak. The bad news is that some 44 patients had been identified with fever, difficulty in breathing and some showing invasive lesions of both lungs. The good news is that there is no evidence of human-to-human transmissions. The WHO reports, "There is limited information to determine the risk of this reported cluster of pneumonia of unknown etiology." The WHO also reports that pneumonia is common in the winter season. I think to myself three things: 1) Brilliant on the pneumonia comment from the WHO; 2) I have no idea what etiology means; and 3) I am glad I do not work in a Chinese live animal/seafood market.

The above three issues are listed in priority sequence to me as I am flying back to the U.S. on January 5, 2020. I guess strange news just comes in threes. I click through some of my camera pictures from the Tortola trip—and happily share a few of those with you now. After all, it was a perfect start to 2020. A little chop in the water but *mostly* smooth sailing ahead!

Island paradise

Smoothies for the smooth sail ahead!

CHAPTER 2: Clouds On The Horizon

When you're weary
Feeling small
When tears are in your eyes
I'll dry them all
I'm on your side
Oh when times get rough…

--Simon & Garfunkel, Bridge Over Troubled Water *(1970)*

March 19, 2020
Foresight 2020 Base Session—Outlook for the Decade

We're about to find out what really matters. Personally. In our families. In our communities. In our work environments. With our information sources. With our leadership. With our global allies. With our faith.

The drumbeat of this not-so-well-understood incident in China is getting louder.

For most of January we all listened into the noise and, I suspect, largely dismissed the seriousness of the outbreak. I mean, Wuhan, China, is a long way away and we have endured a number of these "disease out-breaks" in recent years: SARS (Severe Acute Respiratory Syndrome) was identified in 2003 and emerged in China, and was classified by the WHO as the first severe and readily transmissible new disease to emerge in the 21st century and could be spread directly by droplets and indirectly by *surfaces*; the 2009 swine flu involving the H1N1 influenza virus; MERS (Middle East Respiratory Syndrome) was first reported in Saudi Arabia in 2012 and is *another* coronavirus; the 2014 Ebola out-break in West Africa and the mosquito-borne Zika in 2018 round out the *Recent Viruses for $100* category.

I don't know about you, but I didn't get any of those.

But something different was going on here. Additional cases of the *novel coronavirus* are reported in Japan and Thailand in mid-January, and U.S. airports begin to screen flights between Wuhan and the U.S. On January 21, the first U.S. case is confirmed in the State of Washington. A Chinese scientist confirms that the virus can be transmitted *human to human* and China closes off (as in quarantines) the City of Wuhan. We get a serious lesson in global geography when we learn that this city, which most of us have never heard of, has *11 million people* living it. On January 30, the WHO wakes up a bit and issues a *Global Health Emergency* for just the sixth time in its history. There are now 9800 cases of the virus and more countries are seeing cases.

To add another dark cloud to January 2020, the news of Kobe Bryant's death in a helicopter crash in Calabasas, California, is a gut punch to us all. The clips of Kobe with his daughter Gianna and endless videos of his basketball talent and grace stop us in our tracks.

It just seemed like January, in what was surely going to be the start of the best decade of my life, was slowing down with headwinds and a coat of icy darkness. But perhaps it was just a tapping of the brakes and we would move past January and the storm would subside.

I'm in Park City, Utah, at end of January. My 10th annual hosting of The Griffen Birthday Skiing Event (my oldest brother Pete and I celebrate ours on January 29/30 so a great excuse for the get together). No skiing for me at this year's event as I am recovering from a torn quadricept, but I have vowed to be back by April 1—still some good skiing will be left by then, right? The Phoenix Open wraps up on February 2 with crowds of some 200,000 spectators per day. Super Bowl 54 is hosted in Miami with a sellout crowd of over 62,000, and we all talk about the Chiefs and the commercials. America seems a little more normal on this first weekend in February.

Big crowds at the 2020 Phoenix Open—the infamous 16th hole

But the drumbeat of COVID is getting even louder and sounds now like a bad game of *Jumanji*. Global air restrictions are beginning to be imposed and the U.S. declares a Public Health Emergency on February 3. On February 25, the CDC says this disease (which all are now commonly referring to as "COVID-19") is *heading towards pandemic status.*

I remain optimistic. After all, this is my decade. It's already beginning to feel like this will be a very long year in 2020 and, fittingly, an extra day is tagged on for February 29. Not to be deterred, I jump in (literally) to the Iceman Aquabike event at Lake Pleasant just outside of Phoenix. Thank God for wetsuits. But my spirits are lifted, it's my return to sports events after my own 5-month rehab from quad surgery. I do not tell my physical therapist daughter (who directs my post-surgery recovery) about my return to competition. It is better to ask for forgiveness than permission. I am stoked! Delusional, perhaps, after the cold water and brisk bike. I will go after 20 aquabikes and triathlons this year! Twenty for Twenty! What a great use of my extra day in 2020! This is shaping up to be a terrific year!

On March 13, the WHO declares the novel coronavirus (aka, COVID-19) a *global* pandemic. Just to increase our comfort level, the WHO Director, Dr. Tedros Adhanom Ghebreyesus (let's just go with Dr. Ted), states that the WHO is "deeply concerned with the alarming levels of spread and severity, *and* the alarming levels of inaction." *Mirror, mirror on the wall.*

Houston, we have a problem and it is a lot bigger that the Astros cheating scandal.

On Global Pandemics

As is turns out, *global pandemics* are not new. Prior to COVID-19 the three most well known global pandemics were: the 14th Century "Black Death" or Plague (killing an estimated 75-200 million people); the 1918-1920 Spanish Flu (infecting a *half billion* people and killing an estimated 20-100 million); and HIV/AIDS which originated in Africa with some 32-35 million deaths globally. Although still active, HIV/AIDS is still a pandemic but no longer considered to be an uncontrollable outbreak outside of Africa.

In 2006, nearly 15 years ago, I facilitated a thought leadership session for the well known *Aspen Institute* on "Influenza Surveillance Models and Strategies." It was an in-person gathering of a number of global specialists held in Washington, D.C., that focused on the issues of *pandemic influenzas.* I must tell you that I was *not* one of the specialists, but my role was using advanced (at the time) laptop computer technology to capture simultaneous responses from the participants about how to surveil and mitigate pandemic influenzas. The keynote speaker was Dr.

David Nabarro, Senior UN System Coordinator for Avian and Human Influenza for the United Nations. *Heavy Hitter.*

Dr. David Nabarro--decades of service

In listening to the keynote, I was fascinated to learn that there were only five things that really can create global instability concern for the United Nations (according to Dr. Nabarro). I admit now that I can only remember three of them: a rogue nuclear device, oil above $100/barrel and a *global pandemic.* I'm not sure I want to know the other two.

Dr. Nabarro also outlined—*in 2006*—some seven critical success factors in dealing with surveillance and response to a potential pandemic:

1. Effective strategy: right actions, right place, right time
2. Political direction from the top
3. Ability to rapidly scale up (cash, people, management)
4. Social mobilization (around risks and issues)
5. Incentives for prompt reporting
6. Alliances of governments and partnerships
7. Management: information, analysis, change

Look, I am just stating the obvious. A lot of very smart people had been eyeballing this global pandemic issue for many, many years, and had developed well thought out methodologies, approaches and responses. But they remained largely untested at a global level. COVID was about to lay that bare.

A footnote on Dr. David Nabarro. I Googled him, as I was curious to see if he was still with the UN. He is not, but for good reason. On February 21, 2020, The Director-General of the WHO appoints Dr. Nabarro and five others as *Special Envoys* on COVID-19 to "provide strategic advice and high level political advocacy and engagement in different parts of the world." Nabarro is 71 and still serving the world. *Definitely a heavy hitter.*

And so, heading into the week of March 9, 2020, when the WHO will finally declare that we have hit a *global pandemic*, we are still feeling our way in the dark despite an extraordinary level of research, review and dialogue over countless years. It's like a scene from the book *The Abilene Paradox:* it's not that we are in disagreement, as we all know we are screwed. We just don't want to say it out loud. It would take the NBA to finally get us moving.

The Week When It All Changed

If the early part of 2020, the buildup to the week of March 9, seemed like it was in slow-motion, it was. But the week of March 9 went into *hyperdrive* and changed everything.

I remember the week of March 9 very clearly. Fully into work mode, I had two *in-person* engagements I was facilitating. Most of my work is actually online, facilitating groups virtually on a wide range of issues. *Keeps it interesting.* But years ago, all of my work was in person, using laptop labs and collaborative software. Perhaps 10% of the time now, and mostly for local Arizona engagements, I still do my in-person sessions. So, it was a little unusual that I had two such engagements in the same week.

On March 9-10, I was at the Gila River Indian Community (GRIC) facilitating a session for the Gila River Telecommunications, Inc., Board of Directors to help develop a long-term strategic plan and vision for the organization. A smaller session, seven leaders, but very intensive. I like GRIC and what they are all about as a community and as a sovereign nation. They are proud and progressive. Their land is now at the center point of the Valley in Phoenix. *They are players for the future.*

I can feel that this will be my last week of in-person sessions for a long time. In fact, if my sessions had been scheduled one week later, I am sure they would not have taken place.

In the business world, there was a great deal of awkwardness on how to treat the growing developments of the COVID-19 pandemic. Be aware, be somewhat cautious. But very little clear direction. Do we still shake hands? Is it OK to be in a conference room together? Do you talk about the *pandemic?* And a few people (outside of healthcare workers) are beginning to wear masks. The N-95 kind, like we are on a construction project or something.

On March 8, just ahead of our *week that would change everything*, Dr. Anthony Fauci says, during an interview with *60 Minutes*, "There's no reason to be walking around with a mask," though he adds he's not against masks, but more worried that they are needed for the healthcare workers and those who are sick, and also that wearing masks could lead to "unintended consequences" such as people touching their face when they are putting their masks on or taking them off or adjusting them. *And Dr. Fauci would correct himself soon on mask issue.*

So, no masks in our conference room on March 9-10. But also *fewer* handshakes (it is a really hard habit to break). A few Ebola elbow bumps and fist bumps. I have gone to more of a no-touch but high respect policy: right hand to the heart (a sign of respect in Latin America) and then I remove my hand and point at the person as if to say "I respect you." I really mean "back off."

But the two days go well, and I am quite relieved to have the meetings behind me. But the week is still young and I will be facilitating a major session at Arizona State University on March 12 with an audience of some 30 thought leaders from ASU and Emory University on the role of *compassion* in our society. As you may have read earlier, compassion is not a core strength of mine, so I am really looking forward to facilitating this session—I will be a hungry learner and perhaps a better human being as a result.

On March 11 some very powerful things begin to happen in what I can only describe as a *head-spinning* experience. The WHO formally declares that the COVID-19 crisis is now a global pandemic. Italy, one of the hardest hit countries, announces that all businesses, except pharmacies and grocery stores, would be forced to close. In the United States, the NCAA announces that the "March Madness" championship basketball tournament will be played without fans. *Well, at least the tournament will still be played,* we all reflect with a note of resilience and American pride.

On the evening of March 11 our participant and sponsor guests for the *Compassion Charrette* are gathered at ASU for a dinner event. More than half have flown in and I am convinced that if the session were held *one day later* it would have been cancelled. Still an upbeat event that night, most people still shaking hands and receiving hugs, I continue with my touchless *respect and point* move when I greet people. *This facilitator seems very strange,* many are thinking.

There is much talk of the growing news of the pandemic at the dinner; it seems to actually reduce the tension. *All will be fine, we will work together on this.* Then people begin to look at their phones. The *unthinkable* has happened. The NBA just suspended their season:

NBA Communications Release: New York, March 11, 2020.

NBA TO SUSPEND SEASON FOLLOWING TONIGHT'S GAMES.

The NBA announced that a player on the Utah Jazz has preliminarily tested positive for COVID-19. The test result was reported shortly prior to the tip-off of tonight's game between the Jazz and Oklahoma City Thunder at Chesapeake Energy Arena. At that time tonight's game was cancelled. The affected player was not in the arena.

The NBA is suspending game play following the conclusion of tonight's schedule of games until further notice. The NBA will use this hiatus to determine next steps for moving in regard to the coronavirus pandemic.

I'm not sure what brilliant PR person came up with *hiatus* but the NBA just started a set of dominoes that would fall in rapid succession. Over the next 24 hours *everyone* starts shutting down: The National Hockey League, Major League Baseball, Major League Soccer and multiple tennis associations. The NCAA cancels all of its remaining spring and winter championships *including* the March Madness basketball tournaments for men and women. ESPN notes that the basketball tournament has never been canceled before and estimates that the annual three-week tournament generates nearly a *billion dollars* in revenue.

Careful language is being used. The NHL is "pausing" their season and Major League Baseball will be "delaying" their season for at least two weeks (because a global pandemic can generally be contained in that amount of time?). The Summer Olympic Games are still on (the Games *must* go on), but it is noted that the torch lighting ceremony on the 12th was closed to the public. The Association of Tennis Professionals (ATP) suspends its tour for six weeks but cancels the Monte Carlo tournament globally. *That may not have affected you, but my wife and daughter had tickets for that one and were meeting my son from Vienna there.*

And just when you thought the dominoes were over, there was one last one to fall in that head-spinning 24 hours: Disneyland was closing. *Disneyland was closing.* But don't worry, they said, it's only through the end of the month. That's why it's the *Magic Kingdom.*

But fear not. I would still be facilitating my session on March 12, 2020. DS Griffen & Associates had not suspended operations. But, like for many organizations, that was the week that just about all in-person events wound down. *Until further notice.*

It was actually a very powerful session on the 12th. *Advancing a global culture of compassion.* Perhaps I felt that the cause/subject would be needed with what we might be facing. The Emory team was lead by Geshe Lobsang Tenzin Negi, PhD., as the Director of the Center for Contemplative Science and Compassion-Based Ethics. I was honored to lead the session, but very cognizant of what seemed to be happening around us that day.

On Friday morning, March 13, I met with Dr. Negi and his team to debrief the session. He gave me a bracelet of *contemplative beads* fashioned from wood and leather. He told me, "These have been blessed by his Holiness the Dalai Lama himself." I am not a particularly spiritual person, but 2020 was quickly moving me in that direction. *I put the bracelet on immediately.*

Geshe Lobsang Negi with the Dalai Lama

Dr. Negi (top right) at ASU session 3/12/2020

Foresight Session 1: March 19, 2020

So all of this sets the stage for our first Foresight 2030 session that was held on Thursday, March 19, 2020. A simple proposition we had envisioned back in December of 2019: conduct a series of *online* sessions in 2020 to understand what would influence the decade ahead. A one year lens that would launch a decade of insights.

Things were not going according to script.

But the lens had become infinitely more important. It was clear that 2020 was going to be a year like no other. A global pandemic. A looming Presidential election. A cry for social equality that would lead to unrest in the streets. *Something's happening here, what it is ain't exactly clear.*

I almost pulled the plug on the session. I am going to ask people if they are optimistic about the decade ahead. *Really?* I am going to ask them to set aside the global pandemic for a moment. *Really?* Everything around us shut down last week and I want them to think about this *great decade* ahead. *Really?*

Really. I mean, this is *my decade,* people. The one that I think will be my best decade ever. I am writing a book about it. So, I display a meant-to-be-comforting preamble at the start of the session to let people know that we have not lost the decade yet:

> *FOR THIS SESSION, I ask you to put some boundaries around COVID-19: we will get past it, but it will leave its mark on the future—both in negative impact and in positive implications (hopefully) on how we as a global community deal with it. A WORKING ASSUMPTION/TIMELINE: it's a six-month duration, not 60-day duration. Sports come back online beginning July 1, life is largely back to normal October 1, we will experience one of the largest economic recoveries in history in the 4th quarter and Thanksgiving/Christmas will have an entirely different meaning. And then we will wonder what happens in January 2021.*

I was actually right about the sports thing.

All of our Foresight sessions were one hour in length and had between 30 and 50 participants. I facilitated all 10 of the sessions and used a combination of a web-based collaborative system that allowed everyone to "speak at the same time and be heard" via the digital keyboard, but guided by the facilitator voice for context and clarity. It's an approach we have been using at our Advanced Strategy Center for more than 20 years. It's called *The Advanced Strategy Lab OnLine.*

This first session had 38 participants from across the country whom I considered to be thought leaders, and reflective of a broad set of viewpoints and experiences. For you research types, this is *qualitative research* although we would test a number of key insights with a *quantitative* poll after the series of sessions. But I am a believer in qualitative research and that a set of informed viewpoints matter. For the record, 65% of our session 1 participants were 50 years or older, 35% were under 50. 55% were men, 45% women. 52% considered themselves optimists, while 48% considered themselves realists or even pessimists. Importantly, 52% were also dog owners. *Probably the optimists.*

But, in my mind they were all just interesting people who had meaningful life experiences and were willing to share their views about the decade ahead. Some examples of their responses when I asked them to introduce themselves in a sentence or two:

- "From Colorado (live for the outdoors!) with my wife, two young children and dog. Have worked in brand and corporate strategy for 15 years."
- "I've worked in the health care industry in a variety of capacities for over 35 years, most recently in Federal policy matters. I live in the Boston area and enjoy a wide variety of non-work activities including raising a new Australian shepherd puppy!"
- "Current adjunct professor teaching entrepreneurship and innovation. Thirty years F500 experience as well as multi-time entrepreneur. Originally form NYC, now reside in AZ."
- "Thirty-year resident of Park City. Sales and marketing career, now a senior member of a venture capital/private equity investment fund."
- "I'm a nonprofit leader with degrees in social work. I am married to a professor at a top-tier university. I am a proud Midwesterner and live in a major city. I am a first-generation college graduate and a home owner."
- "I live with my husband and two dogs in beautiful Bucks County, PA. Our two children are spread out on different coasts, one in VA and married to a Navy Seabee, and my son in San Diego."
- "Native of SF Bay Area. In transition to small business owner. Married. A 17-year-old daughter with various hair colors, currently shocking red."
- "I'm a small town dwelling dad, husband, former lacrosse coach, trail hiker, business consultant and strategic networker. I believe in doing well by doing good."

And I have 38 of these interesting people online and ready to help set my baseline for Foresight 2030.

Reflecting Back on the Prior Decade

Before heading into the new decade we asked people about the *prior* decade (2010 through 2019). We thought it would be interesting to see how people were coming into 2020:

Question: *Let's start by looking back. How would you characterize the prior decade—2010 through 2019? What were the biggest trends? The biggest events? What was different about the decade? How did the decade affect/influence you?*

- "Pace of life accelerated dramatically. Crowding in major urban centers. Economy growth. Internet explosion."
- "It was a decade of economic growth. Technology became ever more prevalent, in everyone's hands all day long."
- "What stood out to me about the past decade is the incredible volatility which seems to have become the new normal. The recovery from the financial crisis was incredible, but over the past 4 years we seem to be riding a rudderless ship that's bouncing on huge waves. We also seem to have lost our way as a nation."
- "Biggest trends: recovery from the financial crisis, increasing globalization, increase in disinformation and loss of trust in traditional institutions, growing importance of climate change as a political issue."
- "I believe the decade was defined by the growing divide in our country between the haves and have nots. The middle class began to disappear at a higher rate. The family structure began to shift with more young adults staying at home longer. Science continued to become political. Opinions became facts."
- "This was the decade that brought even more polarization in the U.S. This was the birth of fake news, the loss or decline of many old media models and the growth of new ones. This also was the decade we didn't address the big future issues, i.e., global warming, immigration."

Hmmm. *Maybe I should have tackled "Hindsight 2020" and looked at the prior decade before starting the journey on the decade ahead in "Foresight 2030".*

What was clear to me, in just this initial set of responses, is that some influences for the upcoming decade have been developing for quite some time. Some were on simmer, but some were rapidly heating and getting ready to boil. My quick analysis:

✓ Technology was changing everything. Nearly everyone had access to the level of information *and disinformation* that they wanted.
✓ The pace of life had gone into warp speed. Exciting, but exhausting.
✓ A great divide was shaping up. Social disequity, racial disequity, financial disequity. Polarizing politics.
✓ People seemed to be more focused on themselves and less focused on the world around them. We are numbed by constant images of global conflict, 24-hour cable news, 100-year disasters that happen every year. Let the next generation handle climate crisis.
✓ We seemed to have traded general economic prosperity for an indifference to moral and political leadership and integrity.

But, overall, most people in our initial Foresight session would classify the prior decade as a positive decade, largely due to advances in technology and the economy:

Question: *All things considered, how would you assess that decade?*

No.	Items	Times Selected
1.	**Somewhat positive**	**(38%)**
2.	**Very positive**	**(27%)**
3.	Middle of the road	(19%)
4.	Somewhat negative	(16%)
5.	Very negative	(0%)

Those in the middle or on the negative side were sounding an alarm, though: a loss of our empathy and humanness due to the technology, turning a blind eye to the environment/climate change and an overall political and social divide looming.

Influencing the Decade Ahead
We then asked our participants to look at the decade ahead, and what made them *optimistic* about the decade ahead and what made them *pessimistic* about the decade ahead. We used a technique in this portion of our session where we would pose an open brainstorming question (i.e., "Now, let's look ahead. We are here to consider the NEXT TEN YEARS. Now through December 31, 2029. What makes you OPTIMISTIC about the decade ahead?") and allow for simultaneous open re-

sponses, then a real time summary of themes (referred to as *categorization* in our process) followed by an assessment of those themes. So, 100+ open responses become 10-12 key themes that can quickly be prioritized. Here is the summary of what our participants were optimistic about as well as pessimistic about in the coming decade. The lists are ordered by the group average on a 1-10 assessment of themes:

INFLUENCING OPTIMISM*:* Now, please assess each of the following aspects in terms of how important, IF IT WERE TO OCCUR, it would be in influencing your optimism about the decade ahead. Use a scale of 1-10 where a "1" means a very low level of influence and a "10" means a very high level of influence:

Rank	Theme	Average
1.	Continued economic growth	8.7
2.	More compassionate society	8.7
3.	Positive political change	8.6
4.	We will effectively manage our way through COVID-19	8.5
5.	Positive socio-economic shifts	8.4
6.	Significant medical breakthroughs	8.4
7.	New levels of innovation	8.3
8.	Greater global collaboration	8.2
9.	Real impact on climate change	8.2
10.	We will become increasingly connected as a people	7.9
11.	Continued smart technology adoption	7.7
12.	Positive impact of Gen Z	6.8

INFLUENCING PESSIMISM*:* Now, please assess each of the following aspects in terms of how important, IF IT WERE TO OCCUR, it would be in influencing your pessimism about the decade ahead. Use a scale of 1-10 where a "1" means a very low level of influence and a "10" means a very high level of influence:

Rank	Theme	Average
1.	Level of political unrest	8.8
2.	Our lack of civility	8.4
3.	No climate change progress	8.3
4.	Lack of a moral compass	8.2
5.	Our education system does not improve	7.6
6.	A devaluation of traditional media/journalism	7.6
7.	Lasting impact of COVID-19	7.4
8.	Privacy and security issues	7.2
9.	Wealth gap does not change	6.8
10.	Negative Artificial Intelligence impact	6.4
11.	Overload of social media	6.2
12.	The heavy burden of student debt	6.1

To be certain, our view about the decade is not unbridled optimism. It is clear what an optimistic future might look like, but there are some roadblocks that we, as a country and as a globe, must take on. Many of these roadblocks will be examined in our future Foresight 2030 sessions.

Still in our first session—March 2020—and considering the overall set of factors, we asked our participants for in an initial forecast for the decade:

Question: *All things considered, as you reflect the overall set of factors that might influence your outlook for the decade ahead, what's your forecast for the decade ahead?*

No.	Items	Times Selected
1.	**Somewhat Optimistic**	**(46%)**
2.	**Middle of the Road**	**(30%)**
3.	Very Optimistic	(16%)
4.	Somewhat Pessimistic	(8%)
5.	Very Pessimistic	(0%)

Hedging our bets here. Cautiously optimistic. I'll stay in the middle until I see some sense of our direction for the decade ahead. And while COVID-19 is a factor, it's not a big factor (at least not yet). We can deal with a global pandemic, but the prospect of a long term political divide and inability to address social equality, climate change and incivility temper our outlook. Our participants explain their forecasts:

- MIDDLE: "I don't see political parties coming back together and that will keep our nation divided. However, economic growth will boost everything—technology, advancements in healthcare and improving life to those in the world who are living in poverty."
- SOMEWHAT OPTIMISTIC: "Hopeful but realistic...it's going to be hard to reach the unity and civility we need. But...perhaps this COVID-19 scare will be enough to break down the walls we've been erecting. But to do so we are going to have to address the alienation that drove to their creation in the first place."
- SOMEWHAT OPTIMISTIC: "Somewhat optimistic because we as people have the capability to change and do the right things moving forward...just whether or not we will keeps me from 'very' optimistic."
- MIDDLE: "Hopeful that we will identify leaders who will shift toward solving our issues instead of fearfully moving away from them."
- SOMEWHAT OPTIMISTIC: "I am hopeful that a generational shift will bring about a renewal of sorts. The tools that the next gen is native to, combined with the stark relief of decaying values, may give way to a reawakening of entrepreneurship and innovation with purpose and values."
- SOMEWHAT PESSIMISTIC: "It could be COVID and Trump, but I am overwhelmed with a feeling of doom for our society. We are poorly equipped to work together. We have major challenges to face and I do not believe we can do it well."
- SOMEWHAT OPTIMISTIC: "Too much is happening at once for good people to sit idly by and observe. As with WWII, people all over the world will eventually rise up and reclaim the better part of all of us and win the day. But it is going to be years in the making. My fervent hope is that our children look back in 10 or more years and say we had 2020 vision and earned the right to be part of our global village."

Look, I am feeling pretty good about this first session, especially coming off a particularly head-spinning and mostly negative prior week. It is clear that in 2020 we are at a *tipping point*. This really could be the decade I am looking for, one that will be historic and set the direction for future generations (at least for my four millennials). But what we will need to address will take a *collective will* that we may not have summoned in decades. We have a great deal of faith in the American spirit, our ability to overcome challenge. But we have to find a way to bridge the divide, to re-channel our collective good. We may be clear about the direction we want to head, but right now the water is too calm, too still.

An Early Trial Set of Decade Influencers
So, as part of our first session, we decided to test some elements that might generate the "wind" that we needed to move in the right direction. These were themes developed ahead of the session that were simply meant to solicit reaction. A bit of "what if" analysis if certain conditions were in place. How would you assess these in terms of how important they are, if addressed, for the future of the *next decade?* How likely are they to *actually occur?*

Now, please assess each of the issues in two ways. First, how IMPORTANT you feel that issue will be, if addressed in a meaningful way, for the success of the decade ahead (use a scale of 1-10 where a "1" means not at all important and a "10" means extremely important); Secondly, the LIKELI-HOOD that we will make meaningful progress on or achieve that issue BY THE END OF THE DECADE (use a scale of 1-10 where a "1" means a very low level of progress or likelihood and a "10" means a very high level of progress or likelihood):

Here is how our Foresight session assessed the list. The scenarios are ordered by the *level of positive impact* but then contrasted with the likelihood of occurrence for a gap analysis rating.

#	Scenario Description	Im-pact	Like-ly	Gap
1	HEALTH CARE ACCESS: We finally figured it out. How to provide healthcare to everyone in an efficient and low cost way. No one was denied healthcare and there were still options/providers that people could escalate based on their preferences. A more multi-dimensional healthcare model emerged (body/mind/soul) that dealt with the whole person and emphasized preventative and long term care.	9.2	5.8	(3.4)

2	POLITICAL UNITY: Remarkably, in the U.S., as a model for the world, our political divides had been largely bridged. While there was still room for different approaches and ideologies, there was more common ground and effective legislation and policy in the areas that mattered. The U.S. Congress drew in some of the best and brightest in the decade and became one of the most admired institutions in the country.	9.0	4.4	(4.6)
3	GLOBAL CONFLICT: Governments and leaders leveraged negotiation and long term interests to defuse many long-standing global/regional conflicts. Bodies like the UN were re-tooled to help mediate and resolve conflict. Conflicts that arose were quickly addressed by global interests.	8.7	5.3	(3.4)
4	GLOBAL PANDEMICS: The world learned from recent pandemics such as SARS, MERS, H1N1, Ebola, Zika and COVID-19 on how to better monitor, prepare for and respond to potential pandemics. While new strains emerged post coronavirus, there were no global pandemics at scale during the decade.	8.6	6.7	(1.9)
5	SUSTAINED ECONOMIC GROWTH: While there may be some ups and downs, we were able to sustain measurable economic growth over the decade. Nearly every country participated in the growth and it had a measurable impact on community development and quality of life.	8.6	6.7	(1.9)
6	MIDDLE CLASS: The divide between the haves and the have-nots changed during the decade where a new middle class arose. They were the drivers of the new economy—hard working, but well compensated. The new middle class was easy to get into and a great place to stay. You were welcome to go further and move on to a different wealth category, but many found the middle as the right place to be.	8.5	5.5	(3.0)

7	COMPASSION: A new level of genuine compassion emerged during the decade. People were more compassionate to each other; families were more united; workplaces were respectful and fully supported diversity and inclusion; communities were more civil. We just treated each other a little better in the decade, fewer people felt lonely or isolated.	8.5	5.5	(3.0)
8	RETOOLING EDUCATION: Education was completely re-invented. Early childhood education (ECE) became highly valued and publicly funded, and gave children (birth through age eight) the best start possible. All young people had access to quality higher education with no-cost alternatives for community and state colleges, to reasonably priced private universities. Education was far more aligned with the workforce needs, graduates were workforce ready. The majority of graduates entered the workplace debt-free.	8.4	5.5	(2.9)
9	4th INDUSTRIAL REVOLUTION: The revolution arrived in the decade, but we managed it effectively. We took advantage of artificial intelligence, voice activation, the internet of things and autonomous vehicles in a way that was productive and enhanced our workplace and society. Jobs/tasks that were replaced simply allowed people to be retrained and activate their skills in a new way.	8.3	6.8	(1.5)
10	PRESS FREEDOM: No more "fake news", no more journalists jailed or killed. Journalism experiences a rebirth, the press becomes highly admired and respected across the globe. The news and information that are reported are accurate and consistent, we are a more informed society.	8.3	5.2	(3.1)
11	CLIMATE CHANGE: We addressed climate change in a meaningful and measurable way on a global basis. Corporations and governments were fully aligned on long-term strategies. At the end of the decade, the scientists agree we had turned the corner.	8.3	5.2	(3.1)

12	INNOVATION AT SCALE: We take a page from the Tesla playbook and apply innovation at scale to a broad set of issues, products, processes and services. We change the way we do things in a modern and forward-thinking way. We have really reinvented the way to do just about everything.	8.2	7.3	(0.9)
13	RACIAL INEQUALITY: The decade has created a new and widespread level of understanding about racial inequality as a fundamental divide in our society. It feels like it is in "the rear view mirror" and we feel like one people at work, at school, at our communities and in our neighborhoods.	8.2	6.0	(2.0)
14	ELEGANT AGING: Our boomer populations were well cared for and respected. Long term health care was affordable and available, and the general level of wellness and active lifestyles of those in their 60s, 70s and 80s was the envy of many who were 20 years younger.	7.8	6.5	(1.3)
15	TECHNOLOGY BALANCE: We seemed to have found the balance with the role of technology in our lives and the value of personal interaction and emotional connection. There is a genuine analog balance to digital world.	7.9	6.3	(1.6)
16	MENTAL HEALTH: Mental health was completely repositioned in society. Mental health check-ups were as commonplace as the traditional physical. Treatments and therapies were advanced and well beyond drug therapy. PTSD (post-traumatic stress disorder) could be diagnosed and managed in effective ways with those individuals fully integrated back into family, workplace and society.	7.7	5.7	(2.0)
17	GEN Z INFLUENCE: The impact of Gen Z into the workforce and society, with a new set of values and views, will help solve problems and address social issues. (Gen Z is generally considered to have been born between 1995 and 2015, now 5-25 years old. There are 74 million in the U.S. alone.)	7.3	7.3	(0.0)

18	OPIOID CRISIS: We have addressed the opioid crisis in a significant way and provided treatment to those addicted, and reversed the trend of oversubscribing by the medical community. (Currently, some 130 people a day die from opioid overdose in the U.S. alone.)	6.9	6.1	(0.8)
19	GUN VIOLENCE: A change in attitude, regulation and behaviors regarding gun violence, active shooter situations and mass shootings that significantly reduces gun violence in the U.S. and globally. Schools, especially, feel safe again.	6.8	4.4	(2.4)
20	NEW BOUNDARIES: We have returned to space in a big way. Countries and consortiums have pushed new boundaries of exploration. We have landed people on Mars and established an ongoing base of operations, like the International Space Station, but this one is on the Red Planet. If you want, by the end of the decade, you can go on supersonic craft and orbit the earth and return. It's a party in the sky.	6.3	5.3	(1.0)

I get it. This is serious *pasta against the wall.* But we wanted to get some perspective on what might influence the decade. And we got some surprises, not so much around the top 13 that were 8.0+ on the assessment scale that would have meaningful positive impact if they occurred, but a couple that were well below that mark. In particular, Gen Z Influence and Gun Violence.

Overall, we have a very fundamental problem. 17/20 issue areas are rated at 7.0+ in terms of their importance while only 2/20 are rated at 7.0+ in terms of likelihood. *Houston…*

The top 8 issues by the delta between impact and likelihood:

1. **Political Unity (4.6)**
2. Global Conflict (3.4)
3. Healthcare Access (3.4)
4. Press Freedom (3.1)
5. Climate Change (3.1)
6. Middle Class (3.0)
7. Compassion (3.0)
8. Retooling Education (2.9)

Read this list as some of the major challenges in the decade ahead. But note just how far the divide is on political unity. It is the leader in the clubhouse after this first round.

In one additional test of our list of 20 issues we asked the participants to select the *five issues* from this list that they felt would have the most positive impact if the issue was addressed or achieved. The column to the right indicates the percentage of participants that selected that issue as part of their top five issues. The *top six as a group* are shown below:

Issue	%Sel
HEALTH CARE ACCESS: We finally figured it out. How to provide healthcare to everyone in an efficient and low cost way. No one was denied healthcare and there were still options/ providers that people could escalate to based on their preferences. A more multi-dimensional healthcare model emerged (body/mind/soul) that dealt with the whole person and emphasize preventative and long term care.	61%
CLIMATE CHANGE: We addressed climate change in a meaningful and measurable way on a global basis. Corporations and governments were fully aligned on long term strategies. At the end of the decade, the scientists agree we had turned the corner.	58%
SUSTAINED ECONOMIC GROWTH: While there may be some ups and downs, we were able to sustain measurable economic growth over the decade. Nearly every country participated in the growth and it had a measurable impact on community development and quality of life.	55%
POLITICAL UNITY: Remarkably, in the U.S. as a model for the world, our political divides had been largely bridged. While there was still room for different approaches and ideologies, there was more common ground and effective legislation and policy in the areas that mattered. The U.S. Congress drew in some of the best and brightest in the decade and became one of the most admired institutions in the country.	50%
GLOBAL CONFLICT: Governments and leaders leveraged negotiation and long term interests to defuse many long standing global/regional conflicts. Bodies like the UN were re-tooled to help mediate and resolve conflict. Conflicts that arose were quickly addressed by global interests.	41%

RETOOLING EDUCATION: Education was completely re-invented. Early childhood education (ECE) became highly valued and publicly funded, and gave children (birth through age eight) the best start possible. All young people had access to quality higher education with no-cost alternatives for community and state colleges, to reasonably-priced private universities. Education was far more aligned with the workforce needs, graduates were workforce ready. The majority of graduates entered the workplace debt-free.	41%

Look, we have no shortage of issues for the decade ahead. Imagine for a minute that all six of the above issues were accomplished by 2029. Just a nice checklist at the end of the decade. *A healthy planet. A healthy population. Bipartisan politics. Relative peace on a global basis. An education system fair to all and producing a talented workforce driving sustained economic prosperity for everyone.* That's a pretty enticing decade to envision.

Optimism vs. Pessimism for the Decade Ahead

In one of our final activities in our initial Foresight 2020 session, we asked the group (whom we would begin to refer to as our *Foresighters*) one more time about their outlook for the decade ahead, but this time constrained them to two choices: Optimistic or Pessimistic. Despite the challenges, despite the unexpected impact of COVID-19, we saw that our group was decidedly optimistic about the decade ahead:

Question: *Reflecting again on the decade ahead and considering our session today and the input from your colleagues, how would you assess your outlook for the decade ahead:*

No.	Items	Times Selected
1.	**Optimistic**	**(86%)**
2.	Pessimistic	(14%)

Despite the complexity of the issues we identified and the gaps between impact if addressed vs. the likelihood of addressing, our Foresighters see the decade ahead *very optimistically.* We are, at our base as Americans, an optimistic culture. And we may have to set 2020 aside in a potential decade of optimism, but our group seems to suggest that we *understand* what is ahead of us and we are ready to tackle it. A good economy, continued technology advancement, putting the pandemic behind us—this may create some *serious wind in our sails.*

Finally, in our feedback exercise at the end of the session, we asked participants in this first session on March 19, 2020—the week after the dominoes fell in Sportsland and Disneyland—what the longer term impact of the coronavirus pandemic might be:

Question: *What do you think will be the longer term outcomes of what we are experiencing with the coronavirus and how we have dealt with it? How does this affect the decade ahead?*

- "I think there will be a stronger emphasis on healthcare preparedness as well as access, and more respect for science. I also think we will think harder about compassion, kindness, civility and how important leadership is."
- "Working remotely will increase dramatically, which will force addressing issues around Gen Z, aging, technology and even healthcare solutions. My hope is that we will achieve solidarity in fighting this virus which means we are able to bring civility and leadership closer to becoming the new norm."
- "This has affected the whole world. Depending on how it is dealt with and how flat the curve has gotten, it may shape the future of healthcare and preventative measures that may be put in place."
- "Huge economic dislocation. The American consumer profile will change radically. New industries will spring up to accommodate the remote-of-everything mentality. Significant increase of the population globally will go into poverty."
- "A new focus. Call it God, the Kachina Gods, Buddha, Mother Nature...we are being warned. Wake up, reconnect, row as one. If the current division continues, this polarization globally, we will not have a healthy planet for our children or grandchildren."
- "The economy is going to suffer. There are a lot of people who are out of work and won't get paid, and while the government checks will help, if this lasts for a long time, it will take a long time to bounce back. I also think there is general distrust with the government—I don't know how that can be repaired at this point. Coronavirus will permanently change how consumers shop and how they live. Similar to the Great Depression with my grandparents."
- "Because of how we normally react, we will struggle to adapt in the short term. Overall, we will learn from this and manage them better in the future."

It is remarkable how many of our key challenge themes are intertwined in this small set of sample comments about the implications of COVID-19 for the decade ahead. They point to long-simmering issues that, in a time of true global crisis, will come back to haunt us. Lack of healthcare preparedness and access, the divide in our politics and general distrust of government, the inability to address global issues as a world, the role of compassion and the delicateness of our economy.

Yet, a crisis, regardless of whether we expected it, or in any way were prepared for it, can illuminate these issues in such a way that true leadership, collaboration and innovation can take hold. Crisis can bring us together. A former manager/mentor of mine in IBM, Bob Puskar, always reminded us, "We can either hang together or hang separately." *I get it, Bob.*

So, we have an early global wake-up call in the beginning of 2020 as an unexpected element of the Foresight project. And it puts a magnifying glass on the weak links in our global armor. But an early wake-up call may give us the time and *foresight* needed to retool our collective globe for the future.

Five Foresights From Session 1

There is a lot to choose from in terms of reflecting on what this baseline session tells us about where we are and where we might be headed. Here are five key reflections from session 1 and how they may influence our decade ahead:

1. RIDING TWO WAVES INTO 2020: The prior decade seemed to be a split personality. On one hand, the advancements in technology and a strong economy made this a prosperous time for many. On the other hand, it was not an economic rise enjoyed by all. The wealth divide grew bigger, the social divide became wider, the political divide stretched further. Technology itself was a two-edged sword: great for personal communications and convenience, but easily manipulated to generate disinformation.

2. UNSTABLE POLITICS: It is absolutely fine to have different political parties, policies and ideologies. But there has always been a sense of a common cause, a reflection that America still leads the way as the example of democracy for the world, that we can be counted on. The politics in 2020 are unstable and are, by the accounts of many including those in our first session, becoming *dangerous.* They could lead to social unrest, isolationism from allies/global partners, a devaluing of science and facts, an abandonment of our very principles. How we address this growing instability and political divide will be a primary influencer in the success or failure of this decade.

3. SYSTEMIC INFRASTRUCTURE ISSUES: We have some *deferred maintenance* issues. Not just bridges and roads. A healthcare system that has some of the most outstanding treatments, technologies and practitioners—but is simply out of reach for so

many. Our education infrastructure is in need of a retooling—everything from early childhood education to traditional K-12 through envisioning new pathways to work/career. *Crushing* student debt for those fortunate enough to get through the labyrinth. Journalism and mainstream media seem to have lost their way. Infotainment. Influencing instead of informing. We are going to have to rethink the very concept of *core infrastructure*.

4. THE ELEPHANT IN THE ROOM: Climate change. Look, *I live in a desert.* I know what a heat island is. Natural disasters and 100 year events that are occurring annually just may not be *natural.* This decade—this next 10 years—may be the last window we have to effectively mitigate the impact of sustained global warming. The organization earthday.org warns that, "We have just over a decade to halve our emissions to avoid the most devastating impacts of climate change on our food supply, national security, global health, extreme weather and more." It's a global call to action for our generation to support future generations.

5. RELAX, WE'LL GET 'ER DONE: Despite all of this, we as Americans are an optimistic, glass-half-full lot. *When the going gets tough, the tough get going.* Well, my friends, the going just got tough. And I get that we have a heritage of finding a way, of putting a man on the moon, of jumping into World Wars, a little late, but still saving the day. But this pandemic is the real thing and we have been *really complacent* about a lot of things. And it is *not clear* that the current leadership is up to the task. So I do *hope* that we get it together. But remember: hope is not a strategy. We'll need a lot more action for this decade.

Meanwhile on the COVID-19 Watch

On March 19, the same day as our first Foresight session, California issues a statewide *stay at home order.* Healthcare systems are prioritizing services to those who are the sickest. The United States has reported its 100th death from COVID-19. Later in March, the Senate and House, in a rare but welcome sign of bipartisanship, pass the CARES act and it is signed into law on March 27. It's a two *trillion dollar* rescue package and it won't be enough. Not even close.

Because the slow drumbeats we heard in January and February have been replaced by the slamming of windows and doors. Not just the ticket windows at sporting events, but by big office buildings, retail stores, schools, theaters, restaurants and bars, government services, hotels and resorts—we are slamming the doors shut on our everyday lives.

Batten down the hatches—there's a storm ahead, mates! And it may be the storm of the <u>decade</u>. Everyone below the deck! Arghh!

And we are in *uncharted waters.* We are 90 days into the decade, the one that I am sure *will be the best decade of my life* and we are *adrift.* Kiss that strong economy that propelled us into the decade goodbye. Shape up that home office, guest room or kitchen table because that is your new commute in 2020. Your kids' classroom is next door to your office. Spring Break starts at 10:00pm when you finally go to bed and ends when the sun rises.

And fire up the Winnebago because that is your new *jet airliner* if you want to go anywhere.

I must say that at the end of March, I still didn't know anyone who had tested positive for COVID-19. Not in my family, my circle of friends, people I work with. We have a lot of *open space* here in Arizona and that would become my refuge along with driving trips up to Park City. But some well-known people—sports and celebrities—were getting COVID. Tom Hanks and his wife Rita Wilson. Rudy Gobert and Donovan Mitchell of the Utah Jazz. But I didn't really relate to any of them.

On March 31, Chris Cuomo of CNN announced that he had tested positive. Wow. I keep CNN on in the background of my office and I watch or listen to Cuomo Prime Time on a fairly regular basis. *A really good facilitator* in my professional view. I am sure he thinks the same of me.

But Cuomo does something that I really admired. He opened up his house and his life to us. Actually, it was more like his basement, as he would continue to broadcast his evening show from there. That was big league. *Ballsy.* But it was really revealing. We got a very first-hand account of living with coronavirus. I am also a Sanjay Gupta fan, and he would be on a lot and guide Chris and educate all of us. But coronavirus just seems more real to me now. I suddenly relate.

Our Bridge Over Troubled Waters
We would find out quickly in this first 90 days of 2020 who would really matter to us. The people that we could rely on. There was one group we would rely on big-time. And it turns out that we had relied upon them for a long time before the coronavirus hit. They had always been there for us, but we just didn't need them all the time. But we now *all* needed them *all* the time. They were the *front line* and did not need to be asked to volunteer. They were the healthcare workers. The nurses, the docs, the technicians.

And we all know one, *personally.* I guarantee it. You have one in your family—a wife or husband, son or daughter. Maybe a niece or nephew, could be a next-door neighbor. My nephew Jeff is a firefighter and EMT at Hill AFB in Utah. My niece Ellie is an RN at a hospital in Arizona. My daughter Betsy is a DPT physical therapist. They all deal with *patients*. And they are all exceptionally committed.

In 2019 I had the good fortune to support the Arizona Nurses Association (AzNA) in a project to determine the *Future of Nursing in Arizona*. Interestingly, it was also to understand the trends and influences over *the next ten years* and how to transform the nursing profession for that future. A set of 90 Arizona nurses—novice nurses new to the profession through veteran nurses who had seen it all—participated in our online sessions. While a very wide range of questions and topics, we asked them early on about why they are so *committed* to their work:

Question: *What makes you as a nurse—or someone you know as a nurse—so committed to their profession? Why is nursing so important and engaging to a healthcare professional?*

- "I want to make a difference for others in times they need caring and compassion the most."
- "What makes me so committed to my profession is that nursing to me is not a job or career, but is actually an identity for me, it is part of who I am and everything that I do."
- "The ability to impact a single life in a meaningful manner is a compelling draw to the profession. As a nurse there is the opportunity to influence others during their most vulnerable moments."
- "Nurses are very selfless individuals, like a sponge that takes all the heaviness a patient/caregiver feels and turns that into positivity. It is a very fulfilling job to be able to help people."
- "The satisfaction that comes with making a difference in people's lives when they are at their lowest point. Being able to impact the health of my community."
- "The genuine concern and care a nurse has for other people. The belief that everyone deserves to be treated with kindness, respect and dignity. The ability to be a positive influence on someone's life each day, mentally, physically or emotionally."
- "I love being a nurse. At the end of the day, knowing that I helped or made a difference in someone's life, makes me grateful and my life more satisfying."

Nursing is the tip of the spear in healthcare. And the patient load in this country was about to increase and overwhelm them. But they would not be overwhelmed. It is their calling, it is what they do. And we got to know them again in 2020, the early images of masks and shields, dealing with an unknown. They are all *passionate,* but were already dealing with *compassion fatigue* and being over-scheduled and under-resourced. And yet they held the line for us in early 2020 and would continue to do so.

When evening falls so hard
I will comfort you
I'll take your part
Oh, when darkness comes
And pain is all around
Like a bridge over troubled water
I will lay me down

--Simon & Garfunkel,
Bridge Over Troubled Water

**A 'Rosie the Riveter' inspired mural
at a hospital in Dallas (AP-2020)**

55

CHAPTER 3: The Role of Technology

A just machine to make big decisions
Programmed by fellows with compassion and vision
We'll be clean when their work is done
We'll be eternally free, yes, and eternally young...
What a beautiful world this will be
What a glorious time to be free

--*Donald Fagen, I.G.Y. (International Geophysical Year) What a Beautiful World (1982)*

April 30, 2020
Foresight 2030 Session

Kirk to Enterprise...

Let's be honest. We do not get through 2020 without technology. And I am not just talking about your favorite smartphone that starts with an 'i', but it was the massive confluence of communications, medical and transaction technologies that kept this ship afloat. We *virtualized* nearly everything from business meetings, to employee interviews, to concerts, to doctor visits, to education and probably some things that we better not mention here.

If you were going to have a global pandemic, then 2020 was the right year. In many respects the technology advances were preparing us for some pretty big shifts in how we work, how we search for, buy and receive goods and services, how we manage our fitness and health, and how we are connected with the Internet of Things (Alexa, fire up the Rolling Stones).

But COVID-19 was the *accelerating force*. Things that were interesting from a technology perspective now became *necessary and urgent*. But for the most part, they were not new, they just became new to a lot of people.

Collaborative Meeting/Connection Platforms: Zoom did not magically appear in 2020. You may be surprised to learn that Zoom was founded in April of 2011, nearly 10 years before it became synonymous with the COVID-19 era. There were a wide variety of meeting/screen-share platforms leading into the COVID-19 timeframe: WebEx was the initial corporate forerunner, it would create a virtual "town hall". One hundred people could access the platform, use Voice Over Internet Protocol (VOIP) or a traditional phone connection, but a presenter could mute all lines, share a PowerPoint or video, open up the lines for Q/A, and at least *connect* people fairly efficiently.

Skype was another shared platform that began as a free VOIP capability (I'll *skype* you around 10:00am your time) but then morphed into screen share and further collaboration. Skype was acquired by Microsoft in 2011 as a number of the traditional IT companies and players realized they needed new collaborative solutions. At that time, Skype had over 100 million users and nearly 8 million of those were paying to use Skype to make and receive voice calls globally. It was a great combination of video and voice (video calls were already 40% of Skype usage in 2011).

While Microsoft was endeavoring to advance Skype in the business world, other technologies were springing up: WhatsApp, Messenger, Snapchat and WeChat were grabbing users by the millions and competing on low cost/no cost, ease of use and communication clarity. Eventually Microsoft announced its Teams platform in 2016 and put its development and marketing focus on making Teams its primary collaboration platform. Skype was still out there and remains, according to Microsoft, "...a great option for customers who love it and want to connect with basic chat and video calling capabilities."

Which confused the shit out of most businesses in America who had Skype and Teams and could not figure out which to use and why.

Teams usage was really on the rise as the pandemic took hold (up 110% in the first four months of 2020) and became the choice for many large enterprises that already had heavy investments in Microsoft applications, and there was better attention to security than Zoom. *You might want to be famous for Zoom but you don't want to be famous for Zoombombing.* Wikipedia defines Zoombombing (or Zoom raiding) as, "The unwanted, disruptive intrusion, generally by Internet trolls, into a video-conference call." Just think of it as dropping in a little porn to spice up the CFO's financial update PowerPoint presentation.

But Zoom was at the right place at the right time. Initial security flaws aside, it was easy to use, low cost (and free for anyone doing shorter calls/meetings), and became the platform of choice for many businesses, schools, government agencies *and consumers.* And we quickly realized that all of the people who were completely clueless on conference call etiquette were doubly so when the camera was on. And it became part of our language of the pandemic.

Rounding out the Big Four on the videoconference side in addition to Zoom, Microsoft Teams and WebEx (which was acquired by Cisco in 2007 but just did not seem to catch the usage wave in 2020), was Google Meet. Google Meet essentially replaced Google Hangouts and was free to anyone with a Google Account (up to 100 participants for 60 minutes). Good security and user interface, but probably not as wide-spread or mainstream as Zoom and Teams.

And unless you opted for Antarctica or a remote island in 2020, you used one or more of these platforms to maintain your connections. And not just business, but consumers as well, which spanned from kids connect-ed for education to grandparents connected with their families and their tech-savvy kids. And video allowed us to maintain a level of personal connection. A nice way to start a new client discussion, jump on for a family update or take the place of typical project update. But larger videoconferences became a bit fatiguing. It was just not *that* interesting to watch 35 video tiles of somewhat disinterested people with digital backgrounds of the beach where they *really* wanted to be.

By the way, like many technologies, video conferencing as a technology was in play a long time ago. In 1964, at the World's Fair in New York (Flushing Meadow Park, many of you have seen the iconic *Unisphere* globe if you have gone to Shea Stadium or the US Open Tennis), AT&T debuted the *Picturephone.* You could actually have a video call with someone at a similar Picturephone exhibit at Disneyland in California. On a personal note, I actually *saw* the Picturephone at the 1964 World's Fair.

Interestingly, its futuristic look and feel (Stanley Kubrick in *2001 A Space Odyssey* predicted the Picturephone would make it to space), it was a dismal commercial failure. AT&T spent a half a *billion* dollars on the R&D for the product. AT&T's corporate historian, Sheldon Hochheiser, called it, "The most famous failure of the Bell System." It was simply *ahead of its time.*

Take a look at the picture of Lady Bird Johnson using the Picturephone in 1964…this is zooming in the Sixties!

Virtual Workforce Support: The role of technology in the pandemic went well beyond videoconferencing and connection platforms. Remarkably, many information/services-based industries were able to transition their workforces to virtual "work from home" environments. Big companies simply shut down their office environments for safety. And while some thought that in early 2020 the office exodus might last 3-6 months, others realized that to create focus and operational support for their employees, they needed to send a signal that this was not a vacation. We need you to set up a *serious* home office, put your name outside the door and perhaps put a moat around it so your kids/dogs/Amazon deliveries would not disrupt your work flow.

For many this was really not that new. "Flexible Work Arrangements" have been increasing for years where remote employees can work from home. Many of us in consulting services could work out of a guest office or hotel room while traveling (and too often on a family vacation). Pretty basic essentials—give me a flat surface for a desk, good cell phone connection and solid internet, and the office is up and running. Add a microwave and TV and you have integrated your break room.

But transitioning a national workforce at scale was a different task. And once again technology was there to enable it. Virtual Private Networks (VPNs) for secure connection to enterprise systems, big bandwidth to the home office for the heavy load of business internet transactions, email, videoconferencing and messaging. *And perhaps a little browsing in the background.*

How we work fundamentally changed in early 2020 for many people in information/services jobs *and we may never want to go back to the way it used to be.* We'll save that discussion for another chapter on the future of work, but suffice to say I am glad I don't work in commercial real estate.

And Everything Was Connected: So we connected virtually/visually. We worked virtually. Then we advanced technologies like telehealth and telemed, and we were able to deliver some essential services that way. We shopped virtually and products just showed up on the doorstep the next day. When we did go out we could use contactless POS (Point of Sale) devices or virtual wallet applications. *I mean who uses money anymore?*

And speaking of being connected 24x7, it was really good that we had that big bandwidth coming into the home front. Certainly for the home offices and essential services, but *say Hallelujah* for digital streaming. Hunker down and fire up an eight-season series on your favorite device. My personal favorites thus far: *Bosch* and *Longmire*. And just so you know that I have a little dramatic appeal, I actually liked *The Queen's*

Gambit and *Broadchurch*. Kind of stoked that another season of *Bosch* is going to drop. *But I digress.*

And this Internet of Things (IOT) was beginning to make sense to us. Personal assistants like Alexa and Google could play a song on connected smart speakers, manage the temperature and lights, lock the doors and see *who's at the door*. We were beginning to see the utility of connecting things and how it might change our lives.

And some of us wondered if this pandemic had taken us into a Brave New World that we may not really understand yet. There is a balance that we will all need to learn between controlling technology and technology controlling us.

But make no mistake about it. Technology was at the right place at the right time to enable us to keep a lot of things going in our lives in this pandemic. And if the healthcare workers were the front line of the pandemic, then the IT workers were our unsung heroes. What they did to support and transition workforces, enable telehealth transactions, handle the logistics of massive online ordering and distribution and just, somehow, allow us to stay connected, was amazing.

And if this was just April of 2020, how would technology look by the end of the decade? What role would it play in our businesses? In our government? In our daily lives? This was the context as we headed into our Foresight session on April 30. The role of technology in the decade ahead.

Beam me aboard Scotty.

Heading Into April Foresight

Locked Down. Man, we were really getting used to our homes and families again. So, I would have a pretty captive audience for the April session. People seemed to genuinely appreciate the diversion of a thought leadership session and take their minds off the implications of the virus and *when will this thing end?*

Not soon. At the end of March my home state of Arizona followed the lead of some others and finally issued *stay at home* orders. Goodbye gyms, bars, movie theaters, on-premise dining, in-person education, sports and *haircuts*. We would all get a little shaggy.

I was really excited about April 1. I had circled that day as my target to return to skiing after six months of knee surgery rehab. Wait, what? ALL the ski resorts are closed? Surely this is an April Fool's joke, right?

60

No joke. This was weird and getting weirder. A lot of questions and no answers. We were all in an episode of *The Twilight Zone* and we had no clue how to change the channel. But I still had a book to research and write, so we assembled 50 participants for our Foresight session to explore technology—where we were today and where we were headed.

And, of course, we used technology for the exploration. Fifty people on a collaboration platform: guided by voice, no video. We had learned long ago in our early virtual sessions that video was distracting when trying to truly *engage* people in simultaneous and rapid brainstorming work. Besides, I hadn't worn a shirt with buttons in the last 60 days so I am not sure how I would have looked anyway.

Another terrific set of participants, I once again share a few introductions so you have a flavor of the group that we have assembled:

- "I am an administrator in a higher education setting. My degrees are in social work. I am married and I live in the Midwest."
- "I teach Information Technology and cyber security." (Perfect!)
- "I work in the trial consulting world assisting attorneys as they prepare for trial. My background is social sciences, not law, so geared to understanding how people make decisions. My proudest achievement is my family."
- "I'm an urban planner/PR guy that fell into the e-scooter industry. Currently awaiting social distancing to ease up in Canada to relaunch our fleet of scooters across Alberta."
- "Austin, TX is my home. I am a virtual worker and have been for many years. I love to travel!"
- "An independent researcher and facilitator based in the UK. Father and currently attempting to home-educate—with mixed success!"
- "A Vermonter born, a Vermonter bred, and when I die I will be a Vermonter dead."

Well, you get the picture. A pretty interesting set of participants. And ready to engage on technology.

Reflecting on Technology

How do we think about technology? I mean, is it the great enabler or do we have some concerns that *Big Brother is watching?* One of our initial questions was to explore this fundamental philosophical view:

Question: *Our session today will focus on the influence of TECHNOL-OGY on the decade ahead. Let's start with a bit of a philosophical question: do you see technology as something that is INHERENTLY GOOD or something that is INHERENTLY BAD--or perhaps it's a bit of a HEAD-SCRATCHER--somewhere in between:*

No.	Items	Times Selected
1.	I see technology as something that is inherently good	(57%)
2.	Headscratcher--I am somewhere in between	(43%)
3.	I see technology as something that is inherently bad	(0%)

Most of us have a history with technology. We were analog before we were digital. So we have a perspective on how technology, over time, has impacted us. Often in good ways, but also we have seen the downside of technology. Good intentions, sometimes, with unintended consequences. Some times technology can simplify; some times it can *complexify.*

I began my professional career in 1977 by joining IBM. Formally known as International Business Machines, and, yes, I have heard all of the jokes—It's Better Manually, Itty Bitty Machines and I've Been Moved. But for 19 years it was an amazing opportunity to watch one of the formative periods of technology in this country. Mainframe System/370 behemoths that sat on raised floors in the big organizations; a transition from batch and timeshare systems to interactive transaction systems with—get this —CRT displays. The mainframe to distributed processing transition. The introduction of the *personal computer*. The development of email and voicemail. Mobile phones. The semi-conductor revolutions that would miniaturize everything via the silicon chip. Server technology and the introduction of the Internet. It was the *Information Age.*

So, I have great regard and value for technology. It's always been part of my work—after leaving IBM in 1996 I used a research project from IBM and the University of Arizona on how to leverage technology in group brainstorming to form the basis of my consulting practice. I like technology. But I am really cautious about technology and how it impacts what matters to us. Truth be told, *I am an analog guy living in a digital world.*

And some of you are *digital natives.* I get that. But we have all seen how technology can bring out the good and the bad. Today it's trolls, cyber-bullies, hacking, digital overload/anxiety and massive *disinformation*. But it's also efficiency, personal connection, wealth generation, convenience, the world-at-your-fingers, medical advances, scientific exploration and sending a man to the moon. *And maybe to Mars this decade!*

So, I was not surprised to see over 40% of our participants fall in the middle. No one thought technology is inherently bad and the majority saw it as inherently good. But it pointed out the caution flag that will always be with us as technology moves forward. We asked our participants to explain their POV on technology:

- GOOD: "I use technology every day and it enhances my world view. We need to always be moving forward with new innovation."
- GOOD: "I think tech can add a great deal to our lives in terms of simplifying the things we do. I can't imagine going thru this pandemic without technology we have today."
- GOOD: "Technology has advanced our quality of life over the course of four generations in ways that are simply astounding (life span, health indices, travel, communication). We have to harness and regulate it well, though, in order to ensure it is useful and 'good'. There is always the opposite side of the coin when left unchecked."
- GOOD: "It has allowed human connections across the globe that would not otherwise be possible. It puts information at our fingertips that would otherwise not be possible, which in turn allows for better problem solving."
- GOOD: "Technology has resulted in better environments worldwide, raised people out of poverty, made education universally accessible. Created immense hope for the future."

...on the other hand:

- MIXED: "I don't believe anything is inherently good or bad, but rather how something is used/applied/engaged with determines its ultimate merit. Technology enables amazing life-enhancing solutions AND also creates an existential threat to human relationships and our ability to truly connect."
- MIXED: "I think it is both. It provides so much opportunity for connection, learning, education, etc. I feel it is also negative in a lot of ways and it needs to be more regulated to protect against child endangerment and exploitation, hate speech, etc."
- MIXED: "Technology has provided tremendous advances in the workplace, science and health. It facilitates the opportunities for improving productivity. Unfortunately, its capabilities have invad-

ed spaces in a manner where there is greater disconnect and less productivity than before."

- MIXED: "Technology is good! It moves us to be able to communicate better and faster, to solve problems like getting clean water to more of the earth's population and cures to diseases and illnesses. However, I think it has also made our younger generations less capable of managing themselves appropriately in social situations, I think it has caused anxiety to be more prevalent, and I think it has created a world of "distracted" people. Balance is necessary!"
- MIXED: "Most of my childhood was without technology (digital immigrant). I'm in between because, while I love communication and access to information at your fingertips, it sometimes feels like we are more disconnected from a human perspective with technology than without it."

At a macro level, it has advanced us as a society. At a personal level, it may have changed our *humanness*. It's that delicate balance again between us controlling technology and technology controlling us.

Reflecting on the Prior Decade

To see where we might be headed in the decade ahead we also wanted to see where we had been in the prior decade in terms of technology:

Question: *Let's start by looking back. What were some of the technologies that you feel most influenced our prior decade—2010 through 2019?*

As it turned out the top three responses were:

1. Smartphone
2. Smartphone
3. Smartphone

But there were some *honorable mentions*:

- ✓ Social media
- ✓ Cloud computing
- ✓ Wi-Fi everywhere
- ✓ Online education
- ✓ Advance in personal computers
- ✓ E-Commerce (digital marketplace)
- ✓ Google everything
- ✓ The Internet of Things
- ✓ Simplified Point of Sale
- ✓ Drones

- ✓ The advent of "big data" and analytic software
- ✓ Virtual Reality
- ✓ Artificial Intelligence
- ✓ 3D printing
- ✓ Autonomous vehicles and driver assist technologies
- ✓ Advanced medical technologies and genomics
- ✓ Streaming media
- ✓ Gaming
- ✓ Digital camera integration
- ✓ Apps for *everything*

But hands down, no pun intended, the prior decade was dominated by a blurring advancement in smartphone technology. And our smartphones became *personal* to us. They were always in our hands, on the counter at the bar, in the cup holder in your car, in your jean's back pocket and more than one of you ladies found a new functional use for the brassiere.

And exactly WHY had the smartphone become so essential?

- "Smartphone, because I have access to everything that's important to me: family and friends on social media, pictures and videos of memories, health and finance areas. Everything. Total phone addict."
- "My phone. It provides access to everything I could think of and has almost replaced everything else. I can bank, shop, watch movies, play games and access any information I want—both personal and globally—from literally the palm of my hand."
- "Smartphone: keeps me connected 24/7 to what's going on in the world. Additionally, I love to read and I have an entire library on my smartphone. I can read when I'm in a waiting room or slow grocery store line—it's always there/available. Also love GPS on phone—I'm never lost!"
- "Smartphone. It allows me to work the kind of hours required for me to succeed at my job, while still balancing my life—parenting young kids, helping take care of our parents, exercise, church activity, etc. It allows me to not miss out on life because of work, and vice versa."
- "Smartphone—it is a phone, computer, camera plus photo storage, boom box, email, instant messenger, calculator, map, wallet, keys, ticket, camcorder, alarm clock, video conferencing device/projector, etc." (This may have been Ron Popeil of Ronco fame...*but wait there's more!)*
- "Unquestionably, the smartphone. Importance is CONNECTIVITY...with the world, with the daily (minutely) advancements and activities of the world and nation, and importantly, with family and friends."

Mr. Watson, come here I want you! Who could have imagined the evolution of the phone that began in 1876 with the first phone call from Alexander Graham Bell? The first car phone in 1960?

Now—from your car—you can place or receive calls from any place in the world with General Electric's Simultaneous Duplex Mobile Telephone.

1981 and I would have my own Watson moment. I was the IBM Marketing Representative for all mainframe accounts (Data Processing Division) in Tucson/Southern Arizona. Seven mainframe (System/370) systems with the largest account being Phelps Dodge, the copper mining company with an <u>enormous</u> open pit copper mine in Morenci. 174 miles from Tucson and a true "company town". Just about everything was owned by Phelps Dodge: housing, the hospital, the Phelps Dodge Mercantile—you get it. And Morenci was in the middle of nowhere. Later in my career I would recite the old joke: "If your doctor ever tells you that you only have six months to live, I'd like to recommend Morenci, Arizona—it will feel like a <u>lifetime</u>." Rim shot, please.

But I really enjoyed the drive down and the people at Phelps Dodge. Genuine. No suit and tie, jeans and a western shirt were fine. The best burritos in town were at the Phelps Dodge Bowling Alley. IBM is buying!

So, when it came time in 1981 to select an IBMer in Arizona for their car phone pilot, I was your guy. My largest account was a 3+ hour drive away! So I was blessed with this giant Nokia console phone, handset and cord, plug it into the cigarette lighter. The only trouble was that there was maybe one cell tower that gave you about 10 miles of service as you headed out on the drive. But how cool to get a call on the phone. You can reach me on my <u>car phone</u>. I was part MacGyver and part Bond. James Bond.

So, mobile phones were not new. It's just that in that prior decade (2010 through 2019), everything came together at the right time. The cell connectivity needed, the application platforms and developers, the ad-

66

vancements in screen technology, the camera quality, the chip processing power, the *styling* of the phone, the integration of really good music technology, browser access, navigation, email, etc. And, get this: *you could even make a phone call on it if you wanted!*

Not surprisingly, the overall view about the impact of technology on the prior decade was quite positive as over 75% of our participants indicated "somewhat positive" or "very positive" as noted in the table below:

Question: *All things considered, how would you assess the impact of technology on the prior decade?*

No.	Items	Times Selected
1.	**Somewhat positive**	**(44%)**
2.	**Very positive**	**(35%)**
3.	Middle of the road	(19%)
4.	Somewhat negative	(2%)
5.	Very negative	(0%)

Note that 'somewhat positive' exceeds 'very positive'. *There's that yellow caution flag again.* Where are my "glass half full" participants? But their caution is well noted in their explanations:

- SOMEWHAT POSITIVE: "Many great advances, but deterrents such as cyber crime take away from some of these advances."
- SOMEWHAT POSITIVE: "Overall, very positive, yet some dangerous influences as well, such as "fake news", child exploitation, privacy issues, etc."
- SOMEWHAT POSITIVE: "Technology has enabled major advances across manufacturing, economic well-being and human well-being, while also indirectly creating division in society that has set the stage for today's populist movements."
- SOMEWHAT POSITIVE: "The individual use of technological innovations has enabled more personal independence and achievement, but the aggregation of data from each individual's use destroys privacy and assaults liberty."
- SOMEWHAT POSITIVE: "While technology accelerated quicker time to market and operational efficiencies, improved consumer experiences and the emergence of a social and global exposure, it did change the landscape of personal face-to-face interaction and collaboration."

What Matters Today

Setting aside the prior decade, we wanted to find out the one technology that was most important for our participants and why. It's a good bridge between the prior decade and the decade ahead:

Question: *Thinking about present day, what would you say is the ONE MOST IMPORTANT TECHNOLOGY that you use TODAY that you feel provides value to you? Tell us about the technology and the value, and why this is so important to you personally:*

- "High capacity Wi-Fi. From phone communication to video conferencing to internet searches to texting, none of this would be possible without this technology. You can, in fact, do virtually anything, virtually anywhere."
- "My laptop. For the most part it is my window to the world. Information, news, communications with colleagues/friends/family."
- "iPhone. Not so much for the texting/email/phone part, but for the instant access that it provides me. The Internet as a whole is the driver, but as an interface the iPhone/smartphone is amazing. I am ever curious, and love having a computer in my pocket to be able to research/look up whatever catches my fancy."
- "Virtual Meetings—I can sell, train, interact and encourage clients from afar and not have to travel as much. Would simply not be able to do this without such tele-meeting capability."
- "Today, April 30 (2020), continuing now and working from home for 18 years. The ability to do that from a mountain community is a function of both the internet and computer capabilities. We have continued functioning in this age of COVID-19 without missing a beat relative to work."
- "Social media resources and tools to communicate and market. It is important to me because it is the easiest way to capture and share a brand message to a broad medium while also bringing them into customer view for future conversations and training."
- "Hard to decide between smartphone and my PC. But I suppose my smartphone is slightly more important because it can do more that my PC can do. I am rarely w/o my phone each day. There are times I am without my PC. Rarely, though, it seems."

Well, we are a *tethered* society. But it's a tether that gives us freedom. Smartphone/PC/Tablet as the device, internet and Wi-Fi as the connection medium, to the cloud that contains everything. *Infinity and beyond!*

But there was a certain joy in the statements—look at what I am able to do! Look where I am able to live! Look at how I do my work! Where did all of this *personal empowerment* come from?

Mind-blowing performance. I love the six-foot coiled cable...I was sure the editor of the press release wanted to insert *cobra* for cable and see if anyone noticed. And pop over to a *Sears Roebuck!* A *bi-directional* printer (it really was kind of cool to watch) and 262K of memory. Trust me, your Timex Ironman watch has that beat. And *no IBM manuals* are easily understood.

But this was *personal* to me. I was at IBM in San Jose, California, at our Data Processing Executive Institute (DPEI) when the IBM PC was announced. DPEI was an education center where IBM Marketing Reps brought their DP/IT Managers in for a week-long part education/part entertainment program. I was on the staff, definitely on the entertainment side. But we were expected to know our stuff about technology and do presentations on stage in front of 100 people at a time. The presentation technology of choice at the time: *the foil projector.*

There were two of us on staff that sensed that the IBM PC was a big deal. A tipping point in democratizing technology and *personalizing* the experience. Terry Liffick (*Terrific Liffick* as we called him) was a bit of a mentor to all of us. Older, but a little more techy. Way ahead of the curve on personal computing trends. Could walk into a Radio Shack and hold the employees spellbound...he knew way more than they did. Liffick was *Batman*. And every Batman needs...you guessed it...a *Robin.* A young protégé'. *Count me in.*

We devised a plan on how to engage these mainframe data-processing executive types to the brave new world: *PC a la Carte.* Every coffee break (we had a lot those at DPEI...) Liffick and I would bring out a brand spanking new IBM Personal Computer on a rolling cart. Printer on the bottom, PC and display on the cart and that *ever-so-convenient keyboard and six-foot cable* cradled in our arms. And we put on a show.

"Liff—what do you have there?" I would say.

"Griff—it's the IBM Personal Computer," he would say.

"Personal? In what way? What can you do with it? Does it need a *raised floor*?" I would say.

"No, but you need a raise to buy one!" he would say.

We would go for 30 minutes. Sometimes scripted and sometimes ad-lib. But we got a crowd. We'd show *Visicalc*, one of the first spreadsheets (why, the intersection of a row and a column is a *cell!*) Word processing software—get this—it was called *Easy Writer*. Accounting software from Peachtree. Printing on that *bi-directional* matrix printer. And then the crescendo: we would fire up the Hayes Stack 1200 bps Smartmodem, screeching until it connected with a host, and then we would check in on the Dow Jones News/Retrieval Service. *Check the IBM stock price.*

At the end, I would talk about the future. *This is going to get smaller. Faster. Cheaper. It will become portable. Some day you will slip one of these into your coat pocket.* Liff and I knew that we were showboating the future. I would finish the schtick: "Let me show you the prototype of the new IBM *portable* PC. A simple user interface, only two controls. Lightweight. Stylish. A screen nearly as big as the device. And a powerful screen refresh rate." Liffick knew what was coming. I brought out the *Etch-a Sketch* from my briefcase:

A vintage 'magic' Etch A Sketch

A vintage IBM Personal Computer, circa 1981

But we were making a point. Everything was changing. And we were in Silicon Valley. Apple's back yard. The race was on. And while Apple had Steve Jobs and Steve Wozniak, we had our own visionary—Don Estridge—who led the development of the IBM PC. I often wonder what would have happened if his life was not tragically cut short in the 1985 American Airlines crash at Dallas DFW airport (we lost several IBMers in that crash). It was not an immediate impact, I suppose, nothing ever is in a big corporation like IBM, but was the day the music died for the IBM PC. We would lose that race. But everyone would win in the end.

Years later I would become the Business Unit Executive for the Western United States for the IBM PC Company. We were the official laptop for the NBA. We sponsored the Fiesta Bowl with our OS/2 operating system (I'm not even sure John Junker—Director of the Fiesta Bowl at the time —saw that one coming.) We were really good with businesses, really crappy with consumers. The PC business was eventually sold off to Lenovo. I am typing on a Lenovo laptop now (seriously).

Technology in the Decade Ahead

Well, back to our Foresight session. Having reviewed the prior decade and a sense of technology today, it was time to turn to technology in the decade ahead. We wanted to be balanced in this series of activities, as we knew people were looking at technology in two ways—great if we control it (optimistic), not so great if it controls us (pessimistic). So we simply asked people what makes them *optimistic* about technology in the decade ahead and, separately, what makes them *pessimistic* about technology in the decade ahead.

In both cases we started with an open brainstorming question, followed by a real-time summary of the themes, followed by an assessment exercise about how important that aspect was to your optimism (in the first series), or your pessimism (in the second series).

As a glass half-full person I choose to start with the optimism series:

Question: *Now, let's look ahead. We are here to consider the NEXT TEN YEARS. Now through December 31, 2029. What makes you OPTIMISTIC about the role of technology in the decade ahead and how it might positively impact and influence us?*

There were 142 individual responses which we summarized into 12 primary themes and then assessed:

Now, please assess each of the following aspects in terms of how important it is to you and your family as you think about the positive impact/ influence of technology in the decade ahead. Use a scale of 1-10 where a "1" means not at all important and a "10" means extremely important:

Rank	Idea	Avg.
1.	Our ability to cure disease	9.2
2.	Significant medical advancements	9.1
3.	A safer environment	8.3
4.	Potential to solve global warming	7.8
5.	Clean manufacturing	7.4
6.	Expanded info sharing	7.1

72

Rank	Idea	Avg.
7.	Everyone has access	7.1
8.	Role of AI	7.0
9.	Advanced tele-work	6.7
10.	Role of electric vehicles	6.6
11.	Autonomous vehicles	5.8
12.	New entertainment experiences	4.9

Similarly, we asked our participants what would make them PES-SIMISTIC about the decade ahead, giving balance to our glass half empty friends:

Question: *Now, let's continue to look ahead. We are here to consider the NEXT TEN YEARS. Now through December 31, 2029. What makes you PESSIMISTIC about role of technology in the decade ahead and how it might negatively impact and influence us?*

There were 183 individual responses which we summarized into 12 primary themes and then assessed:

Now, please assess each of the following aspects in terms of how concerning it is to you and your family as you think about the negative impact/influence of technology in the decade ahead. Use a scale of 1-10 where a "1" means not at all concerning and a "10" means extremely concerning:

Rank	Idea	Avg.
1.	Information/news that cannot be verified	8.8
2.	Identity theft	8.2
3.	Tech used for disruptive purposes	8.1
4.	Proliferation of hate	8.0
5.	Lack of privacy	8.0
6.	Data breaches	7.9
7.	Increased government control	7.2

8.	Social isolation	**6.8**
9.	Continued bullying	**6.8**
10.	Intrusion into personal spaces	**6.8**
11.	Lack of equal access	**6.4**
12.	Tech taking away jobs	**6.1**

Ouch. These are pretty heavy concerns. Just the fact that we had 183 open negative comments vs. 142 open positive comments suggests that as much as we value and have become dependent on technology, we recognize the *vulnerability* of that dependency. Once again, the balance: leverage the inherent good, but be cautious about a combination of overuse (i.e., social isolation) and also bad actors (i.e., data breaches, disinformation and *big brother is watching*).

Time will tell in the decade ahead, but I have more confidence in our ability to manage personal over-use (find the analog balance in your digital life) than I do with our ability to safeguard against the bad actors. The idea of *weaponizing* information technology and disinformation is startling and yet it has been front and center in the last two election cycles. Add to that the idea of a digital bank heist of your personal assets (as well as government/business). Then consider the very real implications of *technology-terrorism* by accessing operational control systems of everything from our power grid to our military systems. Whatever we are investing in cyber security as a country/world, we need to double it and fast.

Or keep Bruce Willis (aka, John McClane) on standby. The veteran Die Hard character gave us a good glimpse of what a digital meltdown could look like in 'Live Free or Die Hard' when the bad guys launched a very sophisticated attack on America's information infrastructure. And that cine-scenario was back in 2007. The bad guys have gotten better and McClane has aged a bit.

Rounding out this section of our Foresight session, we asked our participants to reflect on what they felt was the ONE THING that made them most optimistic about the role of technology in the decade ahead and the ONE THING that made them most pessimistic:

Most Optimistic About The Role of Technology in the Decade Ahead:

- "The amount of growth that is possible...we have not even scratched the surface. Lives can be saved, and also lives can be made better, with emphasis ahead of us in technology."
- "The ability to cost-effectively and rapidly solve issues that have been expensive or slow for society to address in the past."
- "Enhanced human intelligence (Steve Job's 'bicycle for the mind')."
- "How it can play a role in improving our lives. From medical advances, space exploration and efficiencies in the workplace."
- "The younger generation's ability to create new ideas around technology—climate change, healthcare."
- "The opportunity to make life better, i.e., medical advances, autonomous vehicles, enhanced information platforms."

Most Pessimistic About The Role of Technology in the Decade Ahead:

- "Destroying people's individualistic tendencies/creativity and ability to think for themselves."
- "Easy...access by others into your privacy, your life, your finances and your 'mind', via social media, hacking, etc."
- "Unintended negative consequences that aren't anticipated and also purposeful bad actors."
- "The role that technology plays in creating social isolation, loneliness and depression, and fueling the worst parts of human nature (aggression, hate, etc.)."
- "Quality of life improvements will generally benefit the 'haves'. The escalation of misuse of technology seems to be on the rise and 'regular' people have few defenses. Misuse of AI and gene editing is downright scary."
- "The possibility of having to make the choice of becoming a house cat or plugging into super computer information and processing power."

I must admit I never thought about it from the perspective of a *house cat*. But I get it. The potential for advancement of the human state is limitless and we all see that in the decade ahead. But so do we see the potential for the diminishment of our *humanness* in the process.

And let's see where our participants ended up on this assessment of the balance for the decade ahead:

Question: *All things considered, as you reflect the overall set of factors that might influence your outlook on the influence of technology for the* *decade ahead, what's your forecast for the impact of technology now that we have considered both sides?*

No.	Items	Times Selected
1.	**Somewhat Optimistic**	**(46%)**
2.	Middle of the Road	(27%)
3.	Very Optimistic	(25%)
4.	Somewhat Pessimistic	(2%)
5.	Very Pessimistic	(0%)

Cautious optimism. It's not about pessimism; we aren't ready to return to our caves, but we are going to keep a close eye on where technology takes us in the decade ahead. The balancing act will be both personal and societal. And the stakes are high. As Jackson Browne might remind us, *there are lives in the balance.*

April of 2020 was a perfect example. Look at the indispensable role of technology in enabling our remote work, the logistics needed to keep our supply chain intact, the value of medical/bio tech to begin the effort to identify vaccine candidates. And, at the same time, there was a great *personal awakening* of what was important to us—family and friends. And what we missed: our basic everyday freedoms, going to a sporting event, a movie, a concert. Great value and respect for the tech, but a reminder of our humanness. *We are not built to be isolated.*

Where I live, in Scottsdale, Arizona, they mostly kept our parks and trails open. Pinnacle Peak, Brown's Ranch, Gateway and Tom's Thumb. You have your set around you as well. What I saw in April of 2020 was amazing. More middle-of-the-day walks with families on the trails (Mom/Dad used to be working and the kids used to be going to school). But now I saw so many dads getting on the trails and showing their sons how to mountain bike (or maybe it was the other way around). Moms and daughters on long hikes. And before you send me one of *them thar tweets,* there were plenty of moms doing the mountain bike instructing with sons/daughters and dads on the quiet walks.

The real winners in April 2020 were the dogs. Seriously, they went from lying around the house all day to constantly being on walks and runs. *Pandemic Exhaustion*, a narrative by Fido.

76

But it was a collective rediscovery of the soul. I would walk every day to a quiet bench on the Pinnacle Peak trail and just watch. Contemplate and reflect. With all the bad of the pandemic, something very good was happening.

Our participants in Foresight also saw the inherent good in technology. There was a sense in their explanations that *good triumphs over evil* in the long run, but we need to keep very mindful of the power of technology—its intentional good and its unintentional consequences and threats—front and center in the decade ahead:

- SOMEWHAT OPTIMISTIC: "While I have concerns, I like to think there are smart people out there who will work hard to address the potential negatives. Such that the good outweighs the bad."
- SOMEWHAT OPTIMISTIC: "Technology is a greens fee, essential for continued progress of humanity. Critical to instill policy and guidelines that support technology advancements while protecting human rights."
- SOMEWHAT OPTIMISTIC: "I think the positive impacts will touch more lives in more fundamental ways than the negative impacts will, because I believe that society and governments will (perhaps belatedly) devise ways to block the truly destructive uses of technology."
- SOMEWHAT OPTIMISTIC: "What a marvelous piece of technology we can all hold in our hands. The only problem is the tendency for technological activities to consume our lives."
- MIDDLE: "We have to be mindful of the impact of technology in our lives and how we allow it to be regulated or abused. Most of us have been indifferent or unaware, but we are frogs in boiling water."

First house cats and now *frogs in boiling water*. The early stages of the pandemic lock down are beginning to take effect.

The Technologies on the Horizon
But we were not done with this *very engaged* Foresight session. What would be the compelling technologies in the decade ahead? What did they see as the *art of the possible*?

Question: *Wide open now. Think about technology in a broad sense—it can be information technology, medical technology, manufacturing technology, military technology, agricultural technology—you get the idea. Our key question is this: What do you feel will be the technologies that will most influence the decade ahead?*

Over 125 responses...it was easy to imagine the potential for the future. We could all sense the *level of acceleration* that was happening with technology in many fields. We summarized the responses into 15 baseline themes and assessed them relative to their *influence* on the decade ahead:

Now, please assess each of the following technologies in terms of THE LIKELY INFLUENCE you feel that each technology will have on the decade ahead. Use a scale of 1-10 where a '1' means a very low level of influence and a '10' means a very high level of influence:

Rank	Idea	Avg.
1.	Artificial Intelligence (AI)	9.0
2.	Medical diagnostics	8.9
3.	Disease detection/cure	8.9
4.	Clean energy	8.0
5.	Cyber security	7.8
6.	Accelerated genome sequencing	7.7
7.	Agricultural advances	7.4
8.	The cloud	7.2
9.	Smarter smartphones	7.0
10.	5G	6.8
11.	Online learning	6.5
12.	Electric vehicles	6.5
13.	Public transit advances	6.3
14.	Autonomous vehicles	6.0
15.	Space travel	5.5

Talk about a *Brave New World*. This is pretty exciting stuff. It's a combination of *enablers* such as AI, 5G communications, the cloud and even *smarter* smartphones. But some important focus areas of medical diagnostics, clean energy, disease prevention, agriculture advance, transportation impact. And space travel made the list.

Space Rebounds in the Decade Ahead

Look, space and NASA were the definition of technology in the 1950s and 1960s. We were in a *space race* with the Soviets and it was a *technology* race. It gave us the first sense of the capability of technology for man, a sense of no boundaries. That "one small step for man, one giant leap for *mankind*" was about technology. It gave us other impressive technology outcomes as well, *Tang* being one of the first tangible consumer outcomes of the massive investment in NASA. Great stuff, I remember it from our cabin in the mountains in Payson, Arizona, as a kid. Practical, too. It had a shelf-life of about a hundred years.

But space travel at the bottom of the list? Are you kidding me? It seemed like once we made it to the moon in 1969 we weren't sure where to head next. The Space Shuttle program seemed poised to take us to the next boundaries of space with a 30-year run from 1981 through 2011. 135 missions that captivated us at the start but then became *routine*. There is an inherent danger when wondrous things become perceived as routine. We forget to marvel about wondrous things. For space travel and its technology we forget to look to the sky and imagine what is possible.

This topic is also personal to me. Of the two space shuttle disasters, Challenger and Columbia, Challenger was probably the one most people remember. CNN was broadcasting it live on January 28, 1986. It was such an anticipated launch. Many of you, I suspect, were children watching the launch live. This was the *education* shuttle. It was the teacher-in-space Christa McAuliffe who would be conducting *lessons in space*. The goal, according to informational site Britannica, "was to highlight the importance of teachers and to interest students in *high-tech* careers." And in 73 seconds, that desired impact was, for a period of time, taken away from us. That live image of the explosion, that Y-shaped billowing trail, was played over and over and over again. The impact of space technology converged with the impact of media technology: 85 percent of Americans had heard about the news *within an hour* of the accident.

And it brought up the difficult question: *was the quest for space worth it?*

After nearly three years of a presidential commission review (Reagan formed the Roger's Commission to investigate the accident) Wikipedia reports out: "The commission found that NASA's organizational culture and decision making process had been contributing factors to the accident." *Remember that finding.*

The Challenger flight was STS-51. (STS stands for Space Transportation System.) While I remember the Challenger accident very clearly, it was the second Shuttle disaster that became more personal to me and more instructional about technology and leadership.

STS-107. 56 flights later. On February 1, 2003, the Shuttle Columbia disintegrated on its way back into earth atmosphere re-entry. Not many people were paying attention to Shuttle landings then. Flights had resumed, things were back to *routine*. The launches barely got coverage, maybe a quick break-away during the cable news broadcast.

STS-107 Columbia at takeoff

I had left IBM in 1996 and was consulting using the *GroupSystems* collaborative technology. It was designed for in-person sessions and was the forerunner of a number of online collaboration technologies, including the one that I was using for the Foresight series. NASA reached out to GroupSystems, as an investigation process was being formed into the Columbia accident (Columbia Accident Investigation Board) and would be based in Houston. Admiral Hal Geyman would head the CAIB and had experience with GroupSystems and wanted to use it for developing cause scenarios and to help ensure candid response and input by the CAIB and guests.

Three of us were dispatched by GroupSystems to manage the CAIB usage of the software in their investigation. We would be assigned rotations of 7-10 days to be onsite in the main CAIB conference room to support the process. The cause of the accident was *suspected* to be a foam strike to one of the wings of the Shuttle upon liftoff—something that would not be detected during the entire flight and would only have its damaging impact upon re-entry when the wing structure would fail due to the strike. Geyman wanted all possibilities to be on the table—internal sabotage, a military strike by an adversary, pilot error and (I am not kidding here) an alien caused event. Aliens?

My son Jack once recited a statement to me that I thought was quite profound. "We are either alone in the universe or we are not. Either of these possibilities is <u>terrifying</u>." So true.

So, if you want to gain an appreciation for space exploration, the technology, the people and the politics, watch it up close for a few months. And watch it with an infographic on the wall in the boardroom that was five feet by seven feet, of the seven astronauts in their orange flight suits before the launch. That is the true *humanness* behind the technology. *Do not forget why we are trying to understand what happened.*

And that very smart and dedicated 13-member Board—physicists, technologists, safety professionals, military professionals and fellow astronauts (Sally Ride was on the Board) were able to determine the *two causes* of the accident by August of 2003:

From my copy of the CAIB Volume 1 Report:

The *physical cause*:

"The physical cause of the loss of *Columbia* and its crew was a breach in the Thermal Protection System on the leading edge of the left wing, caused by a piece of insulating foam which separated from the left bipod ramp section of the External Tank at 81.7 seconds after launch and struck the wing in the vicinity of the half of the Reinforced Carbon-Carbon panel number 8. During re-entry this breach allowed superheated air to penetrate through the leading edge insulation and progressively melt the aluminum structure of the left wing, resulting in a weakening of the structure until increasing aerodynamic forces caused loss of control, failure of the wing and breakup of the Orbiter."

So, two interesting points here: 1) The cause of the re-entry accident was actually at the launch but no one knew that the wing had been breached during the entire flight; 2) The CAIB actually proved the cause finding by firing a piece of foam at a wing model in a warehouse over one weekend. They were actually ecstatic that they had undeniable root cause evidence.

The *organizational cause:*

"The organizational causes of this accident are rooted in the Space Shuttle Program's history and culture, including the original compromises that

were required to gain approval for the Shuttle, subsequent years of re-source constraints, fluctuating priorities, schedule pressures, mischarac-terization of the shuttle as operational rather than developmental and lack of an agreed upon vision for human space flight. Cultural traits and organi-zational practices detrimental to safety were allowed to develop..."

Admiral Geyman summed it up one morning during the daily briefing: "The machines were talking but no one was listening." The "machines" were all of the safety processes, guidelines and even cultural cues that should have alerted people. For example, cameras that were normally focused in on the Shuttle during the launch were off or malfunctioning.

Just as many Americans had thought of the Space Shuttle mission as "routine", so had NASA. Geyman would preach certain leadership princi-ples about technology and space flight. A flight should never be routine, it was *always* developmental in every regard, never "operational". And sometimes we fail to keep important findings or lessons in front of us. Reflect back to the Roger's Commission some 17 years earlier. *A cultural failure.*

Geyman and the CAIB corrected the Shuttle course. Twenty-eight sub-sequent flights went off safely. None were viewed as routine by those responsible for the flights.

So, I know you have a point here, Doug. We should always be in amazement of the wonder of technology. And we should always respect its potential and *watch it carefully.* And space technology should be high-er on our list of technologies for the next decade. And, for some it is. My daughter, Betsy, is a millennial with a keen eye for stars. She is a bit of an amateur astronomer and actually has this massive telescope at our house that she takes out on clear evenings and dials in a planet, a star or even the International Space Station. I have no doubt that if commer-cial space travel does become commonplace in the decade ahead, that she will book a trip. *And I would be delighted to join you.*

Back to the Future
And so we continued with our Foresight session on the Future of Tech-nology, and asked our participants to opine on the one most important technology for the decade ahead:

Question: *As you reflect on all of the technologies that we identified and assessed, and any others that might come to mind now, what do you feel will be the ONE TECHNOLOGY that will most significantly affect the decade ahead? Why that technology and what do you think that impact will be?*

The why is as important as the what, and one technology was dominant:

- "AI: AI will make everything from cars to farmers to the human body run more effectively based upon more efficiency, better decision-making and faster problem detection/resolution."
- "AI/Robotics will fundamentally reshape how we work, how we function, and ultimately raise the question of what is humanity's role going forward."
- "Artificial intelligence—it carries the promise of incredible good (helping us solve large, global, intractable problems) but also potentially devastating negatives (elimination of human work, lack of moral or ethical constraints, exacerbation of economic inequality)."
- "AI to help develop cures for cancers, COVIDs and other long-standing health challenges that we heretofore have been using very blunt objects (like chemotherapy) for treating. Greater understanding and insights will lead to the development of highly tailored, highly targeted cures, therapies and treatments."
- "AI, because that technology would hit so many areas—transportation, medicine, manufacturing, distribution of food across the globe. We can't even conceive of all the ways AI might change us, and it's in such an infancy stage right now."

Keep in mind, I just have 50 *interesting* people on the session, none of whom are physicists, rocket scientists, or heuristic algorithm programmers. They just have a sense that the power of Artificial Intelligence—which happens to be just *one* of the elements of the so-called 4th Industrial Revolution—may represent the next level of technology impact in the decade ahead.

What say you, HAL?

Technology Scenarios
In one of our final activities in this Foresight session, we presented a series of scenarios to stimulate a bit of thought around the future of technology. We wanted to see how realistic the scenarios might be—how likely they might be by the end of the decade:

Now, please assess each of the following future scenarios in terms of how feasible you feel that scenario might be by the end of the decade. Use a scale of 1-5 where a "1" means strongly disagree and a "5" means

#	Scenario Description	Rate
1	UNLIMITED BANDWIDTH: Bandwidth is like air...it is everywhere and everyone has access. You have unlimited bandwidth at home, at work, while you are traveling. We have moved to a smart infrastructure at the regional level where we can adjust the bandwidth thermostat up and down as needed (all automated, of course). There is no more digital divide.	**4.0**
2	THE NEW DIGITAL UNIVERSITY: After the pandemic in the early part of the decade, we never really went back to traditional education. Most education was delivered digitally with virtual reality classrooms that allow us to interact with multiple cultures and learners. Our learning modules were customized and aligned to our career/professional interests and enabled us to be job ready on day 1. Educational content could be streamed and stored with a micro-implant and recalled as needed.	**3.8**
3	AGRI-TECH IS THE NEW TECH: Agriculture technology allows us to optimize the nutrition and yield of nearly any crop while eliminating nearly all of the diseases and threats real-time. Pesticides are no longer needed. All watering systems are automated and highly efficient to provide the ideal growing conditions. Fruit has a longer window for retaining ripeness, which minimizes food spoilage and loss. Home gardens with rapid-yield technology supplement the food needs of many families.	**3.7**
4	HEALTHCARE IS SELFCARE: Home and wearable diagnostics have replaced the need for most doctor visits. Everything is constantly monitored—O_2 level, temperature, heartrate, a monthly scan for diseases, nutrition index and overall health/fitness level. If you do need to see a doctor it is by tele-med with an ability to run advanced remote diagnostics. Nearly all surgeries, if needed, are outpatient and mostly automated or augmented by robotics and micro-surgery devices. Nearly any joint can be replaced and the replacement joint is superior to the natural joint. There has been a measurable and sustainable increase in life expectancy.	**3.6**

5	THE 4TH INDUSTRIAL REVOLUTION WAS A PEACEFUL TRANSITION: It did not happen overnight, but it did happen. By the end of the decade the way that work was done had been fundamentally changed. Artificial Intelligence, Robotics, Big Data, nano-technology, ubiquitous 3-D printing and limitless computational power were working in harmony in development, design and manufacturing. Products were better, people were coordinating and applying new knowledge, and many previously unsolvable problems had been addressed. The new age created new opportunities. There were still plenty of traditional trades and crafts that people could pursue, but many in Gen Z had become the leaders in the implementation of the Revolution, and guided it with purpose and value. The economic divide has been narrowed.	**3.6**
6	WAR GAMES ARE THE REAL GAMES: Most military conflicts are resolved with technology—unmanned aircraft, virtual fences/borders, weapons that are largely controlled by joystick. Advanced cyber approaches allow us to disarm enemies and prevent many conflicts. Stealth advances are amazing...we pretty much know when anyone will make a move before they make it. Shields up, we can avert a strike on any city/location as needed. Our most powerful weapon is technology itself.	**3.5**
7	ALONG FOR THE RIDE: Autonomous vehicles are the norm. We are used to them and we all value them. Enter a freeway and the autopilot takes over and slots you into a speed lane. A voice command moves you to your desired off-ramp. Need a ride in a new city? Reserve an autonomous rental, dispatch your Uber ride with a quick voice request on your iPhone 1000. All trucking is handled by autonomous rigs. Autonomous travel is completely safe and incredibly efficient.	**3.4**

8	A NEW LEVEL OF ENERGY: Solar, wind, thermal and hydro technologies have progressed where nearly all residences and many cities are powered by these alternative energies. Home solar/wind units are compact and include adequate storage capacity for any peaks. Devices come with lifetime batteries (micro-generators) so that replacing batteries or worrying about laptop/phone battery time is no longer an issue. 90 percent of all cars/trucks are electric and efficient, a combination of rooftop solar and ultra-fast drive-by recharging panels have eliminated the need for electric plug in stations. Oh, by the way, the air is MUCH cleaner.	**3.4**
9	INTELLIGENT RECREATION: Weekend warrior? Would you like to ski better, learn to sail, ride a surfboard, cycle on the road (instead of on your Peloton at home)? Imagine the micro-intelligence that could be built into a pair of skis. Autosense the slope, the condition of the snow, see the moguls, set a perfect line. Click on the auto-pilot on your ski pole, record the run with your Google goggle-cam. It autocorrects if you catch an edge. And you can apply this to nearly any sport. Gotta catch that one last ride? Surf's up.	**3.3**
10	VIRTUAL STADIUM: Look, a hot dog and a beer sounds great, but nearly everything else about getting to the ballpark (sport of your choice) is a hassle. Why go to the game when you can be PART OF the game from home. Want to feel what it is like to be the center fielder climbing the wall to rob a home run? Be an NFL running back and accelerate through a narrow gap? Strap in at home and watch the game from any angle, listen to any voice. Everyone on the team has micro cameras you can display, everyone has a mic. Are you a wannabe coach? Well, here's what is really going on in that time out!	**3.1**
11	CONSTANTLY CONNECTED: Mobile connectivity is an entirely different level. A micro device can be implanted in your ear for crystal clear sound and communications—you can connect with anyone, anywhere, with a simple voice command. No need for a video chat, just activate your holographic display for super clear video (with your friends, research a new vacation destination, catch the news...). Another micro implant allows you to transmit what you see. Share a view, share a ski run, share a moment in time.	**3.0**

12	SPACE IS THE COOL FRONTIER: Technology advances and private sector investment ushered in a new travel boom —space tourism replaced eco-tourism. A joy ride was now a quick earth orbit or a sling shot around the moon. Multiple planets had destination colonies that you could book for a week, a month or even a year. Nearly every major city on the globe had a space port to transport you to an outlying destination. While not affordable for everyone, it was within reach of many. Our horizons had been expanded.	**2.8**

I wrote these scenarios because I think *every one of them is possible for the decade ahead.* Actually, I personally think every one of them is *likely* for the decade ahead. And there are plenty of others—how about *drones as first responders* or all money is replaced by *digital currency.*

But this is my Foresight list. We should all envision the future of technology, we should all have a sense of what's possible. But then be cautious about the implementation and any unintended consequences.

And I was a little surprised that more of my participants weren't a little stronger on the likelihood of these occurring across the board. I mean, people, let's talk about space technology...

One thing that I learned since becoming acquainted with technology from my IBM roots back in 1977: do not doubt the pace and potential of technology. We have a *decade* to watch what will happen with technology. We should all be mindful that *Moore's Law* is still in effect. In layman's terms Moore's Law (named after Gordon Moore who created the hypothesis in 1965) is simple: *The number of transistors on a microchip doubles every two years while the cost of computers is halved.*

Yawn. No look, this is serious as you consider the future. We sold (and especially leased) a boatload of IBM mainframes and disk drives because of this guy and this law. Simpler language? Technology will continue to double in speed and be half the price. Every time you blink. Why do you think every person in a third world country may not have fresh water but they have a smartphone? Every time someone thinks that we are hitting a wall in technology, a new innovation/advance happens and we are off to the next level of tech.

How about this: let's see where we are mid-decade, say end of 2025. I'll do an update on technology and my forecasts. I'd say it would be a sequel and I will publish as a book, but we probably won't have any books then and I will just press send and you will receive it via a neuroscience signal...

Balancing Technology

As a whimsical exercise we asked our Foresight participants to take a moment and share how they balance the use of technology within their overall lives:

Question: *Technology can have many positive impacts on our lives— how it connects us, protects us and enables us to see a larger world. But it also has an effect of speeding everything up, of compressing time, of constantly tapping us on the shoulder, of exhausting us. Many of us try to create a balance to the technology impact—a way to slow down, "get off the grid" and unplug for a while. What are some of the things that you do that create that analog balance to your digital world?*

Pretty funny stuff, actually:

- "Tap into my much more exciting inner world exploring my physical intelligence :) ."
- "Have a good conversation with a friend."
- "Visit my siblings, do a jigsaw puzzle."
- "Once in a while READ a PAPER newspaper or magazine."
- "Amateur horticulturist, ride Harley, golf, drive fast cars."
- "Sit in cafe and engage a stranger in conversation."
- "Meditate in my jacuzzi."

Me, I prefer tackling a *Jumble* at the end of a hard day.

Technology and COVID-19

So on April 30, 2020, we are in a scary and uncertain phase of COVID-19. The realities of a government-mandated *lock-down* in our communities. School's out for summer (and it is only spring, Alice). WFH (Work From Home) has become a legitimate acronym in corporate America. We asked our participants about the role of technology early in the pandemic:

Question: *Let's reflect on the role of technology and how it has played out thus far and may play out further in the future on the COVID-19 pandemic. Did it help us prepare? Is it helping us navigate these times? Will it enable us to resolve the crisis? Has it constrained or hindered us in any way?*

It's fascinating to reflect on the responses. It's like an episode of *24—events are happening in real-time:*

- "Technology has allowed large parts of the economy, as well as education, to continue. It will also lead to eventual development of a vaccine."
- "The use of smartphones for contact tracking. The Bio advances using RNAi technology to work to enable virus vaccines."
- "The predictive modeling has been critical in driving plans to flatten the curve and keep us connected to how well it's working."
- "It has helped to prepare and navigate—advanced our ability to quickly move to telehealth, explore cures and vaccines, and to stay connected to others while physically distant, work from home. Careful on moving too fast with solutions without proper testing and trials."
- "Sad to me how LITTLE it has helped. Perhaps it will help now, moving into faster development/testing of treatments and vaccinations. But one would think it would have helped us prepare better up front. One would think it would have helped in the appropriate distribution of testing, etc., across the country (and world), but that did not happen."
- "I cannot imagine going thru this pandemic w/o technology at our finger tips. I've thought often about our grandparents dealing with pandemic of 1918 w/o technology. How did they manage to stay connected? How did they receive information? How did they receive help when needed? I see this contrast between us and them as significant. I am more dependent on tech now than even 2 months ago. I see it as a good thing."
- "We failed at using technology to help the world navigate the pandemic. The access to information, collaborating on protocols, responses and data gathering were all major fails considering the technology tools at our disposal."

Hmmm. *The Machines were talking but no one was listening?*

The Biggest Decade Ever for Technology?

In our last content question, we were curious to see if our participants felt like this would be the *most significant decade ever* for technology and its impact on our lives, or just *another decade of advancement*:

Question: *Every generation experiences the impact of technology advancement and change and (likely) holds it with a certain sense of awe. How it is today, compared to how it used to be. Do you think that THIS DECADE will be the decade where technology had a more profound impact on our lives than any other decade? Or will it just be a decade of advancement, to be followed by the next?*

No.	Items	Times Selected
1.	This decade will see important technology advances but nothing ever moves as quickly as we think it might. It will change some things.	(60%)
2.	This decade will be the most profound technology impact that we have ever seen occur. It will change everything.	(40%)

And the caution flag continues. It's clear that technology is a continuum. There is always something around the corner. There will be big advances in the decade ahead, but it is just one decade. Our participants saw both possibilities:

- CHANGES EVERYTHING: "I think we are on the cusp of a more Jetson's-like lifestyle than ever before."
- CHANGES SOME THINGS: "I believe that it'll be important (the decade) but we won't be vacationing on Mars anytime soon."

Well, at least they are picking up on the space theme.

Five Foresights From This Foresight Session

So there is a lot to reflect on from the session and the Future of Technology. Here are five key reflections from the session and how they may influence our decade ahead:

1. INHERENTLY GOOD BUT POTENTIALLY DANGEROUS: Most of us see technology as inherently good and we value all that it has done for our lifestyle, our economy, our ability to connect, for the medical advancements and for the information/knowledge access it gives us. But we see a dark shadow at times—disinformation, a digital divide that can be leveraged politically, weaponizing of information, military technologies without fail-safes, bad actors that want to breach sensitive information and infrastructure operations. This caution will continue into the decade. And that should make technology *better*.

2. TECHNOLOGY HAS BECOME PERSONAL: Let's face it—we are connected now and forever. We don't just hang on to our smartphones, we have a *death-grip* on them. But that is our new-found level of freedom. And we do not want to lose that freedom. The smartphone has become our personal assistant and access point to everything. And in the decade ahead the

personal technology will only get more personal. More wearable technologies (watches, smart glasses, earbuds that are practically invisible, more medical sensors) and don't be surprised that *imbedded* chips/tech become more common.

3. BIG TECH READY FOR BIG ISSUES: The promise of the decade ahead is how technology can be used at a larger scale to address really significant global issues. Climate change, new modes of transportation, agricultural advances, disease prevention, new energy sources, retooling of education, better healthcare, more global collaboration, an ability for AI to problem solve and predict in a way we never imagined. It should also help on the economic front, giving more people access to information, tools and services. The continued application of Moore's Law should give us optimism that more can be done (no pun intended) at scale to address the big issues and at the same time enable technology to be affordable for more people. Good bye, digital divide?

4. THE MACHINES ARE TALKING, SOMEONE NEEDS TO BE LISTENING: We cannot become complacent with technology nor accept it as routine/commonplace. We must appreciate it, but keep an eye on it. It should allow us to "see around the corner" on trends, but we need to have leadership and apply societal values when we see technology heading in the wrong direction.

5. MAINTAIN YOUR ANALOG BALANCE IN THE DIGITAL WORLD: This is the most important balance for the decade ahead. Leverage and enjoy technology, but do not let it overwhelm you or your humanness. Find and practice the analog behaviors that give you the right balance and perspective. *And teach your children well.*

So, April of 2020 was an important lens from which we could see the implications of technology in the coming decade. All of the above Foresights were in play. As we noted at the start of this chapter, we could not have gotten through 2020 without the role of technology. And, at the same time, we saw a personal awakening about what really mattered to us. It was an important lesson in the balance that we should strive for in technology in the decade ahead.

I remember reading a Time magazine essay back in 1986 when I was still at IBM in the *real acceleration* of the Computer Age. It was by Roger Rosenblatt, a gifted author and essayist who still writes and is currently the Distinguished Professor of English and Writing at Stony Brook University. His 1986 Time Cover Story (December 29, 1986) was entitled *A Letter to the Year 2086* and was a reflection on America in 1986 and how the future America may or *may not* change. I found it to be a fascinating interplay about technology and our humanness:

A Letter to America in the Future: (written in 1986--excerpts)

What would you like to know first? A preliminary sketch? We are not as dead as we seem. On these low slung mornings, your long gone countrymen are attacked in their sleep by emphatic music played on clocks and radios that are yoked together...they proceed to their offices populated with machines designed to give them back the free time they have nearly forgotten how to use. En route they pass people with telephones in their cars, dealing with those they cannot reach because of traffic jams. Some others they pass make homes out of shopping carts, speak the language of the mad, and stare at their loneliness with disbelief...

Children squeal and flutter into schools where the poor are taught poorly and the rich look forward to careers in international banking. Men and women in nearly equal numbers take their stations at jobs that have less and less to do with making things and more with providing 'services' (a service manufactures happiness for the sedentary)...the pace is heady, overwhelming...

There is, nonetheless, a strange suddenness to our times. Days, months sweep by without a ripple, and then from nowhere the news leaps out and grabs one by the collar...this year alone a widowed housewife deposed a foxy tyrant, a stockholder took hold of a giant entertainment company, a space vehicle that was supposed to fly crashed to the earth, a peace meeting between the world's two leaders, a disease took on the look of a plague, a nuclear power plant exploded, a country that keeps blacks and whites separated started coming apart...

Do things sound familiar to you, or has the world advanced so exponentially in these hundred years that our common sights are like fossils? Futurists guess about your life, drawing pictures of robot doctors, television sets that one can talk back to, cars that park themselves. There must be more to you than that...

What did you do to protect the overpopulations we predicted? How did you protect the seashores? What did you do to keep the ozone layer intact, the energy supply, the trees? Have you eliminated ignorance, brutality, greed? You haven't, I know. But one has to ask. Does your world revere the past—not us specifically, but the past in general?

In some ways, then, we are giving you the future in this letter, which seems a right thing to do for one's children's children's children. Look back to us as we look to you; we are related by our imaginations. If we are able to touch, it is because we have imagined each other's existence, our dreams running back and forth along a cable from age to age. Hold this paper to the light. It is a mirror, a delusion, a fact in the brief continuous mystery we share? Do you see starlight? So do we. Smell the fire? We do too. Draw close. Let us tell each other a story.

So, perhaps, in 2020, the future came to visit us early, but helped reawaken us at the same time. And we all found our own ways to reflect on the personal reawakening in 2020.

My "contemplation bench'"
April 2020

My view of Pinnacle Peak
from said bench

CHAPTER 4: The Future of Work

Everybody's working for the weekend!

--Loverboy, <u>Working For The Weekend</u> (1981)

You better not try to stand in my way
'Cause I'm walking out the door
Take this job and shove it
I ain't workin' here no more

--Johnny Paycheck, <u>Take This Job And Shove It</u> (1977)

I love the mornings!
I clap my hands every morning and say, "This is gonna be a great day!"

--Dicky Fox, mentor to Jerry Maguire, from the movie <u>Jerry Maguire</u> (1996)

June 25, 2020
Foresight 2030 Session

Let's get to <u>work</u>, shall we?

How appropriate that our next session would be looking at the *future of work*. I mean, we have just upended every aspect of work in the early stretch of 2020 and we really have no clue where this is headed. Many of us have abandoned the ship where our offices used to be and set up shop at home. Others of you—and thank you—are deemed as essential workers and handling everything from medical care to grocery/pharmacy stores to first responders for fire/police to an army of people delivering *everything* to our doorsteps. And, some of you have experienced that very difficult and emotional reality of losing a job or being furloughed.

My daughter Betsy received her *doctorate* in physical therapy in December 2019 and was hired on full time at a Physical Therapy clinic in Scottsdale in January 2020. In April she was called into the manager's office and advised that she was being furloughed. "Do you know what being *furloughed* means?" her employer asked her. "Yeah," she replied. "It means you get to feel better about firing me."

94

These millennials are pretty sharp.

Look, we all have different views about work—the three quotes at the start of the chapter give us a pretty good spectrum to choose from. And, seriously, your song is *Take This Job and Shove It* and your name is *Johnny Paycheck?* Trust me, friends, if you have ever been in a cowboy bar you'll know that song is alive and well. Usually about 12:30am.

But one thing is clear to all of us. *Work Matters.* I know it starts at the base of *Maslow's Hierarchy of Needs* as in it gives me food, clothing and shelter. But work, for most of us, goes way beyond the base. It gives us *purpose.* It lets me *make a difference.* It creates *pride and dignity.* And probably half of you met your significant other as a result of your work as it creates a *social community.*

Early Research and Lessons on Work
Lesson 1
Back in college (I attended the renowned Northern Arizona University) in 1973 through 1977, I had a number of experiences that would influence my views on work. The first was a book that I read called *Working* by Studs Terkel. *Good Lord. Where do parents come up with these names for their children?* It was subtitled: *People Talk About What They Do All Day And How They Feel About What They Do.*

Terkel's book was an *oral history,* meaning that he relied on one-on-one interviews with people (workers in this case) to tell him about their jobs and what they meant. I must say that I loved the approach of an oral history. It was direct, emotional and showed the art of interviewing, which I later parlayed into the art of facilitating. *Thank you, Studs.*

Studs and his interviewees did not sugar coat things:

From the author in his Introduction:

For many, there is a hardly concealed discontent. The blue-collar blues is no more bitterly sung than the white-collar mean. "I'm a machine," says the spotwelder. "I'm caged," says the bank teller and echoes the hotel clerk. "I'm a mule," says the steelworker. "A monkey can do what I do," says the receptionist. "I'm less than a farm implement," says the migrant worker. "I'm an object," says the high-fashion model. Blue-collar and white call upon the identical phrase: "I'm a robot."

Well, shit. All those jobs are off my list. I mean, I was pretty pumped to get an inside track on the *meaning of work* and I did not like where this was going.

But then Terkel shows a glimmer of hope. That some people really value their jobs and can be an inspiration to others. He concludes the lengthy introduction to his lengthy book (some *800* pages) with a quote from a Brooklyn fireman:

"The fuckin' world's so fucked up, the country's so fucked up. But the fireman, you can see them produce. You see them put out a fire. You see them come out with babies in their hands. You see them give mouth-to-mouth when a guy's dying. You can't get around that shit. That's real. To me, that's what I want to be."

OK, so I will keep fireman on the list.

The 800 pages (and I read the whole thing in 1974) was a head-spinner on work, life and your philosophical approach to both.

Lesson 2
My *second* bit of research was conducted in the summer of 1976 between my junior and senior years in college. Summer school in Guadalajara, Mexico. Twenty-eight hours on a Mexican train from Nogales, Arizona, to Guadalajara, and then I lived with a Mexican family there. *Immersive.*

And I noticed, during my immersion, that there was a pride in work, but a joy in life, in Mexico. There was a reason to take two hours at lunch—you could relax, unwind, be with friends. When work was over, it was *over*. A good meal at home, great discussion with everyone. When it was the *Señora's* birthday on Saturday, *that* was the priority. It was a different sense of *time*. I declared, right then and there, that I would not be bound by a machine on my wrist when I would get my first job out of college. It would be a symbolic commitment to life being more important than work.

When I joined IBM in 1977 I stayed true to that commitment. I did not wear a watch. It made me something that was *different* than the other IBMers I worked with.

It made me late.

On the issue of work and pride about what I saw in Guadalajara, I remember an incident that has always stuck with me. I was on a bus heading back from school (public bus, a noisy diesel). The driver had a crisp white Mexican shirt on. The area around the driver was neat and orderly. He was very polite but very time efficient at the stops. He was very serious and very proud of his work. He did not slouch. He sat straight up ahead with his eyes on the road.

96

During the ride a group of younger riders started messing around on the bus. Pushing and shoving, very loud, very inconsiderate. The driver asked them several times to please sit down and obey the bus rules. There were older riders who were clearly bothered by the group and he could see it. This seemed like a stand-off and, sooner or later, the driver would get to the stop where these kids could exit. *Please.*

But that's not what happened. He pulled over and there was no bus stop. He turned off the engine. He stood up and faced the kids: "No es juego," he said. "Es *trabajo.*" And he repeated it several times. *This isn't a game. This is my <u>work</u>.* No one, and I mean, *no one,* said a word. But we all knew what he meant: This bus ain't rolling until you sit down and settle down. This is my work, and you will not insult it.

We rolled.

I have never seen—in my life—a more genuine example of pride in one's work. And it's a lesson I have taken forward in the work that I do. *No es juego, es trabajo.* What I do matters.

Lesson 3
During my senior year in college, I was taking a class from Dr. Norman Gaither. Business operations and decision making—*something like that.* The NAU business school was actually a gem. They had opened a new campus for the Business School right when I arrived. New, modern, very *business-like.* And they staffed the school with experienced business professionals—not typical academics. I count Dr. Gaither as my first *mentor.* I doubt he would count me a *protégé,* but I am calling the shots here. *I am the Captain now.*

We were talking about what we all should take away, in our senior year, from his classes and his experience. I was expecting an operational algorithm or insight, a secret formula. He said very simply, "There is one thing that will differentiate you in your work ahead and how people see you. It is your *enthusiasm.*" He went on to explain that attitude is everything. "It guides you in your everyday work, it focuses you, it helps you problem solve and it opens doors." He used it in a process example of decision-making steps—identify a problem, develop alternatives, evaluate the alternatives, make a decision. "Then," he said, "implement it *enthusiastically.*" For you math types: a "B" solution with an "A" level of enthusiasm will outperform (is greater than) an "A" solution with a "B" level of enthusiasm.

This is great. I am going to become an enthusiastic fireman who doesn't wear a watch.

We all have certain beliefs about work and why work matters. This session was going to get deep into those beliefs, how the pandemic was rattling and changing those beliefs and what the *future of work* might look like in the decade ahead.

Speaking of the Pandemic

Plenty was happening on the COVID front between our previous Foresight session of 4/30 and our prep for the *Future of Work* session on 6/25. The lockdown for just about everyone was in full force and the novelty was wearing off. Small business was getting shut down big time and big business was trying to figure out a more realistic timeline for how long they would have their office employees continue the WFH (Work From Home) requirement. The smarter and bigger companies knew this was a long way from being over and many began talking about third quarter *2021. 2021?* America had not been in this kind of extended social/health crisis in decades.

A few small victories were being recorded. Remdesivir was showing promising signs of improving COVID-19 recovery in patients according to NIH data at the end of April (a 31% faster recovery time for individuals with advanced COVID-19 and lung involvement). That translated to about a four day faster recovery and on May 1, the FDA granted an Early Use Authorization (EUA) to remedesivir. *This would come in handy later in the year for some of our political leaders.*

On May 9, the FDA broadened the use of the Rutgers saliva-based test for at-home use. It was an effort to remove some of the burden from healthcare workers who were getting inundated with COVID-19 testing demand. *I unfortunately did not see this announcement.*

On May 23, I, like many people who were freaking out from anything that felt a little "off" from a health-care perspective, decided I needed to be tested for COVID. I tried to get in line at a Walgreen's *drive-thru* testing location (I'll have a COVID test and a bag of Fritos please…) but the information about how to register and whether you could just get in line was super unclear. *As was the testing strategy for this country.*

So I did a walk-in at an urgent care facility on a Saturday afternoon. Do I touch the door handle going into the clinic? Do I sit in a waiting room chair? Grab a pen and complete this form on a clipboard…*who used this clipboard last?* Look, just because you are paranoid *doesn't mean that someone's not following you.* This is brilliant. I am going to the one place where there is a likely aggregation of people who have COVID.

And I, like many of you, got the first-hand experience of a *nasal periscope*. Worse, I thought it was only going to be one nostril. I had barely gotten up from an eight count when it was *down-scope* for torpedo tube two. Look, I am not making light of the pandemic or in anyway minimizing the real impact of this for people across this globe that tested positive for this horrible disease. But what a medieval way to approach testing when the test results would take 5-7 days and by then you probably should be tested again. *We failed in this country on how to approach testing as a mitigation effort.*

My test was negative.

On May 28, the U.S. passed 100,000 COVID deaths. On June 10, we reached *two million* COVID cases in the U.S. A June 22 study from *Science Translation Medicine* suggested that as many as 80% of Americans who had sought treatment for the flu in March were actually infected with the COVID-19 virus. If even *one-third* of those people would have been tested for COVID (and remember we had about zero testing capacity in March) it would have resulted in 8.7 million infections. We were a bit underreported. *The object in the mirror may be closer than you realize.*

On June 18 and June 20, the CDC and the WHO, respectively, ended their studies on the testing of hydroxychloroquine as a potential treatment for COVID-19. Later that month I would be prescribed hydroxychloroquine for the rest of my life due to my advancing Rheumatoid Arthritis condition. *Still, I thought, it can't hurt.*

Wrapping up the month on June 29, Gilead Sciences, the developers of remdesivir, set the price of a dosage regimen of the drug at $3,120 (six vials). And finally, Dr. Anthony Fauci, who was the most credible voice on pandemic infections, warned that new cases of COVID (which were around 40,000 per day in late June) could reach a staggering 100,000 cases per day given the trajectory of the disease.

All bets are off. You and I and our children are living one of the most profound events in history. And we do not yet know how this history will be written and how long it will last.

Meanwhile on the Political Front

And if the pandemic was not enough to endure, the politics were weird and getting weirder. Trump, with all due respect to any of you who were supporting him, is sounding like a carnival barker at the task force briefings (which were getting more and more infrequent and polarized).

And something else was happening. This *Biden guy* was making an unexpected run at the Democratic nomination. After a fourth place finish at
the Iowa Caucuses on February 3 and a *fifth place* finish at the New
Hampshire primary on February 11, most of America concluded that he
would *not* be the candidate to face Trump in November. But then Jim
Clyburn, Democratic Congressman from South Carolina, endorses Biden
going into the South Carolina primary on February 29. Biden wins all 46
counties in South Carolina and close to 50% of the popular vote. It is a
catalyst for Biden heading into Super Tuesday on March 3.

And on Super Tuesday, Biden wins Alabama, Arkansas, Maine, Massachusetts, Minnesota, North Carolina, Oklahoma, Tennessee, Texas and
Virginia. 458 delegates and he pulls ahead of Bernie Sanders. *The
polling would indicate that voters may not agree with Biden on the issues, but they think he is the candidate that could beat Trump.*

It was a quick set of dominoes for Biden with the rest of the democratic
candidates. Pete Buttigieg, Amy Klobuchar and Michael Bloomberg drop
out of the race and endorse Biden. Beto O'Rourke, Cory Booker and
Kamala Harris, who had all dropped out previously, endorsed Biden. On
April 8, Bernie Sanders suspends his campaign and on April 13, Sanders
endorses Biden. Biden becomes the *presumptive Democratic presidential nominee,* and on June 9, Biden has enough delegates to secure his
nomination as the Democratic candidate.

*And you and I and our children are living <u>another</u> of the most profound
events in history.* 2020 is giving us a two-fer that will rock this country like
we have never seen before. And I am just trying to get ready for my next
Foresight session on June 25.

*My son Scott and I had a call (that would be a WhatsApp virtual call as
he is locked down in Vienna, Austria) just before the June session. Scott
is a brilliant writer and thinker, a Yale graduate with a global ethics master's degree from King's College in London, and is the Deputy Director of
the International Press Institute in Vienna. I am a Lumberjack from
Northern Arizona University. The acorn fell far, far from the tree. He is a
trusted advisor on the Foresight project.*

*And we decided, going into the June Foresight session, that for this
project and book to be as compelling as possible, to tell a story that
would be the most powerful outcome for seeing the decade ahead
through the lens of 2020, that Biden would need to win the election. And
we revamped our plan for the Foresight sessions and decided, in June,
that our final Foresight session would be held on January 21, 2021. The
day after what we forecasted would be the Biden Inauguration. And we
not only thought this would be good for the Foresight project, we thought*

it was imperative for the country. And we also knew that the divide in our country was about to get bigger.

The Future of Work—June 25, 2020
So on June 25, with a two-pronged timeline of COVID-19 and a presidential election occurring at the same time, we needed to get to work on *The Future of Work.*

Thirty-four participants came together on this particular Foresight session. Once again, 60 minutes and a *workman-like pace.* Let me introduce a few selected members of the work crew:

- "I am originally from the U.S. but living & working in Spain for the last 30 years. I am passionate about cross-cultural experiences and travel extensively for my job, in the education sector."
- "Dog lover, Pilates taker, hard worker. Love people."
- "Entrepreneurial soul trying to make a difference in the world."
- "Civil/Environmental Engineer by training. Currently building custom homes in Seattle area. Married with four grown children."
- "Live in Washington, D.C., part of a great team working to improve higher education outcomes."
- "Based in the Chicago area, focused on helping organizations improve performance or turn around their performance. Find the ever changing pattern of society fascinating, hopeful and occasionally concerning."

Concerning indeed. I would just characterize them all as a bunch of *hard workers.*

Looking Back Before We Look Forward
As we do in nearly each of our Foresight sessions, we asked people to reflect on the prior decade:

Question: *Let's start by reflecting back on the prior decade, 2010 thru 2019. What were some of the jobs/careers that seemed to prosper in the prior decade? The jobs/industries that were net attractors of talent? Well regarded and well perceived?*

This was a fun exercise. Where was the job focus over the prior decade? While we had well over 100 responses, there was a very clear set of themes (not prioritized):

No.	Idea

1. Social media platforms

2. Information technology/software development

3. Gig positions (the 'gig economy')

4. Healthcare

5. Creative services

6. eGames

7. Artificial Intelligence applications

8. Training and development

9. Travel and leisure

10. Some sectors of manufacturing (applied technology)

11. Call centers

12. Social workers

13. Physical therapy and occupational health

14. eCommerce applications

15. Sports and the business of sports

16. Global trade

17. Start-up and small business

18. Ride shares (Uber, Lyft, etc.)

19. Side hustles!

20. Personal trainers for fitness and the overall fitness industry

21. Alternative energy/green economy

22. Shipping and distribution

A little something for everyone, I suppose. But the fundamental point was that the job focus was *broad-based.* Technology, fitness, alternative energy, travel, sports, call centers, entrepreneurism with small business and start-ups. And some *very cool* new language: The gig economy and *side hustles.*

Pssst. What's your side hustle. No, you can tell me. I'm not wearing a wire.

I think Studs Terkel would have his hands full with these interviews. People were, in many respects, *going where they wanted to go.* Technology—as discussed in our previous chapter—was a *huge enabler.* So were innovation and disruptive ideas. And big social trends. Fitness, travel, alternative energy. And it was OK to simply do something you enjoyed. You could be a *gig worker.*

My son Jack is a graduate of the WP Carey Business School at Arizona State University. Supply Chain Management. He is also a really talented golfer. Played in professional "feeder" tournaments for a while. Tried out for the Canadian PGA Tour. Could not quite reach the tour level, Canadian or otherwise. But he is an exceptional people person. Loves golf and is a hard worker. He is now a gig worker. He is a professional golf caddy. Caddies at the Promontory Club in Park City, Utah, in the summer. Caddies at the Estancia Club in Scottsdale in the winter. Headed to the Summit Club in Las Vegas in 2021. Impressive places. Some of you have played there. In caddying a gig is called a "loop". Did you get a loop today? A double? And I must say, he has a pretty good gig going.

So heading into the decade ahead, 2020 pandemic aside for a moment, personal freedom is driving a lot of the *new economy.* A lot of us want a shot at *Shark Tank.* And a lot if us want to be in a job that has meaning and is *purposeful.* And younger people, Gen X and Millennials now and, most likely, Gen Zers in the future, are fine with a resume that will reflect a lot of different *experiences* along the way. Their skills and aspirations are *portable* and can relocate geographically (live where you want to live) and are *transferrable* to different organizations. Maybe they will work for you for a while, maybe they just want to work for themselves.

How We All Became Free Agents
In June of 1977, that was not the environment. If you were lucky enough to go to college, and persistent enough to graduate, you were looking to join a company *for life.* A place to hang your hat (here come some more of *them thar tweets),* in the proverbial sense, where you could move up the corporate ladder, bump your way into the middle class (and maybe beyond), and retire after 20-30 years and receive a nice *pension* and a good send-off party from your company. Perhaps a *gold watch.*

And, truth be known, there wasn't anything wrong with that. Job security and stability. Opportunity to advance. Maybe be offered a relocation in a great place. Build up a lifetime of friends and professional colleagues. *Have a little social status.*

So, in my senior year at the *distinguished* Northern Arizona University, I made the rounds of on-campus interviews at the business college. And for a relatively small school (probably 25,000 students then, but a solid business college), we were getting some good companies up there. I was a dual major in Marketing and Management with a Spanish minor (viva Guadalajara). And, somehow, I ended up with some *pretty damn good* offers. One from IBM and one from Proctor & Gamble. In the marketing department they didn't call them Proctor and Gamble, they were *P&G* and had a certain caché at the business school. In fact the marketing department was putting on a full court press for me to go with P&G. *They mean marketing!*

So it was down to the wire. The P&G recruiters convinced me to head down to Phoenix and go out for a day with one of the P&G marketing reps. *Paper Products Division.* So we hit his territory of big grocery stores and *we did some marketing. And he let me jump right in.*

I set up a Mr. Whipple stand.

Now, some of you have never seen a Mr. Whipple stand. So, I present to you a vintage photo of Mr. Whipple in front of a Mr. Whipple stand. *Please don't squeeze the Charmin!*

I accepted the IBM position the next day.

Nothing against P&G. They were then and they still are one of the best companies in America. *But a man's got to know his limitations.*

And IBM was a great choice. You don't get a better business education. They ship you off two or three weeks at a time to places like Endicott or Poughkeepsie, New York (Poughkeepsie is an old New York word that means "a town with nothing to do.") SYSDM 'A' and SYSDM 'B' (Systems Design and Marketing) technical education, sales call training (Feature/ Advantage/Reaction), presentation skills. All with 35 peers that just graduated from their respective colleges and were all *really smart.* The hotel bar was lively, it was like a corporate graduate school.

The idea was for the company to make a massive investment in you for the long haul. Take two years to train and mentor you before going out on quota. Start as a marketing rep, then take a staff assignment (mine was the DPEI role in San Jose). Move on to be a marketing *manager* which really was a big change (now you were taking care of other people). My assignment was in Portland, Oregon, as the manager in the finance unit. Loved Portland...a running mecca, skiing was close by with Mt. Hood and Mount Bachelor, and the Oregon coastline is phenomenal. *And it really does rain a lot there* but the summers are amazing. *I digress.*

Don't get comfortable. Time for another staff assignment, this time back to San Jose and the Santa Teresa Laboratory. *Relational Data Base. Application Development.* It was another briefing center environment so I was right back in my element. Loved the Bay area and living in Los Gatos. *Another day in paradise. World's greatest weather.* Only two problems: traffic and the cost of living.

So, back to Arizona. Worked for the regional manager. And the region included *Honolulu.* I am all about helping people, so I tried to help the Honolulu branch as often as possible. Right there on 1240 Ala Moana Boulevard. The great thing was that America West Airlines had been expanding service out of Phoenix and was launching a 747 out of there every day for Hawaii. I would get a seat in the *upper deck* of the plane which I referred to as *the living room.* And the best place to stay was the Halekulani hotel right on Waikiki beach.

So, again I say, there was nothing wrong with this corporate life.

Arizona was my last stop on the IBM train. But not my last assignment. IBM was starting the *IBM Consulting Group.* It was an effort to compete with Gartner and Booz Allen and others and move from the implementation level into the *senior decision making level.* And, after some 15 years in IBM, I finally found my craft. Back to education, a *six month* immersion into consulting education and training. Best stuff I had ever seen. This time we were at the new Palisades Education Center on the Hudson River. Set up like a University. Great classrooms and meeting facilities. Board rooms and breakout rooms. Great cafeterias and dining halls. Indoor lap pool and gym.

And I learned the art of consulting.

The Bigger You Are The Harder You Fall

But while I loved what I was doing—being on the leading edge of a start-up business in IBM—the company and the business world was doing a 180 degree change. There were three things that we all said would *never happen* in IBM: 1) that we would hire a CEO from *outside* of IBM; 2) that IBM would ever lay *anyone* off, and 3) that IBM would reduce or eliminate their stock dividend. And they *all* happened while I was still at IBM. I had a birds-eye seat.

Welcome to the 1990s. The Big Ship IBM was taking on water. *A lot of it.* The crew had grown to some 400,000 employees and the organization had become slow due to layers and layers of people and processes. New competitors in PC, servers and software were springing up everywhere. IBM was missing markets and not in tune with what customers were looking for. *When the ship misses the harbor, rarely is it the harbor's fault.*

Earnings were dropping and a level of (seriously weird) panic was setting in. IBM started selling pieces of the company off to stem the losses. To continue the analogy, we were throwing everything not nailed down to the deck overboard to lighten the load. *Not me yet.* In January of 1993, IBM announced an $8.3B loss for the prior financial year. *This was, according to Wikipedia, the largest single-year corporate loss in U.S. history.*

Wikipedia in its summary of the History of IBM: "All told, between 1991 and 1993, IBM posted net losses of nearly $16 billion. IBM's three-decades-long Golden Age, triggered by Watson, Jr., in the 1950s, was over. The computer industry now viewed IBM as no longer relevant, an organization dinosaur. And hundreds of thousands of IBMers lost their jobs, including CEO John Akers." In 1993 the IBM dividend, *a sacred cow*, is cut in half to save approximately $1.5B.

Somehow I remained a stow-away during this period of time. But it was a crazy time to watch an American icon be so diminished. *IBM, not me.*

In April of 1993 IBM hired Lou Gerstner, a former *customer* and CEO at RJR Nabisco, and also at American Express before then. He operated like an outside *consultant* (he was trained in consultancy at McKinsey) and it was refreshing. He reversed the spin-off and sell-off of IBM businesses and recognized that our strength was our integration as a single company. He helped re-build IBM's *reputation* with customers, IBMers and the industry. A level of pride returned and we *hoisted the Jolly Roger* as IBM was back in the black again by 1994 and earned a profit of about $3 billion. We joked internally: *Gerstner was teaching the elephant how to dance.*

From an HR perspective, it turned out that we just needed one new hire to turn things around. *Keep that thought in mind as we watch the presidential politics in 2020.*

But IBM and other companies gave Wall Street credibility to the strategy of *downsizing* as needed. It became a big practice in the 1990s. Big business was *downsizing* at will. They were issuing *RIFS*. These are not the Led Zeppelin type of riffs, these are R-I-F's as in *Reduction in Force.*

And plenty of people in the business world got to experience what a RIF was all about.

It's corporate speak for firing you and for them to feel OK about it.

And all of a sudden, everything changed. The good and benevolent Corporation became *evil*. They broke the bond of *hire for lifetime* trust. In April of 1998, Clark Davis, a writer for the History News Service, summed it up well:

"For most of the twentieth century, American firms kept a bargain initially struck with a generation dubious about the corporate order. The 1990's will be remembered as the decade in which that contract was broken. Work security is no longer an unwritten clause in the job description of salaried personnel."

So, in a blink of an eye, nearly all of us became *free agents*. In 1996 I left IBM to start my own consulting practice. I had joined the *gig economy* before it was called the gig economy. My gigs were then, and continue to be now, *consulting engagements*.

The reality is that it's a *better* system now. You rely on your skills and you can land a gig wherever you want. Some gigs pay more (NFL quarterbacks, lead roles in big movies, CEOs). Some gigs are more visible (mayors of cities, governors of states, the TV news anchor). Some gigs are more purposeful (healthcare workers, members of the military, teachers). But you have to be good at something and, hopefully, over time, love what you do. *If not, change your gig.*

And organizations have to earn your trust and your engagement. They don't have to hire you for life. But they have to matter, they have to stand for something. And when they do, and they create a working environment (aka, culture), and provide reasonable compensation and career opportunities, then they will be *net attractors* of talent. Make no mistake—we *need* good organizations: power utilities, hospitals, universities, governments, technology companies, media companies, retail stores, construction companies, etc.

107

More people need an opportunity to be part of this equation, but it's a good equation now.

Reflecting on the Prior Decade
Well, after that *brief history of work* let's get back to our Foresight session. As we like to do before we get into the decade ahead, we look at the prior decade, 2010 through 2019, and see how the nature of work fared. Was it better or worse for most people? Why?

Question: *All things considered, looking at the past decade, was the nature of work itself enhanced or demeaned for most people who held jobs?*

No.	Items	Times Selected
1	I think it was a MIXED decade for work, completely situational	(50%)
2	I think it was a good decade for work, the nature of work was ENHANCED	(47%)
3	I think it was a bad decade for work, the nature of work was DEMEANED	(3%)

Situational. That suggests that it may have depended on your *gig* and if your skill area was in demand. It also may have depended on how certain organizations developed their work environments and cultures. And some industries were on the rise while market shifts may have really hurt others. *You need to be nimble in these days and times, things can change quickly.* There were interesting insights from our Foresight participants:

For those who saw the prior decade as mixed for the nature of work:

- MIXED: "The gap between haves/have-nots has grown disturbingly, so for some folks, work has moved in a satisfying, rewarding way. For many, though, the ability to make ends meet has declined."
- MIXED: "Technical jobs exploded, but other jobs, especially blue collar, suffered, so the arena was 'balanced/mixed'."
- MIXED: "Expansion of independent, flexible work hours that promoted creativity and autonomy, but also less security due to lack of benefits and the constant specter of needing to be pro-

ductive even in the home or domestic space that once was sepa-
rate."

- MIXED: "Mixed decade because while the job market was good in many sectors it's also clear that automation is having a big impact and will continue to have a big impact, something that hangs over the nature of work and its future."
- MIXED: "Class and race income inequality gap, class and race education gap, etc. The nature of work, I think, was entirely dependent on where you fit in the class and race scale. It was a decade of increasing distance between those who were 'in' and those who remained marginalized."

So, now we see a *work divide* in addition to education, racial equality, economic equality and digital access divides. *Like the last thing we need heading into the decade is another element of division.* A rising tide can lift all boats, but you just may not be in a boat you really like. Or that is going anywhere you want to be. Or even in the boat.

For those who saw the prior decade as <u>enhanced</u> *for the nature of work:*

- ENHANCED: "There was and is a lot of opportunity in the last decade as technology continued to develop and change, and the economy came back on the long expansion from 2008."
- ENHANCED: "In the West, high employment, and a recognition that work had to match the workers preferences—at least for the skilled worker. Think how Google attracts staff as an (extreme) example."
- ENHANCED: "Enhanced. Freedom to work wherever and whenever."
- ENHANCED: "As the demand for workers grew, the "value" of people was more appreciated."
- ENHANCED: "It was a shift to service and information, but seems to be moving forward. Things change, nothing stays the same, and that seems about right to me."
- ENHANCED: "Expansion of social consciousness of the value of work and workers doing that work."

I have found that social consciousness and value for people and their work is proportional to the health of the economy at the time, if you know what I mean.

And there had to be somebody to raise the flag of outright pessimism:

- DEMEANED: "Movement away from the importance of individual value—craft, custom, personal relationships and services—to individuals as commodities that are easily replaced and inter-changeable. Systems and functions became increasingly impor-tant over individual talent and contributions."

This is the theory that we are all just *fungible cogs*. (PERSONAL NOTE: I might be a cog, but I am certainly not *fungible*.)

For many of us, it was a good decade leading into 2020. But there's no reason why it can't be a *great* decade ahead for *all of us* in terms of hav-ing work that is meaningful, that pays a good wage so you can work just *one job* and make ends meet. But we will need to fix a number of things in the decade ahead—early childhood education, restoring the dignity of the blue collar job, increasing the minimum wage to a *reasonable* wage, aligning higher education to the real needs of the industry, increasing focus on skills enhancement and retraining while you are in your job to maintain relevance, and not discarding workers just because they are *older* workers. And we have a long, long way to go toward creating gen-uine *inclusion* in the workplace.

Why Work Matters
And what do you do for a living? Probably the most often asked question that we would get from a new acquaintance. Work is central to who we are, it is part of our identity. And I suppose it should be since we spend a prime part of our day doing it. *What are you going to be when you grow up?*

Older, actually.

So we went right after this existential question: why does work matter?

Question: *Work. Some days we love it. Some days we hate it. But we know it matters. The question is why—why does work matter? Why is it so fundamental to our being, to who we are and what we are? We know the paycheck is important, but we suspect there are many other implica-tions here:*

For this exercise we had our Foresight participants provide quick open responses (nearly 100 responses) and then did a real-time summary. We then asked our participants to indicate how important each theme was to them personally:

Now, please assess each of the following aspects of why work matters in terms of how important they are to you personally. Use a scale of 1-10 where a "1" means not at all important and a "10" means extremely important:

Rank	Idea	Avg.

110

1	Sense of accomplishment	**9.2**
2	Gives us sense of purpose	**9.1**
3.	Can provide for one's family	**8.7**
4.	Produce something meaningful	**8.4**
5.	Personal esteem	**8.3**
6.	Financial return	**8.2**
7.	Can make the world better in some way	**8.2**
8.	Can be fun	**7.3**
9.	Can connect meaningfully with others	**7.2**
10.	Sense of dignity	**7.2**
11.	Good to know I am good at something	**6.8**
12.	Creates challenges to be overcome	**6.4**

Now we are moving up Maslow's Hierarchy. Accomplishment. A sense of *purpose*. Certainly a sense of dignity and personal esteem, but most of us want more than the paycheck: we want to know that *we make a difference* with the work we do; that we *matter*. The open responses leading into our assessment were actually quite revealing:

- "It's strange, seems like being productive is the key to my balance in life in general."
- "When it transforms from just work to purpose."
- "Work translates to an ability to provide for oneself and their loved ones, so a first level benefit of personal and financial security. But at a higher level of purpose—it drives a sense of accomplishment, self-esteem and self-worth."
- "Establishes a sense of value and meaning for yourself as an agent in multiple systems—family, community, society, etc."
- "Whether we like work or not, something that we spend that much time on has at least some impact on the meaning and purpose we feel we have in our lives."
- "It's a counterpoint to dissolution and dalliance."

And how did Kierkegaard get onto my session? Dissolution and *dalliance*? *Shit, I actually had to look up dalliance to make sure it wasn't a typo in the session.*

dal·li·ance: A brief or casual involvement with something. A trifling away of time.

OK—I get it, I think. At least until dictionary.com threw in the *trifling* reference. And while we are on the subject of Kierkegaard (Soren Kierkegaard, the first Existentialist philosopher for those who were *dallying* in your high school English class), he had some other head spinners about the meaning of work and life:

- ✓ "Life can only be understood backwards; but it must be lived forwards."
- ✓ "Face the facts of being what you are, for that is what changes what you are."
- ✓ "The most common form of despair is not being who you are."

Look, the point is this: *why work matters* is a heavy question. Our work is a shared experience we have with each other, it's why we talk about it so much. *How was your day? How is work going?* And when it is an authentic and a meaningful experience, it is incredibly gratifying. To be acknowledged that *I have purpose* is what I would call a come-back shot for life.

A Further Note on Purpose

Organizations have also realized how important purpose is. The consultants would call it *Purpose Based Branding* but it just means that there is more to an organization than making money, than showing a profit. Purpose for an organization can be defined as: "A definitive statement about the difference you are trying to make in the world."

People—as in workers—are drawn to purpose-based organizations. Because just as you and I want to make a difference, the idea that we can part of a larger organization or movement that makes a difference simply amplifies our personal impact and identity. When an organization is clear about their purpose, it aligns with their values, their decisions and even their most fundamental business processes.

One of my colleagues is Haley Rushing, who is the Chief *Purposologist* at The Purpose Institute, a spin-off of the highly successful GSD&M Agency in Austin, Texas. She and Roy Spence, the co-founder of

GSD&M, wrote a visionary book in 1989 entitled: It's Not What You Sell, It's What You Stand For: *Why Every Extraordinary Business is Driven by Purpose.* It provides the rationale and the leadership experiences about those companies that are focused on a powerful and passionate purpose: Southwest Airlines (democratizing the skies—the freedom to fly); Walmart (saving people money so they can live better); The American Red Cross (to enable ordinary people to perform extraordinary acts).

Over the last 10 years I have had the privilege of co-facilitating, with Haley, hundreds of online sessions about purpose with leaders of organizations that wanted to understand how their unique strengths and the needs of the world might intersect to create a unique and compelling purpose. And when that purpose is supported authentically by the leaders in the organization and reinforced with values that are aligned with that purpose, the result is a workplace that attracts passionate and purpose-based individuals who want to be part of that cause. Notes Spence in a description from the book about the impact of purpose to people:

"If you get it right, your people will feel great about what they're doing, clear about their goals, and excited to get to work every morning."

In the decade ahead, being clear on purpose will be a driving factor for us personally as we think about the meaning and value of our work, and it will be a driving factor for organizations who want to stand for something that draws passionate employees.

And What Was Best Job You Ever Had?

You can validate the earlier themes we had assessed with a narrative about what people felt was the *best job* they ever had and why:

Question: *It's time to get personal. Thinking about the various jobs/roles that you have had in your work experience, what's the BEST JOB (could be role or assignment within your job) you have ever had? Why? What made it such compelling and rewarding experience?*

It was fascinating to watch this stream of responses come in. Not just because the jobs were fascinating (and they were), but it seemed *remarkably easy* for people to identify and describe that *best job ever.* Look for the clues in these responses:

- "Press Secretary to Prime Minister of Yugoslavia. Was during the war years so it was an opportunity to help bring peace to a very troubled part of the world. Very high risk / very high reward."

113

- "Providing affordable housing for hard working, low income people. It was life changing for the family (as well as myself) and had generational impact."
- "Program director for an elite undergraduate program. Working with incredibly gifted young people and watching them develop. Many of them have gone on to very successful careers and I have stayed in touch with a few of them—perhaps it keeps you young?"
- "City Manager. I loved being responsible for 240,000 people and 2,600 employees. Building a great city is a legacy job."
- "The best job I've ever had is the current one. It gives me opportunity to get creative and work towards something I personally believe in. This is a "started at the bottom" and worked my way up to a leadership position. I know that job security is not common these days, but I feel heard, appreciated and secure. It's also a wonderful team and the dynamic is very open and welcoming."
- "Running my own business, hiring people I wanted to work with, went after business that meant something to me, and made a difference—fabulous humans to work with and amazing clients on work that was so meaningful (cancer treatment, smoking cessation, etc.)."

And how about you? What was the best job you ever had? Why? Look, you don't have to be a Nobel scientist or be solving world hunger. You just have to feel like you are doing something meaningful and *be acknowledged* that you are making a difference. And sometimes *how* you do your job is just as important as *what* you do.

In July of 2019, I went to Coronado Island to swim in the Coronado Rough Water Swim. As much as I like doing laps in a pool, there is something really freeing about swimming in the open water. Lakes in Arizona, the bay at Rocky Point, an ocean when I can find one. No wait, it's not that I can't *find* an ocean, it's just that I can't often *find the time* to find an ocean. *You know what I mean.*

First of all, there was a reason it was called a *rough water swim*. I should have caught that at the race registration desk. It wasn't just the choppy surf, it was trying to get *into* the choppy surf. This was a mile swim, beach start. Run straight into the water...and get knocked on your *ass* by the waves pounding the shore. It's great to start a race in last place.

But it was a good swim (eventually) and a great event. Fourth of July. Coronado Island. San Diego. Lots of festivities for the day and the island

114

was *packed.* So I wandered into a tavern on the main street where the parade had been earlier in the morning and was ready for breakfast. *I had earned it.* As you may know, I am a counter person, so I sat at the bar. And I quickly noticed that the employees were outnumbered. By like 50 guests to one waitress.

But she was really calm. And despite the growing crowd, she was really happy. And competent. I was in no hurry, just caught her attention at one point and made a quick breakfast order with a coffee chaser...*when you get a chance. No hurry.*

She headed back to the kitchen to grab someone else's order and my eyes caught a chalk board as she headed back. Notes about shifts, maybe an upcoming birthday, a certain burner wasn't working. But in the middle of the chalk board I saw a note that had been hand written. Maybe it was by the owner. Maybe one of the workers. Maybe by the waitress that was handling the place by herself:

Work hard.
Be nice.

And I thought to myself: that is the *best guidance* you could *ever* give your workplace. Not nine core values, a vision and mission statement, a definition of our culture, a mandatory diversity training class next Tuesday. Just four simple words. *Work hard. Be nice.* Because if everybody did that, you would be the epitome of a *high performance organization.* If you work hard, you are *accountable*, and don't tolerate people that slack off. *No es juego, es trabajo.* And if you are nice, then you acknowledge other people, you treat them with respect, you have empathy. And if you are really nice, you are naturally *inclusive.*

So that's my graduation speech to the class of 2020. You want to be successful in your career? Enjoy the journey? Develop a set of friends and colleagues as you head through your career? *Work hard. Be nice.* You will sleep well at night. *Chauncy Gardener could not have said it better.*

Work in the Decade Ahead
In the next section of our Foresight session, we wanted to understand whether people were optimistic or pessimistic about the future of work in the decade ahead and why. And remember, we are seeing the decade ahead from the lens of 2020 and the pandemic which was also influencing how we work and also *whether* we were even working.

Question: *If you were to forecast your view of the future of work in the decade ahead NOW, would you say you were optimistic or pessimistic about the nature of work in the decade ahead for most people?*

No.	Items	Times Selected
1.	Optimistic about the nature of work in the decade ahead--it will be ENHANCED	(79%)
2.	Pessimistic about the nature of work in the decade ahead--it will be DEMEANED	(21%)

Interesting. Going into this question in June of 2020 I could have easily seen this as 80/20 the other way. Too many people without opportunity. The economic divide is big and getting bigger. Technology at scale will take away a lot of meaningful jobs. Big organizations really don't care about the people, they just care about the profits. So I was intrigued that our group suggested, as a strong majority, that the very nature of work might be *enhanced*:

- ENHANCED: "I think that the pandemic is creating a large shift in how we work and treat human beings, and that new ways of working will emerge that are more human and in harmony with the technological development and globalization."
- ENHANCED: "I believe AI and robotics will have a significant impact in what work is done by humans. I am going to stay optimistic and hope this will be uplifting for the workforce and put more 'value' into the work that remains for humans."
- ENHANCED: "Individual talent and contributions from those who have work will be more important than ever because of the crisis-like conditions and economic and health and societal pressures —people who have work will feel very fortunate and needed. Creative solutions, technology—will allow people to work across time and space."
- ENHANCED: "Current social unrest is revealing schisms in our system that must be addressed. That is going to result in meaningful changes to our political reality and willingness to improve our capitalist society to be more accessible and meaningful for everyone—shrink the income inequality gap and opportunity gap."
- ENHANCED: "The COVID experience is revealing both opportunities and cracks in the system. More people are using technology more effectively as we're gaining a better understanding of how it can go wrong. The remote-work phenomenon will create

even more options. The inequity problem is the fly in the ointment."

- ENHANCED: "People will have more freedom to work where and when it suits them. Work will be intellectually challenging as robots will do all the hard work."

Danger Will Robinson! The robots will do all the hard work? Not only am I not buying into that Orwellian view, but it flies in the face of my *Work Hard* mantra. I think people like to work hard. Not burn out, but work hard, be challenged. Be a little out of your comfort zone at times.

One of the most powerful performance models I ever was exposed to was during my time in being trained for the IBM Consulting Group in the early 1990s. For one of the classes, held at the Palisades Education Center in New York, they asked us to bring our tennis racquets. *You would need them for your consulting class.* I am all in, intellectual and physical exercise all in one. And, over a two day period, I learned everything I needed to learn about individual and organizational performance. *It changed my life.*

The consulting team teaching the class was from the InsideOut Development group in American Fork, Utah. *The performance capital of the world,* I was initially thinking. InsideOut was founded by Alan Fine, who, as you may have been thinking, was a tennis coach. It turns out that he was a very *unsuccessful* tennis coach at the start. Because despite all of his knowledge and skill in tennis, he could not make people play better tennis. They were not doing what he was showing them. And it must have been *their* fault.

But Alan learned, through much trial and error, that performance is based on *focused attention.* And often times it is impossible to create focus when there is so much *interference* happening. Like a coach yelling at you on how to hold a racquet, plant your feet, draw the racquet back, hit with *topspin*, step forward, hit the ball on the rise...all at the same time. *Why can't you play better? I am telling you all the things you need to do!*

So, Fine created a simple equation. And you know me, I like simple:

Performance = Capacity Minus Interference.

The model was startlingly powerful, and positive. Most people have a much higher capacity to perform (sports or work), it's just that their capacity is hindered by interference. *Organizational noise,* if you know what I mean.

So, for tennis, we started with an easy drill in the classroom. Pair up, one tennis ball. One person throws, the other catches. *I can do this, I am thinking. Of this I am capable.* But add the focusing exercise: the person receiving the ball says "bounce" when the ball hits the floor, and "catch" when it hits their hand. Bounce/catch. Pick up the speed. Bounce/catch. Switch to catching with your other hand. Bounce/catch. Suddenly everyone in the room was fielding like Cal Ripken. *Interesting, I thought.*

Then out to the tennis courts. A simple variation. Instead of bounce/catch, it was bounce/hit. Call "bounce" when the ball hits coming towards you and "hit" exactly when it hits your racquet. And then do the same thing as it heads towards your opponent. Bounce/hit, bounce/hit. And guess what? You have just changed everything about what you are paying attention to. What you are seeing, what you are hearing, what you are feeling. Suddenly I am in one of the best rallies I have even been in. I didn't realize it, but other people stopped to watch us in this rather epic rally. I didn't see them. *Bounce/hit.*

Have you ever been in the "zone"? When you were performing at your best, maybe beyond what you thought you could do, and it felt *effortless?* It might have been playing a sport, maybe a musical instrument, appearing in a play, giving a presentation at work, *facilitating an online session.* What you felt was what Alan called "the flow zone". That optimum flow when your skills and capacity were at the right level of focus. And all of the interference was out of the way. What if you could do this more often? On an individual level? On an organizational level?

Could anyone compete with you or your organization with that level of focus and resulting performance and the joy of it all being so easy?

The psychological research on the *flow state* was originated by Mihaly Csikszentmihalyi, a Hungarian-American psychologist born in 1934 in Croatia. *We'll just call him "Mick" for short.* His definition of flow was: "a state in which people are so involved in an activity that nothing else seems to matter; the experience is so enjoyable that people will do it even at great cost, for the sheer sake of doing it."

Work hard. Be Nice. *Enjoy it.*

Alan moved all of this to modern sport and modern business.

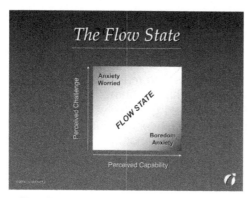

Flow State, from InsideOut Development

Create focus. Reduce interference. Get people into a performance state. And here is the point about why all of this matters: people want to operate at a higher level. They don't want to be in a job that burns them out (upper left, too much stress and interference—aka, micromanaging) and they don't want to do work that is beneath them (lower right, no challenge, meaningless work, anyone could do this). Create that flow state for yourself or for your organization, and your work becomes high performance and high satisfaction.

When I am at my best in my facilitation, I am creating a flow state for myself *and* for my participants.

Back to the Future

And speaking of facilitation, let's get back to the Future of Work. For not all of our participants went down the road of enhancement when thinking about the decade ahead and the nature of work. There were those who were raising a well-articulated caution flag about work in the future:

- DEMEANED: "Unless we address the unbridled greed that typifies so many CEOs, with huge chasms between their earnings and those of their people, it's not looking good. As explained in many of the responses to the last two questions, most people do not look for money as their primary motivation, yet how is it that those who make it to the top are laser-focused on money (mainly their own compensation)? It poisons the water for many of the rest of us."
- DEMEANED: "Worried about the impact of automation. Too early to say whether the job market will be able to compensate for the

job losses because of this, and whether the nature of work will be demeaned, as people constantly fear replacement."

- DEMEANED: "The best part of work involves human interaction and connectivity. We are social creatures. Technology, while making work easier, is also making work less gratifying from the human perspective. This is a paradox."
- DEMEANED: Expanded growth—of both population and economy—will make individual contributions less important. Businesses will be run just by the numbers."

There's that fungible cog theory again.

Influencing Optimism/Pessimism in the Decade Ahead

Let's keep pushing this look at the decade ahead. Two exercises, one about focusing on what might make us optimistic about work in the decade ahead and one that might make us pessimistic about work in the decade ahead:

Question: *Now, let's look ahead. We are here to consider the NEXT TEN YEARS. Now through December 31, 2029. What makes you OPTIMISTIC about the nature of work—why might it be enhanced for most people?*

An open question with plenty of quick responses. We summarized them in a dozen themes and asked our participants to assess the themes:

Now, please assess each of the following aspects in terms of how important you feel it would be, if it materialized, as a positive impact/influence of the nature of work in the decade ahead. Use a scale of 1-10 where a '1' means not at all important and a '10' means extremely important:

Rank	Idea	Avg.
1.	Innovation opportunities for new products/services	8.5
2.	Education opportunities creating new skills	8.4
3.	Role of tech to support work	8.3
4.	Better work/life balance	8.1
5.	Freedom to work in a virtual environment	8.0

120

6.	Greater focus on societal equity	**8.0**
7.	Greater access to online learning	**7.8**
8.	Greater collaboration leads to greater opportunity	**7.7**
9.	Automation of routine tasks	**7.5**
10.	Growth of healthcare	**7.4**
11.	More people will move to their ideal job	**7.3**
12.	Greater focus on safety	**6.1**

Look at the *key enablers:* innovation, education, technology, location freedom, improved social equity, better work/life balance. *More people find their calling, their ideal vocation.*

Question: *Now, let's continue to look ahead. We are here to consider the NEXT TEN YEARS. Now through December 31, 2029. What makes you PESSIMISTIC about the nature of work--why might it be demeaned for most people?*

We kept the process the same—open brainstorming, a real-time summary and then an assessment of key themes:

Now, please assess each of the following aspects in terms of how significant you feel it would be, if it materialized, as a negative impact/influence of the nature of work in the decade ahead. Use a scale of 1-10 where a "1" means not at all significant and a "10" means extremely significant:

Rank	Idea	Avg.
1.	Lack of national/global leadership	8.8
2.	Income inequality	8.4
3.	Prolonged recession	8.1
4.	Lack of healthcare access	8.0
5.	Vanishing middle class worker	7.0

6.	High cost of higher ed	**7.0**
7.	Low paying service jobs	**6.9**
8.	Societal issues—drugs, crime, high housing costs	**6.3**
9.	Isolation from working from home	**6.1**
10.	Continued offshoring of work	**5.9**
11.	Negative consequences of AI	**5.7**
12.	Government intervention in private business	**5.2**

Note what we are *not* as worried about. Government intervention, negative consequences of AI, offshoring and isolation from working from home. But we have some heavy hitters at the top of the list that will influence the direction of this country and future of work: leadership, income equality/vanishing middle class, educational cost and access, healthcare access (talk about *interference*), low paying service jobs. Look, we don't improve the future of work unless we change the game for more people to have the opportunity to access the new economy. And those heavy hitters at the top mean that we have some *heavy lifting* ahead of us.

Question: *All things considered as you reflect the overall set of factors that might influence your outlook for on the nature of work for the decade ahead, what's your forecast for the nature of work now that we have considered both sides?*

No.	Items	Times Selected
1.	**Somewhat Optimistic**	**(52%)**
2.	**Middle of the Road**	**(32%)**
3.	Very Optimistic	(10%)
4.	Somewhat Pessimistic	(6%)
5.	Very Pessimistic	(0%)

Considering both sides, our Foresighters were *cautiously optimistic* about the nature of work with over 80% suggesting somewhat optimistic or middle of the road. It's not a negative view, hardly anyone ventured

122

down the pessimistic view, it's just that there are some *variables* in play that will influence the decade ahead for the nature of work:

- SOMEWHAT OPTIMISTIC: "Lots of opportunities but that may leave many people behind if not trained for new careers."
- SOMEWHAT OPTIMISTIC: "Our trajectory is almost always up, but we've been moving toward a stress point caused by the concentration of economic power combined with the weird political dynamics that are at least partially tied to inequality of opportunity and diverse cultural perspectives."
- SOMEWHAT OPTIMISTIC: "I believe the majority of people in the U.S. want to change our planet for the better and we have enormous potential with the young leadership out there."
- MIDDLE: "I think we know too little about the effects, firstly, of the current economic crisis and, secondly, of technological advances that are rendering many current jobs and tasks obsolete."
- MIDDLE: "More than ever, the issue of national leadership will set the course. I believe we are at a tipping point."
- MIDDLE: "We're really at a tipping point. We have huge challenges that are global in nature and unless we address them in ways that are wise, forward thinking and benevolent, we're likely to slide down a dark tunnel from which there's no return."

This dark tunnel thing concerns me a bit. What is clear is that many in our group tie the future of work to the future of political leadership. It's less about how we balance the future impact of technology and more about how we increase access to education, skills/retraining, wages that can move a large number of Americans out of poverty and how we, as a country, will deal with the level of division that continues to create haves vs. have-nots. When we move out of the pandemic, even in a 2022 timeline, there is little doubt that we will regain our economic growth—the question is more whether there will be equal participation in that growth that opens the door to meaningful work for more Americans. *A tipping point indeed.*

Work Influence Scenarios

My favorite section of each Foresight session—looking at some future scenarios to see how our participants will react. Twelve scenarios this time, with two assessments: the IMPACT to the future of work if that scenario was to occur, and secondly, the LIKELIHOOD of that scenario occurring in the decade ahead:

Now, please assess each of the following future scenarios in two ways. First, the level of positive IMPACT to the future of work if that scenario fully materializes in the decade ahead (use a scale of 1-10

where a '1' means a very low level of impact and a '10' means a very high level of impact); Second, the likelihood that this scenario will fully materialize in the decade ahead (use a scale of 1-10 where a '1' means a very low likelihood and '10' means a very high likelihood):

Here is how our Foresight session assessed the list. The scenarios are ordered by the *level of positive impact* but then contrasted with the likelihood of occurrence for a gap analysis rating.

#	Scenario Description	Im-pact	Like-ly	Gap
1	GENUINE INCLUSION/DIVERSITY IN THE WORKPLACE: The new decade will create a new openness and acceptance in the workplace for all backgrounds. Diversity becomes a cultural strength and you are encouraged to bring "your best self" to work. The old stereotypes fade away ("The Good Ol' Boys Club", loyalty buys you advancement, personal/sexual favors, wait your turn, etc.). You are welcome and included, respected for your talent and work ethic, encouraged to challenge the status quo and your individuality is appreciated.	8.9	6.6	(2.3)
2	COMPENSATION EQUITY: If you do the work, you are compensated at the right level. Pay disequity based on gender, age, race or geography is simply not tolerated any more. Professions that have been constrained in the past by being undervalued by society even when their contributions have been high (teachers, for example) have seen their compensation realigned to reflect that value.	8.9	5.7	(3.2)

3	REALIGNING EDUCATION: The educational environments will fundamentally change to be more aligned with work/career interests. High schools adopt more vocational alignment; you can graduate with a set of skills that you can immediately put into use. Colleges and universities have strong industry partnerships for advanced training where the students are workplace ready and there is a regular return to the campus for experienced workers to further develop their skills. Education and training become more integrated to support lifelong learning.	8.8	6.6	(2.2)
4	UNIVERSAL HEALTHCARE: While workplaces and employers can enhance healthcare plans, benefits and options, the decade ahead sees an implementation of universal healthcare where all citizens have baseline, quality healthcare. Changing a job does not result in the loss of your base healthcare plan—you are free to move about the market and the geography you desire.	8.7	5.8	(2.9)
5	NEW GREEN ECONOMIC DRIVERS: An entire new set of jobs, companies and opportunities come into play with a shift to addressing climate change and environmental sustainability. It's not a trend, it's a global commitment that requires a huge investment in talent, process and infrastructure. It's like the WPA (the depression era Works Progress Administration) for the Planet Earth.	8.3	6.2	(2.1)
6	NATIONAL MINIMUM WAGE: Everyone can get a good start in the workplace with a standardized and fair national minimum wage. If you are willing to work hard, you can earn a good salary and, for many, avoid the need to work multiple jobs just to make ends meet. It's up to you if you want to stay at that minimum wage—most will want to advance their work and careers and earning capacity and find that "dream job", but an entry level hourly job brings a good return and feels like meaningful and appreciated work.	8.2	6.0	(2.2)

7	PURPOSE BASED ORGANIZATIONS: More organizations/brands will adopt a powerful and compelling "Core Purpose" about the difference they want to make in the world. While they will still want/need to be financially successful, they will be guided in all they do by their fundamental purpose and aligned with values that matter. The core purpose and aligned values will be highly attractive to people that want to be part of that cause and purpose. People will feel like they matter and are making a difference.	8.0	6.3	(1.7)
8	MORE ENTREPRENEURIAL OPPORTUNITY: Just about anyone can take their shot on "Shark Tank". More educational institutions and communities are encouraging entrepreneurial activity. Start-up capital is plentiful, the new and small businesses are recognized and supported for their impact to sustaining a growing economy. Innovations are happening at a fast pace and these new start-ups attract passionate people and provide terrific working environments and rewards. Welcome to You, Inc.	7.8	6.8	(1.0)
9	THE ROBOTS DID NOT TAKE OVER: The 4th Industrial Revolution (a fusion of the digital and physical worlds characterized by Artificial Intelligence, Robotics, 3D printing, Cloud Computing, The Internet of Things, Advanced Wireless, etc.) turned out to be more of an evolution that improved the workplace and made it easier to get things done. Repetitive/menial tasks were further automated just as data entry and the switchboard operator went away in the past. Workers simply had better information support, tools and infrastructure. No Danger, Will Robinson!	7.8	6.6	(1.2)

10	VIRTUAL WORKPLACE: The cubicle is dead. The technology, in some ways accelerated by COVID-19, fully enables high impact virtual workplaces. Home offices are productive and secure, collaboration tools are amazing and workers have learned to thrive in the virtual space. Life balance is better, travel is reduced (commute and air) and people feel more in control of their schedule and work flow. It doesn't mean we don't get together, it just means that when we do it really matters and advances our work or sense of workplace community.	7.7	7.5	(0.2)
11	JOB HARMONY: The job matchers (Indeed, ZipRecruiter, Monster, SquarePeg, Glassdoor, etc.) really ramp up their game in the decade ahead. Their technology and ability to match you to an ideal situation is amazing. They can assess and understand what you are all about and what will let you thrive in a work environment. Companies have huge confidence in them, the employees that are placed match the culture and result in high performance and low turnover.	7.2	5.8	(1.4)
12	LONGER TERM CAREER PATHING: More organizations plan and hire for the long term. Their advanced financial planning and support infrastructure (supported by AI and predictive analytics) insulates them from some of the economic waves that might require reactive downsizing. Longer term career planning is in place with an alignment of the company needs and the individual interests. Pace of advancement can be dialed up or down as required, but the idea of long term stability and career growth within a single organization has returned for those who have found the right home.	6.9	5.0	(1.9)

First of all, we have a very strong set of scenarios relative to their potential impact—10 of the 12 were rated at 7.5+ and they are *heavy hitters* on the work front, economic front and on the *political policy front*. Inclusion/ diversity, compensation equity and minimum wage, healthcare access, education access and realignment, the implications of climate change and new energy directions. Other influencers are clear, even if they are less political in nature, they create strong opportunity and impact for the nature of work—entrepreneurial access, purpose-based organizations, virtual workforce, we'll get the 4th Industrial Revolution right. And *maybe* enhanced job matching and longer term career planning will have impact.

But the challenges are significant. Look at the top six gaps between impact and likelihood:

1. Compensation equity (3.2)
2. Universal healthcare (2.9)
3. Genuine inclusion/diversity in the workplace (2.3)
4. Realigning education (2.2)
5. National minimum wage (2.2)
6. New green economic drivers (2.1)

Closing these gaps matters. Not only for the greater individual opportunity and access, but for *society as a whole*. The future of work is tied directly to the future of a better America. We asked our Foresighters to validate this question about the implications of a better work future:

Question: *Imagine that this next decade brings about some of the changes we have described for work and the workplace. More people in their ideal jobs; a new level of inclusion and workplace respect; technology that supports us rather than competes with us; entry level jobs that create a meaningful social wage; education aligned with the needs of the industry; purpose based organizations, and a return to longer term career paths. What's the implication of that Future of Work? How might it affect our communities, our families and our country?*

Here's a quick summary of the implications:

✓ A safer, more stable society
✓ More opportunity for everyone
✓ A more unified country
✓ Healthier, happier people
✓ Few people dependent on government support
✓ High quality of life for more people
✓ Work becomes less stressful
✓ Fewer mental health issues
✓ Lower crime rates
✓ More time for enjoying our family/friends
✓ Better work/life balance
✓ Narrowing the gap between economic classes
✓ More volunteerism
✓ Less illness and disease

128

Look, I know this feels a little utopian, but remember how important work is to our sense of well-being, accomplishment, self-worth, dignity and esteem.

Save The World And Still Be Home For Dinner

We also need to remember that work is a part of life, not the other way around. Americans may have a strong work ethic, which is good, but often are viewed by other countries as being a little out of whack when it comes to *work/life balance.*

I made a decision early on in my work that I would blur the lines between work and life. I wouldn't shut down work at 5:00pm, but I also wouldn't shut life down at 8:00am. That's a tricky balance and has some trade-offs. Even in my corporate life (don't tell anyone) I would balance my day in a way that aligned with my life priorities. In Tucson, I would take two hours on certain work days and go run the trails in Sabino Canyon. In San Jose, I would check the weather on the coast and when the sun looked good I would head to Capitola/Santa Cruz for a combo run and bike. *I'll be right back.* In Oregon, I did my best business planning on the trails of Forest Park.

You pay for this freedom/flexibility with late hours, weekend work and some catch-up early in the mornings. My brother Bruce, a lawyer in Flagstaff, has always been the same way. Our bikes are on the car bike rack and the open area in our cars looks like a locker room—shoes, swimming gear, backpacks, tire pumps. The September 2006 edition of Men's Health *Best Life* featured an article on brother Bruce and his same work/life blur: "Griffen's staff calls him "Superman" because he'll pull over to the side of the road between appointments, slip out of his suit, and disappear into the wilderness for a quick jog, ride or swim."

For us, it was a way to fit work and life into every day. That was our version of work/life balance. But everyone has to find a way to manage that work/life combo—otherwise it leads to massive stress for you and others around you. *I just don't have a life outside of work.* And the technology that connects us also creates an expectation of availability. *Sometimes you feel like Denny's, you're always open for business.*

My friend, colleague and most-important-ever mentor, Will Marré, wrote a book in 2009 entitled, *Save The World and Still Be Home For Dinner. Now that's a title.* I started my consulting career with Will in 1996; he was my gateway from IBM to the consulting world. *I would have paid him just for the privilege of working with him.* An amazing communicator, researcher, writer and the *most balanced* human beings I have ever known. He lived in Escondido, California, and surfed *every day.* The ocean gave him harmony, perspective, balance and joy.

He worked with CEOs and was a coach to many leaders. And he saw first-hand what a lack of life balance could do. Deterioration of health, cynicism, stress, family break-ups. All just to be a leader. The premise of his book was simple: *you can be a leader and still have a life.* The inside of the book jacket provides the context:

"By 'Save the World', Marré asks the readers to stand up for something that really matters to them, to make their unique contributions to a sustainable future, and add value to the lives of others. By 'Still be Home for Dinner' he refers to our ability to enact these changes *in our own way, in our own place, and with those we love*—a way that fulfills the heart and satisfies the soul."

And I think that's a pretty good rationale for how to blend your work and life. And Will didn't just write about it, he lived it. Every day. Will passed away on February 24, 2018. He died on his surfboard. *And so many of us miss his wisdom, guidance and joy for life.*

The COVID Impact on How We Think About Work

In all of our Foresight sessions we ask about how COVID may impact the way we think about the session subject, in this case, the future of work. At least for the short-term, from our lens of 2020, the impact is significant and responses are powerful:

- "Probably exposed the fragility of the economic situation, and provided an impetus for changes that were needed, but seemed too far away before the pandemic."
- "We are learning that technology can facilitate working well without being in a physical office. In addition, it has caused us to understand the value of 'non work' activities often lost in the hurly-burly of working."
- "Certainly COVID forced 'remote work' to happen, quickly, for those roles where remote work can occur. But the service/healthcare workers, they are still face-to-face with potential risks. Does this create/separate two societies/demographics that were less visible previously?"
- "Greatly. COVID has taken away many peoples' ability to work. There needs to be an ability for people to adapt when situations change as well as a greater effort by the government to provide for people when opportunities are taken away from them."
- "It forced us to adapt, pivot way quicker than we would have. We are now using tech seamlessly when we resisted (somewhat) previously."

I think our Foresighters were right. It advanced us in many regards (technology, agility, virtual workplace, the commitment of our essential workers), but it also exposed us (the fragility of our economy, the lack of real crisis planning) and a reawakening to what really matters in our lives.

We even asked our participants about the decade ahead and whether people will think differently about *retirement*. It's another of those somewhat existential questions, so I know Kierkegaard would be pleased:

Question: *How will the decade ahead affect how people will think about RETIREMENT?*

No.	Items	Times Selected
1.	**Most people really don't want to retire, they just want to scale back. More people will continue to work well past the traditional retirement timeline because they want to, it gives them social engagement and purpose.**	(61%)
2.	Most people would prefer to retire or scale back but they can't afford to. Retirement means a return to a minimum wage job to makes ends meet along with any government/social support.	(32%)
3.	No real change, most people who reach their "retirement age" within their company or industry will retire and move to a more leisurely and discretionary lifestyle. Fire up the Winnebago!	(7%)

When my book will be published in 2021 (always the optimistic outlook), I will be 65. I fully intend to maintain my current work/life blur at the same pace until I am 75, then perhaps I will taper off a bit. But I could not imagine not maintaining a level of purposeful work. *Did you realize that Dr. Anthony Faucci, who is guiding us through 2020, is 79?* God bless him.

Five Foresights From This Foresight Session
Wow. Work seems so simple, just *get 'er done,* but it is more than a job task. It influences just about everything we are as a country today and into the future. If we get work *right* in the decade ahead, we will be a far better America. And if we don't, the consequences will be painful and maybe something we simply don't recover from. We really are at the *tipping point.* So here are five reflections from this session and the future of work in the decade ahead:

1. WHAT WE DO MATTERS: Nothing changes in the decade ahead about the fundamental nature of work. It matters for each of us. It helps define who we are and what we stand for. It creates personal pride, esteem, a sense of dignity and purpose. We like to work, we just want to be respected, compensated fairly and given a chance to be successful.
2. TECHNOLOGY IS OUR FRIEND: Just as it was an enabler in the prior decade, it will be an enabler in the decade ahead. It will create many new opportunities and will also create new flexibility for how we do our work. The 4th Industrial Revolution will not be a revolution, it's just the next phase of leveraging technology and adapting to change.
3. WE NEED TO FIX ACCESS/INCLUSIVITY: This is not a fair playing field right now. We cannot maintain the economic and social divide that we have in 2020. More people need access to education and the very nature of education as a conduit to meaningful work has to change. You can be an hourly worker and be a provider to your family via access to a reasonable minimum wage. Everyone can have access to good healthcare. Imagine a decade ahead where *anyone* can pursue the work they want and make a difference *and* they are welcomed into the workplace.
4. YOUR HANDS ARE AS VALUED AS YOUR MIND: The decade ahead will see a resurgence in the value of making things, of physical labor, of vocational careers. Since when did we decide to look down on people who work hard with their hands? There is nothing wrong with being an automotive technician, a construction worker, a miner, someone on a manufacturing line. There is great pride in *making things.*
5. SAVE THE WORLD AND STILL BE HOME FOR DINNER: Find that right balance for your work in the decade ahead. Make a difference, whatever *dent in the universe* you want to make, but do it in way that lets you and others around you enjoy the journey.

I am, at the end of the day, optimistic about this next decade for the nature of work. I am optimistic that each of my four millennial children can choose a meaningful path for their work in a way that is authentic for them. I just want more people to have that opportunity. We will all be better off if we can create that access and remove that economic division.

Now, *get to work!*

My personal thanks to these authors and their books that have taught me so much about the nature of work, of performance and of life balance:

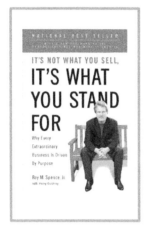 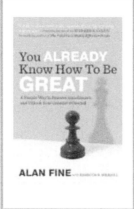 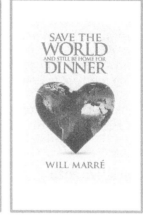

Why Purpose Matters *The Flow Zone!* *Find Your Balance*

CHAPTER 5: A Decade Divided or United?

There's something happening here
What it is ain't exactly clear
There's a man with a gun over there
Telling me I got to beware…

I think it's time we stop, children, what's that sound?
Everybody look, what's going down?

--Buffalo Springfield, *For What It's Worth* (1966)

August 20, 2020
Foresight 2030 Session

First of all, if you have never listened to Buffalo Springfield's *For What It's Worth* song, please put this book down and ask Alexa or Google it, or *ask your mother or father.* They will know it. *They probably still have it on an 8-track cartridge.* When you play it, close your eyes and just listen. It is haunting and powerful. Written by Stephen Stills in 1966 after counter-culture clashes that took place between police and young people, it became somewhat of a national anthem for Vietnam era anti-war protests.

There's battle lines being drawn
Nobody's right if everybody's wrong
Young people speaking their minds
Getting so much resistance from behind

Juxtapose the Vietnam protests in the 1960s with the Black Lives Matter protests in 2020 and play the Buffalo Springfield song. It is the sound-track of protest, of young people and causes. And it is the soundtrack of deep division in America. And, unfortunately, we have to keep playing it.

Vietnam War protests—1960s.

Black Lives Matter—2020

What a field day for the heat
A thousand people in the street
Singing songs and carrying signs
Mostly say, "hooray for our side"

Welcome to the summer of 2020. A summer of *discontent.* A summer of *discomfort.* And a summer of *disconnection.*

More than anything, it was a summer of *disagreement.* But there was one thing we could all agree on: *we are a very divided country.*

Reflecting on American Division

Division is not new to America. It was some 150 years ago when the level of division produced a historic civil war. The American Civil War lasted from 1861 through 1865 between the northern state "loyalists" and the southern state "confederates" that had seceded from the United States. Wikipedia tells us that, "The principal cause of the war was whether the enslavement of Black people in the southern states should continue."

I know this seems like ancient history. But it's not. When I was young, there were still veterans of the Civil War alive. Old, but alive. What would it have been like to experience the American Civil War? Americans divided for passionate causes willing to kill each other. Politics and leadership were front and center. Lincoln was elected President in 1860 largely on an anti-slavery platform and an initial seven slave states declared their secession from the country. It was downhill after that. War broke out in April of 1861, when the Confederate forces attacked Fort Sumter just after Lincoln's inauguration. An additional four states joined the Confederacy and the war was on.

It was the deadliest conflict in American history with some 620,000 to 750,000 soldiers dead and countless civilians caught in the cross-fire. The war ended in 1865 after the Battle of Appomattox Court House. Confederate General Robert E. Lee surrendered to Ulysses Grant. It is one of our most poignant episodes in American history. It showed the high cost of division, and, unfortunately, the American Civil War is not over.

In the summer of 2020 America continues to be divided. Despite 150 years of time since the Civil War, we are still not comfortable with racial equality. *Black Lives Matter* becomes a central point of protest. We are debating about whether Confederate statues should remain. Whether places, be they parks, streets or military bases, should still bear the names of Confederate military leaders. The Confederate flag flew for 54 years atop the dome at the South Carolina State House and later on its

135

front lawn. It wasn't until *2015* that the flag was lowered after then-Governor Nikki Haley took one of her better stands.

In June of 2020, that beacon of American unity, NASCAR, finally banned the Confederate flag from its events. *2020.* Hey, that's *my* 2020 we are talking about and how it may influence the decade ahead. In its statement, NASCAR said the following:

"The presence of the Confederate flag at NASCAR events runs contrary to our commitment to providing a welcoming and inclusive environment for all of our fans, our competitors and our industry. Bringing people together around a love for racing and the community it creates is what makes fans and sport special. The display of the Confederate flag will be prohibited from all NASCAR events and properties."

Gag me with a spoon. NASCAR was founded in 1948. *We just figured out the welcoming and inclusivity thing.* With a little help from advertisers and sponsors that saw the writing on the wall.

The Confederate flag flying at a NASCAR race

Look, I respect history. And for the record, I do not believe that Confederate statues and Confederate history should be *erased* from our history. It is part of our heritage and a symbol of the struggle to create a *United States of America.* The problem is that we are really continuing with that struggle. You can respect history and still *move on.*

That includes the *asshole* who waved a Confederate flag inside the U.S. Capitol on the January 6, 2021, Insurrection. *We'll get to that in a later chapter.*

So, leading up to our August 2020 Foresight session there were a lot of divisional forces lining up. The Black Lives Matter protests accelerated after the highly publicized deaths of Black Americans including Ahmaud

136

Arbery, Alton Sterling, Breonna Taylor and George Floyd. NPR reports that, *"Since 2015, police officers have fatally shot 135 unarmed Black men and women nationwide."* And at least 75% of the officers were white. What does it mean when Americans are killing Americans? It means we are desperately divided.

It was the killing of George Floyd on May 25, 2020, that took everything to another level. Because we all watched the killing. We watched a police officer keep his knee on Floyd's neck for at least 8 minutes and 26 seconds. You could not look away. And you could not walk away.

Protests surged in the summer. And they were massive and they were a different composition than anyone might have anticipated. The New York Times reported that *half a million people* turned out in 550 locations across the United States on June 6. Analysis and polling suggests that some 15 to 26 *million* people had turned out to protest in the summer wave of *discontent.* Another poll from the *Washington Post/Kaiser Family Foundation* indicated that *one in five Americans* had participated in some kind of protest since the start of the Trump administration.

Perhaps you were on the streets. It was a diverse demographic. In many cases a younger demographic with, according to a *Civis Analytics* poll, the largest share of protesters being people under the age of 35. And for many, it was their first time getting involved with a form of activism or protest. *Young Americans have a history of protest and creating movements.* And a new generation was experiencing this.

Black Lives Matter—2020

It was, and continues to be, one of the largest movements in American history. It has at least raised our collective social awareness to a new level. According to Douglas McAdam, an emeritus professor at Stanford University who studies social movements, "It looks, for all the world, like these protests are achieving what very few do: setting in motion a period of significant, sustained and widespread social, political change. We appear to be at a tipping point—that is rare in society as it is potentially consequential."

I would agree that from our lens in the summer of 2020 that we are at a tipping point. I am just not sure which way we are going to tip in the decade ahead. So we convened our Foresight session to get a better sense of where we might be headed.

America Ahead: Divided or United

Thirty-three thought leaders *together and united* to deal with division. I must tell you that our previous Foresight sessions, while significant in their subject content (i.e., Future of Technology, Future of Work), were not really controversial. *We were about to wade into some deep shit.* The divisional fractures that we would be looking at were highly emotional—race, income, politics, gender, etc. And I can assure you I had participants with very opposite views. We could have had some spirited *point/counterpoint* side-bars.

A few introductions from our participants, so you get a sense of our *very diverse* backgrounds:

- "I'm president of a small daily newspaper, married, parent of two grown adults, grandparent of five, thinking about retirement. I live in New Hampshire and have been a resident of the state for about 40 years after having grown up in Vermont."
- "VP Strategic Director/Partner for Sioux Falls marketing firm, 25 years at company; live on an acreage outside of town, married 34 years, two grown children."
- "Entrepreneur & Storyteller." (*Can't wait!*)
- "Husband, father of three girls, work in government contracting."
- "Retired in March, expecting to feel lost without my work—but have been surprised at how much I'm enjoying my free time (read tons of books) and rediscovering volunteer work."
- "I am married with four grown children. I work as the CEO of a telecom company with five diverse subsidiaries in the Phoenix area. I love continued education, golf and contemplating the nature of consciousness." (*Interesting combination...*)
- "Opinion research/market research background. Live in Austin, TX. Happy keeper of cats and plants. There's an SO (Significant Other) in there, too. He makes cartoons!"

Excellent. Perhaps I have found an illustrator for my book.

As we always do in our Foresight sessions, we asked our participants to reflect back on the prior decade and consider what may have influenced our unity as well as our division:

Question: *Thinking about the last decade, 2010-2019, what are some things that you feel brought us closer together—issues, events or causes that helped us to be more UNITED?*

We had some 75+ responses, but there were very clear themes about what influenced us to be more united. Two quick responses:

✓ Obama's election
✓ Trump's election

Facilitator note to self: I am in for a long session… But an overall set of themes emerged:

✓ The advancement of women
✓ The impact of the 2008 recession
✓ Sports and especially the Olympics
✓ The Arab Spring and global quest for democracy/freedom
✓ The advancement of technology and access to the Internet
✓ Medical advancements
✓ A generally good economy
✓ Women's soccer and its impact on young girls
✓ Tragedies and how communities responded (Boston, Dallas, etc.)
✓ Social media and connection, the power of visual/video
✓ The MeToo movement
✓ The Black Lives Matter movement
✓ Progress in public/private space exploration
✓ More people being able to travel globally
✓ How we responded to natural disasters
✓ Accomplishments of young people (innovation and inspiration)
✓ Film, television and greater entertainment access (shared experiences)
✓ Bringing Osama Bin Laden to justice (helping to close a chapter)
✓ Globalization in general

So I am feeling a little better. There were some strong unifiers. Technology was a huge unifier, and so was a generally good economy. Movements and causes—women, youth, Black Lives Matter, respect via MeToo and even global movements such as the Arab Spring. The shared experience of sport (the thrill of victory and the agony of defeat). The role of entertainment and powerful film and TV. And unfortunately, we are sometimes at our best when the worst has occurred—mass shootings, airline crashes, natural disasters. We need to remember why it feels good to come together and do that on a more regular basis—without the disasters.

Our flip side was to look at what influenced division in the prior decade:

139

Question: *Still thinking about the last decade, 2010-2019, what are some things that you feel moved us further apart—issues, events or causes that caused us to be more DIVIDED?*

For you researchers, we had 113 division responses in this question vs. 76 united responses in our prior question. *You kinda know where we are heading…*

Here is a summary of the division themes:

- ✓ The role of social media
- ✓ Trump's election in 2016
- ✓ Polarization of political views
- ✓ Conspiracy theories
- ✓ Gun control debate
- ✓ The growing wealth inequality
- ✓ Police brutality/Police mistakes
- ✓ Lack of equitable healthcare access
- ✓ Global politics and players (Russia, China, North Korea, Iran…)
- ✓ Climate change debate and impact
- ✓ The 24-hour news cycle
- ✓ The continued shift of political parties to their extreme edges
- ✓ Lack of equal access to education
- ✓ Blatant racism
- ✓ Fake news vs. the role of facts
- ✓ Disinformation campaigns
- ✓ Politicization of media outlets
- ✓ Supreme Court nominations
- ✓ Continued gender inequality
- ✓ The power of PACs (Political Action Committees)
- ✓ Distrust of science
- ✓ Generational divides
- ✓ Continued Mideast wars and involvement by the U.S.
- ✓ The technology divide (digital haves vs. have-nots)

It's interesting when some things make *both* lists. Technology, social media, Trumpism. Access to information vs. *weaponization* of information. But one of the most powerful themes overall was the growing sense of *haves vs. have-nots.* How can we ever be unified if a majority of Americans do not have equal access to: technology, education, economic opportunity, healthcare. *How about basic respect and dignity?*

If we don't close these fundamental gaps in the decade ahead we are screwed. And unfortunately the politics heading into 2020 are simply digging these gaps deeper and deeper into the heart and soul of this country.

And if all of that wasn't enough stress, the COVID crisis, which was having a *disproportional impact* on the "have-nots" was simply bad and getting worse and itself was becoming a center of political controversy.

Since our last Foresight session on June 25, Dr. Anthony Fauci appeared before the Senate Education, Health and Labor committee on June 30 and warned that new COVID cases could hit 100,000 cases a day given the current trajectory (we were at 40,000 cases per day at that point). The U.S. hits *3 million* infections on July 7 and on the same day the Trump administration notifies the United Nations that it is beginning its withdrawal from the World Health Organization. The WHO announces that the coronavirus can be transmitted by air (a formal acknowledgement) and can be spread by asymptomatic individuals.

By July 16, the U.S. reports a record 75,600 cases of COVID in a *single day*. By August 17, deaths in the U.S. are exceeding 1,000 per day and COVID is now the number three cause of death behind heart disease and cancer.

On the positive side, the key vaccine developers are into early phase trials and showing promising results. The U.S. Health and Human Services (HHS) and Department of Defense (DOD) sign a contract with Pfizer and BioNTech for the delivery of 100 million doses of their vaccine candidates for December of 2020 with a provision to expand to 600 million doses based on phase 3 clinical trials and FDA approvals.

We are coming together and coming apart at the same time.

Assessing the Prior Decade

So, against a crisis in COVID, replete with its own implications of unifying us and dividing us, we asked our participants to assess the prior decade and conclude whether we became more united or more divided:

Question: *All things considered, looking at the past decade, do you feel we became more united or more divided as Americans?*

No.	Items	Times Selected
1.	**I think it was a bad decade for America, we became more DIVIDED**	(81%)
2.	I think it was a mixed decade for America, call it status quo	(16%)

| 3. | I think it was a good decade for America, we became more UNITED | (3%) |

Ouch. This is not a good trend and does not bode well for the decade ahead. *Over 80 percent concluded we became more divided in the past decade.* This was an activity where we asked people to explain their responses. *And explain they did:*

- DIVIDED: "Things were great under Obama—life was hopeful. In the last 4 years, Trump has created a shambles of this country and what it stands for."
- DIVIDED: "The 2016 election was wrenching and divisive. We saw the ugly side of America. White supremacy moved into the public eye."
- DIVIDED: "Much less sense of a common cause. This has been exacerbated by social media, partisan media, partisan and divisive politicians. A culture that rewards extreme positions with airtime, etc."
- DIVIDED: "Wealth inequality, loss of middle class, lost jobs, and partisanship through social media and 24/7 news cycle topped with a president who fans the flames of division."
- DIVIDED: "Trump and his Confederacy of Dunces destroying norms, institutions and the rule of law to the horror of most and the applause of too many."
- DIVIDED: "As information is presented with ever-increasing targeted audiences, society has Balkanized into groups that only act and think alike. There is little dialogue or appetite to seek out other's points of view that may not be like our own. It's much easier to "un-friend" someone than to practice empathy."
- DIVIDED: "Someone else commented that it was hard to remember when we were united and I agree. The U.S. and the world feel like they are moving back to a tribal, nationalist, splintered 'I have to take care of me and mine' attitude. Really hard to remember the last time something at a country level made me feel united and joyous."
- DIVIDED: "Obama, then Trump, and Congress could not get on the same page on major policy issues. Executive orders became the manner in which policy moved. We as a people retreated to our corners. Moderates disappeared."
- DIVIDED: "Fake news coupled with the proliferation of social media put us all in a frame of mind of not really knowing (or believing) what was going on. Political ideologues (if you disagree, you are wrong, and dead!) on both sides of the aisle mean Congress gets nothing done."

And there were a few that were mixed or leaning towards united:

- MIXED: "Mixed decade with the political polarization leading to some unification and some division through the years."
- MIXED: "I feel some things brought us closer together such as social media, but at the same time things like social media also pushed us apart."
- UNITED: "Unity is within a large silent majority. Make America Great Again is a great vision."

Look, these are all people I value and respect. That doesn't mean I agree with them. One of my mentors, Will Marré, whom I introduced you to in the previous chapter, said it best when he conveyed one of his leadership refrains:

"We can both go to the same movie and have a different experience."

It is one of the most important lessons in respect and diversity of opinion that any of us can carry. I saw the same thing, I just see it differently than you. *I use this often with my family members with varying degrees of success.*

But Will also had another leadership line that many of us can nod our heads to when we think about politics, people, business and life in general:

"How often does a bad movie get better?"

The level of division did not begin in 2016. *But it got magnified big time.* Our polarization and level of *disagreement* seemed to accelerate. And it would all come to a head later in 2020 as we headed into the election season. *Chapter 7 for your Foresight reference.*

By the way, this issue of united vs. divided is not a U.S.-only phenomenon. We do not have the patent on this issue. What happens in the world affects us deeply and will affect our decade ahead. Our Foresight group was only modestly more positive about the global view:

Question: *All things considered, looking at the past decade, do you feel we became more united or more divided as a world (all countries)?*

No.	Items	Times Selected

1.	I think it was a bad decade for world, we became more DIVIDED	(71%)
2.	I think it was a mixed decade for the world, call it status quo	(23%)
3.	I think it was a good decade for the world, we became more UNITED	(6%)

It's not just us. The world is a wonderful, *but really scary* place. We have *borders* and *religious ideologies* and *warring factions* and *autocratic leaders*. We have *nuclear devices pointed at each other.* We have a lot of people who do not like the U.S. for a lot of reasons, and some of those may be well earned. Mostly, I think we are a country and a people who are on the side of creating unity and supporting global human rights and a better life for all. But, right now, in August of 2020, there are also a lot of countries wondering, *what the hell are you guys doing over there?*

And we asked our participants about these global views as they reflected on the prior decade:

- MIXED: "In some ways the world has become more unified, but in other ways it has gotten worse. I think with Trump in office, the U.S. is viewed in worse light globally, which causes more of a divide."
- MIXED: "The U.S. has become separated from most of the rest of the world, but the rest of the world is perhaps more united as a response to that separation."
- MIXED: "We made a lot of progress in the first part of the decade. It's been rougher since a number of the Middle East conflicts and the resulting migrations."
- DIVIDED: "Existing partnerships, like between Europe and the U.S., have frayed. Nationalistic governments are on the rise."
- DIVIDED: "Nationalism: identification with one's own nation and support for its interests, especially to the exclusion or detriment of the interests of other nations."
- DIVIDED: "The rise of nationalism in the USA, UK, Russia, Hungary, Brazil, etc., has led to a decrease in international cooperation with the major powers largely taking unilateral action outside of coalitions and alliances."
- UNITED: "I think the world as a whole wants what's best for all people, rather than just those in their respective countries. The world is a smaller place than it used to be, therefore we have to be more united."

Look, I'm OK with *America First*. I am just not OK with *America Alone*. The world is a smaller place and just as we need to have a higher level of unity in the decade ahead for America, we need to be able to *work together on global issues*. We don't solve or address climate change without a global collaboration. And, not that you need to be reminded, we are in a *global pandemic*. And we really need to have better ways of resolving conflict than wars. *If you have never visited the Vietnam Veterans Memorial Wall in Washington, you should. It is a very long wall. And it's not the only memorial that reflects on the cost of war for our country. God Bless.*

Vietnam Veterans Memorial Wall

World War II Memorial

Division in America 2020

The impact of division, whether in America or globally is real and emotional. And the history of division is important for all of us if we're going to have a shot at being more unified. So we moved our Foresight group in 2020 to look at what is creating the current level of division:

Question: *Let's put emotion aside (for now), and ask you to do some consulting work. Thinking about TODAY (August of 2020), what are the factors/issues most causing division in America specifically? Where are the lines being drawn?*

One hundred sixty-three responses in less that five minutes. No shortage of issues here. For this exercise we did a real-time summary and then assessed the issues in terms of their influence on the level of division:

Now, please assess each of the following factors/issues in terms of how significant you feel they are TODAY in influencing the level of division in America. Use a scale of 1-10 where a "1" means not at all important and a "10" means extremely important:

Rank	Idea	Avg.

145

1.	Trump Presidency	**9.5**
2.	Media overload/disinformation	**8.8**
3.	Lack of bipartisan politics	**8.7**
4.	Level of racism/social injustice	**8.5**
5.	Political/ideological views	**8.5**
6.	Handling of pandemic	**8.4**
7.	Social media influence	**7.8**
8.	Loss of institutional trust	**7.7**
9.	Sensationalizing everything	**7.5**
10.	Economic/wage gap	**7.5**
11.	Healthcare access/affordability	**7.3**
12.	Police brutality	**7.0**
13.	Attitudes towards immigration	**6.9**
14.	Gun control	**6.4**
15.	Climate change	**6.1**

Our assessment seems to track well with our open comments we received. Here's a few for context on the macro level themes:

- "Propaganda masquerading as news, the rise of no-information voters, science denying, education (and the educated) being demonized and the yawning gap between the very rich and the rest."
- "CNN/FOX can take the same topic and have it be something wonderful/terrible at the same time." (*Well, we can both go to the same movie…*)
- "BLM vs. Blue Lives Matter—neither side seeing each other's point of view."
- "We cannot agree if COVID-19 is really a disease or if it is a political ploy."
- "Economic divide between the privileged and the larger proportion that is shut out of achieving a basic standard of living."
- "Leadership. Income inequality. Racial inequality. Gun violence. Healthcare. The culture/goals of America as a nation."

- "Lack of education. Cult of ignorance that feelings and opinions are as good as facts and evidence."
- "Lack of critical thinking in public discourse/media. Everything is sensationalized."
- "Political ideology...disagree and you are wrong! Wealthy vs. struggling financially; education (arts vs. STEM); work and school...virtual or in person; America first or global community; coastal vs middle America; street justice or justice system (including police); defund or educate police, BLM or everyone matters, Yankees or everyone else!"

Those damn Yankees!

There seems to be this same confluence of primary issues affecting the divide: the social, education and economic gap (the haves vs. the have-nots). The media overload and the ability to use disinformation to influence people and issues. The lack of bipartisan politics, working against each other instead of for us. Loss of faith in institutions (media, government, religion). Inability to simply find common ground (my way or the highway). Oh, and the current president seems to be at the top of the list.

Can it be that *one person* can influence that much divisiveness in the country? *It can be.*

But not by theirself. The openness to persuasion is frightening. But it's not new. People do want to be part of a cause that matters. Part of a movement. To belong. The problem is that what you belong to matters. History, once again an important guide to division and unity, has shown the power of persuasion and its implications. The American Revolution was a movement and we seem to feel like it was a *just cause*. Hitler's Nazism was a movement and we seem to feel it was an *unjust cause*. Those are extremes, it gets harder when the movement or cause is in the middle and there can be compelling messages and *persuasion* on both sides.

But remember the adage attributed to Daniel Moynihan:

"Everyone is entitled to his own opinion, but not his own facts."

Facts matter. They matter in how we deal with COVID, how we make decisions on economic growth and strategy. The degree of divide and disequity that exists. There is fault in those who distort the facts to support their own cause. There is fault in the media that chooses fragments of facts to sensationalize. There is fault when you and I are presented with facts and choose to ignore them. *The machines were talking but no one was listening.*

And the lack of civil discourse on issues is a problem as well. It seems like many these days prefer the rather caustic approach that the *Urban Dictionary* takes when they define the term "You are entitled to your opinion":

Term: "You are entitled to your opinion." *Considered a safe phrase—1) To agree to disagree. 2) "You have the right to your opinion, but at the same time go fuck yourself and the horse you rode up on."*

Welcome to civility in America, circa 2020.

Surely Things Have Been Worse

Let's move on, shall we? For the most part our discourse in this Foresight session has been reasonably civil. But it's easy to get caught up in the moment. Surely we have been at this level of division before in this country, it's just amped up a bit due to the politics and ease with which we can turn up the volume with technology. I will grant you that in 1861 the level of division in America was higher. And the level of unity in 1941 was higher as we entered into World War II. But once again, those are the extremes. Where are we today compared with, say, the last 64 years?

Question: *We all have our own experiences and historical perspectives. Let's give you a horizon of 64 years to play with--1956 thru 2020: All things considered do you feel that AMERICA is more divided today than any time in the last 64 years, or vice versa?*

No.	Items	Times Selected
1.	**I think America is MORE DIVIDED today than any time the last 64 years**	(84%)
2.	I think America is LESS DIVIDED today than any time the last 64 years	(16%)

Some of you are wondering about the 64 year timeline. Check the epilogue for context.

I get that there may be some "in the moment" bias. But these were private responses, the participants did not see each other's responses until after they had submitted their own response. And, keep in mind that we are in a global pandemic, a level of political polarization that we may have never experienced in our lifetime, we have massive protests in the streets and we have a growing social and cultural divide. *So I was not surprised.*

148

- MORE: "We are more divided than we have ever been in my 50 years, but it is very close (barely more or less) to in the '60s with race riots and Vietnam. Very close, but I'll say more divided."
- MORE: "I think perhaps in earlier times people could avoid major issues of the day more easily. Today, the issues that are tearing this nation apart are EVERYWHERE, inescapable, affecting EVERYONE. Pandemic and the lack of leadership are inescapable."
- MORE: "The Vietnam era was the closest we have to today's political and social unrest. I think it was probably a close second, so we aren't too much more divided than we have been in the past. But it's not the norm by any means."
- MORE: "I don't necessarily think that the topics we are facing today are more significant than problems we've faced in the last 64 years, but I will say we are more divided on the current topics than any others..."
- MORE: "I think that there has always been division, but the difference today is that the mechanisms of spreading division—especially through social media—are just greater. So the division becomes louder and seems like it is the status quo."
- MORE: "The Trump presidency, fueled by a vast array of media sources, has created the biggest divide in my memory. Facts are no longer trusted. Science is questioned. Having certain conversations with family and friends are guarded or avoided. We do not have leadership that seems to want to solve the problem."
- MORE: "There has been a lot of division in the last 64 years, and I feel that the division was strong for the issue in question, but society as a whole was able to find common ground on other things. Now, seems like there are more things dividing us at the same time and among more groups."
- MORE: "It may be perspective because I am more aware today and have more information to draw upon than when I was 18, but it seems more divided. I think the housing crisis created more of an economic divide in America. There is a backlash today with BLM and MeToo even though things have probably gotten better today, but it is because of the past coming out. There is an anti-intellectualism movement going on that social media platforms help. This is dangerous."
- MORE: "Political parties are so far left and far right that there is no middle ground. There is never agreement because the voices that are heard are the extremes. The media is very left and very right as well which just makes it more divided."

Welcome to the age of *extremism.*

Unity in the Decade Ahead

So far, the responses to our Foresight session do not bode well for the decade ahead. We should retreat to our point of view. Retreat to our tribes. Hell, let's just head back to our *caves*.

But one thing I have already seen in our Foresight sessions is that Americans are uniquely *optimistic*. We may push things to the brink, but we usually figure it out in the long haul. We will swing the pendulum back when it gets a little out of balance. But I was not sure in this case (and admittedly I am still quite uneasy about the decade), but I was encouraged by our Foresighter responses on what they felt about the decade ahead:

Question: *If you were to forecast your view about the level of unity in AMERICA in the decade ahead NOW, would you say you were optimistic or pessimistic about our level of unity?*

No.	Items	Times Selected
1.	**Optimistic about the level of unity in the decade ahead—it will PROGRESS**	**(81%)**
2.	Pessimistic about the level of unity in the decade ahead—it will DECLINE	(19%)

This can't be the same group of participants. *Pass the pipe.* How can you say that we are at the low point of division in 2020 but say that you are optimistic about our unity in the decade ahead? The explanations were powerful and really quite rational:

- PROGRESS: "We will get through COVID together and that will unite us ultimately."
- PROGRESS: "Coming out of COVID, coming out of what will be a bad economic period, coming out of historic federal debt, and coming out of a decade where Gen-Z and everyone else realizes the problems with social media and the 24/7 biased news media cycle, we will be in a position to collectively pull together."
- PROGRESS: "Looking at the long arc of history, the strength of this country is its self-correcting characteristic. A trait of the American people is to take action and that is happening."
- PROGRESS: "The current level of disunity is unsustainable. Something will have to give and both sides will have to crawl towards the center to survive."

- PROGRESS: "I am optimistic because I choose to be. I don't want to be part of the problem if I succumb to the negativity. I "feel" as if Rome is burning but hope that we can put out the fire before it is too late."
- PROGRESS: "My view is contingent on the result of the presidential election, which currently favors Biden. If Trump is reelected then there will definitely be more division and the U.S., I fear, will move firmly toward authoritarianism. If Biden is elected it will potentially increase unity but there will continue to be forces that resist efforts toward achieving common ground."
- PROGRESS: "It will be a slow progression but progress will happen. I believe we will get younger, smarter leadership. We will work on climate change, which will bring new jobs, clean air, sustainability for our planet."
- PROGRESS: "There is much work to be done in healing our nation, but the common bond of the COVID experience and the common exhaustion of the Trump presidency has given us the gift of being able to empathize with every other citizen in the country on these two topics."
- PROGRESS: "We can only improve from where we are now. I think we'll have a different voice in leadership. I think the dangers of having ineffective leadership and polarized parties are obvious, and more working together across the aisle will, in time, return. Or, maybe we just won't be a country any more."

You had me for most of that last response. A little concerned about the loss of country idea.

Nature abhors a vacuum. *What? Kierkegaard back on your sessions?* No, it's just that I agree that the level of division is not sustainable. It doesn't feel right. The whole mood of the country could change by early 2021 *if* three things happen:

1. Biden gets elected.
2. We have a successful vaccine rollout and have a sense that we can defeat COVID.
3. The economy begins a genuine recovery.

You want to add a *moonshot* to creating optimism about the decade ahead? Rally around climate change and a younger generation that takes it on as *their* cause. All of that may move us in the right direction, but it won't move *all* of us in that direction. The extremists may stay extreme. And we can't make this a decade where just the "haves" are united. That is a false summit.

By the way, we are actually *more optimistic* about America progressing on unity in the decade ahead than we are the world. But we are still optimistic:

Question: *If you were to forecast your view about the level of unity in the WORLD in the decade ahead NOW, would you say you were optimistic or pessimistic about our level of unity?*

No.	Items	Times Selected
1.	**Optimistic about the level of unity in the decade ahead—it will PROGRESS**	(69%)
2.	Pessimistic about the level of unity in the decade ahead—it will DECLINE	(31%)

It's interesting to see that a different level of generational thinking is coming into play on this. It's also a little concerning that if we don't create the level of unity globally that the results could be catastrophic. Some thoughts on both sides:

- PROGRESS: "Not sure to call it UNITY, but once the U.S. straightens up a bit, and stops tormenting the world (allies and foes), we will begin to come to a leadership position again. Not sure what nuclear will mean if it comes to Iran/Iraq, but if that does not erupt, other nations will try for peace, including North Korea and China and Russia."
- PROGRESS: "Again I believe, for the most part, that we will reach out globally to deal with the world problems, in my opinion we have no choice. Otherwise we can't sustain this planet."
- PROGRESS: "Contingent on U.S. election. If Trump is re-elected it will embolden authoritarianism and will erode the international organizations that have bound the world in common purpose since WWII. If Biden is elected we will return toward traditional diplomacy that both parties have pursued for 75 years."
- PROGRESS: "It may get worse before getting better, but in the long run I believe that the next generation will have a more global view of the world and the issues they face will need global responses."

- DECLINE: "Trump administration will take a long time to repair. Also there will be immigration and war threats due to climate change and inequality."

- DECLINE: "The effect of climate change on where people live and how they grow food, access to water, etc. We are entering into the era of mass migrations. It has started and will continue in the decade and decades ahead."
- DECLINE: "Concerned about the rise of nationalism and lack of ability to help other nations...especially as far as the COVID crisis goes immediately, but also as water issues, global warming become more prevalent. Countries will be taking care of their own before they can help other."
- DECLINE: "It will depend on the outcome of this election, whether we continue to promote capitalism or take a turn towards socialism. If the U.S. is not strong, there are a lot of bad actors out there who will create trouble."

The stakes are high. Our level of American unity will have influence on global unity. I prefer that we hang together as a planet. It's kind of the only one we have at this point in time.

Influencing Factors for the Future

And what might really drive our future reality on unity vs. division in the decade ahead? We posed two questions about the future—why we might be *more united* and why we might be *more divided* just to test our previous level of optimism.

Question: *Now, let's look ahead. We are here to consider the NEXT TEN YEARS. Now through December 31, 2029. What makes you OPTIMISTIC about our ability to be united as Americans—why might we be more UNITED?*

After open responses we did a real-time summary of the factors that might influence optimism in the decade. The following is the summary (factors were not prioritized):

No.	Idea
1.	Moving beyond the pandemic
2.	Our level of resiliency
3.	Improved economy
4.	Space exploration
5.	Close the gaps in wealth and education
6.	Stronger national leadership

7.	Improved access to healthcare
8.	Positive role of technology
9.	New generation's input/ideas
10.	Science-based decision making
11.	Visible progress on climate change
12.	Less bias in mainstream media
13.	The next generation of leadership taking hold
14.	Improvements in health and wellness
15.	Racial equality, diversity acceptance/inclusion
16.	Less social media influence and bias
17.	New modes of transportation (hyperloops, high speed rail, electric everything...)
18.	The advancement of women in leadership roles
19.	Real advancement on gun control
20.	Improvements in education access
21.	Rallying around common challenges
22.	The values of our youth (Gen Z) and their impact

Get 'er done. A to-do list for the decade. At least it's a *starter* list. You will note that we are shifting a fair amount of burden to this *next generation and younger generation* of leadership. I'm OK with that, they will need some guidance along the way, but, after all, *it is their future.*

Question: *Now, let's continue to look ahead. We are here to consider the NEXT TEN YEARS. Now through December 31, 2029. What makes you PESSIMISTIC about our ability to be united as Americans—why might we be more DIVIDED?*

I probably should have quit while I was ahead. But if we are going to be successful in the decade ahead we need to be real about the roadblocks. After open responses we did a real-time summary of the factors that might influence pessimism in the decade. The following is the summary (factors were not prioritized):

No.	Idea
1.	Wealth divide continues
2.	Negative influence of AI
3.	Mainstream media bias continues
4.	Trend of anti-intellectualism
5.	Race inequality is not addressed
6.	Political divides grow stronger
7.	Lack of equal education/healthcare access
8.	Lack of social media accountability
9.	Continued mistrust of leadership
10.	Lack of vision for the future
11.	Climate change not addressed
12.	Lack of bipartisan politics
13.	The "cult" of ignorance and anti-intellectualism
14.	Generational political and values differences
15.	Global threats and conflicts
16.	A move towards socialism in the U.S.
17.	Trump being re-elected
18.	Trump not being re-elected
19.	Anti-immigration policies and attitudes
20.	Too much power by a small number of tech companies
21.	General cynicism
22.	Not re-establishing our position as a member of the global community

You will note that as a wise facilitator I chose to keep a little peace in the session with factors 17 and 18. Remember, we can both go to the same movie and have a different experience. *I am just choosing not to watch that movie again.*

There is also a strong theme about resolving some of the fundamental gaps that exist. We don't create that level of sustained unity without a stronger base of equity. Racial equity, gender equity, educational equity, economic equity, healthcare equity. This is *not* about socialism. It's about what this country should stand for. The country's commitment should be to create that access and fairness and acceptance. The individual's commitment is to work hard, earn that level of equity and pay it back to others around you.

Our "dose of reality" seemed to refine the level of optimism about the unity in the decade ahead. I also chose to change the scale from a binary optimism/pessimism scale to more granularity. It was quite revealing:

Question: *All things considered, as you reflect the overall set of factors that might influence your outlook for how united we might be in the decade ahead, what's your forecast for the future now that we have considered both sides?*

No.	Items	Times Selected
1.	**Somewhat Optimistic**	**(61%)**
2.	Middle of the Road	(19%)
3.	Very Optimistic	(10%)
4.	Somewhat Pessimistic	(7%)
5.	Very Pessimistic	(3%)

Back to the view of *cautiously optimistic.* Few were really ready to declare victory or defeat (very optimistic or very pessimistic), but the strong majority feel like we have a shot at this. Let the decade play out. Let's see if the positive influencing factors resonate and reward.

Some comments from our 80% that were Somewhat Optimistic or Middle of the Road:

- SOMEWHAT OPTIMISTIC: "At some point we collectively will realize that after 10 years of division (that was really exposed in 2016 and has accelerated since) we need to pull together as Americans."

156

- SOMEWHAT OPTIMISTIC: "To borrow (and mangle) a quote: The arc of the unlighted universe is long, but tends toward cooperation."
- SOMEWHAT OPTIMISTIC: "We may be down right now, but Americans course-correct well when we've made a mistake and/ or not lived up to the values and promise of the nation's founding."
- SOMEWHAT OPTIMISTIC: "Hope people can get around their differences and look for commonalities or at least respect differences. Seems like historically we took pride in being a "melting pot" of people and ideas, and currently that is not a good thing."
- MIDDLE: "Uncertainty of the moment. Now could end up being 4-5 years or half of the decade."
- MIDDLE: "Some of the things I have heard I very much agree with and can see as positives, but I just don't feel like the ones making the decisions will do so with what is truly best for this nation. Everyone is looking out for themselves and their party first. We need to look at our citizens and be looking at what is best for America first, and I just don't see that happening."

What if we really did what was best for the entire nation? We have a long way to go on inclusivity, but it's a powerful promise. For you as a person, for an organization you are part of, for a country that we want to be better in the decade ahead.

Unity Influence Scenarios

As we moved to the end of our *emotionally exhausting* Foresight session, we presented our set of scenarios that might influence the unity of the decade ahead. These were developed by our Center prior to the session to test the reaction of our participants on the IMPACT to the future of unity if that scenario was to occur, and secondly, the LIKELIHOOD of that scenario occurring.

Now, please assess each of the following future scenarios in two ways. First, the level of positive IMPACT to American unity if that scenario fully materializes in the decade ahead (use a scale of 1-10 where a '1' means a very low level of impact and a '10' means a very high level of impact); Second, the likelihood that this scenario will fully materialize in the decade ahead (use a scale of 1-10 where a '1' means a very low likelihood and '10' means a very high likelihood):

Here is how our Foresight session assessed the list. The scenarios are ordered by the *level of positive impact* but then contrasted with the likelihood of occurrence for a gap analysis rating:

#	Scenario Description	Im-pact	Like-ly	Gap
1	BIPARTISAN POLITICS: While the decade did not see an end to the traditional two-party system in the U.S., it did see an end to damaging partisan politics. New leadership on both sides of the aisle focused on common ground for Americans—the economy, education, healthcare, racial equality and the environment. There was a new level of responsiveness to issues when they arose where the U.S. government could take decision and bipartisan action. The respect for government as an institution was one of the most remarkable turnarounds of the decade.	9.3	4.5	(4.8)
2	PROLONGED ECONOMIC RECOVERY: Starting in 2021, and influenced by a post-pandemic level of consumer demand and confidence, we experienced a prolonged economic recovery and level of growth that was one of the strongest on record. It was a recovery that nearly every sector and every demographic participated in. A rising tide lifts all boats.	8.8	6.9	(1.9)
3	THE PANDEMIC IS BEHIND US: In the 1Q2021 an effective vaccine was validated by phase 3 trials and made available to any American who wished to be vaccinated. The country finally moved to a national set of measures on masks and protocols that helped to achieve a significant reduction in COVID cases. There was an element of herd immunity that occurred and even after the availability of the vaccine Americans were careful to adhere to published protocols. By the summer of 2021 the COVID pandemic was largely behind us. Schools, sports and social activities were fully normalized by the fall.	8.8	7.7	(1.1)

158

4	A NEW RESPECT FOR MEDIA AND JOURNALISM: The "sensationalized" news and journalism trend (infotainment) came to an end in the decade where a new level of journalism and media excellence emerged. Mainstream media became a trusted source of news and information, and there was minimal political bias in the reporting. Americans were more informed in the decade through a combination of mainstream media and a more accountable social media. Oh, you could still fire away your opinions but you were more like the corner speaker at Hyde Park in the UK. Loud and tolerated, but unlikely to sway significant public opinion when the facts were not present.	8.5	4.1	(4.4)
5	THE REBIRTH OF THE MIDDLE CLASS: The highest growth of any economic segment in the decade was the new middle class. Strong economic growth and new opportunities enabled nearly every American family willing to work hard to have a strong level of earning power and financial security. In many respects, the new middle class was the place to be—financially comfortable, a balanced work/life environment, career growth and a terrific environment to raise a family. The Gen Z crowd fully endorsed the lifestyle.	8.3	6.0	(2.3)
6	UNIVERSAL HEALTHCARE: After decades of effort we finally moved to a well-designed healthcare system that guaranteed basic/affordable healthcare for every American. It was not only a relief to many lower/middle income families but it seemed to spark a stronger interest and commitment to wellness and preventive measures. There was still room for enhanced company health care benefit programs and private insurance, but for many the basic universal healthcare program provided the care needed for themselves and their families. It removed one of the fundamental divides that Americans had been dealing with for many generations.	8.3	6.9	(1.4)

7	A CHANGING OF THE GUARD: A new wave of young leaders, diverse as America itself, stepped forward in America with new ideas and a new vision for the future. They were welcomed and mentored by existing leaders, a new level of civic engagement and commitment to service seemed to develop in the country. Millennials and Gen Zers accepted a new mantle of leadership and also helped engage a broader set of Americans in the democratic process.	8.1	7.7	(1.4)
8	RACIAL INEQUALITY WAS FINALLY ADDRESSED: Buoyed by the activism and outcry from events in 2020, including the street protests, sports activism, political change, corporate cultural changes, police policy changes and strong leadership from Black and other minority groups, the decade saw a fundamental reversal of racial inequality in the country. Our leadership looked like our communities. While we might still value and appreciate our racial heritages, we valued being equally treated Americans above anything else.	8.0	5.5	(2.5)
9	IMMIGRATION REFORM MOVED FORWARD: Long standing issues on DACA (aka, 'dreamers'), pathways to citizenship and immigration policies were resolved. Border security was strong and appropriate, but a new message emerged that America valued the diversity and the commitment of a new wave of immigrants to our country. The welcome mat was out for those who shared our values and wanted to be part of the American Dream. New immigrants were a strong part of the economic growth during the decade.	7.8	6.5	(1.3)

10	EXTENDED PUBLIC EDUCATION ACCESS: Another long-simmering debate was addressed in the decade where free public education was extended through the state college level and community college structure. Any student who was willing to work hard could attend a public two-year or four-year program at no cost to earn their basic degree. In the process of having a higher volume of students (and more consistent volume) the colleges became more aligned with career-ready programs for these students to align specific curriculums with the job requirements of the students. Private colleges and universities never skipped a beat; their market was still strong.	7.8	6.0	(1.8)
11	A NEW UNITED NATIONS: Strengthened by global collaboration and success in addressing two of the most significant issues facing mankind—climate change and the COVID-19 pandemic—the world moved to a new level of cooperation. The United Nations and other global organizations such as the WHO enjoyed a new level of attention and investment. You could still flex your nationalistic muscle and protect your borders, but the world realized that a peaceful and more united globe allowed leaders to focus more on their people, economic strategies and social agendas. Conflicts, when they occurred, were short and were quickly addressed by global leaders.	7.2	5.8	(1.4)
12	A WOMAN AT THE HELM: The decade finally saw the election of a woman to the U.S. presidency. It was an election that was supported by nearly every demographic, and the new president ushered in a new respect for women's leadership and equal footing. For younger girls/women it was a sign of great hope for their futures, for the world it was a sign that the U.S. had finally caught up. It created pride for all Americans that we had moved past one of the last gender biases.	6.9	7.3	+0.4

13	COMMON SENSE GUN SAFETY: Led by a bipartisan Congress, an engaged president, and supported by the NRA, responsible gun owners and young voices/activists, a common sense set of gun safety measures were adopted, including universal background checks, a ban on assault weapons and a new level of support to better understand and deal with mental health issues in the country. Mass shootings were reduced significantly and, overall, guns were in the right hands of responsible people. The right to bear arms was better balanced with the right people to have those arms.	7.2	5.5	(1.7)
14	WE UNITED ON THE CLIMATE: The U.S. rejoined the Paris Climate Agreement and served as a catalyst to move the world to aggressively address the challenge of climate change. Countries and companies committed resources and set strong goals for carbon reduction and also to meet the scientific goals of limiting global warming. While it will take decades of continued work, there was agreement that we had reversed the course of climate change and our globe looked positive again for future generations.	6.8	5.8	(1.0)
15	HOW ABOUT THAT MARS LANDING: The bold goal of reaching Mars with a manned mission was achieved with spectacular success. A combination of NASA, private firms such as SpaceX and a global collaboration pulled it off with the landing being one of the most watched moments of the decade. It was not going to be a one-shot deal, it was determined from the landing and exploration that Mars was suitable for a colonization effort in the next decade (2030-2039) and there was a sense that we had reopened the universe. Adding to the national pride, an American was first to walk out of the landing vehicle. In an odd twist, a small potato field previously farmed was found in a valley near the landing vehicle.	6.3	6.1	(0.2)

A lot to unpack here. First, our Foresighters saw a lot of merit in the scenarios in terms of potential impact to American unity over the course of the decade. 13/15 were rated at 7.0+ and all 15 were 6.0+. *Even space travel was getting a little respect.*

But the top three would really be the catalyst for the decade: 1) A new level of bipartisan cooperation on the political side to put our country above politics. To move forward after such a divisive period in our history. To restore trust and faith in our government; 2) A prolonged economic recovery. Talk about creating hope and opportunity. Companies that are growing and hiring, new economic segments taking hold, entrepreneurship on the rise; 3) The pandemic is in the rear view mirror. A collective sigh of relief, a declaration of victory where Americans had to pull together. *If we can defeat COVID, we can do anything.*

And it turns out, in our assessment on likelihood, that we look pretty good on 2 out of 3. Which would be OK if we were talking about a batting average for baseball, not the future of unity in the decade ahead.

Mars aside (you already know my view on the value of space travel/exploration), the one most troubling assessment in terms of impact was the issue of climate change. The second lowest in our assessment. *It's just the future of the planet.* I am afraid we have a long way to go to persuade the average American about the urgency of action. The assessment was about the impact to American unity and I think quantitative surveys and research will likely show immense generational differences on this issue. On this note, it was gratifying to see the scenario of *The Changing of the Guard* (a new generation of leaders) be assessed highly at 8.1. My view is that the *Changing of the Guard* will have a significant impact on *We United on the Climate.*

But let's get to the real dilemma about the prospect for unity in America in the decade ahead. Some of the most important influencers—rated very high in terms of potential impact—seem to slip out of our grasp when we look at the likelihood of them materializing.

Here are the top gaps:

1. Bipartisan politics (4.8)
2. A new respect for media and journalism (4.4)
3. Racial inequality was finally addressed (2.5)
4. A rebirth of the middle class (2.3)
5. Prolonged economic recovery (1.9)
6. Extended public education access (1.8)
7. Common sense gun safety (1.7)

The impact of bipartisan politics was 9.3, a half point (on our 1-10 average) ahead of anything else. And one of the *least likely* to materialize. What's the implication of *ten more years of partisan politics* on everything from immigration reform, to voting rights, to addressing racial inequality, gender inequality, climate change, gun control, healthcare reform, Supreme Court nominations, education reform...

We have to find some middle ground in our politics.

And two of our other top rated gaps are the subjects of future Foresight chapters—*The Future of Media/Information* and *Rethinking the Future of Education and Learning.* We had a sense that they would be fundamental influencers on the decade ahead. But at least we were giving Education a chance in our assessment here...we seem to feel that the likelihood of a meaningful reform of media and addressing it will be an uphill climb. *Perhaps the Myth of Sisyphus will inspire us to feel there is hope in pushing this boulder up the hill.* Once again, and unfairly so, I put my bet on the change to younger leadership.

Reflecting on the Struggle for Equality

As we stand in August of 2020, our summer of *discontent, discomfort and disconnection,* I would add *discouragement* to the list. On the positive side, the Black Lives Matter protests drew in a diverse demographic and massive media coverage. It also drew in significant corporate, sports, entertainment and political leadership to say that *once and for all* we must create an environment of social equality and inclusion for *all Americans.* I believe the outcry was genuine, but Americans *and especially American leaders* can have short attention spans. Systemic racism, sexism and gender bias will not be changed in a summer of discontent. This country is simply not comfortable yet with the implication of true social equality.

Look at our history. The original baseline in America for voting was *white males who owned property.* The U.S. Constitution originally looked to the states to determine who would be qualified to vote. After the Civil War, Congress passed the Fifteenth Amendment, which was ratified by the states in 1870:

The right of citizens of the United States to vote shall not be denied or abridged by the United States or any State on account of race, color, or previous condition of servitude.

By the way, we forgot about women being able to vote, but we got around to it 50 years later with the 19th Amendment in 1920. The year before my mother was born.

164

The right of citizens of the United States to vote shall not be denied or abridged by the United States or any State on account of sex.

But at least we fixed the *racial inequality* side of things in 1870, right? Pop this term into your browser: Voter Suppression. It began with poll taxes and literacy tests and southern states were particularly egregious in their use of the barriers over decades. According to a historical analysis published by the Carnegie Corporation, "The struggle for equal voting rights came to a head in the 1960s as many states, particularly in the South, dug in on policies—such as poll taxes, English language requirements, and more—aimed at suppressing the vote among people of color, immigrants and low-income populations."

In 1964, the states ratified the 24th Amendment to target poll taxes:

The right of citizens of the United States to vote in any primary or other election for President or Vice President for electors for President or Vice President, or for Senator or Representative in Congress, shall not be denied or abridged by the United States or by any State by reason of failure to pay any poll tax or other tax.

Poll Tax in America, circa 1947

Poll taxes, begun in the 1800s, were outlawed in *1964.* But there were a lot of clever people at the state/local government level who could find new ways to create *voter suppression.* It took the visibility and the violence of the Selma marches in 1965 (from Selma, Alabama, to the state capitol, Montgomery) to trigger national attention and action with the passage of the landmark Voter Rights Act. *History will show that this was a true _bipartisan_ effort with a 79-18 vote in the Senate and a 328-74 passage in the House.*

In 1971, we decided to add young people to the voting privilege as most states required voters to be 21 years of age. You see, it was OK to draft 18-year-olds for the Vietnam war to fight and die for their country, but voting was off the table. It took student protests and activism to push the 26th amendment:

The right of citizens of the United States, who are eighteen years of age and older, to vote shall not be abridged by the United States or by any state on account of age.

And Doug, once again we appreciate this history lesson but what does it have to do with the decade ahead?

Everything. The granting of *social rights* in this country is a slow and painful process. There are many who have and will continue to block the opportunity for social equity to Black Americans, women, LGBTQ+, immigrants, LatinX, Native Americans, Asian Americans...the list is way too long. And the process and the pain has been especially acute for Black Americans.

I must tell you that for a good part of my life I was uncomfortable around Black Americans. I grew up in Arizona. That's a clue. The number of Black students in my grade school—zero. The number of Black students in my high school—zero. Sure, there were some Black students at my college but, well you already know, it was in Arizona and it was the smallest of the three state universities. More than zero, but not many more. Surely there must have been some Black recruits in your first IBM class? Well, it was 50% female, which I think made IBM feel that they were making progress in diversity. I think there were one or two Blacks in my first two IBM education classes. The first Black IBMer I worked with was Randy Roberson at the DPEI program. DPEI was unique and tight; we depended on each other. He was a damn good mentor.

Later, after DPEI, I remember IBM conducting mandatory diversity training. The most uncomfortable thing I have ever experienced. Trying to teach us what diversity means and how to accept others. Role playing. It was, with all due respect, a program checkoff for HR.

Sometime after I left IBM, I was asked by a friend to facilitate a strategic planning session for the Greater Phoenix Black Chamber of Commerce in 2011. I was uncomfortable at the start, unsure of how to act and unsure of how they were perceiving me. I found the harder I worked, the more comfortable I was and they seemed. It wasn't that hard. Then the

166

Board Chair asked me to facilitate the strategic planning for the U.S. Black Chamber organization and their Board. These were some very visible leaders, headed by Ron Busby, the President and CEO, out of Washington, D.C. I hosted them at my Center in Scottsdale. What was I doing? Now I was _really_ out of my comfort zone. They didn't really know me, but they were _depending on me_. So, I just focused on helping them develop their plan. They were committed and passionate about the future of Black Chambers and the impact to Black Americans. We brainstormed on areas of strategic focus for USBC. We developed 21 focus areas (I forgot to say they were ambitious as well). Same approach then with the collaborative software that we use now in our Foresight sessions in 2020. I looked back at their planning document and one of the focus areas stuck out to me:

COMPELLING MESSAGES: Create and communicate a clear set of compelling messages about the US Black Chamber, the opportunity ahead for our chambers and overall Black communities, and the larger implication of the impact we can have on America's future.

The larger implication of the impact we can have on America's Future. This wasn't just about Black Americans it was about all Americans. These guys were leaders. Ron invited me to run a leadership session in Washington the following summer at the U.S. Black Chamber Leadership Institute. I was honored. We were just working together to move ideas forward. It wasn't that hard. You don't learn about diversity and inclusion from an HR class or program. You learn about it from working together on things that matter. That's why it works in sports, the military, music. While I haven't seen Ron since 2012, I am still on his email update list. That guy has a picture with every leader in Washington. He is making a better America. That's how I learned to be comfortable around Black Americans.

2012 US Black Chamber Leadership Institute

It's not that hard when you just work together

So, in August of 2020, we are trying to assess and forecast the issue of division and unity in America in the decade ahead. We are seeing some of the largest protests in American history with *Black Lives Matter* and we are faced with a prospect of a sustained political divide, and unsure if we can address underlying education, healthcare and economic issues. American companies are *still* trying to create "diverse and inclusive" workforces and cultures (and mostly still trying to do it with education programs). White Supremacist groups are coming out of the shadows fanned by presidential rhetoric. An *anarchist movement* was attaching itself to the Black Lives Matter protests and blurring the message for change. QAnon is a far-right extremist group that alleges there is a deep state conspiracy that is trying to undermine Trump's presidency. *I'm not making this up.*

And social media and mainstream media just keep turning up the volume and inviting more people to jump into the fray. *Sensationalize the division.*

How about just working together on things that matter?

Politics For $100

At the time of this Foresight session, we are just *seventy-five days* away from the November 2020 presidential election. And one thing is clear: the outcome of that election will set the tone for America United or Divided for the decade ahead:

Question: *In just SEVENTY-FIVE days, we will hold the next presidential election in the United States. What impact do you feel the outcome of this election will have on whether we become more united or more divided?*

No.	Items	Times Selected
1.	**Massive—regardless of the outcome it will set the tone for the decade.**	**(69%)**
2.	Significant—it's an important election and there are very clear divisions in America on the candidates and their implications. But every election is important and it always seems like the stakes are high.	(22%)
3.	Modest—regardless of the outcome it is only one factor in a series of social, economic and information trends.	(9%)

168

As if we even needed to ask. Once again, the emotion was high:

- MASSIVE: "I cannot imagine an event with more impact than the election, both at the president and senate levels. What happens will determine what can be done politically and could restore some polish on politics."
- MASSIVE: "If Trump wins, I think the country is going to burn down. Not really, but still, I think there will be riots and no one will believe that he has actually won. And if Biden wins, I think the silent majority will all die inside. Unfortunately, I don't think either option is good, and I think the outcome will be a shock regardless of who wins."
- MASSIVE: "If Trump/Pence win, the economy will roar back; this will be the cause for many great effects in the decade."
- MASSIVE: "It is always tempting to say that this election is more important than previous, but it truly is, in that we have had an anomalous president who has been hostile to traditional, bipartisan principles of American democracy and a challenger who supports those principles."
- SIGNIFICANT: "I am hopeful for a change in administration, but the issues are great and complex. I can hope for, at best, incremental change that will set a foundation for more progress going forward."
- MASSIVE: Trump wins, we lose. See Obama's speech last night, he said it better than I ever could. Biden wins, what a wonderful outlook. Will be a great, great cabinet, young people, Latinos, Blacks, women. Fresh ideas. SMART leaders, woke leadership. Ready to get to work."
- MODEST: "We are divided, I am not sure an election will bring us together."
- MASSIVE: "Regardless of outcome, the losing party is going to be PISSED OFF!"

There's something happening here
What it is ain't exactly clear

COVID's Impact on American/Global Unity
In our last question for this Foresight we asked our participants about the impact on America and the world:

Question: *How has the COVID-19 pandemic affected the way we think about America and the world today and our ability to work together or work apart?*

Once again our participants provided emotional but insightful commentary:

- "We're still figuring that out. If we're honest we should feel humbled as a country that we've discovered our own Achilles tendon. It puts a humiliating dent in our view of American exceptionalism."
- "We have learned just how fragile our economy and quality of life are. That is a big incentive to cooperate and collaborate."
- "One would hope that the pandemic would facilitate our ability to work together toward a common goal(s)... But in the U.S. we have politicized COVID and, as a result, once again hampered our cooperation."
- "It separated us even farther apart—when it should've and could've brought us together."
- "I have been dismayed with the manner in which the federal government has responded to this crisis. The states have had to do it themselves, which, in a sense, has created unity there. But we've only been able to show the world how *not* to do it."

Five Foresights From This Foresight Session

Kind of a heavy session, eh? Well, kind of a heavy topic. The United States of America: *as divided as we have been in at least fifty years.* And while we are somewhat optimistic about the level of unity in the future we are also extremely realistic about the challenges. We are working against powerful forces that have created barriers to access for *over 200 years* and it's a little naïve to think we can redirect that in the next 10. But we better try. Your children and mine are depending on us to move this country forward. So here are my reflections from this session:

1. THE POLITICS OF UNITY: You cannot put politics aside in the next decade. They are front and center in addressing almost every influential issue that might unite or divide us. I am not sure if this current two-party system will survive the decade. How about the *Common Ground Party*. We need leaders of the primary two parties—current and future—to be willing to address the hard issues and find that common group. The extreme edges are just too damn sharp.
2. SOCIAL RIGHTS: We need a new Bill of Rights—a fundamental set of *social rights* that every American *and everyone legally in this country who is trying to be an American* is entitled to. How about basic dignity, being heard, being accepted, being valued, being *seen*. That's a good start.
3. SHARED EXPERIENCE MATTERS FOR A WHILE: Do not underestimate the impact of the shared experience of COVID-19 as

170

a unifier for this country. But don't rely on it to go much beyond 2022. We all stopped for a while, and it has been and will continue to be a reawakening as we try to put the pandemic behind us. But it's the *systemic issues* that will need to be addressed in the decade ahead.

4. A GENERATIONAL TRANSITION: It is really hard to change people's behavior. Especially *older people.* I mean, don't stop trying. I have changed my views on a lot of things by being more informed, having new experiences, just being open to different views. But, by and large, I am not sure we move on from some of our conscious and unconscious biases until our Millennials and Gen Zers really kick in.

5. WE ALL WANT EQUAL ACCESS: Do you think that those who fall into the *have-not* category want to be in that category? Equal access starts really early—early childhood education, a good living environment, healthcare, a good family structure. But the biggest access that we all want is *opportunity.* To earn a good living via a fair wage, educated/trained in a meaningful skill, open a door to a first job, be accepted and included in that job. That's a uniting thought, you know, *the land of opportunity.*

A Personal Note: How I Spent My Summer in 2020

I am a lucky dude. I get to bounce back and forth between Scottsdale, Arizona, and Park City, Utah, pretty much any time I want. I have been doing it for 10 years. Plan on riding out the next decade doing the same thing. *I like the drive—it creates analog balance.* Besides, it gets *really* hot in Arizona in the summers. I need an escape hatch. Especially in a pandemic.

So I relocated to Park City for much of the summer of 2020. It seemed a little calmer, but even on Main Street in Park City there were protests. The city allowed some local artists to create a BLACK LIVES MATTER mural on the street. I thought that was quite cool. It was vandalized two nights later. I thought that was quite uncool. United and then Divided.

I like to walk around my neighborhood when I am in Park City. it is called Pinebrook. Nice to say "Hi" to everyone. I have a 45-minute loop. I started noticing some signs popping up in the yards. Colorful. First just one or two, then more. *There was a movement being started in my neighborhood.* Just another element of 2020, I suppose.

It turns out it was a bit of a movement, though it didn't start in Park City in 2020. It was an effort by a group of women in Wisconsin that began on November 9, 2016—the day after Trump's election. It was led by Kristin Garvey who researched the messages and then wrote them on a white foam board with a sharpie. A local artist converted it into a set of rainbow colors 24 hours later on a yard sign and the messaging took off. It popped up at the Women's March in January, 2017, and then at Black Lives Matter protests in June of 2020.

Then it popped up in my neighborhood in Park City in August of 2020.

The sign was powerful. It seemed to parallel many of the themes we had developed in our Foresight session. Simple, direct. Children walked by the signs every day. Maybe they took a minute to read them. I did. It gave me a renewed sense of optimism that we might make some progress in terms of unity in the decade ahead:

On my walk in Park City, August 13, 2020

HERE WE BELIEVE:
BLACK LIVES MATTER
WOMEN'S RIGHTS ARE HUMAN RIGHTS
NO HUMAN IS ILLEGAL
SCIENCE IS REAL
LOVE IS LOVE
KINDNESS IS EVERYTHING

I think it's time we stop
Hey what's that sound
Everybody look, what's going down

Peace out

CHAPTER 6: The Future of News, Media and Information

Ending Scene from <u>Three Days of the Condor</u> (condensed):

<< Street scene, New York. Turner and Higgins have arranged a meet. A CIA car can be seen tailing them in the background. >>

TURNER (aka Condor): *Hey, Higgins. Let's say, for the purposes of argument, I had a .45 in one of my pockets. And I wanted you to take a walk with me. You'd do it, right?*

HIGGINS (CIA Deputy Director): *Which way?...*

TURNER: *Do we have plans to invade the Middle East?...*

HIGGINS: *No. Absolutely not. We have games. That's all. We play games. What if? How many men? What would it take? Is there a cheaper way to destabilize a regime? That's what we're paid to do...*

TURNER: *Boy, what is it with you people? You think not getting caught in a lie is the same thing as telling the truth?*

HIGGINS: *No. It's simple economics. Today it's oil, right? In 10 or 15 years, food. Plutonium. Maybe even sooner. Now, what do you think people will want us to do then?*

TURNER: *Ask them.*

HIGGINS: *Not now, then. Ask them when they're running out. Ask them when there's no heat in their homes and they're cold. Ask them when their engines stop. Ask them when people who've never known hunger start going hungry. You want to know something? They won't want us to ask them, they'll just want us to get it for them.*

TURNER: *Seven people killed! And you play fucking games!*

HIGGINS: *Right. And the other side does too. That's why we can't let you stay outside.*

TURNER: *Well, go on home, Higgins. Go on. <u>They've got it</u>. Come on, you know where we are. Just look around. They've got it. That's where they ship from. They've got all of it.*

<< *Pan back to see the New York Times offices.* >>

HIGGINS: *What? What did you do?*

TURNER: *I told them a story. You play games. I told them a story.*

HIGGINS: *Oh, you poor dumb son of a bitch! You've done more damage than you know.*

TURNER: *I hope so.*

HIGGINS: *Hey Turner. How do you know they'll print it? You can take a walk, but how far if they don't print it?*

TURNER: *They'll print it.*

HIGGINS: *How do you know?*

<< Fade to credits, street scene in the background. >>

-- *Three Days of the Condor, 1975. Directed by Sydney Pollack.*

September 24, 2020
Foresight 2030 Session

<u>Three Days of the Condor</u> is one of my all-time favorite movies. You can't go wrong with Robert Redford (playing Joe Turner, code name *Condor*). He works for the CIA at the *Modern Literary Historical Society*, a front for a CIA team that, well, reads books. On everything. They are an analog version of today's digital analytics tools that scan social media traffic. They are looking for signals that other countries, terrorist cells or previously undiscovered spy networks have caught onto CIA programs. And Condor found an undiscovered rogue network. The problem is that the organization was a spin-off of the CIA itself. And they did not want to be found out.

174

1975 release poster   *Condor at the CIA* American Literary Historical Society

Everyone but Condor is killed inside the *Historical Society*. He was literally out to lunch. The rest of the movie is the interplay between Condor and Higgins (the CIA Deputy Director), Joubert (the professional assassin hired by the CIA to take out the *Historical Society*), and Kathy Hale (played by Faye Dunaway), who unintentionally becomes Condor's accomplice. It's complex and terrifically acted. And it is a timeless story. *The end justifies the means.* At least in the CIA's eyes. Condor eludes Joubert and the CIA and is on the lam. He is a *loose end.* He is a bookworm, not an experienced operative. He's an *amateur* and that's what makes him so hard to take down.

He knows that he cannot trust the CIA to bring him in. They will kill him. His only playing card is that he knows the *story.* And the story is the *truth.* And, at the end of the movie, he is placing a bet, a big one, that the media will tell the story. And tell the world the truth.

After all, that's what we look to the media to be. The unbiased source of truth. Never to be intimidated by the power of government, politics, business or self interest.

But we have a problem in 2020. The media has blurred between information and influence. Social media has blurred with mainstream media. News anchors have blurred with entertainers. Breaking news, which once would stop everyone in their tracks, is just a gimmick. Everything seems to be sensationalized. The media in 2020 has been *weaponized*.

Journalism is supposed to be a sacred profession. Beyond reproach. Noble and purposeful. *Three Days of The Condor* was not really a movie

175

about the media, it just had a powerful scene at the end that made you wonder if The New York Times would bow down to the CIA or stand up for the truth. The 2017 drama *The Post* was a little less subtle. Tom Hanks plays Ben Bradlee, The Washington Post executive editor, who forces a decision by the Post publisher Katherine Graham (played by Meryl Streep) on whether to publish the Pentagon Papers, which reveals the deception by the U.S. Government on the Vietnam war.

The Post publishes the Pentagon Papers in 1971. The White House retaliates and The New York Times (also a cohort in the publishing) and The Post take their case to the Supreme Court which ultimately rules 6-3 in favor of the media's rights. Then President Nixon famously declares that the Washington Post be forever barred from the White House. *At least until Watergate.*

And look, if you don't choose to watch those two well-acted and directed movies, how about Tom Cruise and Jack Nicholson in <u>A Few Good Men</u>. The classic courtroom scene where Nicholson delivers one of the best movie lines ever:

LT. KAFFEE (Cruise): *Did you order the Code Red?*

JUDGE: *You don't have to answer the question.*

COLONEL JESSUP (Nicholson): *I'll answer the question. You want answers?*

KAFFEE: *I think I'm entitled to answers.*

JESSUP: *You want answers?!*

KAFFEE: *I want the truth!*

JESSUP: *<u>You can't handle the truth</u>.*

——*A Few Good Men, 1992. Directed by Rob Reiner.*

Americans not only can handle the truth, they *deserve* the truth. The problem these days is we are not sure what the truth is anymore. Everybody wants it their way. Everybody wants to put a spin on things. Much of the media is as complicit as the politicians.

If we are going to get this next decade on track, we need to deal with the age of disinformation. The mainstream media needs to regain their credibility and focus on surfacing truth without spin. The social media companies need to help people connect, share and engage—but not be used for ulterior motives by other parties. Their *algorithms* need to change. And we as Americans need to be better at discerning truth and fact from spin and political ploys. Seriously, *we are smarter than we have been demonstrating in 2020.*

And the truth is, we are watching a movie in 2020. It's not <u>Three Days of the Condor</u>, <u>The Post</u> or even a <u>Few Good Men</u>. It's the global pandemic in tandem with one of the most bizarre political periods in history. And at some point, we all need to agree on the facts. Because, simply put, *facts matter.*

So, for our next Foresight session, we tackle the Future of News, Media and Information, and *why being informed in the decade ahead* matters to all of us.

A Personal Context

When I was in high school, 1969-1973, I had a button that I would wear on my shirt every once in a while. Simple, red letters on a white background: *Survival in the seventies depends on you being informed.* I felt kind of *intellectual.* But I believed it. I mean, the age of innocence was over by then—Vietnam had taken care of that for a generation and then *Tricky Dick* gets his hands caught in the cookie jar in 1972 with the Watergate break-in.

I watched the *CBS Evening News With Walter Cronkite.* Now there was a guy who would tell it to you straight. A 1972 poll named him as, "The most trusted man in America." Supremely objective, he was the journalists' journalist. But he would share a personal view or two. In 1968, after covering the Tet Offensive in Vietnam, he declared that the Vietnam war could only end in a "protracted stalemate". Then President Lyndon Johnson told his staff, "If I've lost Cronkite, I've lost middle America." According to the Brittanica.com, "Some held that Johnson's decision not to run for re-election that year was a direct result of Cronkite's reporting." *Another heavy hitter.*

I also read the newspaper in high school. I still read it every day. But I have a vested interest. My first job (other than mowing a few lawns) was as a newspaper carrier. I delivered the *Phoenix Gazette,* which was the afternoon edition from the publishers of The Arizona Republic (the morning paper which continues as of today). Why deliver newspapers? *Only newspaper carriers had those cool bikes with the spring on the fork.* Plus newspaper bags on the front and baskets on the back. Like a freight train when fully loaded.

But, *I delivered the news.* Not as well as Walter Cronkite, but *I was in the club, right?* There is something about the smell of the ink, the feel of the paper, the sound when it hits the driveway *just right.* I was helping to keep people informed. It turns out that this issue of *being informed* was as critical in 2020 as it was in when I was just *wearing that button* and *riding that bike.*

Cue the Foresight Session

As we assembled our Foresighters in September, it seems like everyone in America was *disinformed*. Fake news. Social media. CNN on one side and Fox on the other. In our most recent session in August when we looked at the divide in America, our participants put "Media overload/disinformation" as the number two issue influencing the level of division in America. *Just a tad behind the Trump presidency.*

Media overload? Surely in 2020 with all that is happening, we couldn't be *over-informed*. Wait, a new button pops into my mind: *Survival in 2020 depends on you being non-informed.* Just ignore all media. Maybe not a bad idea at the time.

Thirty-five participants on this session to examine the *Future of News, Media and Information*. A rather informed group, actually. As we always do, a few introductions:

- "I have worked in media my entire life. For the greater part in commercial television, some cable television, and now public television."
- "Market researcher, New Englander, tired."
- "I am a believer in enjoying life and playing golf. Keep it simple."
- "I work in economic development as CEO of the Scottsdale Area Chamber of Commerce. Married with two children."
- "Passionate pursuer of clarity amidst chaos! Started in journalism, expanded to political campaigns, and have spent the last 25 years in consulting on marketing, communications, advertising, and customer experience strategy across many sectors."
- "I work hard in work times, but I need free time after work to drink a beer and talk to friends. I love music, I love sports, I am a leader and am used to deciding things immediately rather than waiting for the future."
- "Phoenix native. Software developer, activity enthusiast. Can't sit still."

Wait, what? Where did I get this group? Passionate pursuer of clarity? You are either tired or you can't sit still? Enjoy life and play golf? Look, one thing I can tell you from personal experience, if you play a lot of golf, it does not necessarily correlate with enjoying life. *Fore!*

178

Why Being Informed Matters

We began our session with a very fundamental question: *Why does being informed matter?* Not a trick question, not one of my existential analogies:

Question: *Let's start with a personal reflection: why does being informed today matter to you personally? What does it allow you to do or do differently as a result?*

For the record, this was a pretty savvy and well educated group:

Please indicate the highest level of education you have attained:

No.	Items	Times Selected
1.	Master's Degree	(45%)
2.	Four year Bachelor's Degree	(34%)
3.	Doctorate	(8%)
4.	Some graduate school but not graduate degree at this point	(5%)
5.	High school diploma or equivalent	(2%)
6.	Some college but not a degree at this point	(2%)
7.	Two year Associate's Degree	(0%)

So, my expectations were pretty high that there would be some solid rationale for why being informed matters. We generated some 110+ open responses, but were able to develop a fairly net set of themes. A dozen to be precise, and then we asked our participants to assess them in terms of how important the themes were:

Now please indicate how important each of the following aspects of being informed are to you personally. Use a scale of 1-10 where a "1" means not at all important and a "10" means extremely important:

Rank	Idea	Avg.
1.	Allows me to make informed decisions	**9.8**
2.	Helps me understand issues affecting the future	**8.5**

179

3.	Helps me navigate life in general	**8.1**
4.	It's about preserving democracy	**7.8**
5.	Helps keep my family safe	**7.7**
6.	Keeps me mentally sharp	**7.3**
7.	Creates healthy conversations	**6.8**
8.	Allows me to contribute to society	**6.6**
9.	Helps me provide guidance to friends/family	**6.1**
10.	Gives me confidence in my beliefs	**6.1**
11.	Gives me a career advantage	**5.5**
12.	Allows me to participate in social events of my choosing	**5.5**

Well, if there was ever a time to make *informed decisions* and *understand issues* affecting the future it was 2020. A global pandemic and a critical presidential election. And, yet, our very ability as Americans to get unbiased information to help understand those issues and make those decisions had never been more under attack. But our participants understood why 2020 had to be an informed year and why they had to work at it:

- "Too many places to get misinformation these days, and you must work hard to stay informed. It's important to seek out unbiased opinions."
- "Being informed allows me to understand and make sense of today's landscape, various facts and opinions, and improves decision making. Helps to identify opportunities, trends, issues and potential road-blocks."
- "Separating facts from alternative facts when it is most important."
- "I can't claim status as a critical thinker if I am only 'informed' in the comfortable vacuum of my own thinking. Or the thinking of others 'like me'. Staying informed means doing the work to get out there and find other perspectives."
- "The world has become more highly differentiated and cluttered. More product brands, company brands, political brands and idea brands. It isn't just a choice between chocolate, vanilla and strawberry. The differences are subtle and small, so being informed is essential to good and consistent decision making."

180

- "Life is a constant battle. Without fast, good, reliable 'intel' you will lose the battle."

Reliable intel. So, it's a little cluttered in 2020, but one thing is clear: it's really important to be informed. And here's the first strong foresight: *it's your responsibility to be informed.* There's a big difference between being *uninformed* and being *disinformed.* Uninformed is on *you.* Disinformed is on *them.* And, the more informed you are, the less likely you are to be disinformed.

Look, take another look at the dozen themes that our group developed and assessed in 10 minutes. It's not rocket science, it's pretty common sense about the value: career advantage, guidance to my family, contribute to society, navigate life. And the reality is, it's never been easier to be informed. To have that good intel. Most of us have a 100-500 meg internet broadband pipe coming into our homes. You can search on *anything.* Have news feeds. Look at historical perspectives. Track research polls and trends. And you can be *selective* about your sources. Find sources that you find to be credible. That you can *trust.*

Meanwhile Back at The Pandemic and Political Fronts

Here's a quick example of the challenge of staying informed while deflecting disinformation. This is an excerpt on the pandemic update and timeline from the American Journal of Managed Care:

August 23, 2020
Convalescent Plasma is Cleared for Use by the FDA:

The FDA issues another EUA (Early Use Authorization), this time for convalescent plasma from recovered patients as a therapy to fight COVID-19. There is ongoing debate about the treatment, which is rooted in experts' skepticism that all patient populations will derive benefit from it, due to a lack of efficacy data. Meanwhile, White House Press Secretary Kayleigh McEnany claims it is a therapeutic breakthrough.

Just to be clear, I did not have Kayleigh McEnany on my list of trusted sources of good intel.

But there are some promising developments that we will need to *stay informed on* as 2020 progresses: Pfizer and BioNTech are expanding their phase 3 trials. Johnson & Johnson is beginning their phase 3 trial. The U.S. Health and Human Services and the Department of Defense have a plan to make COVID-19 vaccine free for all Americans with a target initial roll out of January 2021. *The plan does not yet have guidance on who would be the first to receive the vaccine.* Stay tuned to be *informed.*

The country is gearing up for the first presidential debate on September 29, only a few days after our current Foresight session. A country-wide opportunity to become more informed. I mean, what could go wrong?

Cue in the disinformation:

From the Wikipedia timeline of the Biden 2020 Presidential run: "Since Biden's successful nomination in the Democratic primaries, Trump attempted to cast doubt over Biden's abilities, claiming that he was suffering from dementia and that he was taking performance-enhancing drugs in the primaries. Trump called for Biden to be drug tested before the presidential debate; Biden declined. Trump also claimed that Biden would use a hidden electronic earpiece for the debate, demanding that Biden's ears be searched. Again, Biden declined."

I'm not making this up.

Reflecting on The Prior Decade
Back to our Foresight session, we asked our participants to reflect on the prior decade and to see where we *gained ground* as well as *lost ground* on terms of being more informed:

Question: *Thinking about the last decade, 2010-2019, in what ways do you think we GAINED GROUND on being more informed?*

It was all about <u>access</u>:

- ✓ Increased access to media via the internet
- ✓ Distribution of content via mobile platforms
- ✓ Increased number of media outlets
- ✓ Customized news feeds
- ✓ Massive amounts of data at our fingertips (search/analyze)
- ✓ More real-time news and events being broadcast
- ✓ The ease of sharing information
- ✓ Smartphones that are, well, pretty smart
- ✓ 24 hour news channels
- ✓ Social media distribution, i.e., Twitter
- ✓ Increased wi-fi coverage (constant access)
- ✓ More integration of multiple news platforms (newspaper, radio, digital, TV, etc.)
- ✓ Increased ability to fact-check
- ✓ Higher quality cameras and video, YouTube as a sharing channel
- ✓ Technology enabled research (e.g., text analytics)

Clearly, the *opportunity* to be more informed had just been democratized by technology. But what got in the way?

Question: *Still thinking about the last decade, 2010-2019, in what ways did we LOSE GROUND in becoming more informed?*

It was all about <u>discerning the truth</u>:

- ✓ The development of left and right media
- ✓ Too many voices (too much noise)
- ✓ Media bias
- ✓ Poor quality reporting
- ✓ Lack of filtering and control over what was real and what was manipulation
- ✓ Opinions as news
- ✓ Lack of fact checking—a rush to publish/distribute
- ✓ The advent of the "cancel culture"
- ✓ The news industry lost its professionalism
- ✓ Algorithms feeding information on social media
- ✓ Volume of information impairs insight
- ✓ Internet trolls
- ✓ Less utilization of traditional/credible sources: network news and newspapers
- ✓ Sensational coverage of news—drama over content
- ✓ Lack of overall public trust of the media
- ✓ We didn't have a Walter Cronkite to guide us
- ✓ Venture Capital ownership of media
- ✓ The ability to "gaslight" just about any issue
- ✓ Failure of major technology platforms to police their content/usage
- ✓ Lack of high integrity leaders at the top of some news companies
- ✓ The loss of local newspapers
- ✓ The use of technology to skew what I see (bots, cookies, etc.)
- ✓ The race to be first in breaking a story
- ✓ The intentional broad based use of social media with false information

One of our participants summarized it perfectly: *"You have to work harder to discern what's true."*

Or, as the *Boss* so eloquently sang:

Man came by to hook up my cable TV
We settled into the night my baby and me
We switched 'round and 'round 'til half past dawn
There was fifty-seven channels and nothin' on

--Bruce Springsteen, 57 Channels (And Nothin' On) (1992)

So, more access in the prior decade (which is good), but way harder to discern what is real (which is not so good). So, if you were mindful of this dilemma, it was a great decade to be more informed. If you were on *auto-pilot* it was a decade to become *disinformed*.

Question: *All things considered, looking at the past decade, do you feel YOU became more or less accurately informed about the issues that were important to you?*

No.	Items	Times Selected
1.	**I became MORE informed**	**(71%)**
2.	I became LESS informed	(29%)

And for our Foresighters, you could see that they had to put some work into managing that fine line:

- MORE: "More informed with the caveat that more time is spent now on reading from multiple sources to get to the actual truth."

- MORE: "Definitely more news out there and am more informed, but is the information accurate? It's hard to know sometimes."

- MORE: "I increased the range of news sources that I take my information from and this allowed me to better balance perspectives on issues. And I don't really follow news on social media."

- MORE: "I find it increasingly important for me to hear points of view from both sides to help me form my own opinions, and so I spend a lot more time fact checking and digging into issues and news. Overall desire to make more informed decisions and to not be a sheep."

- MORE: "I have access to more information. But, I have to work to confirm that what I am reading and learning is credible and reliable. It has made me a better informed person and a better researcher, as well."

- LESS: "I get lost in the 'noise' and extreme views/behaviors and the general nastiness of everything going on, and it makes it harder for me to want to engage."

- LESS: "Media is more opinionated/less fact-based but I also became less engaged for the same reason."

- LESS: "It is the accuracy that is the issue here for me—I regularly consume a newspaper a day, at least one news bulletin on TV and another on radio plus a news magazine or two a week and always have—but now I feel that I don't know the 'full story'."

It makes it harder for me to want to engage. I get it, and that concerns me. Not only for my generation, but for the younger generations—Millennials and Gen Z specifically. We cannot afford for them to tune out—not because they don't care, but because it is just too damn hard to get to the truth.

Question: *All things considered, looking at the past decade, do you feel MOST AMERICANS became more or less accurately informed about the issues that were important to them?*

No.	Items	Times Selected
1.	**They became LESS informed**	**(77%)**
2.	They became MORE informed	(23%)

Now remember, this is a pretty highly educated group. And a group that feels, for the most part, very well informed. *Just ask them.* So, there might be a little bias on their part to have completely flipped the question results, but I am afraid that they were pretty dead-on with their explanations:

- LESS: "Less informed—most people just hear what they want to hear in order to reinforce their position and be right. And it's easy to just take the headlines at face value—whether they represent the right or the left."

- LESS: "Getting most of their 'news' via the Internet. The speed that occurs makes digesting and evaluating the accuracy of the 'news' more difficult."

- LESS: "It depends how you interpret the question. Americans became more informed in the sense that they have access to more information. However, they became less informed in the

185

sense of receiving quality information. The overall amount of information available grew, but quality information stagnated, or even dropped."

- LESS: "The social media programming has skewed what people see, thus driving extremism that is frequently based on fictitious information. And, people are being overwhelmed by the flow of information."

- LESS: "Too many people accept anything they read as true and only seek out news sources that confirm their predispositions. I also think too many people have too little understanding of/appreciation for our history and principles and don't recognize their deterioration."

- LESS: "Not sure I'd say MOST, but MANY are not willing to do the work to explore the true facts. MANY assume something to be true (or not) simply based on the SOURCE of the information. Many count on social media (or comedy news) to get their facts."

- LESS: "Information bubbles. Echo chambers. The ease with which you can find a point of view that matches your own and don't have to search any further. The comfort of continued living in our own biases."

- MORE: "I feel like overall they have become more informed, though that can depend on which sources they choose to use. They have the ability to have been more informed."

Maybe we have yet another example of the haves vs. the have-nots. Those who have the time, experience and desire to discern what is true and what is manipulative, and those who depend on a certain source or choose to *find a source* that is of their liking to echo a certain view. At some point this extreme difficulty in determining what is true is going to become dangerous.

The Gift That Keeps on Giving
I reconnected with the media in 1998, after I had left IBM and had formed my own consulting company, *DS Griffen & Associates.* World headquarters in Scottsdale, Arizona. Snappy name for a company, I have been employee of the month twice now.

In June of 1998, I had the good fortune to appear in an *earned media* placement. It was a story that appeared in the June edition of the Delta Sky magazine. Some of you may not appreciate this now, but the airline magazines that were placed in seat back pockets were pretty heavily browsed in those days. Lots of business folks traveling and just about everybody, at some point on the flight, would look through the current

186

monthly edition. And Delta airlines was a good business traveler airline. *A good placement.*

The article was a bit serendipitous. A freelance writer had called Group-Systems, whose software I was using for my collaborative sessions. GroupSystems was a result of a joint project with IBM and the University of Arizona—I became acquainted with the project while I was part of the IBM Consulting Group. The writer, John Grossman, had heard about GroupSystems and wanted to talk with someone about how the platform worked. They routed the request to me. *Well, I know how to take advantage of a blue-bird opportunity.* Trained by IBM, you know.

Well, it turns out that John lived in New Jersey. *John—this is great!* I told him that I was doing a session for KPMG in a week *in New Jersey* with one of their teams and I would check to see if he could sit in and observe the session. KPMG was my first consulting client in 1996 (*still* a client in 2021!), as I had joined forces with my good friend Will Marré (see chapter 4) who had landed a leadership contract with the KPMG State and Local Tax Team (SALT). We were using my laptop lab in a number of activities to support SALT as a *high performance team. ReaLeadership* according to Will.

So, John joined us for a session, just sat back and watched. He seemed to really get the concept of collaboration. In 1998, we were pretty leading edge with what we were doing and he was sure he could place an article. He never had me review the article, he just wrote it and then (which was brilliant) had a series of illustrations done (by Hal Mayforth) that were really eye catching. John entitled the article: *The Sounds of Silence.* With a subtitle of: *Can be the most productive idea-driven meeting you'll ever conduct.*

A copy of the article showed up in my mail with a note from John. It was a full Delta Sky magazine, the article bookmarked with a yellow sticky. I booked a Delta flight the next week and took a backpack with me. *Stuffed 36 of those magazines in the backpack.*

It was a great article, a full three pages. Great teasers for the traveling business executive. *Example from John in the article:* "In a typical meeting, only one person can talk at a time. Here, theoretically, all two dozen of the KPMG managers can 'talk' simultaneously. Moreover, they do so anonymously." He adds: "In eight minutes, the group identifies 130 leadership issues. And it does so without uttering a single word." *Ah, the sounds of silence. I get it.*

But John's real gift to me and my relationship with media was an inset box at the end of the article. The ultimate call to action for a business exec reading the article:

Getting Wired: If you are interested in setting up a computer-mediated meeting through DS Griffen & Associates, call 480.585.8039 or send an email message to DSGriffen@aol.com.

The Sounds Of
Silence
Can be the most productive, idea-driven group meeting you'll ever conduct.

Getting Wired

If you're interested in setting up a computer-mediated meeting through D.S. Griffen & Associates, call 480-585-8039 or send an e-mail message to *DSGriffen@aol.com.*

Delta Sky article, June 1998   *The gift that keeps on giving*

That's right, America Online—AOL. People wonder why I still use that email ID (among others). *I worship it.* Holy shit! *You've got mail!*

One of the first emails was from the Newspaper Association of America (NAA), well known to everyone in the newspaper industry and headed by CEO John Sturm. *They saw the article and wanted to know if we could do a similar session with editors/publishers of North American newspapers at an upcoming session in Dallas.*

Well, of course. After all, I have a background in the newspaper industry. *See, I knew the newspaper delivery route would come in handy.*

And it was a very powerful session. Thirty participants from some of the largest newspapers in the country. They wanted the answer to one question:

What was causing the decline in newspaper readership in North America?

And thus began a connection with the news and media industry that continues through today. Over 1000 sessions across 15 countries. *Word of mouth advertising.* A lot of times in the early days we would drag our cases of laptops to the meeting location. *Try doing that in Venezuela. When Chavez is heading the country and doesn't like the newspaper group you are working with.*

188

But it was a tremendous seat at the table. Gannett. USA Today. The Arizona Republic. The Denver Post. Cox Newspapers. The Corporation for Public Broadcasting (NPR/PBS). Hearst Newspapers. The MediaNews Group. What I learned is that news and media, as they headed into 2000 and the new millennium, were entrenched and not ready to change. Newspapers were just that—*papers*. Not ready to go digital/multi-platform. Watching the core readers slowly get older, with little engagement to a new generation of readers/listeners/viewers/visitors. To them, the Internet was the *enemy*. Until they decided that they really weren't in the newspaper business, they were in the *informing business. Voila!* They were no longer bound by the printing press.

The Newspaper Association of America is now the News Media Alliance.

And, as we stand in 2020, a lot of people are in the informing business. Or maybe that is the *influencing business.* I have great regard for the journalism profession. But a lot of people were muscling in on their territory. And a lot of those new players did not have the kind of principles and integrity that the true journalists have.

The Issues Affecting News and Media Today

Back at our Foresight session I feel like I have gone into the *wayback machine.* Instead of asking what was causing the decline in newspaper readership, we just wanted to find our what was *wrong* with the state of news, media and information:

Question: *Let's ask you to do some consulting work. Thinking about TODAY (September of 2020), what are the factors/issues that are most concerning to you about the News, Media and Information? What's not working the way it should?*

This was one of our questions with open responses (more than 100), but then a real-time summary of key themes that we could assess.

Now, please assess each of the following factors/issues in terms of how significant you feel they are TODAY in affecting the quality/accuracy of the News, Media and Information that we might consume. Use a scale of 1-10 where a "1" means not at all concerning and a "10" means extremely concerning:

Rank	Idea	Avg.
1.	Role of disinformation	**9.3**
2.	Speed of news without fact checking	**8.6**
3.	Difficulty to determine what is NOT accurate	**8.5**
4.	Sensationalism	**8.4**

5.	Negative influence of social media	**8.3**
6.	Inherent source bias	**8.1**
7.	Lack of in-depth analysis	**8.1**
8.	Judging news rather than reporting it	**7.9**
9.	Loss of reporting/interviewing skills	**7.0**
10.	Every story has an agenda	**6.9**
11.	Influence of advertising	**6.2**
12.	Diminishing number of news sources	**4.7**

Note that it's NOT about the number of news/media sources. Today, it seems like *everyone* is trying to be a news/media source. I remember being at a conference for the World Association of Newspapers (more on them later) and it was the real start of *citizen reporting/journalism*. Anyone with a smartphone, laptop and internet connection could now be a news source and a de facto extension of the industry. Great, right? The speaker had one of the most memorable lines of the conference:

"We need citizen journalists about the same way we need citizen dentists."

There is a reason why professional media organizations have *editors*. And that doesn't mean that you *bloggers* out there are not good at what you do. Many of you are. But when *everyone* on social media decides that they are in the informing business then we have a problem.

But, to be fair, the issues around professionalism and quality reporting/ informing are not just the domain of our "citizen journalists". It's a huge problem in mainstream media. Look at our list. Disinformation, sensationalism, speed over accuracy, lack of in-depth analysis, poor reporting skills, inherent bias. How many of you watch your 10:00pm local news? If you do, how *informed* do you feel? How many of you read your daily newspaper? *It's gotten a little thin, eh?*

Thin if you can even find your newspaper. Less than 30 days after our Foresight session, one of the largest cities in America decided to *stop printing a daily newspaper*. The *Salt Lake City Tribune* had been published for nearly 150 years. But they would switch to a *weekly* paper delivered by mail. *That should be stocked with today's top stories.*

The Associated Press reported: "The change won't result in cuts to the newsroom staff of about 65 people, although some would be redeployed," the newspaper said. Nearly 160 press operators, carriers and other employees will lose their jobs.

Some would be redeployed.

Look, I get that digital news coverage is the dominant media. I hit my AzCentral app every day (the app produced by *The Arizona Republic*) and it is current, updated and links me to a thousand other information sites and sources. I get the *New York Times* "The Morning" email every day. But we don't want to lose the balance of traditional mainstream media in the decade ahead.

The Tribune was redeployed in 2020

But maybe the *Tribune* is just an aberration. A necessary pawn in the modern world and the quest for a *more informed society*. So we asked our Foresighters about the quality and accuracy of news and media today compared to 10 years ago:

Question: *Back to our consulting work. Overall, as you reflect on the News, Media and Information today, do you feel that the quality/accuracy is higher or lower than, say, 10 years ago?*

No.	Items	Times Selected
1.	**I think the quality and accuracy of the News, Media and Information is LOWER than it was 10 years ago**	**(94%)**
2.	I think the quality and accuracy of the News, Media and Information is HIGHER that it was 10 years ago	(6%)

We already agreed about how important *being informed* was to our lives. Just don't look to your news, media and information sources to be informed accurately. *Are you serious?*

- LOWER: "There really is too much fake news masquerading as real news. I feel good about my ability to fact check and parse sources, but I don't have faith in others to do the same...based on experience."

- LOWER: "The media have fewer resources; the loss of shared belief in reporting the facts leading to deterioration of the accuracy and insights."

- LOWER: "Less professionalism. The craft of journalism has been degraded. With a president who has over 20,000 lies attributed to him, the environment is so sad for people who remember when reporters really could be counted on for getting the truth."

- LOWER: "Priority on being first, sensationalism and grabbing eyeballs/screens vs. in-depth, high quality and factual information. Attention span of public is weak—looking for soundbites and 'snackable content'."

- LOWER: "Across all news media, it has probably diminished but there are wide differences. Some are fabulous sources of objective, accurate information, but huge numbers of news sources are totally biased by design."

- LOWER: "Unfortunately, I think it is lower. There are obviously great sources of quality and accurate news out there. The problem is that there is a huge rush to get stories out and huge incentives to tell certain stories that fit audience's preexisting perceptions or that fall into existing conceptions. Media outlets are also forced to compete with social media so they end up borrowing some of their characteristics: sensationalism (especially in headlines), polarizing angles on stories. Galvanizing/energizing audiences FAST in a certain direction counts more than carefully delivering nuanced stories."

- LOWER: "Social media, online access, etc., have made the need to get news out fast and to be sensational to get attention seemingly more important than being accurate. Influencers are now who young people look to for information."

That last comment bears repeating: *Influencers are now who young people look to for information.* Not reporters, news anchors, broadcasters or writers. *Influencers.* Social media influencers are a big business. They can have *millions* of followers. They can make or break products and brands. They can influence and raise the visibility of big-time political issues, candidates and races. *Full disclosure: one of my sons, Sam, is a talented full-stack IT programmer. He worked in 2020 for—you guessed it—a social media influencer company.* Shit! It's influence powered by technology! My influence used to be powered by a Schwinn paperboy bicycle.

But I think there may be a race brewing here in the decade ahead. *In this corner:* the power of social media, digital news, customized news feeds, smartphones and ubiquitous news sources, that, if manipulated for the wrong reasons, could create a level of disinformation that makes 2020 look like child's play. *And in this corner:* advanced artificial intelligence that will filter all of that much like your PC security software fights malware today. Automates fact-checking, blocks disinformation, selects the best and most credible news and information sources.

I know, I know. Who is going to keep influencers from mis-directing the AI?

Trusted Sources

Let's move on. AI may be in the future for helping us with determining trusted sources, but for now we are kind of on our own. So we asked our Foresighters about their most trusted sources. Here were some of the most frequent responses:

- ✓ The New York Times
- ✓ The Washington Post
- ✓ The Wall Street Journal
- ✓ National Public Radio
- ✓ BBC (British Broadcasting Company)
- ✓ Google as a search site
- ✓ The Atlantic
- ✓ CNN for quick updates
- ✓ TLDR Newsletter (curated daily newsletter on tech and science)
- ✓ Fox News

CNN and Fox News. *Well, you gotta trust somebody, right?* The above was not just a subset of the responses. It was basically *the list.* This is really unscientific research but for many people, it really is a short list when it comes to trust.

We decided to take this idea of *trust* in a different direction and ask our participants about the **level of trust** they have about certain people, organizations and entities *that are in a position to influence us.* We purposely mixed in some media people and entities, but we came up with a pretty interesting set of 25 possibilities.

Now, before you read ahead to the Foresighters' assessment, what are the top five for you? The bottom five for you? You can mark with a pencil or pen or memory ... up to you!

Entity/Organization/Person (original order in Foresight session...)	Top 5	Bottom 5
Your largest daily local newspaper		
Your network news TV stations		
Newspapers with a national reach such as USA Today, NY Times and Washington Post		
The major social media platforms		
Cable news networks such as CNN and Fox		
Public Media stations (PBS and NPR)		
The Federal Government		
Your State and Local Government		
The U.S. Supreme Court		
The World Health Organization (WHO)		
The Centers for Disease Control and Prevention (CDC)		
Dr. Anthony Fauci		
Anderson Cooper		
Sean Hannity		
Bill Gates		
Barack Obama		
Bill Clinton		
Donald Trump		
The two major political parties (Democratic Party and Republican Party)		
The U.S. Congress		
Airline pilots		

The United Nations		
Global news organizations such as the BBC		
Your church or place of worship		
The leadership at the company/organization you work for		

Now let's take a look at how our Foresighters look at the list:

Please consider each of the following entities/people that might be in a position to influence/inform us. Please indicate the extent to which you trust the entity or person. Use a scale of 1-10 where a "1" means a very low level of trust and a "10" means a very high level of trust. If you are not familiar with a particular entity or person you may mark "abstain":

Rank	Idea	Avg.
1.	Airline pilots	8.1
2.	Dr. Anthony Fauci	8.1
3.	Public Media stations (PBS and NPR)	7.9
4.	Barack Obama	7.8
5.	Global news organizations such as the BBC	7.6
6.	Newspapers with a national reach such as USA Today, NY Times and Washington Post	7.6
7.	Bill Gates	7.4
8.	The leadership at the company/organization you work for	7.4
9.	The U.S. Supreme Court	7.1
10.	Your largest daily local newspaper	7.0
11.	Your church or place of worship	6.7
12.	The World Health Organization (WHO)	6.6
13.	The Centers for Disease Control and Prevention (CDC)	6.4
14.	The United Nations	6.2

15.	Anderson Cooper	**6.2**
16.	Your network news TV stations	**6.0**
17.	Your State and Local Government	**5.6**
18.	Bill Clinton	**5.5**
19.	Cable news networks such as CNN and Fox	**4.3**
20.	The U.S. Congress	**3.9**
21.	The Federal Government	**3.7**
22.	The two major political parties (Democratic Party and Republican Party)	**3.4**
23.	The major social media platforms	**2.8**
24.	Sean Hannity	**2.2**
25.	Donald Trump	**1.8**

We did a lot of short snap polls/assessments in our 10 Foresight sessions. This may be one that I truly was most fascinated to see—I had some hunches, but I am not sure I wanted to put a wager down. You could have easily expanded this list to 100 people, organizations and entities, but for our purposes, this 25 seemed to make a few rather interesting points. First, look at the top ten vs. the bottom 10:

Top 10 (in order from most trusted)	Bottom 10 (in order from least trusted)
Airline pilots	Donald Trump
Dr. Anthony Fauci	Sean Hannity
Public Media stations (PBS and NPR)	The major social media platforms
Barack Obama	The two major political parties (Democratic Party and Republican Party)
Global news organizations such as the BBC	The Federal Government

Newspapers with a national reach such as USA Today, NY Times and Washington Post	The U.S. Congress
Bill Gates	Cable news networks such as CNN and Fox
The leadership at the company/ organization you work for	Bill Clinton
The U.S. Supreme Court	Your State and Local Government
Your largest daily local newspaper	Your network news TV stations

My God! Could you imagine if Fauci had a pilot's license?

Think about the implications (and again, just our assessment, but some pretty smart people with a lot of experience). Look at the power and trust we have in three specific people: Anthony Fauci, Barack Obama and Bill Gates. *Informers and big-time influencers.* Several mainstream media entities: Public media stations (specifically the Corporation for Public Broadcasting company—they bring you Sesame Street as well), global news stations like BBC, the big national newspapers and your local newspaper. *I feel somewhat vindicated here.*

We still have regard for the U.S. Supreme court on the government side, but not much else. Federal Government, the U.S. Congress, the major political parties and even state and local governments are all on the suspect list. I personally like Bill Clinton, but look, the Monica Lewinsky line was a little weak. But look at the *bottom of the list.* It's pretty hard to score a 1.8 on the Foresight 1-10 *trustmeter.* Congratulations to the <u>current</u> President of the United States of America.

We'll take that up in the next chapter.

Personally, and especially when there's a *global pandemic* going on, I would like to have trust in our government. The stakes are pretty high. Even when we don't have a global pandemic going on, I would like to have trust in our government. But we know the divides that exist from our previous Foresight chapter. Little faith in a return (to any degree) of bipartisan politics. I continue to place my faith on a new and younger generation of leaders that will get involved, hear the call of service and bring fresh ideas and collaboration to the table. *I like collaboration.*

The Role of The Media

Back to the gift that keeps on giving, we received an invitation to facilitate a session of futurists in media in 1999 at the Chicago Tribune. Sponsored by the McCormick Foundation, it was entitled *The Next Big Idea*. The newspaper industry leaders knew they had to start a transformation process. A revolution had begun with the internet, but it wasn't clear how the great newspaper companies would partake in this revolution.

It was not only made up of U.S. companies; the newspaper industry is a true global industry. And one of the participants cornered me after the session. Distinguished. From Spain, with a thick Castilian dialect. He *loved* the laptop lab and the idea of collaborating on new *innovations*.

His name was Juan Antonio Giner. He was the CEO and co-founder of INNOVATION Media. A prestigious global media consultancy. He knew, for his company to transform global newspapers and their media companies, they would have to think differently. *This laptop digital collaboration thing might be the answer.*

"Dooooglas," he said in his Castilian accent. "Can you and Patrick bring these computers to Caracas?" Patrick was my cohort at the time, Patrick Garrett, a former IBMer and the technical facilitator (we made up the term technographer) for our system. I turned to Patrick. "Caracas?" He replied, "Pretty sure this guy is talking about Venezuela."

I moved quicky to my semi-fluent Spanish. "Absolutamente, Juan Antonio. ¿Cuándo?" "Dooooglas. Nos vamos la próxima semana." Patrick has no clue. Clearly, I don't either. But I'm in. And Juan Antonio already had a name for this new consulting tool: *Computer Assisted Brainstorming Sessions (CABS)*.

One of the greatest privileges in my career. Working with Juan Antonio and his team, Patrick and I (and some other cohorts over time) traveled to many of the great global newspapers to conduct CABS sessions. Venezuela, Columbia, Chile, Mexico, the Dominican Republic, Costa Rica, Spain, Portugal and the UK. And INNOVATION had a special relationship with the World Association of Newspapers (WAN) that held an annual global conference. INNOVATION would publish an annual set of articles, interviews and insights called the Innovation in Newspapers World Report (later changed to Innovation in Media World Report).

Now the travel got *really interesting*. Moscow, Capetown, Hyderabad (India), and Vienna.

The story of Chicago and CABS from Juan Antonio's 2019 book

For several of the WAN sessions, I had the opportunity to co-present a session to the conference. In 2009, I was also working with the Harris Interactive company (they produce the long running Harris Poll) and we were able to do a special poll with some *eight thousand* participants on trends in news and information and media *credibility.* We turned it into an article as part of the 2009 World Report. I titled it: "The 2009 Innovation/ Harris Poll Survey on Newspaper Readership: *Readers Want The Truth, The Whole Truth and Nothing But The Truth.*"

There. That's it. That's all you have to do if you are in the media. *Just tell the truth.* That was the case in 2009 and it's the case in 2020. We also identified 11 key roles for media for readers and their communities, and assessed how important the roles were to these 8,000 global survey participants. It's a compelling list, relevant then and relevant today. The assessments are shown for the United States and for Europe (percent indicating very important or important—top 2 box):

Role	US	Europe
Provide news and information about events in your local region and community	90	91
Provide news and information about events in your country	90	93

199

Provide news and information about events in the world	89	92
Hold public officials accountable for what they do	89	87
Report the news as quickly as possible	86	91
Provide news and information that you can use in your daily life	87	90
Protect the public from abuses of power	84	89
Provide news and information that's interesting to know	83	91
Provide news and information that you need to decide how to vote	83	78
Point out problems that need to be solved	83	90
Help society solve its problems	60	82

What if this is what the media did today? And did it accurately. In our country and in the world. Seems to me we would be better served and *better informed.*

2009 WAN Article: The Truth, The Whole Truth And Nothing But The Truth...

2009 INNOVATION/HARRIS POLL SURVEY ON NEWSPAPER READERSHIP: READERS WANT "THE TRUTH, THE WHOLE TRUTH AND NOTHING BUT THE TRUTH"

INNOVATION has once again teamed up with Harris Interactive and their innovative Harris Poll to gain a fresh perspective on the attitudes of Americans and Europeans on the subject of news, media, newspapers, and what newspapers can do to differentiate themselves in today's exploding media environment.

Douglas Griffen
Consultant, INNOVATION International
Media Consulting Group (USA)
griffen@innovation-mediaconsulting.com

The poll, taken during January 2009, is a follow up to a similar effort undertaken by INNOVATION and Harris in conjunction with the 2007 Congress of the World Association of Newspapers (WAN) in Cape Town, South Africa. Harris Interactive, developers of the long running Harris Poll and internet based panel for global

• How the media landscape is changing: what respondents saw as their sources of news and information NOW as well as what these sources might be FIVE YEARS form now;
• How CREDIBLE are newspapers, on an 0-100 index;

RVANT in the lives of readers.
    The 2009 results show that while newspapers have not stood still in the last two years, neither have the attitudes of our public or the world in which we live. An unparalleled confluence of issues is facing us on a global

	USA %	UK %	France %	Italy %	Spain %	Germany %	Europe %
TV Network News	26/25	32/36	30/29	30/30	31/22	26/28	30/29
Online news and information	22/18	18/14	17/17	21/22	17/18	18/18	18/17
Cable network news	14/14	2/2	2/0	7/5	3/2	9/7	8/8
Radio	10/12	17/15	21/20	11/11	14/16	16/18	16/10
Major Daily Newspapers	10/12	6/6	9/7	7/8	11/13	12/13	9/10
Local community newspapers	7/6	6/6	5/3	8/7	3/3	8/4	5/5
Magazines	4/4	4/3	7/5	5/5	4/4	8/5	5/4
Personal Daily Newspapers	4/3	11/11	8/8	10/8	12/12	6/5	9/9
School and web newsletters	1/1	1/1	2/1	1/1	2/1	1/1	1/1

NOTE: 2008 poll / 2007 poll

TABLE 2 What will be your sources for news and information in FIVE YEARS?

	USA %	UK %	France %	Italy %	Spain %	Germany %	Europe %
TV Network News	23/20	29/32	27/30	24/30	26/31	26/26	26/30
Online news and information	33/22	27/18	25/17	30/21	27/17	25/18	26/18
Cable network news	14/14	8/2	3/2	9/7	3/7	6/9	6/5
Radio	9/14	14/17	18/21	9/11	13/14	14/15	14/16
Major Daily Newspapers	7/10	5/5	7/9	6/7	9/11	11/12	7/9
Local Community Newspapers	5/7	4/6	4/3	5/6	3/3	6/5	4/5
National Daily Newspapers	3/4	8/11	6/5	9/10	10/12	5/5	8/9
Magazines	3/4	4/3	7/5	5/4	4/3	5/4	5/4
School and web newsletters	1/1	1/1	2/2	1/1	2/2	1/1	1/1

NOTE: 2008 poll / 2007 poll

The Future of News, Media and Information

Back to the future and our Foresight session. We wanted to know if our participants were optimistic or pessimistic about the direction of media:

Question: *If you were to forecast your view about the News, Media and Information in the decade ahead NOW, would you say you were optimistic or pessimistic about where it is heading?*

No.	Items	Times Selected
1.	Pessimistic about the News, Media and Information in the decade ahead—it will DECLINE	(59%)
2.	Optimistic about the News, Media and Information in the decade ahead—it will PROGRESS	(41%)

Somewhat of a split vote, leaning a bit pessimistic. Here's some selected explanations from our Foresighters…optimists first, please:

- PROGRESS: "New regulations and industry ethics will emerge and will largely be industry motivated. Potential new standards of certification for truthfulness/accuracy vs. opinion based presentation."

- PROGRESS: "Awareness is the first step in change. It's obvious we are all aware this is NOT working. Now more than any time in history we are willing to accept change."

- PROGRESS: "It can't get much worse. I am encouraged to note that the mainstream newspapers are significantly expanding their online readership. I also believe that Social Media might get wound back a bit, by making them responsible for what appears on their websites."

- PROGRESS: "It will happen in several years, I think, but I am cautiously optimistic there will be a reckoning. I think people fundamentally want the truth and will find ways to get it delivered. For every action, there is a reaction."

- PROGRESS: "The masses are revolting and smart people are engaging for the right reasons. Unfortunately, the problems are getting big enough that they will have to be confronted for us to maintain our civil union and address the issues that are being ignored right now due to the current state of affairs. So, I think revolutionary forces will demand change as our ancestors have done in the past. That will bring about a reset, and the tech can be channeled for good in driving an informed, democratic republic."

- DECLINE: "Lean toward more fragmentation, polarization, worsening of current state unless we see fundamental change in the leadership of the country and the standards to which we hold news and media organizations."

- DECLINE: "This is a very difficult question. Would have preferred to say somewhere in the middle. I don't see the sensationalism and polarization improving in the short term because, at the moment, this is the business model that feeds both traditional and social media, and because public media literacy (which is especially difficult in the online sphere anyway) is low. That needs to change in order for quality information to become more viable, but that is a long-term issue."

- DECLINE: "Unless there are major structural changes, such as tightening libel laws so there is a significant penalty for falsification of facts, the news media/social media pattern is likely to continue in the skewed, headline-grabbing, extremism-fueling reality. Reform can occur, but there appears to be little organized focus on achieving it."

- DECLINE: "There will be more confusion, more channels/sources and we'll have less time to evaluate and consider what we read/see/consume. Many of the larger media organizations are VC (Venture Capital) owned and don't have democracy in their thinking."

- DECLINE: "I am pessimistic that Biden will win the vote but Trump will somehow prevail and keep in power. And with that power, what tyrannical things will be schemed up to protect himself and grow power of his party? How will media be controlled?"

Damn. That was a pretty close forecast on September 24, wasn't it?

What I will say, is that the future direction of news, media and information in the decade ahead is *in play*. The current state is unsustainable. I am going with the minority view on this—I say that it will progress. *It has to.*

In a follow-up activity, we asked our participants what would make them *most optimistic* about the future of news, media and information (if it were to occur) and the one thing that would make them *most pessimistic:*

What Would Make You Most Optimistic?

- "I think there is an increasing energy and interest among young people to work in journalism and information gathering and dissemination. I think they will lead a needed resurgence in passion and professionalism."

- "There is increasing pressure on social media companies to address clearly false and dangerous facts. In addition, the European Union is playing an increasing role in fighting for consumer privacy and information protection."

- "Change of administration. Return to responsible, ethical and intelligent leadership with respect for the Constitution and the role of science in the world."
- "I think there are some experienced journalists who are still trying to tell the story, to report the news and base the information on the facts determined by good investigative reporting. I think things have swung so far to the extremes, that the natural course will be to gain some balance and hopefully that happens."
- "Mobile technology documents events today in unprecedented ways, and therefore allows the truth of events to be captured and told accurately."

What Would Make You Most Pessimistic

- "At the moment business model that feeds sensationalism and polarization has not changed, and it's getting worse. We need to see some significant developments here but I don't see a game-changer on the horizon."
- "If anyone came out with a truly neutral news platform, it probably wouldn't get the advertising dollars needed to allow it to compete with the extreme ends of the other sources."
- "The lack of passion across the political and social entities for fundamentally reforming how we get, process and use information. If there are not some structural changes to help drive more accurate information (while keeping a fee low), things will become more problematic in our society."
- "We will most likely continue down the same path. Too many big companies are allowed to own too much media. Walter Cronkite once said that the worst thing that happened to the CBS news division is that it started to make a profit."
- "It is so noisy and fragmented out there, it will take a Gandhi or King or some other inspired leader to bring a measure of focus. That is a thin thread to hang hope on."

Thin indeed. But I still have faith that we will move this in the right direction in the decade ahead. These are powerful opposing forces. One final assessment on the optimism vs. pessimism:

Question: *All things considered as you reflect the overall set of factors that might influence your outlook for the News, Media and Information in* *the decade ahead, what's your forecast for the future now that we have considered both sides?*

No.	Items	Times Selected
1.	**Somewhat Optimistic**	**(36%)**
2.	**Somewhat Pessimistic**	**(36%)**
3.	Middle of the Road	(18%)
4.	Very Pessimistic	(10%)
5.	Very Optimistic	(0%)

Dead heat, as of September 2020. And you know why optimism is shown ahead of pessimism in the assessment? *O comes before P in the alphabet.* Let it be a sign for the decade ahead.

Why Press Freedom Matters

We saw some real danger signs over the past couple of years with President Trump often repeating the rhetoric that the "fake news media" is the *enemy of the American people.* On August 16, 2018, the United States Senate passed by *unanimous consent* a resolution affirming that the media is not "the enemy of the people" and reaffirming "the vital and indispensable role the free press serves."

This is serious shit. In many countries in the world there is a very diminished press freedom. Journalists have a target on their backs. According to the International Press Institute (IPI), there were 55 journalists killed in 2020 alone. In the prior decade, 2010 through 2019, the global death toll for journalists was *997* killed. Some were more visible like Jamal Khashoggi, murdered by a team of Saudi agents in the Saudi consulate in Istanbul in October 2018. But that is only 1 of 997 stories in the past decade.

We know something about press freedom in the Griffen family. My son, Scott, is the Deputy Director of the IPI which is based in Vienna, Austria. Haven't seen him this year. They are locked down harder than we are. But his IPI team, and others like them, are fighting against the tyranny of anti-press leaders in countries around the world. *Never thought that the U.S. would need to be on that list.* Unfortunately, it is a long list.

Press freedom and societal freedom are completely aligned. Many of you have seen it first-hand in your travels or with media members you may know. The first WAN conference I attended was in Moscow in 2006. Courtesy of my colleague Juan Antonio Giner. Russia wanted to put on a good propaganda backdrop that all was good there in terms of access and freedom. We were VIP big time. Dinners and tours, a concert with the Moscow Strings. But the most powerful event for me (one of the most powerful in my life) was the event in the Kremlin. Yes, *that* Kremlin. Several hundred of us for a tour and then into the main presentation hall. Formal. Serious.

Must be a big-time speaker. *The biggest.* Putin. No shit. I was frozen in my seat. A long speech, audio translation in our earpiece. Man, I am waiting for Jack Ryan to come busting through the doors. And then, it happened. Not Jack Ryan, but two rows in front of me three members from an opposing political party unfurled a protest banner. *In the Kremlin in front of Putin.* They were smothered by green clad Russian guards in about 10 seconds and *hauled out.* Putin paused, for a moment, smiled and continued his speech. *Did not see that in the morning paper.*

Media Influence Scenarios

Customary in our Foresight sessions, we bring a few ideas to the table. *Potential influence scenarios* for the decade ahead.

Now, please assess each of the following future scenarios in two ways. First, the level of positive IMPACT to the future of News, Information and the Media in the decade ahead if the scenario was to occur (use a scale of 1-10 where a "1" means a very low level of positive impact and a "10" means a very high level of positive impact); Second, the LIKELIHOOD that this scenario will fully materialize in the decade ahead (use a scale of 1-10 where a "1" means a very low likelihood and "10" means a very high likelihood):

Here is how our Foresight session assessed the list. The scenarios are ordered by the *level of positive impact* but then contrasted with the likelihood of occurrence for a gap analysis rating:

#	Scenario Description	Im-pact	Like-ly	Gap
1	MAINSTREAM MEDIA REGAINS TRUST: You simply can't make it in this decade if you can't be trusted. Mainstream media re-prioritizes accuracy, source validation, fair visibility to both sides of an issue, less focus on sensationalism and more focus on balanced reporting. Mainstream media returns to watchdog journalism, getting ahead of issues and helping to shine the light on truth. Breaking news is REALLY breaking news.	8.7	4.5	(4.2)

2	GLOBAL PRESS FREEDOM USHERS IN A NEW POLITICAL REALITY: Oppressive leaders and oppressive governments are simply no longer a match for the people and their fundamental right to be informed, and for the free press to be supported. New global organizations—think of them as the UN for the press—emerge to protect journalists and their methods. The pen (or keyboard) is truly mightier than the sword.	8.6	4.5	(4.1)
3	NEGATIVE POLITICS DISPLACED BY ISSUE BASED CAMPAIGNING: Politics undergoes a fundamental change. Americans no longer tolerate negative campaigning, dis-information approaches and fear-based communications. You campaign on, and are elected on, your knowledge and position on issues that are important for the future. You are measured on your commitments. You can still be very persuasive on your issues and their impact, but a more informed and discerning electorate will determine whether you are on the right track for the future.	8.6	3.3	(5.3)
4	SOCIAL MEDIA CLEANS UP ITS ACT: The major social media companies take important steps to safeguard the accuracy, security and intent of information on their platforms. New leaders emerge in the companies with stronger values on privacy, mis-use of robotics/trolls, unlawful intent and influence. The dark side of social media retreats.	8.5	3.7	(4.8)
5	THE TRUTH NETWORK: A new digital news/information network emerges as a brand that differentiates itself by being completely objective, non-biased, fact based and respected for its research and journalistic integrity. They deliver on a consistent basis, and have a broad base of viewers/followers who simply value their programming and dial into "The Truth". And here you can handle it.	8.3	4.4	(3.9)

206

6	JOURNALISM EXPERIENCES A REBIRTH: The importance of quality journalism to inform our society experiences a rebirth as a profession. More influential schools and universities emphasize journalism as a vital profession and role for the future. Business leaders and their companies advocate and support journalism, and existing media companies provide more funding and support for future journalists.	8.2	5.0	(3.2)
7	A NATIONAL REINVESTMENT IN PUBLIC MEDIA: There is a new recognition that the principles embodied within our public media system (The Corporation for Public Broadcasting that supports PBS and NPR) have long been aligned with fairness, truth in broadcasting and supporting local community engagement. New federal funding is added to strengthen the public media role and voice as a trusted source of news and information, and its audience grows substantially.	7.8	4.6	(3.2)
8	A NEW WALTER CRONKITE EMERGES: In the 1960s, during his time as CBS News anchor, Cronkite was often cited as "the most trusted man in America." During our new decade, a new Cronkite emerges that a majority of Americans believe is informed, accurate, relevant and unbiased. Likely using a combination of traditional media and social media platforms, their voice is an essential part of us staying informed.	7.6	3.8	(3.8)
9	INFORMATION FITNESS IS THE NEW TREND: It just matters more in the decade ahead to be informed. Education at all levels refocuses on the importance of informed and engaged students, people actually work out their minds and knowledge at least an hour a day just like they were at the gym, technology provides alert information on a real time basis. Informed Singles—no joke—becomes one of the most successful new online dating sites.	7.5	4.5	(3.0)

10	GENERATION Z COMES TO THE RESCUE: A new generation of information consumers takes hold with Generation Z (those born in 1997 and later). They become known as the "Informed Generation." They tackle critical issues such as climate change, education reform, healthcare access and even global conflict with fact-based and research-based approaches. They are problem solvers but they use information, fact and science along with a refreshing dash of optimism.	6.8	4.9	(1.9)
11	NEURALINK ADVANCES THE BRAIN IMPLANT INDUSTRY: Elon Musk was right. The Neuralink concept of a micro implant in the brain to work with neuroscience principles becomes an affordable reality. Imagine programmed chips that transmit information and expertise to your brain in way that enables you to perform tasks you never thought possible.	4.8	3.7	(1.1)
12	YOUR OWN PERSONAL CHANNEL: Technology in the decade ahead comes to our rescue. We are able to customize the information topics, sources, level of detail and essential integrity of the news and information we receive. A daily summary, specific alerts, scenario forecasts, detailed research insights. It's an aggregation of global sources, filtered by interests and guided by artificial intelligence.	4.4	7.9	+3.5

Now, we have had some gaps in our previous Foresight session on the influence scenarios, but, man, *this is breaking news*. How were we even close on optimism vs. pessimism early in the session? Some of the areas—while clearly impactful—just seem like a long reach. But *Negative Politics* aside (5.3 gap), most of the others could be influenced by a combination of leadership and *constructive* new technology. It's hard to really forecast fully out through the decade and see the possibility of turning some of these areas around. But I have a strong faith in the media—the *real media*—that they can swing the pendulum back.

The media impact divide. Look at the top 6 gaps between impact and likelihood:

1. Negative politics displaced by issue-based campaigning (5.3)
2. Social media cleans up its act (4.8)

3. Mainstream media regains trust (4.2)
4. Global press freedom ushers in a new political reality (4.1)
5. The Truth Network (3.9)
6. A new Walter Cronkite emerges (3.8)

My hypothesis is simple. It all rests with mainstream media. If they regain trust, align with many of the key roles we articulated in our 2009 WAN article, they could impact many of the other influences in the list.

And, I am a little surprised about *Your Own Personal Channel*. Not the likelihood at 7.9, I agree with that. I would have expected the impact to be higher. Maybe it feels a little too impersonal. A little too Orwellian. Finally, don't bet against Elon Musk. *On anything.*

COVID Impact on the Way We Think About News, Media and Information

As we wrap up our Foresight session, we wanted to see how the COVID environment is impacting our perceptions of news, media and information:

Question: *How has the COVID-19 pandemic affected the way YOU think about the News, Media and Information?*

Facing a global pandemic puts the media in an especially visible and vital role. We are depending on information to guide our daily lives and understand what our country and the world is doing. If there was ever a time for truth and clarity, 2020 needed it in covering COVID:

- "I think it's just perpetuated some of the issues, but overall it is a reminder of just how important quality information is. This is a serious moment for which we need serious news. Disinformation is not just a nuisance, it's a health risk."

- "Increased the noise level. Everyone competing to get out 'information' the fastest (micro-seconds), and it is conflicting from moment to moment and source to source, so I don't have a whole lot of trust in what I am reading out there other than a general sense of what's going on."

- "I'm definitely more engaged with news more often. I do believe that initially the media was trying to get as much accurate information as possible, but once it turned political (which it did very quickly) it became difficult to sort out the true facts from the spun stories. I don't know how health and safety ended up being divided among party lines, I don't believe it is really the case, I just think it's been reported with a skewed angle."

- "We have more time during COVID, hence we've likely spent more time on various media, which has helped to provide for a

209

more critical eye of which are trusted sources, also greater chance to explore a variety of sources."

- "COVID-19 coverage has literally impacted the health, welfare and safety of the public and led to lives being saved and lives being lost. What is striking to me the most is the politically-aligned disinformation that is presented to the public (face masks, hydroxychloroquine, injecting household cleaners, etc.) as fact and has killed people who believed it. The fundamental First Amendment rights we espouse as a nation must be balanced with consequences for those in the media who would continue to shout 'Fire' from a crowded room while there is none. COVID reinforced the importance of news and how the consumer responds to the news."

I know that, sometime in the future, we will be past the pandemic and one of the things that media must do is objectively rate their performance in providing the right level of news and information, and if they had the right impact. Were we as Americans *more informed* about the pandemic and able to make choices and form clear views, or were we saturated by politically biased information and influence? In the decade ahead, there will be new crises where we need the media to inform and guide us. We are not yet to the needed level.

Five Reflections on the Future of News, Media and Information in the Decade Ahead:

1. MAINSTREAM MEDIA MUST LEAD: If we are to regain the public trust in media and higher confidence in news and reporting, mainstream media must lead the way. This is their domain, they have the journalistic principles, resources and reach. There are issues in the decade ahead where we will depend on the media and their information.
2. NEW GENERATION OF JOURNALISTS: We have done a pretty good job of attracting the next generation to STEM (Science, Technology, Engineering and Mathematics) careers, we also need to attract them to journalism. Journalism is a *purpose-based* role and a higher calling. These new journalists can help us be more informed to understand new challenges and live our lives better.
3. GLOBAL PRESS FREEDOM: Global press freedom, in the decade ahead, will be a mega-issue on the same level as climate change, pandemic preparedness and social justice. We need to maintain it in the U.S., but also be an active proponent globally. That press freedom must also avoid the trap of disinformation and bias.

210

4. FILTER OUT THE DISINFORMATION: You can't have counterfeit currency in the economic system and you can't have *counterfeit information* in the media industry. Social media companies play a role, traditional media plays a role and technology itself will play a role. You are entitled to your opinion, but not your own set of facts.
5. COMMIT TO BE INFORMED: Our ability to personally navigate the decade ahead requires a commitment to be *informed*. It's just not OK in these days and times to say, "I don't know anything about that," when *that* is affecting the future of your family, your community, and society. You will have more confidence in the journey you take.

An Arizona Reflection

I have mentioned Walter Cronkite many times in this chapter. But so have many of our participants. His impact cannot be understated in terms of media trust and credibility. And we do need the *next Walter Cronkite* in the decade ahead. Arizona State University is the home of the Walter Cronkite School of Journalism and Mass Communication. It is co-housed with KAET Channel 8, the PBS public media station. It's a terrific building. I've done some sessions there for the Arizona Republic as well as for KAET 8. I am telling you it is *eerie*. I know "Cronkite" is on the building, but it feels like he is *in the building* as well. Ask anyone there. He is keeping an eye on us. He expects you to do your best work when you are there. His standards are high.

We can't let him down. Not in that building and not in this country. I think he would want us to deal with the complexity of where we are today. Struggle with it. But simplify it at the end of the day. Tell the truth. Inform people. Help them with their lives.

Thank you for reading this chapter. I hope you enjoyed it. It's where we are today. But we all have some work to do in the decade ahead for a better media and for us to be personally better informed and address the issues ahead.

And that's the way it is.

The Cronkite School of Journalism—ASU

Walter Cronkite

CHAPTER 7: 48 Hours—The Whole World is Watching

Doctor, my eyes
Tell me what is wrong
Was I unwise to leave them open for so long?

'Cause I have wandered through this world
And as each moment has unfurled
I've been waiting to awaken from these dreams

People go just where they will
I've never noticed them until I got this feeling
That it's later than it seems

--Jackson Brown, Doctor My Eyes (1972)

November 5, 2020
Foresight 2030 Session

It's time for the gloves to come off. This is the main event everyone has been waiting for: Trump vs. Biden. America is ready. The world is ready. Our *Foresighters* are ready. I played out a hunch for this session: that the hype would deliver and that the election would not be called on the evening of the vote. Too many variables with all of the voting methods and even the media would have to be careful not to pull the trigger early on a swing state. We chose to have the session two days after the voting began—hence the 48 hours label. Kind of a CBS thing.

But *The Whole World is Watching.* You have to have the right historical context for that one. Some of you can hear that chant right now. *The whole world is watching! The whole world is watching!* Back to the volatile '60s in America, but an appropriately political context. The 1968 Democratic National Convention at the Conrad Hilton Hotel in Chicago. Anti-Vietnam war protesters rallied around the chant on the evening of August 28, 1968, the third day of the convention. Notes Wikipedia: "Demonstrators took up the chant as police were beating and pulling many of them into police vans, each with a 'superfluous whack of a nightstick' after the demonstrators began to come into Michigan Avenue in front of the hotel."

1968 Anti-war demonstrations—Chicago Convention

A superfluous whack of a nightstick. In other words, the Chicago police *beat the shit out of these kids.* But welcome to the emerging age of video and real-time media. The goodness of America was broadcast for everyone to see. *The whole world was watching.*

There are some events, some points in time, when everything you do is under a magnifying glass. The 2020 presidential election was just such an event. My personal view was that the balance of the decade was at stake. *That's my decade and the subject of this book.* We held our Foresight session 48 hours after the opening of the polls. And we were right—as of November 5, the election had not yet been called.

Events are happening in real-time. It's just the future of the free world. More Americans will vote in this election than in any previous presidential election. New voting methods to accommodate a pandemic—early voting, mail-in voting, drive-by voting. Trump would tell you after the election that *even dead people could vote.*

The Role of the Pandemic
My own view (which you get to have when you author a book), but this election would not have even been close were it not for the pandemic. It still would have been loud, noisy, nasty. But Trump would have been re-elected. He survived the Mueller investigation, the *first* impeachment trial and everything mainstream media could throw against him. Prior to the pandemic, the economy was relatively good (although hugely inequitable) and the world was largely at peace. We all laugh at the combination sideshow and car wreck, it's hard to look away.

214

But throw in a global pandemic that requires real leadership...now you have a problem. On September 28, a few days after our previous Foresight session, the world surpassed *one million* COVID deaths. And then COVID hits the presidency hard and close to home: on October 2, President Trump and First Lady Melania Trump announce that they have both tested positive for COVID (yes, this time it was OK to click on the link). It's bizarre, *poetic justice* many think, but it is still an incident that *surely* will affect the president's understanding of the leadership implications of COVID and what has to be done.

Trump survives via a cocktail mix of remdesivir and dexamethasone, and that stirring drive-by to say hello to his followers wishing him well at the hospital. He leaves the hospital on October 5, but on October 8, in an editorial published by the New England Journal of Medicine, 34 editors call out against Trump and his handling of the pandemic, stating that, "The Trump administration has taken a crisis and turned it into a tragedy." *It is the first time in its 208 year history that the publication has either supported or condemned a political candidate.*

On the same day, October 8, a poll conducted by <u>Gallup-West Health</u> finds that more Americans trust Biden to lead the U.S. healthcare system through the pandemic. Oh, and the number of people infected by the COVID-19 outbreak during the Rose Garden ceremony for Supreme Court Justice Amy Coney Barrett has grown to 34 including a number of White House staffers. *A classic case of lead by example.*

Global cases of COVID top 40 million on October 19 with 220,000 deaths in the U.S. as the hardest hit country on the planet. The U.S. closes in on 100,000 cases a day as we head into the November 3 election.

What a fucking nightmare.

Look, I, for one, thought that Trump *might* turn out to be a pretty good president after the first election. *I am an optimist, you remember.* I recall watching the election results in Mesquite, Nevada, in 2016. My son Jack, the golfer, was playing the Nevada Open. About everyone in the tournament was packed into the bar at the Casa Blanca Resort and we were watching the results. *This cannot be happening!* Hillary could lose this thing. This was not the way the movie was scripted. *Kirk to Enterprise: set coordinates for the Klingon planet.*

My niece, Keven Griffen, was attending Brown University. She said that the next morning the girls in the dorm had taken four sheets and strung them together and hung them down four floors on the outside of the dorm building. One word on each sheet from top to bottom:

WHAT

HAVE

WE

DONE?

Well, that kind of summed things up. But I initially saw it like a style change for a baseball team. *Time for a new manager.* Sometimes you just need to mix it up. Change out a nice guy manager for a hard core asshole that will hold people accountable.

Besides, if it doesn't work out you can just fire the manager and bring someone else in. *Oh, you can't do that with a President?* Well, you can try. It just takes four years.

I never expected Trump to change his personality. But I thought he would make some adjustments to the office itself. He actually did, the first time he addressed a joint session of Congress in 2017, and we all breathed a sigh of relief. Even CNN thought we might be OK. But that turned out to be an aberration. On the positive side, I don't think any world leaders wanted to mess with us. *That guy Trump is nuts...we have no idea what he might do.*

So, here we are on November 5, 2020. The pandemic has changed the momentum going into the election, and now it is the critical 48 hours: The Whole World is Watching. And that includes our Foresighters.

Meanwhile Back at the Ranch

I am conducting this session back up in Park City. Frankly, it was getting weird in Arizona. We are a Republican state, after all, and the Trumpsters were getting a little too visible for me. In the early part of the pandemic, around late April, all the pools had closed down, so I improvised my lap swimming workouts and found one of the only lakes in Arizona that you could still (legally) gain access to. Bartlett Lake is still in the desert, but at the fringes of the Tonto National Forest and only 35 minutes from my house. The Bartlett Lake Marina was a private marina with some public access and parking, but I felt like a *private person*, so I parked there and swam in the cove off the marina. Said hello to the County Sheriff and he said no problem with the swimming.

And then I saw my first Trump truck and Trump flag in the marina parking lot. Brash, I guess, but kind of weird at the same time. Like a modern *Rat Patrol* vehicle. But look, I am probably not 100% authorized to be on the marina grounds and it might be a secret Trump training camp, so when the guy drove by me I raised up a fist and nodded at him: *right on brother!* I figured that would suffice as a daily swim pass. He nodded back. I was in the swim club; he assumed I was in the Trump club. *Bipartisan politics circa April 2020.*

When I headed up to Park City for this trip on October 17, the Trump truck flag party had gone on steroids. Earlier that week I was driving down Scottsdale Road and I saw 100+ Trump trucks head up Scottsdale Road. *Every one of them had a Trump flag.* The new Confederate Army. They were heading north—maybe there was a convention at the Bartlett Lake Marina. I was tempted to flip a bird with an outstretched hand via my sunroof but wisely reconsidered that move. Gave them a double fist pump through the sunroof. *After all, I needed to keep my swim privileges at the marina.*

And then there were the *Trump Zombies.* Perhaps you saw a few of these in your geography as you headed into the 2020 election. Trump Friday Maga Meet-Ups. Reminded me a little of the Hare Krishna movement. In North Scottsdale, every Friday night, a group of Trump supporters would gather at the corner of Alma School Road and Dynamite Road. I have no idea why that corner, but I went by that corner every Friday on my way in and out of the Brown's Ranch Trailhead at the end of Alma School. My Friday afternoon mountain bike escape. It started with 5-10 people and by October it was 50-75 and growing. It was basically a cocktail party with Trump signs and flags. Maybe a tambourine or two. I drove by on the evening of October 16. I live five minutes from the Zombie corner—I smiled and gave them a honk and a cordial fist pump. *Enjoy your Friday night.*

Look, everyone likes to be invited to a party. I get it. The trucks were a little scarier than the Zombie corner, but it was all the same thing. The summer Black Lives Matter protests were real protests. The August 1968 student protests at the Democratic National Convention were real protests. The Trump trucks and street corner gatherings were *social occasions.* But they were a visible sign of the American Divide heading into November. My sense, watching all of this in late October, was that the Trump truck procession was more like a funeral procession and the festivities on the corner were winding down. Don Meredith in the background: *the party's over.*

A Trump truck procession, October 2020

The Whole World is Watching

So, let me introduce you to a few of our 38 Foresighters who had gathered on November 5, in the midst of our *48 Hours—The Whole World is Watching* session:

- "I'm a speaker, author, purpose consultant and mother."
- "Opinion leader, community thought leader. Long time civil servant, trend watcher."
- "Former brand strategy executive, retired (as of March) and working for diversity & economic equity."
- "Arizona based consultant/mentor for exec teams and adjunct instructor in GCU Business School. Father of 3 girls living in NYC and LA."
- "A mature guy who has been in the television and media business my entire career. Currently lead a PBS station in the Midwest."
- "Young marketing and strategy professional with an outgoing personality and optimistic outlook on life."
- "Consultant based in the Midwest, love to cycle, hike and spend time with family."
- "Retired CEO of Int'l Research firm. Married, two children. Love to travel, frustrated now by the COVID. Sports fan. Avid reader. Very interested in the election...need toothpicks today to keep the eyes open!"

Or an energized facilitator.

Where We Stand

I shared the following screen to set the stage:

As of 11:00am EST on November 5 (the start of our session):

No.	Idea
1.	ELECTORAL COLLEGE VOTES: 270 needed to win, Biden leads 253 to 213
2.	STATES STILL UNCALLED (6): Alaska, Arizona, Georgia, Nevada, North Carolina and Pennsylvania
	1. BIDEN leading in Arizona and Nevada
	2. TRUMP leading in Alaska, Georgia, North Carolina and Pennsylvania
3.	LEGAL CHALLENGES: A number of challenges already filed and more are likely, unclear if any will have impact but it may be a while before a final resolution
4.	RESULTS COMING IN REAL-TIME: Voting results are coming in throughout the day with most of the attention on Arizona, Georgia, Nevada and Pennsylvania
5.	POPULAR VOTE: Biden leads 72,161,772 to 68,673,708

We began our session by conducting two *Point of View* activities. Wide open, step up to the virtual mic and let it fly:

POV Question 1: *It's now been about 48 hours since the polls officially opened and the 2020 presidential election day began. Imagine you were being interviewed on your favorite national or local newscast, a set of "focus group" participants reacting to the election and the last 48 hours. How do you interpret the last 48 hours—what did it tell you about the country and the issues we have been dealing with? What's your analysis?*

- "We are very divided as a nation. It is a tight race. Tensions are high. People are scared regardless of the result."
- "The country is more divided than we might have thought. We really need to understand how Americans see our country so differently. Going forward it's going to be a challenge to find a way back together. And BTW, how amazing that we're doing this session while the Presidential vote hangs in the balance and the Senate is 48/48!"

219

- "We are incredibly divided and pollsters were wrong about the Biden landslide. In addition, it appears that there is voter fraud occurring in mostly Democrat run states. Worried about the outcome regardless of who is declared victor."
- "We are deeply divided and largely intractable in our views. The divisions are beyond political affiliation and encompass culture, values, aspirations and behavior."
- "We can no longer see Trump as an aberration. Despite his odiousness, his repugnance and his lying, 68 million people voted for him. We have to find ways to accommodate the view of the world those people see."
- "It tells us the country continues to be more divided than we thought, or perhaps hoped. We are in an unknown point in our election, and it is disappointing to see our current elected official(s) already disputing results of an election that has not yet been called. It says we are a nation divided—not united."
- "We have an undetermined status that appears to be contested before it's over. Hard to know what the final results will be, seems likely Biden will win. Seems likely there are and will be more fights about this. Has been relatively calm thus far, other than crazy Arizona with Trump supporters protesting outside the vote tabulations. Wondering what they think that accomplishes."
- "That we couldn't be more divided. That the party system is a huge failure. That the guy in the White House is the worst in history and I am not even a Democrat. We may be on the verge of a civil war. That most white Americans are racists."
- "As a country we are not 'listening' to each other. It blows me away that 68,000,000 fellow citizens voted for someone even they think is an asshole. Yes, President Trump and most Republicans have inaccurately characterized Democrats as quasi socialists, but that seems to have worked."
- "Uncertainty at every turn. Conflict and clashes over opinions, accusations and conspiracy theories abound. And also a little glimmer of humanity and people remembering (perhaps) that people are people, and that is what is most important. I'm shocked to hear how some friends are reacting to the rolling results of the election. It baffles me to hear the ignorant statements by both sides."
- "Frankly, no surprises. As expected, it is close and chaotic. Disappointed in the fanning the flames of distrust with the process. Turnout reflects tremendous passion about our political situation. Voting trends reflect significant party loyalties and increased partisanship. Trending to reflect a vote leaning toward a rejection of the President relative to the overall support of the Republican party."

220

- "If the United States is the role model to the world of how the democratic process works, we are a big embarrassment this year."
- "The nation is holding its collective breath—waiting to see the election results—with each side trying to imagine what the next four years will look like if their side loses. This moment feels like being stuck outside in a blinding snowstorm—it's hard to know in what direction to proceed."

Pretty much every statement is followed by a mic drop. Looking through the full set of nearly 40 POV statements, there are some very clear themes:

- ✓ Few people have ever seen this country as deeply divided as we are in this election.
- ✓ The most positive aspect of the election thus far is the level of turnout.
- ✓ It's not an election that you just "win and move on". Half of America will not be happy with the outcome.
- ✓ Emotion is fueling the electorate. That can be very dangerous.
- ✓ Despite all of the emotion, the process seems to be holding up so far.

What About "Crazy Arizona"

I resemble that remark. As I was watching the coverage on election night, and texting with family members and friends, it was clear that Arizona was going to be in the national spotlight. Most people assumed Arizona—a traditionally Republican state—was going to be somewhat close but would end up supporting Trump. But the vote was far too close on Tuesday night and now there was a possibility that Arizona could end up supporting Biden. So close that Fox News—a staunch supporter of Trump, actually called the race for Biden on Tuesday night—something that even CNN and other (generally speaking) pro-Biden media outlets were not yet prepared to do.

God, I would have loved to have been a fly on the wall when Fox called the race in Arizona and Trump was watching the tube. The man's head must have exploded.

But if you were paying attention to Arizona, before the election, you might have seen what was coming. I think one person changed this race. One person sent up a flare to say that we had had enough of the Trump show even in Arizona. A staunch Republican stepped up in Arizona.

Cindy McCain.

On September 22, Cindy McCain, the widow of Senator John McCain, endorsed Joe Biden for President, in a very public and impactful rebuke of President Trump:

"I decided to take a stand, and hopefully other people will see the same thing. You may have to step outside of your comfort zone a little bit, but Biden is by far the best candidate in the race. He supports the troops and knows what it means for someone who has served. Not only to love someone who has served, but understands what it means to send a child into combat. We've been great friends for many years, but we have a common thread in that we are Blue Star families."

The AP interview with McCain notes, "Trump has had a fraught relationship with members of John McCain's family since he disparaged the Arizona senator during his 2016 campaign."

Fraught relationship. That would be an epic understatement.

Trump crossed a pretty fundamental line of decency when he famously said during his 2016 campaign of McCain, "He's not a war hero. He's a war hero because he was captured. I like people who weren't captured." McCain famously returned the favor with his dramatic thumbs down vote against the repeal of Obama's health care law on July 28, 2017:

Almost as dramatic as the vote from McCain, is Mitch McConnell's stance with his arms folded. He knows he will be getting a call from Trump in about two seconds.

That Maverick grin

What Trump failed to understand is that you don't mess with *The Maverick*. Not only is McCain a beloved hero/legend in Arizona, but he has a Navy Destroyer named after him (The USS John McCain—DDG 56). The ship's nickname is *Big Bad John*.

USS John McCain (DDG 56)

I think Cindy McCain just asked the crew to fire one more round on John's behalf in 2020.

What Was Really on the Ballot

One thing was very clear on November 3: there was a lot more on the ballot than Biden and Trump. America's future was on the ballot. We asked our Foresighters what they thought was on the ballot:

Question: *We all know that the presidential election was on the ballot (Biden vs. Trump). But this was not a typical presidential election. It was a confluence of powerful movements and issues. WHAT ELSE do you think was on the ballot on November 3?*

In this exercise we generated more than 120 responses and then summarized them real-time into a set of themes. The very length of the summary—26 line items—was an indicator on the scope and complexity of the election and why it would be so influential on the decade ahead:

Now please indicate how important each of the following issues are in terms of influencing the decade ahead (use a scale of 1-10 where a "1" means not at all important and a "10" means extremely important):

Rank	Idea	Avg.
1.	American democracy	9.2
2.	Information vs. disinformation—whether truth can still be seen	9.0
3.	The essence of America—what we stand for	8.9
4.	The character of leadership	8.7
5.	Racial equality	8.5
6.	The economy	8.4
7.	America's role on the world stage	8.3
8.	The future of the Supreme Court	8.2
9.	Balance of power in the Government (Executive/Legislative/Judicial)	8.1
10.	The role of science	8.0
11.	Climate change	7.9

224

12.	A woman's right to choose	7.7
13.	The balance of the right to protest vs. law and order	7.3
14.	ObamaCare (the future of healthcare access)	7.3
15.	The management of the COVID-19 pandemic	7.1
16.	Immigration reform/DACA	7.1
17.	Wealth equality	7.1
18.	Civility	7.0
19.	The role of young voters	6.9
20.	Reducing the Federal deficit	6.5
21.	Taxes	6.5
22.	Social Security solvency	6.4
23.	The process of increased early voting	6.1
24.	Gay rights/gay marriage	5.4
25.	Second amendment rights (bear arms)	4.9
26.	Cannabis (legalization of marijuana)	3.0

And you thought you were just voting for a presidential candidate. We also asked our participants to indicate how influential the issues were to them and their vote personally:

Now please indicate how important each of the following issues were in terms of the degree to which it influenced YOU on your vote or the candidate you supported (use a scale of 1-10 where a "1" means not at all influential and a "10" means extremely influential):

Here are the top ten from the assessment:

Rank	Idea	Avg.
1.	The character of leadership	9.2

225

No.	Items	
2.	The essence of America—what we stand for	**9.1**
3.	American democracy	**8.9**
4.	Information vs. disinformation—whether truth can still be seen	**8.8**
5.	The management of the COVID-19 pandemic	**8.3**
6.	America's role on the world stage	**8.2**
7.	Racial equality	**8.1**
8.	The role of science	**7.8**
9.	The economy	**7.7**
10.	Civility	**7.7**

Rarely has a single election had so much riding on it. The whole world *was* watching this election, it was about the future of America, but also about how America affects the future of the world.

How the 48 Hours are Impacting Us

Now for the second POV question. A two-part question, how the 48 hours have affected your level of optimism for the future and *why*:

Question: *All things considered, as you reflect on the 48 hours since the polls opened, have these 48 hours made you more optimistic or less optimistic about the decade ahead (now through December 2029)?*

No.	Items	Times Selected
1.	**LESS optimistic**	**(45%)**
2.	**MORE optimistic**	**(37%)**
3.	Really has not changed my outlook from where I might have been prior to the election	(18%)

A divided America, why not a divided set of Foresight participants? It's interesting that for more than 80% of our participants, those 48 hours moved the needle from where they were before the election. Here are some explanations about the moves in both directions:

- LESS: "Without meaning to, I believed some aspect of the notion of a blue landslide. This clearly did not happen."
- LESS: "Our country is too divided to accomplish what it needs to."
- LESS: "There is a fundamental disconnect between educated urban voters and less educated rural and small town voters. We lack common dreams for America and our families."
- LESS: "While I thought the election would be close, seeing the sheer number of people who voted for Trump is scary and disappointing. Makes me realize I have a lot less faith in my fellow citizens who can't stand up for basic human rights and choose to stand up for, and defend, a racist, sexist, discriminatory leader."
- LESS: "Slightly less optimistic insofar as it's hard to understand how people can turn such a blind-eye toward so many acts of incompetence, character defects, autocratic tendencies...shows the power of confirmation bias to see what we want to see and ignore any facts to the contrary. Hard to imagine a future where Truth has the power and influence that it once had."
- LESS: "I'm dismayed about the divide in this country. Many are perplexed about how I cast my vote. I am equally perplexed about those voting for someone who appears to suffer from dementia with very questionable financial ties to China. So, while others do not understand my stance (voting for pro-life), I don't understand theirs."

Whew. I think I am glad that this is a virtual session and that I am not in the same room with everyone. Emotion is running a tad high.

- MORE: "At least we are still struggling to choose the right person. A lot of voters came out based on the numbers, which is good. At least it means something to people, I guess."
- MORE: "Voter turnout and engagement. It's as though a sleepy electorate was hit over the head with a 2x4 and is suddenly awake. Now the question is how can we channel that energy and engagement for positive ends."
- MORE: "The election process works. Every four years we can change power in the U.S. peacefully."
- MORE: "Just barely more optimistic. If Biden can pull this out, then I feel an overwhelming relief and a surge of optimism that it's a start. It will take longer than I would like for change, but again, a new president with forward leaning ideas can kick start our country."

227

- MORE: "I am optimistic given how involved many Americans are voicing their opinions, let's hope this continues to happen! I am also optimistic that as a nation we will work together to break the divide that is so apparent in our country. It will be hard work, but can be done!"
- MORE: "Increased voter turn-out is encouraging. Addressing social issues is very front of stage. Lack of character in some leadership is motivating new potential candidates for public office to step forward to all levels of public service."

Finally, there were those who simply felt the election reinforced their existing views:

- SAME: "I saw things that both concerned and encouraged me. Concerned that there was no voter repudiation of Trump and also the systematic efforts in some states to suppress voter turnout. Encouraged that Biden looks to ultimately win and that there was not widespread voter intimidation as threatened by Trump and his supporters."
- SAME: "Seemingly no willingness to work together to address the major issues facing this country."
- SAME: "I hoped otherwise, but what's going on is proof positive that we are a nation divided and one election cycle is not going to magically address it."

While the election had not been called as of our session, it was generally viewed that Biden was likely going to win when all of the votes had been counted and the states called. Even for the Biden supporters, that did not call for unbridled optimism. It would not be a clear mandate. It just seemed to magnify the level of division. Addressing the division, trying to find common ground as Americans, feels like the real challenge of the decade ahead, no matter what side of the aisle you are on.

Surprise, Encouragement and Discouragement

It appears that there was something for everyone in this 48 hours. Rather than lengthy POV statements, we decided to do a quick lightning round with three questions—what *surprised* you, what *encouraged* you and what *discouraged* you. There were very clear themes from the three questions:

What's the ONE BIGGEST SURPRISE to you about the 48 hours you just experienced?

- ✓ That we are here 48 hours after the election with no winner
- ✓ The degree of popular support that Trump has

- ✓ The urban vs. rural divide
- ✓ How wrong the pollsters were in forecasting the election
- ✓ The Arizona surprise in appearing to support Biden
- ✓ The impact of mail-in voting
- ✓ The level of down ballot suport for Republicans
- ✓ The record turnout in voting
- ✓ The lack of a clear mandate against the president
- ✓ The "Blue Wave" never materialized

What were you most ENCOURAGED by in the last 48 hours?

- ✓ The level of civility that we are seeing
- ✓ The sheer interest in the process
- ✓ The level of patience shown by mainstream media
- ✓ The record turnout of voters
- ✓ That states, previously aligned with one party, are open to change
- ✓ The overall integrity of the voting process
- ✓ The commitment of openness of the poll workers
- ✓ The overall diversity of the electorate
- ✓ That the media was willing to show patience
- ✓ The real-time counting and updates

What were you most DISCOURAGED by in the last 48 hours?

- ✓ Not having a definitive result yet
- ✓ The lack of condemnation from the Republican party towards Trump
- ✓ That we are becoming a conspiracy chasing country
- ✓ The armed crowd at the Maricopa County Vote Counting Center in Arizona
- ✓ The attempts to already discredit the voting process
- ✓ That this was the best we could do in terms of presidential candidates
- ✓ That the divide in America is as big as it is
- ✓ Lack of uniformity on how we count ballots
- ✓ The lack of turnout by certain demographics (e.g., black men)
- ✓ The continued role of disinformation

Quote of the series—in responding to the question on what they were most encouraged about:

"That Biden is most likely going to win. As I read this morning, the only way Trump is getting to 270 is if he loses 30 pounds!"

Come on…that was pretty funny.

At the end of the day, elections matter. You can have all of the media commentators share their views, all of the pollsters give it their best shot, look at all of the historical analogs, look at early exit polls. But election day matters. We are at a different and complex point in American history. Every vote, no matter how it was cast, mattered. As it is said in sports, *you still have to play the game.* Stick around for the fourth quarter of this one.

The Consequence of 2020

So how big was this election? Don't they all feel like massive events that will change the future? Let's ask our Foresighters:

Question: *Many have said that, "This is the most consequential election of our lifetime." Reflecting on YOUR lifetime and your awareness of prior presidential elections, do you agree with this or not?*

No.	Items	Times Selected
1.	**Yes, I feel this is the most consequential election of my lifetime**	(81%)
2.	No, I don't feel it is the most consequential election of my lifetime	(19%)

Finally—a clear winner in a vote! This was a group that has seen a few elections in their lifetimes and many that are pretty astute about history, politics and the media. *Most consequential of my lifetime.* It didn't feel at all like that in 2016, at least not to me. Interesting, potentially historical in the sense of a woman president in Hillary Clinton (and a *first dude* in Bill). It was a surprising result, perhaps dismaying for some, but I didn't feel like it was the end of the world. I voted for Hillary, but I didn't love Hillary. *A little goofy for me at times.*

So it wasn't the most consequential in 2016, but Trump won. But now it is the most consequential because *Trump is running.* Someone has been turning up the tension of the Vise-Grip of issues confronting this country.

For those of you younger folks who don't know what a Vise-Grip is, here is a picture. Suffice to say when you lock down the jaws it is really hard to unlock them. America probably feels like it has a big pair of Vise-Grips locked on its...

230

The Classic Vise-Grip by Irwin Tools

Let's move on, shall we? Metaphorically speaking, that one makes me a feel a little uncomfortable.

So, for those who indicated it is the most consequential election, here were the explanations:

- YES: "It is the one I remember caring the most about, feeling passionate about."
- YES: "Yes, we have reached a moral watershed."
- YES: "Because Trump is the most consequential and comprehensive disaster in my lifetime."
- YES: "No doubt; this was an opportunity to repudiate not just Trump as a leader, but an entire leadership style that others will emulate for a long time to come."
- YES: "I find that people value their own political issues more than they value decency and that is a shocking realization, and can lead to even more polarization and inequality."
- YES: "I have never felt as much pressure and obligation to vote as in this election."
- YES: "We have reached a tipping point. Are we going to revere leaders who threaten our democratic republic, or are we going to reject it for leaders with vision for the country and its complexities?"
- YES: "We are in a pandemic that is about to approach a horrible period, with a current president that has disregarded science and lacks compassion for all citizens. The pandemic and economy are interrelated, and without solutions that take both into consideration, we will fail as a nation. Not sure the nation could withstand four more years of this."
- YES: "The 2008 election was important because it was a changing of the guard. But this just feels like more is on the line. I don't think the world can handle four more years of this circus, which is tearing apart our institutions."

And just when you thought it was safe to go outside, along comes a sobering thought for the future:

- NO: "This always gets said every four years. Prediction: the presidential race in 2024 will be the most consequential election in our lifetime."

And I have to admit: that actually may be the case in 2024.

Enduring Outcomes From the 2020 Election

If indeed this was the most consequential election of our lifetimes, then surely there must be *enduring outcomes* as a result. I am not speaking of the person who will be elected (our Foresighters have a 90% confidence level that Biden will eke this out within the next 48 hours), but the implications of what we have experienced will likely influence our decade ahead.

We looked at both the positive enduring outcomes as well as the negative enduring outcomes. First, the *positive enduring outcomes:*

Question: *Regardless of which candidate will emerge to win, we'd like you to consult on what you feel will be the enduring outcomes of the 2020 election cycle. Think about the full year and what has occurred: the party nomination process, the role of sports, civil unrest, the role of media (mainstream and social), how voting methods changed, final debates and their coverage, gender and race issues and crisis management. What do you feel are the POSITIVE enduring outcomes from this election cycle?*

For this activity we solicited open responses and then did a real time summary of the themes:

Positive Enduring Outcomes (not prioritized)

No.	Idea
1.	Increased voter turnout
2.	The role of early voting
3.	Recognition of the importance of racial equality for the future
4.	Younger generations getting involved in the election issues
5.	Civic participation in the key issues

No.	Idea
6.	The political influence of sports teams/players
7.	Law and order matters
8.	The importance of civil debates
9.	Climate change on the agenda
10.	New ways of reaching/engaging voters

Looking at the opposite side, the *negative enduring outcomes:*

Question: *Now, still thinking about the full year, what do you feel are the NEGATIVE enduring outcomes from this election cycle?*

Similarly, for this activity we solicited open responses and then did a real time summary:

Negative Enduring Outcomes (not prioritized)

No.	Idea
1.	The influence of dis-information
2.	A nation divided
3.	Inability for the two party system to find meaningful compromise
4.	Uncivil behavior becoming accepted
5.	Pressure on the electoral system as the determinant of voting in the future
6.	Whether debates really matter
7.	The continued lack of trust in the government and major institutions
8.	Violence as a way of pushing agendas
9.	A politicized Supreme Court
10	Self interest over national interest

Glass half empty or half full for the decade ahead? How would you assess the positives vs. the negatives? We asked our Foresighters:

Question: *All things considered as you reflect the overall set of enduring outcomes that may be a result of the 2020 election cycle, do the positives outweigh the negatives or vice-versa?*

No.	Items	Times Selected
1.	**The negatives somewhat outweigh the positives**	**(41%)**
2.	**The positives somewhat outweigh the negatives**	**(24%)**
3.	The negatives far outweigh the positives	(16%)
4.	The positives and negatives largely balance out	(14%)
5.	The positives far outweigh the negatives	(5%)

This is fairly easy to read: 65% of the participants were in the *somewhat outweigh* category. That just means it is too early to tell. I'll take that as a win for America. Here is some selected rationale from our Foresighters:

- NEGATIVES SOMEWHAT: "The division aspect is more dangerous than a good voter turnout. At least in the short term."
- NEGATIVES SOMEWHAT: "In my opinion, as a nation what makes us so unique is that people can (supposedly) freely share their opinions and views, now if we the people can't freely express who we are and our views because of intolerance, what does America even stand for?"
- NEGATIVES SOMEWHAT: "One election cycle will not fix the pandemic, systemic racism, climate change, perceived entitlement and disenfranchisement of white people, etc. . . . we have a LOT of work to do."
- NEGATIVES SOMEWHAT: "The negative influence of fake news spread through social media is ruining our ability to think, discern and make reasonable choices. It is tearing apart relationships, families and communities caught in the grips of misinformation fueling hate/fear."
- NEGATIVES SOMEWHAT: "Unfortunately, the extremist viewpoints are splitting the country apart. No common sources of information anymore and lack of trust."

- POSITIVES SOMEWHAT: "I still have faith in the goodwill of the American people and their desire to continually create the 'shining city on a hill'."

- POSITIVES SOMEWHAT: "Despite Biden being a relatively weak candidate, he was able to get the victory; if the Dems had supported a more leftist candidate this might not have happened, so they were willing to sacrifice some of their more controversial points to get Trump out..."
- POSITIVES SOMEWHAT: "We are Americans and can figure this out. We have to learn to work together regardless of party affiliation."
- POSITIVES SOMEWHAT: "Well, it can only get better. I have to hope the Lincoln Project plays a role in the future, and we become more balanced."
- POSITIVES SOMEWHAT: "Again, if Biden wins, I believe the turn toward civility will begin, with, finally, a civil president who knows how to interact with people. Then I believe, if this happens, slowly but surely he will surround himself with people dedicated to a future that will help our planet."

- BALANCED: "More voters is good. More misinformed voters is not good. Not sure how we get voters to more critically filter the messages that they receive, whether by domestic or foreign sources."
- BALANCED: "Regardless of who wins, victory comes with many issues. It is difficult to feel very positive about anything after this whole kerfuffle..."

And I rarely feel positive after a *kerfuffle*.

Improving National Elections

One thing is for sure. This election had some serious dynamics to it and we already look at some enduring outcomes—both positive and negative. Keep in mind that every country on the planet conducts national elections (perhaps some fair, and some not...). But we should lead the world on how to do it right. Participation, technology support, security, balanced media coverage, etc. So we were curious about how our Foresighters would *improve* our national elections.

Question: *I hate to tell you this. There are going to be two more presidential elections in the decade ahead (2024 and 2028), and congressional elections every two years along with annual state elections. Let's just focus on the national elections (presidential and congressional) which, by and large, determine the policy leadership of our country. How do we IMPROVE national elections in the decade ahead?*

It's a relevant question for our focus on the decade ahead. It does sound exhausting but we have two more presidential elections ahead this decade. We took some 85 open responses and did a real-time summary of the themes and then assessed the list:

Now, please indicate how effective (assuming they were implemented) each of the following approaches might be in improving national elections in the decade ahead. Use a scale of 1-10 where a "1" means not at all effective and a "10" means very effective:

Rank	Idea	Avg.
1.	Better fact checking	8.1
2.	Better process for declaring winning states	7.2
3.	Better debate formats	6.9
4.	Make election day a national holiday	6.9
5.	Leave electoral college behind	6.9
6.	No more political action committees (PACs)	6.8
7.	More people engaged in local level voting	6.7
8.	More vetting of candidates	6.6
9.	Enforce term limits	6.3
10.	Better info on party platforms	6.2
11.	More time for in-person votes	6.1
12.	Eliminate robo calls	5.9

Better fact checking. A point above anything else. What if our national elections were guided by information and not *disinformation.* I get that we have a responsibility to be an informed electorate, but you should have some expectation that someone running for the *President of the United States of America* and their political party and campaign team will tell you the truth. Let us battle it out on policies and approaches, but at least base your platform on facts not *PACs.*

Some observations from our participants:

- "Sunday elections. Fact checking. Mute button for debates."
- "A more streamlined way to count/process votes in each state. Mail-in voting is here to stay."
- "Innovate secure on-line voting."
- "Federal mandates on how federal elections are handled."
- "Have a more cohesive national voting and vote-counting process agreed to at the state level."
- "Make election day a national holiday, give people the day to vote."
- "National fact-checking site where people can easily turn to find the facts/truth of a situation."
- "Adopt term limits, abolish the two party system in favor of 'ranked choice voting'. Invite young people into the process and people of color. Stop trying to implement voter suppression."
- "The electoral college needs to go the way of Trump University."
- "There should be a centralized single authority declaring states being won...not multiple biased news outlets."
- "Uniform early voting windows with consistent rules. No characterizing election results in any state before 60 percent of both early and day of votes are counted. Ultimately, mandatory spending limits based on public financing for all campaigns would be most helpful."

All things considered, the 2020 election appears to have been executed quite well. More people engaged in voting, new voting methods, good security, a more patient media and *exceptionally* committed local polling workers and election officials. Healthcare workers will still get the award for their commitment and compassion in 2020, but hats off to all of you who worked the tireless hours with cameras and "poll observers" in your face.

The concern we should all have is how the political parties, consultants and politicians themselves will look to game the system four years from now. *Maybe they should check with the Houston Astros.*

Political Influence Scenarios

Customary in our Foresight sessions, we bring a few ideas to the table. *Potential influence scenarios* for the decade ahead.

Now, please assess each of the following future scenarios in two ways. First, the level of positive IMPACT to the future of America in the decade ahead if the scenario was to occur (use a scale of 1-10 where a "1" means a very low level of positive impact and a "10" means a very high level of posi-

tive impact); Second, the **LIKELIHOOD that this scenario will fully material-ize in the decade ahead (use a scale of 1-10 where a "1" means a very low likelihood and "10" means a very high likelihood):**

Here is how our Foresight session assessed the list. The scenarios are ordered by the *level of positive impact* but then contrasted with the likeli-hood of occurrence for a gap analysis rating:

#	Scenario Description	Im-pact	Like-ly	Gap
1	BIPARTISANSHIP COMES BACK IN STYLE: 2020 showed that we had put the needs of Americans at risk while we gridlocked many key issues. The decade ahead showed a slow but steady return to a level of bipartisanship where crossing the aisle meant you were will-ing to put American issues above party is-sues.	9.3	4.5	(4.7)
2	MEDIA RETURNED TO A ROLE OF IN-FORMING: Mainstream media and, in many cases, social media, recognized that an in-formed electorate moves America in the right direction. The media understood the danger of mis-information and dis-information to the values and security of the country and dou-bled down on informing rather that influenc-ing. A level of trust returned to the media.	9.0	4.1	(4.9)
3	AMERICA'S STATURE ON THE GLOBAL STAGE RETURNED: The balance was struck between our important self interests as a country and the importance of American lead-ership and influence in world issues and events. Not everyone likes us, but we are re-spected in our leadership role. Our allies (new and old) value this role and a renewed com-mitment to partnerships.	8.8	6.2	(2.6)

4	YOUNGER LEADERSHIP STEPS FORWARD: While it's OK to have some elder statesmen in the picture, it was clear that we had gone too far. A fresh set of younger leaders stepped forward, many in their late twenties and early thirties, to provide new energy and ideas for America's future. It was like entrepreneurism meets politics. It was disruptive but effective. These young leaders will be influencing the future for an entire new generation.	8.4	7.3	(1.1)
5	CIVICS RETURNS TO THE CLASSROOM: Government and education leaders realized that too many young people were not taught the fundamentals of civics in the classroom nor that the vital role that exercising civic responsibilities matters for everyone. Civics became a required educational component in middle school/high school and it influenced more young people to be engaged in community/government issues and increased young voter turnout.	8.4	5.8	(2.6)
6	WE STOPPED TALKING ABOUT GENDER/RACE/DIVERSITY: Not that we didn't care and value diversity, it's just that diversity was simply accepted. Leaders were leaders, lives were lives. We turned an important corner in American history in the decade ahead and fully embraced all that a diverse people can provide.	8.3	4.0	(4.3)
7	SCHOOL'S OUT FOR THE ELECTORAL COLLEGE: It was a spirited debate but the country left the electoral college behind in the decade ahead and the popular vote was used for Presidential elections. It served to increase the perceived value of the individual vote (my vote matters) and helped support strong and consistent voter turnout.	7.8	4.1	(3.7)

8	ONLINE VOTING FINALLY ARRIVES: While in person and mail-in voting are still options, we have implemented online voting for all state and national elections. It's simple, secure and it has measurably increased voting turnout. Clear processes are in place (i.e., voting begins 30 days prior to the election and stops on election evening). You are given a clear confirmation that your vote has been received and validated.	7.8	6.1	(1.7)
9	A NEW AMERICAN PARTY EMERGES: Frustrated by the lack of bipartisanship and disillusionment with the traditional two-party system, a new party/movement emerged in the decade ahead called the "American Party". It developed a set of values, principles and platform issues that drew in many independents but also attracted forward thinking Democrats and Republicans. It was not a fad, and a New American Agenda emerged and was largely enacted upon as result.	7.4	4.3	(3.1)
10	SPORTS REALLY LEARNED TO PLAY: The 2020 election showed the power of sports in engaging in social and political issues that mattered to the players and their leagues. Sports became a powerful influencer on issues in America (and globally) and candidates and their parties sought out their support and endorsements. It's what we play for and what we stand for.	4.8	5.2	+0.4

Pretty interesting. 9 of the 10 potential influences rate 7.4+ on the potential impact, while *none* of the 10 rate as a 7.4+ in terms of likelihood. In fact, on the issue of sports in politics and social issues, its likelihood is higher than its impact. *Don't tell Lebron.*

We can see what could have impact, but the divide in America, our entrenchment, our political realities and biases constrain our ability to make progress. But we are mere pollsters here, and remember that the pollsters were way off for most of the election cycle. *It's why we play the game, it's why we engage in the decade ahead.*

Here is what we must tackle. Look at the top seven gaps between impact and likelihood:

1. Media returned to a role of informing (4.9)
2. Bipartisanship comes back in style (4.7)
3. We stopped talking about gender/race/diversity (4.3)
4. School's out for the electoral college (3.7)
5. A new America party emerges (3.1)
6. America's stature on the global stage returned (2.6)
7. Civics returns to the classroom (2.6)

We've dealt with media in a prior chapter—we understand the gap and also what media—mainstream and social—could do to change the game. It's just frightening to see the low level of confidence that we can make progress on the issue. I have more optimism on this than others, but I see the challenge. Getting to genuine diversity acceptance in this country seems way harder. Maybe a little more optimistic on the gender side, but 2020 showed just how divided we are on race/ethnicity and how one person can set us back years. Let's hope the reverse is true. And bipartisanship to round out the top three. Don't hold your breath, just keep voting in a younger generation of leaders who understand that this is how we move the country forward. Common ground and shared ideas for success.

Five Reflections on Finding Common Ground in America in the Decade Ahead:

1. A RETURN TO COMMON VALUES: Americans have historically had different points of view but shared common values. Respect for family, respect for hard work, a value of independence, how we can come together in times of need, American ingenuity, willing to give a neighbor a hand when needed. We need a return to common values. If you immigrate here, you need to respect and be part of those values. Decency matters.
2. POLITICS WITH A PURPOSE: We have a huge number of challenges in the decade ahead. Climate change, education reform, healthcare access, economic development, global politics. There is no reason that two political parties can't agree on a shared agenda of common issues for the country. It's called a Venn Diagram. That intersection is what we agree to do together.
3. DROP THE DIVIDE: Urban vs. Rural, Black vs. White, Wealth vs. Poor. We live in the most amazing country on the globe; try a few of the others if you don't believe me. Just drop the division. That doesn't mean America becomes socialist. If you don't want to get educated and work hard, figure it out another way. We

241

give you access and opportunity, you can live your life the way you want. On the ranch or in the city.

4. PREPARE FOR THE NEXT DECADE: Guess what? Other countries want what we have. Economic prosperity, technology superiority, transportation efficiency. We really do need to rebuild our infrastructure for the decade ahead. And we need every able-bodied American to get that done. Set some bold goals, restore the great American Dream, grab some global expertise and land them here.

5. AMERICANS SERVE THEIR COUNTRY: Our previous generations understood the importance of serving their country. I so respect young people today who have chosen to serve America. *Thank you for your service.* Every young American needs to create an individual service plan. Healthcare work, military service, Peace Corps, be a volunteer in a school, run for office. There is no racial, sexual, gender or faith prerequisite for that job.

The Whole World's Watching: Dear World

I couldn't resist this one. If the premise of this session was that the whole world was watching our election in 2020 and the cycle we have gone through, then perhaps our Foresighters had a message for the world:

Question: *Now, imagine it is the end of the year, a final reflection on December 31. The whole world really was watching this election and the impact it would have on America. As you reflect on how the election played out, how people reacted, how America reacted, what would you tell the world about this election and what it meant, and what it said?*

DEAR WORLD...

- "We're back! Sorry for the weirdness and inappropriateness of the last four years, but you can start to count on us again."
- "While democracy can be chaotic, passionate and confusing, the system we have in place always works out the way it was designed to work."
- "Dear World, Biden's election reflected that most of us Americans care about the soul of the nation and are willing to support a candidate who promises to restore that soul."
- "Dear World, please don't think that Trump reflects all of our thoughts; it was only half of ours, which is horrifying in and of itself. However, we are moving back towards a rational, reasonable being. We will not have random tweets in the middle of the night or espouse lies every time we open our mouths. We welcome you back to a non-altered reality."

- "Dear World, we don't have our shit together. Sorry about that. Democracy is messy and imperfect. Let's remember what President Obama said about the moral arc of the universe being long and bending toward justice. Let's keep that in mind and take it to heart even as we struggle with the short term."
- "Dear World...we are actually good people. The president that was in office the past four years doesn't truly represent us. We want to be inclusive, we want to work together, we want to tackle important global issues together with you. Please don't judge us for our bad decisions, we want to make it right."
- "Dear World, please forgive us for we know not what we do. Grant us the strength, resiliency, compassion and wisdom to do our part for the greater good."
- "America is divided. This is uncomfortable but it happens periodically in a democracy. We have had a very divisive president for four years who drove people further apart, although he did not necessarily create the divisions. America is trying to turn the corner with a more unifying president, but unity will not happen quickly."
- "We are not really as screwed up as it looked. We can and should get better. Hang with us..."

Remember—we can either hang together or hang separately. I think the world has seen this movie play out a time or two. I think America has a deep reservoir of good will with the world. I personally think America will be back on track with the world by the end of 2021.

The Impact of COVID on the 2020 Election

We always ask our participants how COVID—as we consider the decade ahead through the lens of a 2020 global pandemic—affected the subject of the session. From my personal POV, it not only affected it, it decided it. No pandemic, no problem for Trump. At least in terms of a final election outcome. Here's what our participants said:

- "Well, it just added to the divide."
- "It probably cost Trump re-election...There is a God?"
- "It has delivered mail-in voting more broadly in the U.S., thereby increasing convenience and voter participation."
- "Increased mail-in votes. Increased fear. More blame on government for not doing more or not doing enough. Increased polarization between parties—masks or no masks. All of it has added to the tension."

- "It's turned science into a partisan issue. Have heard from Republican family members that COVID was manufactured by world leaders to see how much control they could exert over people's lives...so they don't wear a mask as a sign of personal liberty and freedom. Huh?"
- "It is the only reason there was a close election and possibly a change in leadership. The failure of leadership in this pandemic is the only reason there might be a change in leadership."
- "I think it played an important role, but only by a small margin. I don't think that most people voted one way or the other because of the pandemic. But I do think a small group of people changed their vote because of it, which in some states, especially in the Midwest, helped tip the scales."

Pandemics should not be politicized. Drop everything and lead. *There are lives in the balance.* If Trump had turned his ego down and *led for one year* he would have been re-elected for four. It's that simple. And he actually did in two respects: Operation Warp Speed probably saved the world (to a certain degree) with the acceleration of vaccine development. The economic stimulus efforts with the Paycheck Protection Program, SBA Economic Injury Disaster Loans and the direct stimulus payments probably saved our economy from collapse. He just forgot about the people. A consistent policy on how to protect Americans with simple measures like mask wearing. It cost *hundreds of thousands of lives* and cost him an election.

He can run again in 2024. We don't get the lives back.

How it Played Out After the 48 Hours

On Friday, November 6, I headed back from Park City to Arizona. Still no final call on the election, but a Biden election seemed imminent. America was actually pretty chill. No riots in the streets, no civil war. The Trump trucks were there, but a little subdued. I know the Zombies were on the street corners but it was kind of like your last semester in college...nice to see everyone but reality was around the corner.

On Saturday I was at Tusayan outside of the entrance to the Grand Canyon. My son Sam was running a trail half marathon with some friends, one of the first events I had seen staged since April. I was at the 11 mile mark, I had ridden my mountain bike. I was just waiting for him and I had lots of time to wait: he and a friend had taken a wrong turn at mile six and added about five miles before they realized they were off trail. Peaceful out. Texts started coming in. It was official, CNN and other outlets had made the call. Biden would win the final electoral vote 306 to 232.

Arizona's 11 electoral votes went to Biden. I swear I looked up at the billowy Arizona clouds and saw John McCain. That impish grin was back. No words were needed.

I was pretty exhausted after the week, the session, the 48 hours. This stuff mattered to me and I know it mattered to everyone, regardless of what side you were on. I had committed to myself that I would hike a few hours in the Grand Canyon that day and test out the rehab on my knee, now over a year since a torn quad. I know the Canyon well. I hike it every year, stay at Phantom Ranch, get off the digital grid. I have a lifetime National Parks pass, courtesy of my daughter, and I cruised through the south entrance of the park. As I headed towards Grand Canyon Village and my favorite parking place near Bright Angel Lodge, the cloudy skies parted. I had the sun roof open (I always do) and had just gotten to the edge of the rim—I still had about 5-10 minutes before getting to the actual village.

Sometimes a song comes on the radio at the right time. You know me, I am a bit nostalgic about my music. This one was from the Beatles:

Little darling, it's been a long, cold, lonely winter
Little darling, it seems like years since it's been here

Here comes the sun do, do, do
Here comes the sun
And I say it's all right

Little darling, I feel that ice is slowly melting
Little darling it seems like years since it's been clear

Here comes the sun

--The Beatles, Here Comes the Sun (1969)

There were quite a few people on Bright Angel trail that afternoon. I only had time to get down to the three-mile rest house and then head back. The sun was out for a while, then the clouds would come back. A little early sleet/snow, and then the sun again. I think McCain was still messing with us, just having fun up there. I could see it, though, in people's eyes as I passed them on the trail—me going down, them going up, then the reverse. They all knew. Something had changed, a load had been lifted. We were still in a pandemic, but it felt like we had a little wind at our backs.

I drove back home on Arizona 64 south towards Williams. Pretty classic Arizona. Rural country, farms and ranches and a lot of open space. By and large Trump country. But I went by one big ranch and noticed a big American flag in front of the ranch. Not unusual. What was unusual was that a lot of the other ranches were flying a Trump flag as well, but he was not. I smiled. No way of really knowing, but I was thinking that this rancher decided one flag was enough in 2020. I think he made the right choice. Doesn't mean he might not consider another flag in the future. But for now, November 7, 2020, we were all flying the same colors.

Author and Sam Griffen—Tusayan Trail

Bright Angel Trail, November 7, 2020

CHAPTER 8: Get Smart! The Future of Education and Learning

No more pencils
No more books
No more teachers, dirty looks
Out for summer
Out 'till fall
We might not come back at all

School's out for summer
School's out forever
School's out with fever
School's out completely

--Alice Cooper, School's Out (1972)

December 12, 2020
Foresight 2030 Session

Alice Cooper's *School's Out* was a bit of a national anthem for young people in the 1970s. He may have been one of the first to formally declare that there is something fundamentally wrong with the American school system and approach to education. I don't think he was *really* focused on education reform, but school was part of the establishment and anything associated with the establishment in the 1970s was fair game. And how eerie was the line that *School's out with fever* when we think about 2020 and the pandemic. Alice wrote this in 1972.

The Complaint Against Education

My daughter Betsy is a complainer. She carries that as a badge of honor. She is *really good at it*. Tune her in at FM station K-MPLN. But she mixes in good humor with it so it is both expected and tolerable. One day when she was in high school she was on a real tear about school and education. The teachers were all against her. The classes were *stupid*. Some of her classmates were *just the worst*. The text books were so outdated. The assignments were just *too hard*.

"Betsy," I said, in my best fatherly voice (low and stoic) to a high school daughter, "you think education is hard, try not having one."

Oh, that was good for the dadster. Epic. Impactful. Betsy just looked back at me, somewhat quizzical: "*Whatever.*"

To Betsy's credit, she went on to earn the highest credential of any member of the *Griff Squad*. She earned her doctorate in Physical Therapy and now wears the coveted white jacket and practices in the Bay Area.

She recently called me to complain about her work commute across the Bay Bridge.

A more well-known complainer in education was James T. Hart in <u>The Paper Chase</u>. Released in 1973, a terrific movie about the rigors of law school. The student (James Hart) was played by Timothy Bottoms and the stoic/traditionalist law professor, Charles W. Kingsfield Jr., was played brilliantly by John Houseman. My brother Bruce, the lawyer in the family, advises that the movie is required viewing by any budding law student.

The classic complaint comes in the classroom as the pressure of the first year law course at Harvard is really mounting. Hart *complains* and gives Professor Kingsfield a flippant answer to a legal question. Kingsfield calls the young law student to his desk, a full class of student *witnesses* look on:

KINGSFIELD: "Mr. Hart. Here is a *dime*. Take it, call your mother, and tell her there is serious doubt about you ever becoming a lawyer."

The classic scene in <u>The Paper Chase</u>. "Here is a dime…"

248

The Real Complaint: The System is Broken

Look, education is hard. It's *supposed to be* hard. But it is also supposed to prepare you for your work and life ahead. Some people will not want to work hard, and that is on them. Your chance of getting *anywhere* without a decent educational base is a steep uphill climb and many will give up the hike far too early.

But many in America simply don't get the chance to even get started on their educational journey. Little or no access to early childhood education that prepares them for learning. Poor educational facilities and marginal instruction in traditional K-12 classes. Many never graduate from high school. Many never get the chance to go to college and, if they do, they are often unprepared for the rigors and then find themselves with a mountain of debt. Many do not understand the emerging set of *educational pathways* that include vocational training as alternatives to a traditional four-year college experience.

And even if the *student* gets it right, is a hungry learner and ready to put in the hard work, the American educational system seems to be failing in front of our eyes.

Here are a few educational stats (a quick scan of online articles) to get us warmed up for the chapter:

- ✓ 30 years ago, America was the leader in quantity and quality of high school diplomas. Today, our nation is ranked 36th in the world.
- ✓ Every year 1.3 million high school students don't graduate on time.
- ✓ Students who graduated from college in 2019 had an average debt load of $29,800.
- ✓ 14% of new teachers resign by the end of the their first year; 33% leave within the first 3 years and 50% leave by their fifth year.
- ✓ A third grade student who does not read at an appropriate reading level for the third grade, compared to a student who does, is four times less likely to graduate by age 19.
- ✓ Only 1 in 4 high school students graduate *college ready* in the four core subjects of English, Reading, Math and Science.
- ✓ 90% of new jobs require some level of college/post-secondary education.
- ✓ Roughly half of the students who enter a four-year school will receive a bachelor's degree within six years.

Oh, there are so many things wrong with that last statement!

In the decade ahead, we need to *completely rethink* our approach to education, from early childhood education to the role of traditional K-12 systems to expanding the pathways to the workforce coming out of education. Not everyone needs to—nor wants to—go to a traditional four-year college or university. We need to take away the stigma of the blue collar professions. Surgeons are skilled workers who use their hands. Welders are skilled workers who use their hands. Both need good educations, and our system needs to have the *foresight* and flexibility to support a full range of educational needs that enable people to be ready for the workforce and for life in general.

How American Students Are Holding Up in 2020

Our *Foresighters* have largely recovered from the stress and emotion of our November session covering the presidential election. I am sure they are up to the task of rethinking American education. I wonder, though, how our *students* who are part of the American education system are faring. Heading into the pandemic, most of them were already hitting the wall at some point.

A survey by the American College Health Association in the spring of 2018 found, "Almost two-thirds of college students said they had experienced 'overwhelming anxiety' within the previous 12 months. Almost 57% reported higher than average stress levels." Further, the survey noted that—among students seeking help from counseling centers—"anxiety and depression were the most common *complaints*."

And now most of them have come back to the *home dormitory*. At least for the holidays. The CDC advises, "Amid national spikes in COVID-19 cases and hospitalizations, the agency recommends that people avoid mingling with people who have not resided in their household for the last 14 days. As cases in the United States surpass 11 million, CDC officials worry that the situation could worsen during the holiday season."

School's out completely.

Let me introduce you to a few of our highly educated and stress-free Foresighters for the session on the future of education and learning:

- "Philanthropic consultant helping clients achieve their missions and the greater cool, a philanthropic activist."
- "I am a retired RN and am enjoying retirement immensely! I golf, run, hike, read—all those sports one can do while being isolated."
- "I'm a strategic planner, facilitator and speaker on topics of public participation and customer engagement."

250

- "I work in the automotive industry and live in Michigan. I have two children—a boy who is 8 years old and a daughter who is almost 2 years old. I've been married to my wonderful husband for 9 years."
- "I am an artist/artisan/educator. I have my own business in the design, engineering and manufacture of clothing and accessories for women (and a few men). I prefer to make wearable art clothing, but also make tailored clothing."
- "Work globally from California's Central Coast. Founder and CEO of a full service marketing agency dedicated to lifestyle and hospitality industries. Enjoy hiking and biking in the surrounding trails and exploring the area's wine country."
- "Market researcher, New Englander, *tired*."

Tired? Of what? Being a market researcher? Being a New Englander? Have the *complaints* begun already? *Here's a dime…*

But it is a terrific group. Forty-two Foresighters, an even mix of gender, a really *smart* group with 93% having at least a college degree and 64% possessing an *advanced degree*. Twenty-seven advise they are *optimists*, 13 are *realists* and two admit to being *pessimists*. Over 70% are parents, so they should have some good stories about the challenges of education.

Reflecting on My Education Pathway

How did I get to where I am today? *The existential questions are beginning to creep back in.* But it's a fair question for all of us, especially as it relates to our education experiences and their influence on where we ended up in work and life. Was it environment that influenced all of the experiences—where you lived, your family structure, your income and access, the quality of schools in your system, etc.? Or did you change that environment—how you learned, how hard you worked in class, the extra reading you did, how you created your high school experience, how you approached the decision of where to go to college and even if you wanted to go to college? And some of you reading this book (*advanced learners!*) are still in high school/college—how will you decide your next steps?

Like many in my *boomer* generation, our family was pretty influential on our education decisions. I think I had a bit of a head start on expectations. My mother, Barbara, went to Smith College in Northampton, Massachusetts, a private liberal arts women's college. My father, Frank, went to West Point, the U.S. Military Academy in New York, some 50 miles north of New York City on the Hudson. Both served in the military in

World War II. Education was not a given for their peers; *their* families influenced their choices and commitments. That education allowed them to serve their country and, later, allowed them to head west to Arizona and settle into a good middle class lifestyle.

The first decision I had to make about education happened to me in kindergarten. Seriously. My mother was a homemaker at the time but she had mandated that the three Griffen boys (I was the youngest of the three) would attend a good pre-school kindergarten. I actually remember it quite well: *Tutor Hall.* Pretty close to a full day—get dropped off in the morning, carry a *very cool* metal lunch box, get picked up in the afternoon. An early childhood education for me and my brothers and some sanity for the madre during the day.

And then they called my mother into the principle's office one day. *This cannot be good, even in pre-school.* But it was good. They wanted me to take a special test to see if I should skip the next year of kindergarten. *I am all for skipping school, this is like an early opportunity for Ferris Bueller's Day Off.* And, in the Spring of 1961, I am a robust five years old and seated in front of an *entrance exam* for first grade.

I actually remember the test...comparing long words to see if they were the same, picking out certain objects, some simple arithmetic, reacting to written paragraphs. And the good news is that I passed the test. The bad news is that I was supposed to decide whether to skip the next year of kindergarten and head into *post-pre-school graduate school:* first grade. And my mother—seriously—bows out of the discussion. *It's up you, Dougie.* Dougie? It's *Doug,* Madre. So I decide right then and there we drop the Dougie at Kindergarten and pack the Doug and move on to the big time.

So now I am the youngest person in every class from first grade to senior in high school. But kind of a cool badge of honor. Except that I didn't get to drive until my last semester in high school.

I had a great elementary school and public high school experience. Madison Simis and Madison Rose Lane for elementary. Well rounded—good classes, great teachers, lots of good friends. Plenty of time for PE (physical education) and sports. All the boys took shop, the girls took home economics. *I did say traditional, did I not?* But on the subject of shop, we all learned to *make things.* How to use a drill and a saw, sand wood and plastic, build a bookshelf, hammer a nail.

252

And the other interesting thing about our shop in elementary school is that *behind the shop* is where the school fights were. A little out of the way, hard for the teachers to see it. *Meet you behind shop, butt-head.* Mostly I was a spectator, but I ended up 1-0 in my career. Went against Dale Howk, notorious for his choke hold. Had defeated many a bigger adversary. Onto the ground after some preliminary punches, and sure enough, he is on top of me and had me in the choke hold. *It's over, murmured the crowd.* I am about to black out when I grab his elbow and twist him straight down and over (reversal) so he is now on his back and I am on top. The *death-grip* is released. I take a few short celebratory, soft, punches to his face (we were friends, mostly) and proudly ask...*do you give?! Well, do ya?*

I would later become a varsity wrestler in high school.

Central High School, one of the largest in the Phoenix Union High School district. Seven-hundred-fifty in my senior class. How absolutely cool this was. Big campus, modern classrooms, a great generation of class-mates to be with. Most of my friends were big-time athletes—we played together in grade school and the grade school coaches and PE teachers would let the high school coaches know who was the next quarterback, point guard or pitcher. I tried a lot of things my freshman year: tennis, swimming, track, wrestling and cross-country. I stayed with wrestling and was pretty damn good. My friend Dale Howk would become the top cross-country runner for Central. My friends on the football team (it is good to have friends on the football team) would win the state championship my senior year. We sipped *Bacardi 151* watching the games from the stands, but it was all a classic high school experience.

I enjoyed my classes. I graduated 21st out of 750. In those days, everything changed after high school. And I guess it still does. The friends that you grew up with from grade one through your senior year in high school all head off in different directions. No social media; maybe you would see them in the summer, but usually only at the high school reunion. *My fiftieth will be coming up in 2023.* I'll be there.

So I have three choices on what to do next. *Door Number 1:* I have applied to some of the Ivy League schools (the intellectual in me) and I am *wait-listed* at Dartmouth. A nod to my mother. Cool campus, very New Englandy.

Door number 1

Door Number 2: I go down to Mexico fairly often with my friends to Rocky Point and scuba dive, hit the beach, sample a little *Jose Cuervo*. One of my brother's friends tells me about the Universidad de Las Americas in Puebla, Mexico. Well known for its programs in international business. *Interesante.* I apply and am accepted.

Door number 2

Door Number 3: We all need a backup, what we refer to in negotiations as a BATNA (Best Alternative To a Negotiated Agreement). My BATNA is Northern Arizona University. Two-and-a-half hours away in Flagstaff and also where both of my brothers went for their undergraduate education. I get an academic full-ride scholarship. I think the madre likes this door.

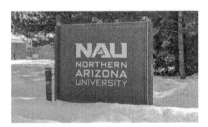

Door number 3

It's only my second real choice on what to do in education. My first was skipping the year in kindergarten, really an easy, but very influential, decision in my life. *Never looked back on that one.* But, shit, three doors *is* a dilemma. I can make a good case for each door. I am feeling a bit of stress now. I take myself off the Dartmouth waiting list. *You should have just accepted me in the first place.* I am envisioning driving my 1966 Ford Bronco (half cab, roll bar, Muntz 8 track stereo, tow bar on the front... *should have kept that one...*) from Arizona to Puebla (about 100 km southeast of Mexico City). What a drive that would be. I imagined that I would write my first book: *Mexico on a Shoestring.* As in a shoestring budget, like no money at all. The book cover would be me bouncing along a dirt road in the Bronco with Federales, *señoritas* and bill-collectors from the university all chasing me.

I literally shut door number two one week before I was supposed to start the drive south. There was some unrest in Mexico City and some serious unrest in my mind. By then, though, I had told NAU that they would *not* have a third Griffen to deal with. But then I called them back up and asked them if they would reinstate my application. And my scholarship. A "yes" would open door three. A "no" would take me through door two and off to Mexico.

My book writing would have to wait. NAU graciously chose to take me back. *I would become the highest ranking scholar at NAU in the freshman class of 1973.* Not Dartmouth, I get that. But a point of pride in my education journey.

And you already know what happened after I graduated from NAU. Straight into IBM. What I didn't tell you in that earlier chapter is that, after college, I had applied to and was accepted to the Thunderbird Graduate School for International Management to pursue a masters in international business. My third real decision on the education front. IBM was too hard to turn down. They were *International Business.* So that became my master's degree, it said so on my business card for 19 years. But, rounding out the journey, I then finally made it to my international business dream and conducted international engagements when I left IBM in 1996. Some of them in Mexico City. I checked off door number two.

Earth to Dougie. Fascinating, but what the hell, you are supposed to be setting the stage for the future of education. And I am. Because all of that set the context for my life. I was fortunate that I had parents and siblings who valued education. I was fortunate that we lived in a modest middle-class neighborhood and had access to good public schools in grade school and high school. I was fortunate that my mother invested in *early childhood education* for me. I genuinely enjoyed school and was extremely fortunate that I had *options* for college. Three doors to be precise. And then I chose a company in IBM that was exceptionally dedicated to ongoing professional education. And I graduated from college, remarkably, with no student debt. Just a high level of *student gratitude*.

So this should be a wonderful and upbeat session on education, as I am sure that America has simply enhanced what my opportunities were so that *everyone* can have access to those same doors in 2020, right? Right? *We'll ask our Foresighters.*

The State of Education in America—2020

Our first question in our Future of Learning and Education Foresight session was simply to gain a perspective from our participants on what they felt was the state of education in America today:

Question: *Imagine you are on a panel discussion (albeit a virtual panel). Education is the topic. How would you describe the state of education in America today? Where do you feel we stand and why? Please be as descriptive and persuasive as you can:*

Well, class is in session and the students had some strong opinions:

- "Overall poor. Our education objectives have not evolved over the past 50 years, teachers are underpaid and under-appreciated. College and graduate school is more or less a requirement to work in the world today, yet attending will put you in crippling debt for decades to come."
- "Struggling. The divide in the country is illustrated by quality of education and what is being placed on the schools. The pandemic has brought out the cracks in the system."
- "I think the education system is broken in many ways. Our children aren't getting the education they need, and many are excluded from participating in our education system. I worry about classrooms moving away from teaching facts."
- "Outdated. Classroom and teaching styles are, in a lot of ways, similar to the way it was 100 years ago. Furthermore, an education is merely a checklist for a lot of people."
- "Under threat—state tuition cutbacks. Top schools will sail above —many second or third tier schools will struggle. Threat of microcredentials and "as-needed learning". COVID-19 may disrupt living away from home expectations. Online classes may become more prevalent."

- "Deplorable. Unequal. Overpriced. In addition to little real STEM focus, I'd like to see all levels of education teach 'students' how to solve problems. How to *think*. Not just learn or memorize."
- "I think we are at a crossroads re: education. Even prior to COVID, it seems to me that education costs are ridiculous and based on a pre-technology model. On-line learning should be far less costly and better prepare kids for a future in this technology-based world. COVID requirements may actually help in this regard, forcing educators to explore more on-line approaches."
- "Weird is the best word I can choose at this point. Obviously education is of huge importance but, with the disruption COVID-19 has caused, the way education is happening at all levels is different than ever before. Online learning at all ages presents challenges, special education needs are a huge challenge and a huge burden has been placed on parents to supplement and support their children's education."
- "Segmented. Private schools are at the cutting edge and if they are available to you, your kids will get a great education and be well prepared for life. Public schools are failing by all possible metrics. There is no drive or understanding to fix the problems. Schools are instead focused on 'feel good' metrics that don't actually improve learning or skill development. The division between those who can leave the system and those who can't is widening and having lasting implications. Education used to be an equalizer—if you put in the work, it would give you a better life. That isn't true in the current system."
- "The educational system is broken. Parents have decided they know how to educate their children and do not trust the system designed to educate their children. They expect the system to work the way they believe is best. In fairness, the educational system is outdated and outmoded and underfunded. Instead of giving the system the resources needed to adapt and change, societal prioritization has minimized, impeding the system to move in the direction it needs to go."
- "Education beyond high school is the key to economic opportunity in this country—but access to that opportunity is extremely inequitable, particularly for people of color and low income communities. Higher ed fails too many people, graduating on average 58% of those who are first-time, full-time students—yet somehow that is seen as a failure, not of the system, but of individuals. Most drop out and many are left with debt. False meritocracy. Engine of reproducing privilege in this country."
- "Broken, undervalued and falling behind among the major players in the world. Higher ed has lowered in the value while skyrocketing in the cost. Public schools are sorely underfunded and

educators are paid nothing. COVID has brought tech adoption rapidly across all levels, but they are not prepared to deliver in an effective way or in a way that truly drives to learning and growth."

Woah. These are not responses. They are *essays*. We have struck a nerve here. I know the statements are a lot to read so let's just go with *CliffsNotes* version:

The state of education in America: poor, struggling, broken, outdated, under threat, deplorable, unequal, overpriced, weird, segmented, a false meritocracy, undervalued, at a cross-roads and falling behind.

I must tell you, this is not a divided point of view. This is a serious consensus by our Foresighters that the basic American education system is in deep trouble. Which means America is in deep trouble if we don't address some of the fundamental issues that were raised:

✓ Lack of access for many Americans
✓ Deteriorating instructional quality
✓ Rising costs leading to crippling debt
✓ Teaching to the test, not teaching the fundamental skills
✓ Lack of teacher compensation and support
✓ Outdated methods
✓ Failing higher education graduation rates
✓ Underfunded and undervalued by our states and local communities
✓ Disparities emerging between private schools and public schools
✓ Lack of parent involvement and support
✓ Lack of updated technology (amplified in COVID period)
✓ Non-traditional methods undercutting base educational tenets

To be fair to the educators and the education system, if you have been in a classroom in the last five years, I suspect you have been a little concerned about the attention span and learning rigor shown by the students themselves. *You need to be an active participant.*

So, do we have any chance of addressing the issues, of improving education in America? We asked our participants to give Education in America a report card. A classic A through F scale:

Question: *If you were handing out a report card on the state of education in America today and how we are performing, what grade do you give it?*

No.	Items	Times Selected
1.	**I give it a 'C'**	**(48%)**
2.	**I give it a 'D'**	**(30%)**
3.	I give it a 'B'	(18%)
4.	I give it an 'A'	(2%)
5.	I give it an 'F'	(2%)

This may have been generous. Somewhere between a C minus and a D plus. But it is not a report card that you are eager to show the parents at home.

Reflecting on the Prior Decade

So, how did we get to this point in 2020? *Well, we worked really hard in the prior decade to achieve this very mediocre performance:*

Question: *Thinking about the prior decade—2010 through 2019—would you say that education in America progressed or declined overall?*

No.	Items	Times Selected
1.	**Education in America declined somewhat**	**(51%)**
2.	Education in America progressed somewhat	(26%)
3.	Education in America declined significantly	(23%)
4.	Education in America progressed significantly	(0%)

So, just over half of our participants suggested that it declined somewhat and another 23% suggested that it declined significantly—74% combined on the decline. Just over a quarter suggested that it had progressed somewhat. Let's consider their explanations:

- DECLINED SOMEWHAT: "Grade inflation, lack of funds for technological facilities and equipment."

259

- DECLINED SOMEWHAT: "Higher education continued to progress, it is still world-class, although the cost is an issue. The quality of public education appears to have declined, opening the door to a more patchwork system."
- DECLINED SOMEWHAT: "Not keeping pace with world in high school. Universities have a very biased political framework. Have not made investments in skills training—instead the folly that everyone needs college."
- DECLINED SOMEWHAT: "There is extreme competition and high cost for private schools for primary and secondary education which contributes to the gap between rich and poor. Many opportunities for a good education are out of reach for lower incomes, many schools in poor areas are just babysitting, and without this foundation, professional opportunities later in life are very limited."
- DECLINED SOMEWHAT: "Budgets have necessitated cutting many arts/humanities curricula, which may train people for jobs, but not enrich them for life. Also the 'teach to the test' has contributed to this. It seems that when I hear about education in other countries, they seem to be doing a better job than the U.S."
- DECLINED SIGNIFICANTLY: "School choice has been a thinly disguised attempt by Republicans to weaken and disenfranchise public education, and it has been working. Meanwhile the costs of higher education reached levels that cannot be sustained by society."
- DECLINED SIGNIFICANTLY: "That we haven't made SUBSTANTIAL advances in the scope, funding and quality of education suggests that we are necessarily declining—and losing opportunities that are incalculable and irretrievable."
- DECLINED SIGNIFICANTLY: "The educational divide is no different from any of our other sociopolitical and economic divides. We are not teaching children critical thinking skills. Instead, we are programming them to believe what we want them to believe, not exploring and learning. It is getting exponentially worse and this is the second or third generation of isolated (home school) education activities."
- DECLINED SIGNIFICANTLY: "Continued lack of funding for public schools, teachers are woefully underpaid and under-appreciated, rise of charter schools contributes to lack of direction, focus and right priorities. Education should be a basic human right (along with healthcare) and provided consistently and fairly across the board (K-12, university is a different conversation)."
- DECLINED SIGNIFICANTLY: "Higher ed focused on $ and not learning. Value of degree has lowered significantly while costs have been driven out of this universe."

260

- PROGRESSED SOMEWHAT: "Access to higher ed improving, completion rates improving (slowly, too slowly) but equity gaps (income, race) not closing."
- PROGRESSED SOMEWHAT: "Seems like we have added new 'industries' to study (cloud computing, fintech, etc.) and we brought back some trades at junior colleges."
- PROGRESSED SOMEWHAT: "We had children in secondary and college environments and observations were that it was more advanced and comprehensive than during our era. AP courses, level of work, complexity all significant."
- PROGRESSED SOMEWHAT: "America, by not censoring the internet much and having many people teaching online, has made education more accessible than before."
- PROGRESSED SOMEWHAT: "Tapping my optimism, young people still have lots of opportunities for personal growth. Education may not be leading, but it is at least evolving to adapt to the technological trends in the world."

So, perhaps some room for a little optimism. Not as stagnant or declining in all areas, but this is an industry that is exceptionally slow to change. In the decade ahead it will need some *disruption* to change the status quo, good political leadership, local community engagement, some serious parental involvement and some financial approaches to help bridge the access gap.

Some Reflections on the Last Decade

I have two general sets of reflections over the last decade in terms of education in America: one set is *personal* and the other set is *professional*.

Let's start with personal. All four of my children graduated from college in the prior decade and all had different experiences, but all have been set up (I think) for future success. All of them had elementary public school experience in Arizona, but then all went to private school for high school. It is my very strong belief that the quality of their high school experience set the stage for opportunity and academic success in college.

✓ Scott, my oldest, attended Phoenix Country Day School for high school (actually started there in 8th grade). Awarded the Teacher's Prize for outstanding performance, studied Latin and now speaks six languages, gave a graduation address on globalization (global before global was cool) and then attended Yale University and later earned his Master's degree in Global Ethics at King's College in London. I am deeply in debt to him for his

261

academic excellence and commitment, and deeply in debt because of the same. *Just kidding, Scott.*

✓ Jack, my second oldest, attended Notre Dame Preparatory High School in Scottsdale, graduated with honors, and attended Arizona State University and their highly acclaimed Barrett Honors College. Graduated in Supply Chain economics from the W.P. Carey Business School. Works in the golf industry as a professional caddy. Tee to fairway to green is the supply chain he manages, and it's a pretty good gig.

✓ Betsy, tied for third oldest (a twin), attended Notre Dame Preparatory High School where she *complained frequently* about the rigid structure of a Catholic school and has several letters of 'commendation' on her complaining. Nonetheless, graduated with honors and also attended the Arizona State University Barrett Honors College, graduating in *kinesiology*. That's right, *kinesiology*. Which sets you up well for a three-year pursuit of her doctorate in Physical Therapy. *There is a doctor in the house.*

✓ Sam, the other half of the twins, likewise attended Notre Dame Preparatory High School, graduating in the top quartile of his class. Counters the ASU Sun Devil trend and attends the University of Arizona in Tucson, a *Wildcat*. Chooses a business major and focuses on economics at the Eller Business School, adds a technology (computer science) minor and parlays that into a full time technology development position. He has a bright future ahead to *converge* his business/technology skills.

Look, we are all proud of our children, no matter what. But each one was able to create a unique career path by a common dedication and opportunity within *education*. They were all involved in their schools, all varsity athletes in high school. *This is good, as not a single Griffen, aside from my wife Janet on the piano, has a musical muscle in their bodies.*

On the professional side, during the last decade, I was involved with three aspects of education that suggested to me that disruption and change were possible in this industry:

1) **The Growth of Community Colleges:** A four-year college is simply not the right option for many people (young students as well as adults). I had the opportunity to work with Pima Community College on the development and launch of their set of "Centers of Excellence" in six key curriculum areas: Applied Technology, Public Safety, Health Professions, Information Technology,

262

Hospitality and the Arts. In each case Pima aligned with the industry, the community, the teachers and the students to develop strategies and pathways to enable a two-year college to create relevant skills and career opportunities for their students. It was a win/win/win—great for the students, great for the industry that hires the students and great for the faculty/college;

2) **The Power of Vocational Training:** Around 2010, I was introduced to Kimberly McWaters who was the CEO of Universal Technical Institute (UTI) that has a series of vocational campuses in Arizona and across the U.S. The primary focus of UTI was training the next generation of automotive mechanics for dealers, but they also had institutes/training centers for HVAC, marine and motorcycles. This was a completely different track than basic academic education. These were vocational schools that would draw from high schools as well as disenchanted college students, and give them a fast path to a highly valued skill. Their biggest challenge, in many cases, was convincing the *parents* that a mechanical trade was relevant, a great career and a big-time earnings opportunity for their child;

3) **The Advent of Online Education:** Online education was not invented in 2020 with the pandemic. Many schools were developing online as a strategy for the institutions and to extend global access. Many also felt that online students could become hybrid students, mixing in the physical campus and also creating a life-long learning opportunity for that student as they progressed in their career. One of the first was Western Governors University (WGU) which was launched in a strategy session in 1997 by a meeting of the Western Governor's Association that felt the internet was a strong emerging strategy and could change the way students could access education. I facilitated a session for their students in 2010 that raved about *online convenience*. WGU is highly recognized for their pioneering efforts in "distance learning" and set the stage for nearly every major American university to add online education to their programs.

WGU: Some early wise online Owls

All of these are alternatives to traditional four-year education pathways. They are creating new, and generally far more affordable, access points to a broad range of students, including adult learners. And they are just one piece of the education reform puzzle.

Why All of This Matters

Back to our Foresight session, we wanted to do a little academic analysis on why all of this focus on education was so important. Why it really matters to the country and the decade ahead:

Question: *As you reflect on your experiences and viewpoints in education, why is this such an important area of focus for the decade ahead for America? Why does it matter so much—what's at stake?*

In this activity we brainstormed a set of open responses, then summarized them on the fly and assessed the summarized list. We had over 125 open responses and a summary of 15 themes which we assessed as follows:

Now please indicate how important each of the following reasons are for why addressing education in America matters for the decade ahead. Use a scale of 1-10 where a "1" means not at all important and a "10" means extremely important:

Rank	Idea	Avg.
1.	Preserves an informed public and democracy	**9.5**
2.	We have significant issues requiring critical thinking	**8.8**
3.	Social cost of poor education	**8.8**
4.	Foundation of a strong society/culture	**8.8**
5.	Creates level of economic security	**8.6**
6.	It's our future talent pipeline	**8.5**
7.	Allows us to adapt to new challenges	**8.5**
8.	It's the innovation driver	**8.3**
9.	It's about our global competitiveness	**8.2**

10.	American Dream...that our children will do better than we did	**8.0**
11.	Preserves our quality of life	**7.7**
12.	Creates the right level of equity	**7.6**
13.	Reinforces our position as a technology leader	**7.5**
14.	Reinforces importance of sustainability	**6.7**
15.	We can't burden the next gen with debt	**6.1**

This is a *very* powerful list. It's not just about individual opportunity, it's about global competitiveness for the country itself. *An informed public and democracy. Critical issues ahead. A strong society. Preserve our quality of life. A driver of innovation.*

Some observations on the collective importance of education for the country from our participants:

- "It builds the foundation for progress, leadership and innovation into our future as a nation. It also helps break down divisions and brings a higher level of empathy in human interaction."
- "If we are to maintain our status as a people who can think, invent, create, be entrepreneurs, do great science and medicine, etc., we MUST begin with education."
- "Education will provide a common means to transcend challenging societal and cultural barriers here at home and internationally."
- "Lack of education tends to breed many social ills, most obvious in the inner city areas of the largest cities...crime, shootings, drugs, low quality of life, children without food, etc. And the cycles continue unabated. Education is only one of the answers, but it is a big one to help the youth climb out of the morass of generations."
- "Civics, service and climate change are critical, democratic areas of future concern/focus. We need an educated, engaged population to be able to contribute to the common welfare and create a sustainable country and world for future generations."
- "Knowledge is increasing so fast and being incorporated into everyday life experiences so deeply that without broad-based quality education, an increasing majority will fall behind in literally every facet of life."

- "What's at stake, I think, is that it is critical—as demographics shift—that the next generation have the skills to think independently to support innovation, support how we function as a society."
- "Everything is at stake. Education is the basis of future entrepreneurship, creativity, American participation on the global stage, leadership, the economy. It is critically important that we educate our citizens well."

I hereby vote for the positive consequences. But what if we *don't* get this right? What are the *negative consequences*?

Question: *What is the ONE MOST NEGATIVE CONSEQUENCE for America if we DON'T rethink learning and education in the decade ahead and we get it wrong? How will it affect us?*

The course title of this elective class is *Educational Armageddon*. From our attending students:

- "A compromised, rapidly declining quality of life particularly for anyone outside the top 5% people of wealth. Even the wealthy will be threatened as the economic and social divide increases, threatening political stability."
- "Increasing division within our country, educators opting out of teaching for better paying jobs and professions, lack of talent for our industries/companies, global disequity in skillsets, lack of economic security."
- "We will continue on the current path of greater gaps in knowledge, income, access to education and health and social services."
- "We descend further into polarization and leave even more of our citizens without the opportunities we want for ourselves."
- "We will fall behind other countries in terms of competitiveness, the social fabric will continue to tear."
- "Our country will no longer be a worldwide power. We lose our advantage. Life as we know it will be very different."
- "We become an inequitable society like third world countries."
- "Division. Loyalty to faction over fact. Fall of the Democratic Republic in our role in the world and the fundamental tenets that keep our society together and strong."
- "Ultimately, the collapse of the American way of life."

It's remarkable to see the role that education decline could have with the division in America. Too strong of a downside? Fear-mongering by our Foresighters? It's like we are talking about the fall of the Roman Empire!

Yeah, we kinda are. That's why the decade ahead is so crucial to address education.

But remember, our Foresighters are nothing if not optimistic. They have seen a few things in their experience where America has had to dig in, re-invent itself, rethink its future:

Question: *Are you optimistic or pessimistic about the ability for America to really address education and learning in the decade ahead?*

No.	Items	Times Selected
1.	**Optimistic**	**(65%)**
2.	Pessimistic	(35%)

Academically speaking, that's a *two thirds majority*. Haven't seen that in America in a while, so we asked our participants about that optimistic view:

- OPTIMISTIC: "Tough nut to crack, but I think we'll at least have smart sensible people involved in policy decisions affecting education."
- OPTIMISTIC: "I'd like to think that younger generations are becoming more aware of the importance of education."
- OPTIMISTIC: "I'm not saying it'll be easy, but I am hopeful that Americans share the value of investing in and empowering our children and future generations."
- OPTIMISTIC: "I am always optimistic—one can't go into something like this feeling like things cannot change—they always can! At my heart, I believe everyone wishes for a better world and education is key to this."
- OPTIMISTIC: "Just barely optimistic and that's totally a function of my perpetual outlook. The short term trends are worrisome. I just hope the pandemic acts as a catalyst for change to improve our current path."
- OPTIMISTIC: "I want to believe. I'm hopeful that the masses will move past the greed that currently dominates all spending and focus and we will get to working together to solve those things

we face. But selfishness will have to be defeated by unity and collectivism."

Admittedly, there is a lot of conditional language attached to the statements. But likewise on the most ardent pessimists as well:

- PESSIMISTIC: "We are SO divided—on the one hand, it seems to buffer us from radical changes for the better or worse (depending on your point of view) but it also doesn't let us join with the better angels of our nature to do the right things where we SHOULD be able to agree."
- PESSIMISTIC: "We have been on a decline for decades in education. COVID has influenced some radical changes, such as publicly funded alternatives to antiquated approaches to education more of a possibility, but the public school system is now an industry that is more concerned with self-preservation than education. They will fight hard against change."
- PESSIMISTIC: "Reformers have been trying to address shortcomings in education for decades. The improvements that get made may have small impacts with such a massive system. On the other hand, forces beyond policymakers (such as COVID and remote learning) may provide a significant realignment with big improvements for some. Overall I believe many will be left behind."
- PESSIMISTIC: "We, as a country, have so many things to address in the years ahead, education being just one of many. I think some progress might happen, but given the sheer scale of change that is needed in so many areas, I think progress will be slow and generational, not something that is 'fixed' in a decade."

One of the most important lessons from the global pandemic is that we really can accelerate change in this country and *turn on a dime* when the urgency is upon us. How we developed a vaccine strategy and the trial results in under 12 months, how we moved forward with telehealth and telemed when it seemed like it was such a slow and arduous implementation, how we rallied around successive economic stimulus measures, how we transitioned much of education and work into a virtual environment. Imagine if we take the same urgency towards climate change, education *reform* and social equity. *A lot of things could be different in the decade ahead.*

What Needs to be Addressed

I suspect that many of you have been involved in some kind of *education summit* or process team to *improve educational outcomes.* Maybe at a local level, a state level, nationally or just part of a specific school effort. *Frustrating, eh?* Hey, I have facilitated a few myself. A few high fives at the end of the session, some good energy, and then it seems like the air just goes out of the balloon as time passes. It is hard to make systemic change, but the only way you can change it is to commit to that change.

Our Foresighters were ready for their version of a *virtual* education summit. Let's take a swing at this education piñata and see if we can hit it straight on:

Question: *Education is a broad topic—it can span from early childhood education (birth to age 8) all the way through adult learning after traditional education and work experiences. What are the issues that you feel are most important to address as you think broadly about education and learning in the coming decade? Where do we need to put our attention?*

Forty-two people, passionate about a subject, letting it fly simultaneously. But I think it felt good to talk about solutions, about what could be addressed. Nearly 150 individual responses and then our real-time summary process which yielded 20 themes, which we would address two ways:

First, the IMPORTANCE of addressing this area in the decade ahead to improve education/learning in America (use a scale of 1-10 where a "1" means not at all important and a "10" means extremely important):

Rank	Idea	Avg.
1.	Enhancing education in lower income areas	9.2
2.	Equal access to quality education	9.2
3.	Increase focus on critical thinking skills	9.0
4.	Access to/quality of early childhood education	8.8
5.	Increase teacher pay	8.8
6.	Increase funding for public education system	8.8
7.	More focus on practical workforce skills	8.3
8.	Encourage intellectual curiosity at all levels	8.3
9.	Better technology access to support learning	8.1

10.	More pathways after high school	**7.9**
11.	Reestablish a priority for civics/history/arts	**7.9**
12.	Continue advancing efficiency/impact of online learning	**7.8**
13.	More opportunities for higher education	**7.7**
14.	Increase teaching of life skills	**7.6**
15.	Smaller classroom sizes	**7.6**
16.	Increase focus on necessary soft skills	**7.1**
17.	Better integration of business/industry with education	**7.0**
18.	Advances in lifetime learning	**6.5**
19.	Align people with their passions	**6.5**
20.	Allow for school choice	**5.5**

Hit the recess bell! Send this to the school principal, the Governor, the incoming Secretary of Education, drop a copy off to Jill Biden and ask her to get this in front of Joe at her earliest convenience.

Wait, what? It's a two part assessment? Well, bring it on, we are here to change the future of education!

Second, the FEASIBILITY of addressing this area in the decade ahead (use a scale of 1-10 where a "1" means not at all feasible and a "10" means extremely feasible):

Rank	Idea	Avg.
1.	Continue advancing efficiency/impact of online learning	**8.4**
2.	Better technology access to support learning	**8.3**
3.	More focus on practical workforce skills	**8.1**
4.	Increase teacher pay	**8.0**

5.	Access to/quality of early childhood education	**7.6**
6.	More pathways after high school	**7.4**
7.	Increase focus on critical thinking skills	**7.2**
8.	Reestablish a priority for civics/history/arts	**7.2**
9.	Increase teaching of life skills	**7.0**
10.	Equal access to quality education	**6.9**
11.	Better integration of business/industry with education	**6.9**
12.	Increase funding for public education system	**6.8**
13.	More opportunities for higher education	**6.7**
14.	Encourage intellectual curiosity at all levels	**6.7**
15.	Increase focus on necessary soft skills	**6.6**
16.	Allow for school choice	**6.5**
17.	Enhancing education in lower income areas	**6.5**
18.	Advances in lifetime learning	**6.4**
19.	Smaller classroom sizes	**6.1**
20.	Align people with their passions	**4.9**

All things considered, it's not as bad as I might have thought. Most were within a 2 point gap in terms of importance vs. feasibility. Here were the top 10 gaps:

#	Educational Area Description	Im-pact	Fea-sible	Gap
1	Enhancing education in lower income areas	9.2	6.5	(2.7)
2	Equal access to quality education	9.2	6.9	(2.3)
3	Increase funding for public education system	8.8	6.8	(2.0)

4	Increase focus on critical thinking skills	9.0	7.2	(1.8)
5	Encourage intellectual curiosity at all levels	8.3	6.7	(1.6)
6	Align people with their passions	6.5	4.9	(1.6)
7	Smaller classroom sizes	7.6	6.1	(1.5)
8	Access to/quality of early childhood education	8.8	7.6	(1.2)
9	More opportunities for higher education	7.7	6.7	(1.0)
10	Increase teacher pay	8.8	8.0	(0.8)

Look, compared to some of the gaps we have seen in our other assess-ments in previous chapters, these give us a chance. The top three are the big three: funding, equal access, improving education in lower income areas. I would argue that access to quality early childhood education is a bigger gap than is perceived, but I have done some specific work there.

The McCormick Center for Early Childhood Leadership (at National Louis University) is one of the most prominent organizations trying to create change for early childhood education (defined as birth through age eight, roughly third grade). They advance a *Theory of Change* that, "Enhanced leadership competencies and increased leadership capacity within orga-nizations will yield substantial improvements in program quality, which will in turn improve outcomes for children and families served."

Strengthen the leaders and the support for those leaders and you change the game for everyone. But that is all about *systemic change* for the credentials of the leaders, the degrees required, compensation equity and state level oversight. Early in the pandemic, in May of 2020, we con-ducted sessions with key Early Childhood Education (ECE) leaders in establishing a *Unified Framework for Early Childhood Program Leaders*. There was strong buy-in, but a recognition that the funding to get there will be challenging.

I do not underestimate the role of the incoming First Lady (Jill Biden) on early childhood education, equalizing access for education in general and increasing our public funding and awareness on the critical impor-tance of education for the decade ahead.

Lastly, in terms of the analysis of our assessment, I am not clear why the gap on *increasing critical thinking* skills is so high. I will have to think about that some more.

Choosing a Major

Twenty areas is a lot to go after, so we asked our participants to consider five different aspects of learning and education in America and choose ONE of them to focus on in terms of improving education. Declare a major:

Question: *Imagine you had unlimited funds and resources and could focus on a particular aspect of learning and education in America in the decade ahead. Which area from the list below would you choose?*

No.	Items	Times Selected
1.	**TRADITIONAL K-12 EDUCATION: Focus on the support for students from kindergarten through high school, and how you might enhance the environment, learning methods and outcomes.**	**(51%)**
2.	**TRANSITION TO THE WORKFORCE: Focus on the options and support to transition high school graduates effectively into the workforce. Options could include community college, traditional colleges/universities as well as vocational training models.**	**(24%)**
3.	**EARLY CHILDHOOD EDUCATION: Focus on the support and learning environment for children from birth to age 8 (typically through the third grade).**	**(22%)**
4.	ONGOING WORKFORCE TRAINING: Rethink the way we continually train and update skills within a workforce setting. A sense that your company/hiring organization will constantly invest in your work/career to maintain your value/relevancy.	(3%)
5.	ADULT ELECTIVE LEARNING: Create new methods and opportunities to enable adults to learn elective skills and interest areas that maintain an intellectual and emotional vitality throughout life.	(0%)

The top three areas cover a lot of group but have good rationale by our participants:

- TRADITIONAL: "It's just the foundation for everything. Strong K-12 education that provides equal opportunities and an equal footing to all students is the building block for our society."

- TRADITIONAL: "The value of education is cumulative. I'd invest early intending to affect their entire lifetimes—with the expectation that their generation(s) would grow into a smart, vibrant, thriving and opportunity-laden adulthood."
- TRADITIONAL: "These are the foundational years. We need to establish good habits and skills early so that they can properly enter the workforce or continue on with higher education. If the foundation isn't good, nothing else matters."
- TRADITIONAL: "It is either the only formal education people may get, which means it is our only shot to give them the skills they will need to make it through life, OR it is the essential foundation for higher education acceptance, learning and successful completion."
- TRADITIONAL: "Without a solid, stable K-12 education, a nurturing school environment, informed and compassionate teachers, and education and services for parents, our kids don't have a chance. Their underperformance and inequity will increase, contributions to society will decrease."

- TRANSITION: "This would have the most positive impact on employment rates, poverty, crime, equality."
- TRANSITION: "Not everyone is meant for college. HS kids are getting more informed and closer to making these choices. Plus, we've been doing K-12 learning methods and outcomes and not really getting as far as we used to. Seems like time to change."
- TRANSITION: "It spans things, and when you look at current U.S. workforce, by reaching down through school years to prepare graduates, it would seem we would be much better off with people being positioned to get a start in life as young adults."
- TRANSITION: "I think finding your passion for what you want to actually work on in life could have the best impact."
- TRANSITION: "Things are out of balance. Getting it right will make businesses more efficient and reduce costs. More students will be aligned with country needs (and pay for skills will rise)."

- EARLY CHILDHOOD: "There is very compelling research that early childhood education has the highest lifetime (and societal) ROI."
- EARLY CHILDHOOD: "Early childhood is when the mind does a large of chunk of its learning and there is large brain development. This is the time in a life to really hone in on proper education."
- EARLY CHILDHOOD: "Enabling the learning foundation as early and consistently as possible would allow for future learning im-

274

provements and lifelong learning opportunities to unfold more organically. Everyone starts from the same base."

- EARLY CHILDHOOD: "Ninety percent of a child's brain develops by age five. Incredibly, it doubles in size in the first year and keeps growing to about 80 percent of adult size by age three and 90 percent—nearly full grown—by age five."

- EARLY CHILDHOOD: From pre-K to third grade sets the course of success and failure for many students—it is essential to get this right, provide equal access to all young children, regardless of where they live, the income of their family, their ethnicity. Educate our pre-K to third-grade teachers well and pay them an equitable wage."

I think professor Charles W. Kingsfield, from our Paper Chase setting, would be proud of the arguments for all three of the areas. And here is the point: this isn't a choice between the three, it's a choice and a mandate to improve *all three* at the same time. We don't have time to be sequential; these need to be done in parallel.

Investments and Innovations

If we are going to change the game for education and learning in the decade ahead, we have to be *disruptive*. Accelerate change with selected strategic investments and innovations. So we asked our Foresighters to identify the changes they would make—no constraints on funding, resources or political constraints:

Question: *What do you feel is the ONE MOST IMPORTANT investment/ innovation or change that could be made that would have the most positive impact in education in America in the decade ahead? Why would you champion or advocate for this area?*

- "Life skills, budgeting, financial intelligence. People do not understand debt management, saving for the future, delayed gratification, investment returns, taking care of oneself."

- "School choice. Anyone in a less-than-ideal situation can just get out of it. No financial or logistical barriers, they just pick a better future."

- "Free education. Education is for the benefit of our nation and world as a whole. Students should not be penalized and burdened financially for receiving it. Education should be looked at as an investment in the country, not an opportunity to make money off loans."

- "Paying K-12 teachers more would push the smartest and best students to choose to have a career in education."

- "When you let your children in schools, you trust and believe teachers will help them to grow and be better people. We NEED to invest in teachers' capacity, quality and knowledge. They have our future in their hands."
- "Making state college free. College education is basically mandatory to even consider getting a job these days, and graduate school is highly suggested. If someone comes out of school with 70K plus in debt, how are they expected to highly contribute to the economy for years to come? Buying a house, etc., are all much more difficult with so much debt as you are just starting your life."
- "An educational system that considers the whole person and the whole family—holistic learning, exploring new ideas, STEM-Civics-Culture, critical thinking, finding your passion and being able to make a living from it, AND services to help a kid's family support and nurture that learning at home."
- "Invest in closing equity gaps by race and income at all levels of education. This would lift all boats and revitalize our economy, our innovation, our happiness. There is something so corrosive to our nation's soul in the unfairness. Plus, with more people thriving and contributing, we'd all benefit."
- "Bring our children back into the public school classroom. Home school, private school and charter school programs represent and support the beginning of our socio-political divide. Eliminate it!"
- "Credential-based education—it would open up higher ed to more people, increase the value of an education as it links directly to jobs in the private sector and it would dramatically lower the costs."
- "Investment in closing the digital divide. Ensuring that all students and schools have the technology they need to enable in-room and remote learning."

These are some bold ideas, but on a basis of common sense when you peel them back, it would seem that education itself should be considered as part of America's *infrastructure*. Let's keep an eye on that discussion in 2021.

The Challenges in the Way
There seems to be strong agreement in America that the status quo in education is not tolerable. So what's in the way of sweeping changes? Serious restructuring to make significant impact...we asked our participants:

Question: *It's difficult to make an argument against investing more in education and learning for America in the decade ahead. And yet it seems difficult to create the level of national mandate to be willing to re-direct the investment needed. What's in the way of enabling significant change for education and learning in the decade ahead?*

It was easy to throw a lot of one word answers at this—*politics, tribalism, budgets, selfishness, debt, greed*...but we summarized all of the responses into 15 themes. Just for consideration, we didn't prioritize them, but the magnitude was clear:

No.	Idea
1.	Divided politics in our country
2.	Lack of adequate budget/funding
3.	The growing deficit in our country
4.	Lack of urgency—not seeing the value in moving education forward
5.	Lack of trust in educational institutions
6.	Leaders who may not make education a priority (Federal/State/Local)
7.	Generational attitudes (I worked my way up, so can they...)
8.	That the payoff is so far down the road (long term investment for the ROI)
9.	The lack of an educated society (they just don't get it...)
10.	Divergent POVs on the best path forward
11.	That "market forces" will just fix this over time
12.	Unwillingness, as a country, to invest for the greater good
13.	Inability to address teacher pay as a catalyst
14.	Not having the right people in the right leadership positions (e.g., Secretary of Education)
15.	Those who may be profiting on the status quo of education

Pick your favorite. At the end of the day, it will take strong and sustained *political leadership* to guide the country to elevate the priority of education. If it's not done at that level, we will see passionate, but very limited, incremental change. This will be at the top of the list for the decade that begins in 2030. *We cannot let that happen.* No, seriously, I really don't think I can get this group together again. *They will have moved on.*

Welcome Back to Your Freshman Year in High School

OMG. Please no. Just for a few minutes, why not? Imagine that *you* were about to start your freshman year in high school but it was 2020, our current reality. Pandemic aside for now, we were interested in what might impact your success over the next four years:

Question: *Let's change the context for a moment. To a large degree we have been focused at the macro level about the impact of improving education/learning for America as a country. Imagine yourself as incoming freshman in high school. It's a public high school. Which of the following do you think will most impact the trajectory of your success over the next four years?*

No.	Items	Times Selected
1.	**The quality of the teachers and their teaching methods**	**(49%)**
2.	**The support from my family**	**(21%)**
3.	Quality counseling to understand my interests and help me make a good post secondary education decision	(13%)
4.	My own goals/ambitions/personal drive	(10%)
5.	Have access to and being involved in extra-curricular activities (sports, music, drama, student government, etc.)	(5%)
6.	Running with the right friends/social crowd	(2%)
7.	The technology available to support my learning	(0%)

Pretty simple. This group is pretty comfortable with their ambitions/drive...they need an environment that comes with great teachers, resources and methods. Parents matter, they will play a support role. But they are not in the classroom eight hours a day:

- QUALITY OF TEACHERS: "At the end of the day, if teachers aren't there to support their students, provide motivation and offer them the tools and resources they need—students will likely

278

fail. They need the guidance and structure that a good teacher can provide."

- QUALITY OF TEACHERS: "We can all remember that most memorable teacher, whether a small or large action that made a difference in our lives and potentially helped us find our passion, supported us when others did not, saw the good in each of us, taught us more than what is in books alone, focused on our success. All of these things are important—teachers are a differentiator."
- QUALITY OF TEACHERS: "Everyone needs a mentor. The only way I made it through HS was my desire to stay academically eligible to be on the swim team. That was my motivation. But, my coach was the one who made sure I didn't lose my way."
- QUALITY OF TEACHERS: "The quality of the teachers and teaching methods would help me succeed, despite difficult circumstances. Good teachers in high school have made a significant positive impact on my life."
- QUALITY OF TEACHERS: "Teachers that are great educators you always remember and make an impact."

I suppose it's the same for many high schools; at least it was in my day (1969 through 1973). At our high school reunions, *the teachers all attended*. Well, I am sure not all, but a lot of them. They knew they made a difference and they were so excited to see how these *experiments* turned out. A lot of laughter, a few tears, but an open recognition, by us as students and them as teachers, that they were mentors. I know that's the big reward in teaching, and they were lucky to experience that. We were lucky to have them. In the decade ahead we need a new generation of teachers to join the ranks, be well compensated and supported and play that essential role. I, for one, do not think that you get that today in a typical high school, nor in an online environment.

And, reflecting back one more time in our *Return to Freshman Year* (nightmare) scenario:

Question: *All things considered, do you think it would harder, easier or about the same for you if you were to be a high school student today than it was when you were actually in high school?*

No.	Items	Times Selected
1.	**Harder**	**(56%)**
2.	About the same	(39%)

| 3. | Easier | (5%) |

I think harder as well. Here is how our participants explained it:

- HARDER: "SOOO many more pressures for kids and families today. I would hate to be in middle or high school today."
- HARDER: "Social pressures seem way harder than they were 30 years ago! I think that would be a huge challenge for me. Technology makes things easier in a lot of ways, but the social side, yikes."
- HARDER: "I think teachers are overwhelmed and simply cannot navigate all the distractions which prevent them from effectively connecting with and educating their students."
- HARDER: "Distractions. The world is significantly more chaotic now thanks to mobile phones and dopamine rushes."
- HARDER: "The tyranny of social media as a tool for bullying or at least causing a student to question their stature among their peers."
- HARDER: "I think there is less direction/support/quality education in the school systems themselves and definitely less support/encouragement from parents (who are busy working)."
- HARDER: "Today's students have many more issues facing them at a young age."
- HARDER: "Technology (e.g., social media) makes being a kid these days SO hard. Nothing is secret. There is no grace for making mistakes."

Read the last part of that last explanation again: *Nothing is secret. There is no grace for making mistakes.* That genuinely makes me sad. I know I am a bit nostalgic and an admitted analog guy living in a digital world, but I would take the experience of what I had in 1969 thru 1973 *hands down* over trying it in 2020. *But our kids do not have that option.* We have to make the system better and be there when they need us.

Education Influence Scenarios
Customary in our Foresight sessions, we bring a few ideas to the table. *Potential influence scenarios* for the decade ahead. Fun list. Call it extra credit:

Now, please assess each of the following future scenarios in two ways. First, the level of positive IMPACT to the future of education and learning America in the decade ahead if the scenario was to occur (use a scale of 1-10 where a "1"means a very low level of positive impact and a "10" means a very high level of positive impact); Second, the LIKELIHOOD that this scenario will fully materialize in the decade ahead (use a scale of 1-10

280

where a "1" means a very low likelihood and "10" means a very high likelihood):

Here is how our Foresight session assessed the list. The scenarios are ordered by the *level of positive impact* but then contrasted with the likelihood of occurrence for a gap analysis rating.

#	Scenario Description	Im-pact	Like-ly	Gap
1	EQUALITY IN EARLY CHILDHOOD EDUCA-TION: Government, policy-makers and public/ private partnerships collaborate to create a new level of access and equality for early childhood education. EVERY young child experiences a supportive and qualified learning environment regardless of who they are and where they live.	9.2	5.9	(3.3)
2	AMERICA RE-INVESTS IN ITS PUBLIC EDU-CATION INFRASTRUCTURE: The number one infrastructure project for the decade ahead is a massive investment in our K-12 infrastructure. Facilities, classroom space, technology support and learning methods all go through one of the most significant upgrades imaginable. It is a partnership at the Federal/ State and Local government level that really works.	8.9	5.6	(3.3)
3	TEACHER COMPENSATION ACHIEVES WORKPLACE EQUALITY: Teaching becomes one of the most sought after professions in the decade ahead. In addition to creating compensation equality to other professions, their own professional development is enhanced/supported, their level of administrative support is expanded to enable more time on core teaching and new career pathways are developed to retain them in the profession.	8.6	5.1	(3.5)

4	THE VALUE OF VOCATIONAL: The stereotype of a traditional college experience changes in the decade ahead. Technician skills become highly valued as many campuses create partnerships with industry for construction, automotive, mechanical and industrial positions where the compensation, training and benefits help drive the new middle class in America.	8.1	7.1	(1.0)
5	WE RE-IMAGINE LEARNING TECHNOLOGY: The great technology companies that have led so many advances in core technology, communications and social media turn their attention to re-imagining learning technology. The components of the Fourth Industrial Revolution are harnessed to create a learning revolution. Strap on a set of learning goggles my friends!	7.7	7.0	(0.7)
6	PUBLIC COLLEGE IS FUNDED AS A BASIC RIGHT: The burden of a base two-to-four year public college expense is removed by a nationally funded program. It's not a free for all approach, it's a free-for-those-who-need approach and those-who-want-to-work-hard approach.	7.5	5.4	(2.1)
7	EDUCATION AND INDUSTRY CREATE A NEW ALIGNMENT: New partnerships and alliances are created between industry and education. Curriculums are aligned with the skills and entry level positions that are in demand. There is an unprecedented level of resource exchange between schools and industry.	7.4	5.9	(1.5)
8	TRADING DEBT FOR SERVICE: The heavy debt of advanced degrees (law, medicine, technology, education doctorates, etc.) can be off-set by students or the hiring organization via a new Federal program that will waive or significantly reduce degree debt by applying that skill for a specified duration in a service environment. The environment could be military service, government service, foreign service or critical public service roles. It creates a new transition for young people between the education and their industry placement.	7.3	6.0	(1.3)

9	EARLIER ALIGNMENT TO EDUCATION/CAREER PATHING: Less of a roll of the dice on where to go to school and how you end up in a job/career. A new focus at the high school level upscales traditional counseling with AI, industry expertise and skills assessment to develop and define a combination education and career pathway that greatly increases the likelihood of success for a young person. There is often early funding from industry and state/local government to support the educational pathway.	6.8	5.1	(1.7)
10	THE UNIVERSITY OF V: That would be the University of Virtual. Accelerated by the COVID pandemic in 2020, virtual access and learning changed the game. Students anywhere can now access education everywhere. It broadened the reach of education and created new equity in education and learning.	6.6	7.1	+0.5
11	THE WORKPLACE IS THE NEW CENTER OF LEARNING: In the decade ahead, a new level of investment in continual education emerges within companies/organizations. It is recognized that a career is not fueled by politics or seniority but by continual skills and career shifts that are supported by the organization. It becomes one of the key factors for why a young person will choose a certain company to work for. The education journey is part of the workforce journey.	6.3	5.5	(0.8)
12	ADVANCES IN NEURAL PATHWAYS TO ACCELERATE LEARNING: At a very core scientific level we progressed the understanding of how the brain learns and retains information via neural pathways. It led to a better understanding of behavioral learning and methods that significantly improved the capacity to learn.	6.3	4.9	(1.4)

Pretty interesting. 8 of the 12 potential influences rate 7.0+ on the potential impact, and several of the 10 rate as a 7.0+ in terms of likelihood. Virtual (The University of V) looks like a lock on feasibility at 7.1 but that actually exceeds the perceived impact at 6.6. *Really interesting.*

I think this was one of our most intriguing influence scenario lists. Touches a lot of aspects of education and learning and suggests some big possibilities on disruption. I give it an "A" for originality, but likely a "C" for reality. *But the decade is still young.*

Here is what we must tackle. Look at the top six gaps between impact and likelihood:

1. Teacher compensation achieves workplace equity (3.5)
2. Equity in early childhood education (3.3)
3. America re-invests in its public education infrastructure (3.3)
4. Public college is funded as a public right (2.1)
5. Earlier alignment to education/career pathing (1.7)
6. Education and industry create a new alignment (1.5)

Look, if you want to draw in the next generation of committed teachers to engage, instruct and mentor our children, you need to create a competitive work environment. Create career paths that retain these teachers in the education profession. Bring them hungry learners that have received quality early childhood education. Invest in facilities and infrastructure that create a learning environment for our students and a point of pride for our communities.

Five Reflections on the Future of Education and Learning in the Decade Ahead:

1. EDUCATION STARTS EARLY: Every study about early childhood education says the same thing: educate early and you will create a lifelong learner. We cannot afford to miss the window for young kids because of unequal access, uneven instruction and lack of community investment/support. Educate our parents and educate our leaders on why early education matters. The kids are the easy part.
2. YOUR VOCATION MATTERS: I don't think many students in grade school are ready to figure out what they want to be yet, but once you hit high school it is time to expose our students to a wide range of opportunities. We need to step up counseling and advising, let students know that traditional college is one option, but so is a two-year community college or vocational school. Create pathways early that match interest and aptitude.
3. TEACH YOUR CHILDREN WELL: Nothing replaces a quality teacher. They are this wonderful bridge between home/parents and the real world that awaits. I think higher education can take care of itself—invest in culture, values, develop an education brand. But in K-12, we need to lend a hand and up the ante for

teacher pay, skills development, career opportunities and resources. Raise the bar, appeal to a new sense of purpose.
4.   BALANCE TECHNOLOGY AND EXPERIENCE: There is still
     something wonderfully communal about a campus. I know not
     everyone can check out for two-four years, but for those who can
     and are committed to the learning and passionate about a voca-
     tion, it is a rare opportunity. The pandemic caused the pendulum
     to swing a little too far to the technology side. Whether it's a
     campus or kindergarten class, add a little experience.
5.   INVEST IN THE DECADE AHEAD: Everything in our sessions
     suggests that we have some big-time issues to address in the
     decade ahead—climate change, social change, rethinking trans-
     portation, healthcare access and, yes, *solving world hunger*. We
     need critical thinkers in the decade ahead—kids in high school
     and college today who can jump in and be part of a new *prob-
     lem-solving generation*. It starts with education excellence.

The Impact of COVID on the Education in America

We always ask our participants how COVID—as we consider the decade
ahead through the lens of a 2020 global pandemic—affected the subject
of the session. I can only imagine what it must have been like to be a
teacher or a student in 2020. Here's what our participants said:

- "Pulled back the curtain for a lot of parents. Hopefully they de-
  mand more, especially as schools continue to flounder nearly a
  year in."
- "It has shown us that remote learning is possible, and how valu-
  able teachers really are."
- "It's obviously driven a lot online—but the jury is out on whether
  that's all good. There's a lot to learn from this experience."
- "Huge impact. Students have lost a year's worth of learning.
  Many unable to access computers. Or have access to teachers.
  We really need to catch up this next year."
- "Fundamentally changed it. Harshly highlighted every structural,
  glaring weakness. The challenge is ours for the taking or the losing."
- "It has made it obvious to me, as a parent, that teachers are absolutely vital to my children's success! It has flipped the way kids
  learn, required so much more use of tech, which is going to
  (IMO) have some negative impact on students."
- "Has exposed great weaknesses in online learning...for the most
  part the technology is there, and will get better, but students do
  not seem to have "grabbed the baton" with how to equalize the
  learning they get "on the net" with in person learning in the class-

room. Many have "dropped out" (Betsy DeVos, today, said 3-4 million have). Also, there are 21 million people in the U.S. who have no access to internet. What cracks do they fall into?"

- "We have set back a generation of students right now, intellectually and socially. I think it will create the imperative to jumpstart some changes to bringing students and teachers back into the system. I think it has also taught us the importance of equal access to technology and also to the potential for virtual learning to work alongside in-person learning, providing more opportunities to people to learn (students can sign up for "competing" courses, students/adults who work have some flexibility of access, and some courses may just be better offered virtually)."

- "I'm afraid it will have long-lasting repercussions. Every student in school right now will have half an education for this school year. There will be fewer people willing to go into teaching, after hearing the nightmare stories. There will be trauma (PTSD like) in many who were affected so closely (i.e., those who had COVID, had friends with COVID, attended school, then didn't attend, then attended again); the list goes on."

Hey! Here's an idea for 2020. Let's just pull the plug on all in-person education and see what happens? Well, if you ever wanted to conduct the ultimate chemistry lab experiment, we just did it in 2020. And to be honest, we have no idea what the results are yet. This is likely a two-year experiment. On the bright side, we just really exposed some weaknesses in the system. On the dark side, we may have sacrificed a year of learning for our kids. But perhaps it was a life experience that taught some unexpected lessons for our kids. Perhaps a more genuine appreciation of what a wonderful opportunity learning is and the importance of the personal relationships that in-person education can offer. Maybe, just maybe, it influences a new generation of teachers to join the system.

One Final Scenario—Northern Arizona University, Business School, 2030

Fall semester, 2030. Day 1 of *Social Trends and Their Influence on the Decade Ahead (2030-2039)*. Fifty bright students, a tiered classroom. A beautiful fall day on campus, lots of energy in the room. *Hungry learners, no doubt.*

Finally, the side door opens, straight up 9:00am. A little quieter now. *Professor Douglas S. Griffen* walks in slowly. An NAU issued backpack. Tweed jacket. He brings out a spiral notebook and checks a few handwritten notes. Slowly, methodically, he looks up at the class. *I was in your seat at one time,* he wants to say. But that's not the right tone to set. He touches the control panel at his desk and displays a graphic that is a combination of a welcome and a first scenario assignment to have the class consider.

GRIFFEN: Good morning, ladies and gentlemen. I trust that you are well rested and eager to consider the merits of this morning's assignment. 2030, and we are now into year three of President Harris' and Vice President Buttigieg's administration. You have been asked to advise the administration on which priority for America will be most influential for the decade ahead, where their leadership acumen should be focused. There are five potential scenarios. You have five minutes to create your notes before you argue your selection in front of the class. You may begin your consideration.

THIRD ROW STUDENT (Phil Sobel): Professor? Professor?

GRIFFEN: Yes, Mr...and what might be your name, young man?

STUDENT: Sobel, sir. Phil Sobel. Look, no disrespect but I think that *day one* is supposed to be an orientation, a little sense of what we are going to be covering in the semester ahead. I mean, some of us are auditing today to see if we want to actually *take* this course. (A few snickers from the other students.)

GRIFFEN: Mr. Sobel, would you come forward for a moment?

STUDENT: Sure, *Professor G*, happy to...

GRIFFEN: Mr. Sobel...(reaches into a *jar* on his desk). Here's a *dime*, Mr. Sobel. Go call your mother and tell her...

Fade from the classroom, an outside shot of the business school. A green mountain bike is leaning against a tree. The professor still pedals.

CHAPTER 9: States as Brands—
The Arizona Leadership Edition

Well, I'm a-standing on a corner
In Winslow, Arizona
Such a fine sight to see
It's a girl, my Lord, in a flat-bed Ford
Slowin' down to take a look at me

…
Lighten up while you still can
Don't even try to understand
Just find a place to make your stand
And take it easy

--Eagles (written by Jackson Browne), Take it Easy (1973)

December 17, 2020
Foresight 2030 Session

Just find a place to make your stand. I found mine in 1956, or I suppose, more accurately, it was found for me. I was born and raised in Arizona. Third generation. That's always a good conversation starter. *A native Arizonan* I say. *Nobody's from Arizona*, they say.

State 48. Officially added to the U.S. flag of state stars on February 14, 1912. That was the last state added until *after* I was born. God, I sound old, like I was in the Civil War or something. But, yes, you are right, Alaska and Hawaii were added in 1959 to round out the top 50. A few efforts underway these days for Puerto Rico, Guam and the District of Columbia (DC). I would agree that DC often acts like it is not part of the U.S., but that's a different chapter. Personally, I think we are just enamored with the idea of an *even* 50 states. No flags or history books to change. Or maybe you need to vote a state out to add a new one.

I like that twist, I have a few in mind.

Three Cultural Influences

So, Arizona must be a pretty new place to have just been added as the 48th state. Actually, it has a very rich history and deep heritage which influences it to this very day. The *Arizona Republic* reports that, "The Hohokam people began building villages along the Gila River around 1 A.D." Odd, since the Arizona Republic newspaper was not founded until 1890, but this was excellent early reporting. *And how did you know that it was "1 A.D."?*

But I digress. Along with the Hohokam, there were additional Pre-Columbian peoples in the state including the Mogollon and the Ancestral Puebloans (also known as the Anasazi). The Mogollon Rim was named after one of the early groups and is a major feature on the state topology. These cultures would develop and last over some 1400 years, and many of their structures and ruins are part of Arizona historical preservation sites. *I went to more than a couple of those as part of early school "field trips".* I still take field trips as an adult, I just call them *road trips*. Rarely to Hohokam ruins.

As the early cultures faded, additional Indian (aka Native American) groups developed in Arizona, including the Navajo, Apache, Southern Paiute, Hopi, Yavapai, Akimel O'odham and the Tohono O'odham. Many of our counties are named after these tribes, and many of the tribes are established in reservations that have now emerged as economic players in the state. We will need to talk a little more about the entire issue of how we treated Native Americans as a country and created *reservations* for them, but we'll get to that. Suffice to say, though, that the Indian influence on Arizona's culture is a rich and powerful influence that affects our history, art, culture, values and norms to this day.

It has not always been a proud past in terms of our treatment of the American Indians. As the white settlers came into the West, including Arizona, there were fierce battles for sovereignty and land. The Apaches kept the settlers off of their tribal lands for 30 years before Geronimo surrendered to the U.S. Army forces in 1886. He is considered the last American Indian warrior to surrender, and it marked the end of the Indian wars in the Southwest. The Bureau of Indian Affairs now administers over 55,000,000 acres of land held in trust by the U.S. government for the Indian tribes. There are some 574 federally recognized tribes in the U.S. and 21 tribes are recognized in Arizona itself.

Apache Indians en route to imprisonment in 1886.
Geronimo is third from the right in the front row.

I have had the privilege of working with one of the Arizona tribes, the Gila River Indian Community, for the last four years. Strategic planning for their fire department, their utility authority, their telecommunications company and for their commercial development authority. The tribe is committed to improving the lives of their community members. They have three casinos in the Valley with another recently granted. They are not just in the gaming business, they are in the *event* business, the *sports promotion* business, the *technology* business and the *commercial development* business. They are nearly 100% fiber to the home for broadband, they just landed the Phoenix Rising Soccer Club and its stadium, their fire department runs a modern fleet and uses GPS for emergency location services, they are building a solar farm, and they are partnering with big commercial entities for real estate, hotel and real estate development. They also have a heritage of respecting the land, of sustainable agriculture and farming, and of family orientation.

Gila River is just one example of the heritage of the Native American/Indian peoples and the impact they will have on the future. The tribes and their *sovereign Indian nations* will be important partners for the growth of Arizona in the future. Their lands, in many areas of the state, are strategically located. Their leaders are strategically positioned for the future. They are the first of three important cultural influences on the state.

Our Mexican Heritage

Arizona was part of Mexico before it was part of the United States. The Spaniards were the first Europeans to explore Arizona, and Spanish missionaries began to settle into the southern geography of the state in the 1700s and established Tucson (aka, "The Old Pueblo") in 1775. In 1822, Arizona became part of Mexico and the state of Sonora.

Let's be clear here. For a period of time, Arizona had its own beach and port in Rocky Point.

All of that ended with the Mexican-American War, which lasted from 1846 to 1848. It was incited by the U.S. annexation of Texas in 1845. There was a lot of confusion back then, which ultimately led to the armed conflict. Mexico considered Texas to be Mexican territory at the time. The Republic of Texas was considered to be a *de facto* country at the time, but apparently its citizens wanted to be Americans and be annexed. Domestic politics were involved as the annexation of Texas would change the balance of power between the northern free states and the southern slave states (Texas would have been a slave state). President James Polk apparently was not confused and ran on a platform of U.S. expansion, including Texas via the annexation. Which sounded clear, but was not, as the U.S. claimed that the boundary between Texas and Mexico would be the Rio Grande River, and Mexico said it was the Nueces River to the north.

Just leave the beach in Arizona alone, whatever you do.

Then Polk tricks Mexico into starting a conflict so the U.S. could declare war on Mexico. War is declared and the U.S. moved against Mexico on many fronts including a Naval blockage on the Pacific Coast on the lower Baja California Territory, lands beyond Texas such as the regional capital of Santa Fe (Nuevo Mexico), and even occupied Mexico City in September of 1847. Mexico was outnumbered for traditional warfare and eventually signed the Treaty of Guadalupe Hidalgo in February of 1848 to end the war. As part of the treaty, Mexico recognized the *Mexican Cession,* which were the areas not part of the disputed Texas territory, but conquered by the U.S. Army.

You guessed it. This included the present day states of California, Nevada, Colorado, Utah and *most of Arizona.* The U.S. paid Mexico some $15M for the land and assumed another $3.25M for debts that Mexico owed to U.S. citizens before the hostilities started. We did not get the beach in this initial deal as there was a southern third or so of Arizona and a sliver of western New Mexico that was still retained by Mexico.

Another chance for the beach?

Actually, yes. Driven by the interest of the U.S. for a transcontinental rail-road along a southern route, the U.S. then negotiated a second deal to acquire the lands in Arizona and New Mexico in the Treaty of Mesilla in 1854. The treaty was signed by the U.S. Ambassador to Mexico, James Gadsden, and the Mexico President, Antonio Lopez de Santa Ana, and referred to as the "Gadsden Steal" at a price of $10M. *OK, it was referred to as the Gadsden Purchase, but seriously...*

Maybe another $1M on the table and we would have had the beach?

Who knows. But this was the last major territory acquisition for the U.S. in the continuous states and finally defined the current border of Mexico and the United States. Arizona moved from Mexico to the U.S., but re-tained a cultural and historical background of the Mexican culture and people. We share a border with Mexico, but also a colorful past and im-portant international future. Mexico is the second of three important cul-tural influences on Arizona.

The Mexico Cession and Gadsden Purchase

Rocky Point—Arizona's Southern beach

And just a couple of final points on the Arizona Beach. The reality is that I *prefer* to have our beach in Mexico. Everyone in Arizona knows about Rocky Point (Puerto Peñasco). You can drive there in about 3.5 hours from Phoenix. Another country, a different culture. It's like flying internationally to some far off destination but it's really just a simple *road trip*. Cold *Tecates* await you, good swimming/snorkeling, great fishing, plenty of beach, the estuaries, Sand Hill and a couple of my favorite watering holes: *Wrecked at the Reef* and *JJ's Cantina*. My brother and I head down every year for the Rocky Point Triathlon staged out of the Las Palomas resort. Ping-pong at *Wrecked at the Reef* is always the fourth leg.

And yes, you cross the border. I am all for good borders. I am all against tall walls on borders. I get that good fences make good neighbors, but, cartels aside, most Mexican people I know are hard working, family oriented and not trying to re-enact the Mexican-American War. We were led astray on this one, and I predict that by the end of the decade much of that wall will be taken down. *Where is Reagan when we need him?*

Cowboy Up!

I think if you sent out a national survey about the images that come to mind when people think of "Arizona", the *Arizona Cowboy* would rank high on the list. I'm not talking about the *drug store cowboys* you might see in some parts of the country (and certainly not the *naked cowboy* in New York City), but I am talking about the genuine deal. Weathered skin, cowboy hat, old Levis or Wranglers, cowboy boots and some spurs. *My horse is parked out front.*

We had some very famous cowboys in Arizona—most notably on the list would be Wyatt Earp. Perhaps the best known gunfight of the West which took place at the O.K. Corral in Tombstone, Arizona. On the side of the law were the Earp Brothers—Wyatt, Virgil and Morgan—and along with Doc Holliday they went toe-to-toe with *them outlaws* Ike and Billy Clanton, Tom and Frank McLaury, and Billy Claiborne at 3:00pm on Wednesday, October 26, 1881, in Tombstone. The McLaury brothers were killed along with Billy Clanton. Ike Clanton and Billy Claiborne *ran from the fight* and Virgil and Morgan Earp, along with Doc Holliday, were wounded. Virgil Earp, by the way, was the Town Marshall.

Score one for the law that day, one of the most famous 30 seconds in the West. But score a bigger one for the Town of Tombstone that lives off of that famous event to this day. In fact, you will see a re-enactment of the gunfight *every day*. One day, a few years ago, one of the cowboy actors forgot to load blanks in his gun and shot one of the other guys. I hope the *Town Too Tough to Die* had a pretty good lawyer working for the Mayor.

Memorabilia from the OK Corral

Author Griffen as a young lawman

Arizona is a genuine player in the American Wild West. Many of us grew up watching the Hollywood version of the West—Gunsmoke, Bonanza, The Rifleman (Pa! Pa!), The High Chaparral, The Big Valley and even the Lone Ranger. But one actor epitomizes the West: John Wayne. And, *look here, Pilgrim,* John Wayne filmed dozens of his movies in Arizona including *Stagecoach, Angel and the Badman,* and *Red River.* And he was a resident at times as well with a 50,000 acre cattle ranch near Eager, Arizona.

So, Arizonans have a heritage with the American West and the American cowboy. A pioneering spirit, a rugged individualism, a welcoming tip of the brim, a bit of *maverick* in many of us. Plenty of cowboys in our towns and cities—Prescott, Tucson, Flagstaff, *Winslow* and one of my favorites, Payson, near the base of the Mogollon Rim.

My dad leased land from the Forest Service in 1956 and started the Three Pines Griffen cabin along Ellison Creek just north of Payson. Built it from scratch, along with my mom and, eventually, a little help from the three Pines (which were the three Griffen boys). The cabin is still there and we own the land now. The land and the cabin look exactly the same now as it did in 1956 (the land is great, the cabin could use a little update). We spent a lot of time up there as kids and got to know Payson as well. Famous for its summer rodeo (claims to be the oldest continuous rodeo in the world).

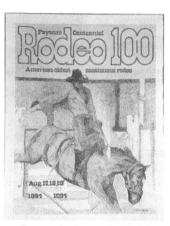

The "Three Pines" Griffen cabin, established 1956   *Payson Rodeo poster, 1984*

But on a summer afternoon with your cowboy boots and hat on, sitting on the fence rails that surround the rodeo arena, a cold A-1 Arizona beer and perhaps a pinch between your cheek and gum, *there ain't nuthin' like bein' a cowboy*. Hang on for eight seconds!

So, that's our third influence—The American Cowboy. And that's a hell of a trio: the American Cowboy, the Native American Indian and our Mexican friends from the south. All have respect for the land and the sky, an innate pride, family orientation. *A streak of independence.* They influence our past, but they also influence our lifestyle today and our path for the future.

States as Brands
Wait—the future—you mean like the decade ahead? Now we're getting somewhere with this *journey of a chapter*. The premise is very simple: there will be winners and losers in the decade ahead when you look at the 50 states (assuming we stay at 50). And Arizona will be a winner, easily in the top five and maybe at the top of the podium at the end of the decade. They will be a *bellwether* for the country, an early trend setter on

politics, technology, healthcare, social equality, international trade, renewable energy and sports/entertainment.

Arizona's flag and "brand logo"

The Authentic Arizona Cowboy
(Megargee)

In the decade ahead, states will become brands. Some will be authentic brands, they will stand for something and draw people. Some will be marketing brands and people will see through them. I see Arizona as the brand that mixes innovation for the future with an understanding and respect for its heritage of the past. We'll explore this premise about the future with a set of *Arizona branded* Foresighters. A tip of the cowboy brim to John Wayne for this insight:

"Tomorrow is the most important thing in life. Comes to us at midnight very clean. It's perfect when it arrives and puts itself in our hands. It hopes we learned something from yesterday." (J. Wayne)

Saddle Up.

The Foresight Arizona Leadership Edition

Author's Note: In addition to our normal sharing of insights and assessments from our interactive Foresight session, we are including five "Featured Foresights" from Arizona leaders who shared a view on the future of Arizona in the decade ahead. These Featured Foresights were collected after our Foresight session via email request and an approval for attribution for the book. Enjoy!

There were some *pre-qualifications* for this "special edition" of our Foresight interactive session. You had to either be a resident in Arizona now, or be a previous resident (and perhaps wonder why you moved to South Dakota or Minnesota...). So we found 38 *Arizona Foresighters* for our special edition, here are a few backgrounds to introduce them:

- "I am a long time management consultant, parent of three adult children, originally from the East Coast/Mid-Atlantic now loving life in northern AZ."
- "I am the Executive Director for Scottsdale Leadership. I live and work in Scottsdale. I am married with three grown daughters and two wonderful grandchildren!"
- "An Arizona native and long time community leader. Served on Scottsdale City Council for two terms."
- "Farm kid from Iowa, CPA and CEO of two large companies; now an insurance broker in AZ. Married, with two high school kids."
- "Hi there, I am currently living in Tucson, AZ, and am from Flagstaff, AZ. I just finished attaining my bachelor's degree from the University of Arizona and have plans of attending law school in the near future. In the meantime I am working and saving money."
- "Defense lawyer in Northern Arizona for nearly 40 years. Native of Arizona and an avid skier, triathlete and occasional fisherman on the Tonto. Also developing a vineyard on Oak Creek near Page Springs (Echo Canyon). First bottles this December!"
- "I love the desert, Arizona, and the small things in life."
- "In a world that can sometimes be dark, isn't it wonderful that we get to spread the light. Let's light it up..."

Woah, there pardner! I love these sessions too, but I am a little concerned about what you are planning to light up. Nonetheless, let's spread a little Arizona sunshine!

For the record, 85% of our participants in this session were currently living in Arizona and over 80% (regardless of whether they are currently in Arizona) had lived in Arizona for over 20 years. So, we have some serious experience on the session to look at Arizona now and in the future.

What Makes Arizona Arizona

A reasonable first question. After all, if our premise is that *states are brands* in the future, then we need to be clear about the attributes of this brand:

Question: *All of you on our session today are current Arizonans or have an Arizona connection in the past. As you think of Arizona as a state, what makes Arizona an attractive place to live, work or visit? What makes Arizona Arizona?*

I know this phrasing drives the grammar police crazy—*what makes Arizona Arizona*, but it is intentional. A brand needs to be distinctive and authentic. It has to be something that *resonates*. If you are a first time

297

visitor to Arizona, you have to immediately feel something unique. *Other than it is 115 degrees in July in the desert.*

So here are a few "brand attributes" that were identified by our Arizona Foresighters:

- ✓ The Western heritage
- ✓ The Sonoran Desert
- ✓ The desirable climate for most of the year
- ✓ Access to the outdoors throughout the state
- ✓ The Grand Canyon
- ✓ A welcoming culture, you can assimilate from anywhere
- ✓ The open skies
- ✓ The independent spirit and "pioneer" spirit
- ✓ The Hispanic and Native American cultural influences
- ✓ The silhouette of a saguaro cactus
- ✓ The distinctive sound of an Arizona *rattlesnake*
- ✓ Less government by design
- ✓ Proximity to California but not with the "crazy of California"
- ✓ The mix of the old west and the metropolitan high tech west
- ✓ World class airport (Phoenix Sky Harbor)
- ✓ The heritage of the 5 Cs (more about the Cs later)
- ✓ Arizona sunrises and sunsets
- ✓ The diversity of the topology—deserts to forested mountains
- ✓ Modern infrastructure (transportation, internet, services, etc.)
- ✓ Abundance of National and State Parks
- ✓ The overall quality of life
- ✓ The relatively good affordability of housing and education
- ✓ Strong job/professional opportunities
- ✓ Great sports and entertainment options
- ✓ Excellent state university system

One of our participants described it this way: "The spiritual nature and connection to the earth. There is a real sense of place. From the Grand Canyon to Sedona, the Sonoran desert, the Chiricahuas and the history of this place from the Anasazi to present day."

A sense of place. Isn't that what we all want when we think of where we live and what we call home? Arizona is all about a sense of place. If you have lived or visited here, you know what I mean. Perhaps you have hiked the Grand Canyon, visited Sedona, hit a round of golf on one of the many desert-style courses, stayed a weekend at a Scottsdale resort, mountain-biked in the Sonoran Preserve, watched an Arizona sunset or just admired the vastness of the Arizona sky.

The vastness of the Arizona sky. I was running a trail race one Saturday many years ago (the older we get the faster we were) near Prescott. Wide open country, a combination of desert/mountain terrain. To be honest, I was kind of zoning out. I was 35 miles into a 50-miler and grinding up Mingus Mountain on a back road. You spread out pretty quickly in one of these Arizona ultras. Mostly I was looking down at my feet, but around a curve I caught sight of a fellow runner. Didn't know him, but I knew he was leading the race. I came up along side of him, no words for a few minutes.

He looked over. "Scott Modzelewski," he said and smiled. "You can just call me *Mojo.*" Great, *Mr. Mojo,* I thought. *You can just call me ass-tired.* But there was a bit of *mojo* about him. Spirited, taking in the solitude and the beauty of the Arizona terrain. We passed the time for the next 45 minutes as we continued the long climb.

Seeing the top of Mingus Mountain ahead, Mojo pointed up and simply said, "Arizona Blue." *I am kind of looking around for a sign or something.* "The sky," he said. "Arizona Blue. There's nothing like it in the world." And he was right. A deep, clear and inviting blue sky set against the mountain topography. I locked in on the sky. *It's what makes Arizona Arizona,* I thought. I zoned out for a while, and then turned to say something to Scott.

Mojo had taken off as we crested Mingus Mountain. I think he has pulled the "Arizona Blue" trick on a few other competitors in the past. But he was right. *There's nothing like it in the world.*

Picturing Arizona: 100 Years of *Arizona Highways*
Long before social media kicked in, the world learned about Arizona and our *Arizona Brand* through the *Arizona Highways* magazine. Begun in 1921, it had a unique coffee table style size that was meant to be left out for others to enjoy. World class photography, no advertisements for most of its published life, and an amazing chronicle of Arizona's outdoors and its history. Ansel Adams contributed photos, so did the *very accomplished amateur photographer,* Barry Goldwater.

Subscriptions of the magazine reach all 50 states and two thirds of the countries on the planet. One of my prized possessions in my Center is a large framed black and white picture of the Grand Canyon, signed in the margins by the long-time publisher Win Holden and his management team after a planning session we conducted in 2006. I asked Win, now retired from Arizona Highways, his view of what makes Arizona Arizona:

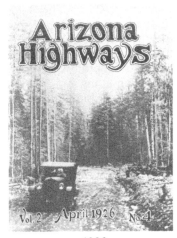

1926

1954

1986

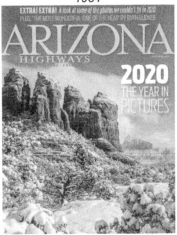

2020

Featured Foresight—Win Holden, Former Publisher of Arizona Highways:

"Arizona's compelling array of strengths and assets underscores how well the state is positioned to not just survive, but thrive, in the future. Consider the obvious physical beauty of places like the Grand Canyon, Sedona, the Mogollon Rim, Monument Valley, Saguaro National Monument, Lake Powell, Lake Mead and scores of others. It's simply impossible to identify another state with such abundant and stunning vistas. And that's not idle hubris. Over 42% of Arizona is public land which provides limitations on private development, ensuring the breadth of natural beauty is preserved for future generations."

A Legacy of Arizona Leaders

In September of 2005, in a meeting that turned out to be the impetus for this book, I ran a session with Arizona leaders for The Phoenix Business Journal to look back at some of the most important stories and leaders over the last 25 years (1980 through 2005). The session was sponsored by their publisher, Don Henninger, whom I consider to be a friend and an authentic Arizona leader. It was a fascinating session with notable leaders such as Ed Beauvais, Karl Eller, Ira Fulton, Kathy Munro and Jack Pfister. These leaders knew Arizona and reflected back on some of the most significant stories and accomplishments:

- ✓ The development of the Central Arizona Project (transporting Colorado River water)
- ✓ The building of the Palo Verde nuclear power plant
- ✓ The development of a modern freeway infrastructure
- ✓ The passage of a groundwater management act for the future
- ✓ The Translational Genomics Research Institute (T-Gen)
- ✓ The arrival of Michael Crow to transform Arizona State University
- ✓ The impact of the Mayo Clinic on our healthcare reputation
- ✓ The launch of America West Airlines (later merging with US Airways/American Airlines)
- ✓ The development of the Indian Gaming compact and casinos
- ✓ The development of major sports in the Valley along with Jerry Colangelo
- ✓ Intel's decision to bring in the first $1B chip fabrication plant
- ✓ The development of the Fiesta Bowl
- ✓ The preservation of large amounts of state trust land for open spaces

All of these developments, cited in 2005 as having been some of the most significant stories and impacts for Arizona over the last 25 years, have been essential for the development over the next 15 years into 2020 and will continue to set the stage for Arizona's leadership for the decade ahead. These were Arizona's original *Foresighters*. I asked Don, the session sponsor in 2005, to reflect in 2020 on Arizona in the decade ahead:

The point here is simple: it takes long term vision and leadership for a state (or any organization) to develop and sustain a compelling brand. Most leaders are focused on the short-term, on results they can expect to see in the next quarter or fiscal year. Long term leaders, some call them *servant leaders*, are focused on years ahead, even decades and generations ahead.

I was in a session in 2008 with the Mesa City Council and their mayor, Scott Smith, where we were developing a new vision for Mesa, Arizona. Mostly known as a slow-paced retirement community with lots of wide streets, Smith and the council wanted to transform Mesa and their brand. It was about placing a series of long term bets around education, business attraction, retention of their *beloved Chicago Cubs* spring training facility, mass transit and a regional airport. Smith explained the context of the long-term leadership moves: "Leaders plant trees under whose shade they do not intend to sit."

Now I don't know if the mayor came up with that himself but it was *damned impressive* to me as their facilitator for the session. I mean, *I'm* supposed to come up with those *pithy* leadership statements. I fired up a hand: "Mayor Smith! Mayor Smith! I've got it!" I blurted out:

"Bigger trees. Sooner shade."

I mean, give me a rim-shot. A round of head-nods. *Nothing.* But I knew what the mayor was saying. And they planted those trees (the smaller

302

versions) and grew them into the new Sloan Park, housing the Cubs, developed Mesa's Riverview Park, went forward with light rail when other Valley cities did not, attracted new education players and have been prominent in the development of the Phoenix-Mesa Gateway Airport. It's still a *flat city geographically*, but it is a city *on the rise economically* and poised to be a leader in the state in the decade ahead.

The Arizona Leaders We Admire

So, back to our 2020 Foresighters, we asked them about the Arizona leaders they admired most:

Question: *We'd like to start our focus on leadership by asking you to think about an Arizona leader—past or present—you really admire. Who is that leader and WHY do you feel strongly about their leadership and impact?*

The attributes about independence, the pioneer spirit and long-term leaders, often ahead of their times, were apparent in the statements:

- "Barry Goldwater—A true believer in Arizona with genuine interest in the land, people and future of the state. An authentic leader."
- "Herb Drinkwater—I think of him as the embodiment of Scottsdale's many wonderful facets: friendly, welcoming, Western, accommodating, patient, charismatic, smart and trusted. His legacy is strong because he was so committed and so able to connect with people throughout the community."
- "Sen. John McCain. The Maverick. You might not align with all of his policy positions, but his life, his example, and his commitment to trying to build the best world for Arizona and our nation is unassailable. Not afraid to swim upstream—a man of integrity."
- "John Rhodes for his vision for Arizona's water supply. He worked for decades to get the CAP aqueduct funded and built."
- "Jeff Flake. Clear about his principles and stuck to them. Represented a libertarian streak that fits well with Arizona."
- "Goldwater. He loved the land of Arizona. He loved the American Indians of Arizona. He loved the independence that attracted people to Arizona. He relied more on his fellow human than he did institutions."
- "Mo Udall—He managed to work with those in the opposition party to achieve results that not only advanced his own agenda, but ensured that both Arizona and the nation would benefit as well. He was a true statesman and many current politicians can learn from him."
- "Sandra Day O'Connor—represented Arizona on Supreme Court."

- "John Wayne, he introduced the west to the world and supported Arizona as a land owner and rancher, and he filmed movies in the state."
- "John McCain—fighter, principled, rugged, durable, caring, honest, empathetic, independent, even though anchored in a party, respectful of others. I believe his leadership style is inclusive while still charting a course. And I believe it is sorely needed nationally."

Look, these are *big names*. Goldwater, McCain, Udall, Drinkwater, O'-Connor, Rhodes, Flake and even *The Duke* John Wayne. But look at the set of *political mavericks*. They did big things in Arizona but also played on the national stage. Goldwater and McCain ran for President. Both a victim of circumstance and timing. Barry Goldwater was taken down by Lyndon Johnson as too independent and reckless, epitomized by LBJ in the "Daisy Ad" in 1964: "These are the stakes. To make a world in which all of God's children can live, or go into the darkness. We must either love each other or we must die." *Boom*. (Google "Daisy Ad" for one of the most chilling ads ever.)

McCain, ever the Maverick in 2008, running against Barack Obama, made history when he selected Alaska Governor Sarah Palin as his running mate. *A little too maverick on this one.* I am convinced to this day that a John McCain/Mitt Romney ticket might have propelled McCain to the presidency. Or at least given him a shot.

Another Arizona legend: Sandra Day O'Connor. Smashed the legal glass ceiling with her nomination in 1981 as the first woman Supreme Court Justice in 1981 and served until 2006. *Tough and principled*, another classic Arizona leader. You don't mess with Justice O'Connor.

I found this out first-hand. I was running a session for The Arizona Republic newspaper and the O'Connor House Foundation at the Walter Cronkite School of Journalism at Arizona State University in 2009. Justice O'Connor was not only one of the sponsors, but she was one of the *participants* in the laptop lab session that I was facilitating. *All rise.* I mean, this was cool. I had just launched a brainstorming question to the laptops and I noticed that Justice O'Connor seemed puzzled about the use of the laptop and perhaps how to enter her responses. *The facilitator becomes the help desk.* I walked over, very respectfully and very quietly, and said, "Justice O'Connor...would you need any help with the laptop?"

She paused, and *ever so slowly*, looked up from the laptop and turned towards me. "Young man," *Oh shit! Nothing good ever comes after "young man".* She paused again. "Do I *look* like I need your help with the laptop?" That was like arguing in front of the court and getting a 9-0 verdict against you. And then, *ever so slowly*, she turned back to the laptop. I turned and ran.

Author Griffen with Justice O'Conner--2009

Positioning Arizona For The Decade

Back to our Foresighters. Our next activity was to look at how Arizona might be positioned to lead for the decade ahead:

Question: *In what ways do you feel Arizona is well positioned for the decade ahead?*

So, if you are a brand that will lead and endure for the decade ahead, then you need to have some strong evidence. *May it please the court:*

- ✓ Attraction of technology-based companies (The Silicon Desert)
- ✓ New leaders for the Senate (Kyrsten Sinema/Mark Kelly)
- ✓ Strong tourism assets
- ✓ Plenty of room (available land) for growth
- ✓ More balanced politically than we were in the past (i.e., SB1070 days)
- ✓ All four of the major sports teams in the Valley
- ✓ The global attraction of Arizona State University and its leadership
- ✓ Relatively affordable housing
- ✓ The lifestyle and welcoming culture
- ✓ Sky Harbor airport and growing global connections
- ✓ Relatively low state tax, more business-friendly
- ✓ Becoming a leader in autonomous/electric vehicles
- ✓ A diversified economic base

✓ An expanding healthcare industry including bioscience
✓ A growing and diversifying population
✓ Taking smart steps on water management
✓ Making it easy for business to relocate

Growing forward. The U.S. Census Bureau in July of 2020 indicated that Maricopa County in Arizona was the fastest growing county *in the country.* And the Phoenix-Mesa-Chandler metro area was growing at the fastest pace of any of the top 10 metro areas in the country. On the job economics side, the Arizona Office of Economic Opportunity estimates that Arizona will add 550,000 jobs by 2029, *four times the average U.S. growth rate.* I'd say those trees that were planted over the last 25 years are getting *mighty big.*

Featured Foresights—Sandra Watson, President and CEO of the Arizona Commerce Authority:
"Over the last ten years, it's been exciting to see Arizona transform into a globally-recognized hub for innovation. Ten years ago, Arizona was struggling under devastating job and revenue losses as one of the hardest-hit states during the Great Recession. Today, our economy is diversified across several high-tech industries, with more jobs in manufacturing than construction, our startup ecosystem is attracting global attention and our state is competing at the highest level for economic development projects.

Looking ahead, opportunities abound. As companies around the world look to bring more manufacturing to U.S. shores, Arizona has emerged as the go-to destination for advanced manufacturing. Emerging technologies that have found a home in our state include semiconductors, electric vehicles, automated vehicles, artificial intelligence, quantum computing, fintech, cyber security and more. With a robust and growing workforce, modern infrastructure, reliable energy, a low-cost business environment and thriving innovation ecosystem, Arizona is poised for explosive growth in the years and decades to come."

Adds one of our Foresighters: "We are Arizona—wild, free, great climate, great diversity, great opportunity. Our fast growth, livability and affordability, compared to the left coast makes us a natural leader."

Nice jab at the left coast (aka, California).

Arizona as a Bellwether

OK, looks like some good sailing ahead for the state, but we are in competition with 49 others in terms of leading the country for the decade ahead. How do our Foresighters feel about Arizona as a *bellwether* for the country for the decade ahead?

Question: *A "bellwether" is defined as a leader or indicator of trends. A premise for this session is that Arizona is well positioned to be a bellwether for the country for the decade ahead—a leader in many areas and a state to watch as a trend-setter in leadership. To what extent do you agree with this premise?*

No.	Items	Times Selected
1.	**Somewhat agree**	**(47%)**
2.	**In the middle on this one**	**(22%)**
3.	**Strongly agree**	**(20%)**
4.	Somewhat disagree	(8%)
5.	Strongly disagree	(3%)

So, our Foresighters lean positive on this, but there is some wait and see going on as well. After all, Arizona has a bit of a legacy for *Boom and Bust*, so this idea of sustained leadership for the decade ahead will have to be demonstrated over time:

- SOMEWHAT AGREE: "Arizona is rapidly becoming a microcosm of the country, politically a very centrist state now but with a strong economy, meaning that leadership also needs to be more middle of the road."
- STRONGLY AGREE: "The amount of people moving to Maricopa County is proof Arizona is a bellwether. People are voting with their feet."
- SOMEWHAT AGREE: "Our population growth is impressive, but I believe we need to enhance our business climate and culture so we evolve into a popular destination for industry. It seems like when you mention Arizona, most people think of retirement or outdoor activities like travel."
- SOMEWHAT AGREE: "As former hubs throughout the U.S. reach their capacity or their costs become too high (LA, NY, San Francisco), companies and people turn to locations that meet their needs but don't break the bank. Phoenix, especially, is an attractive city to these groups--growth in Flagstaff and Tucson also represent this change."
- MIDDLE: "First of all, we currently have excellent leadership in the Senate who are both open minded and intelligent. This will

give instant credibility to our state in so many ways. Arizona has also proven itself to be willing to consider new and innovative ideas and policies, and this makes it a very attractive location for those considering moving here. Two specific powerful areas are health care and what Michael Crow has done for ASU."

- STRONGLY AGREE: "Arizona has it all at an affordable cost of living for nearly everyone. As we have grown at record pace, we have a balanced mix of views that include both conservative and liberal agendas."
- IN THE MIDDLE: "AZ has historically been a follower state. We are a bandwagon state without any documented history of real innovation or leadership. We should be the solar capital of the universe, the center for understanding drought and climate change, and capitalizing on the fact we are rarely visited by natural disaster. We just have never appealed to the "big fish" who swim in the global economic ocean."

Big fish that swim in the global economic ocean? Yet another vote that we should have annexed Rocky Point so we have a port to land that big fish.

But, we are clearly in the running. And it will take real innovation and leadership for the decade ahead. Some other *states as brands* will be competing hard in the decade ahead. The top ten states that our Foresighters see as competition for the decade ahead (alpha order):

1. California
2. Colorado
3. Georgia
4. Michigan
5. Nevada
6. New York
7. North Carolina
8. Tennessee
9. Texas
10. Utah

Improving Arizona for the Decade Ahead
And what will it take to improve Arizona's odds to be that bellwether? We asked our Foresighters where Arizona should focus its leadership:

Question: *Let's get some strong consulting advice from you now. Imagine you are part of a bipartisan taskforce to develop strategy for the state in the decade ahead—2020 through 2029. Where do you feel Arizona should focus its leadership, resources and strategy?*

Clear themes here and it looks like we'll be planting some more trees:

Now please indicate how important each of the following reasons are for the future of Arizona in the decade ahead. Use a scale of 1-10 where a "1" means not at all important and a "10" means extremely important.

Rank	Idea	Avg.
1.	Improving education across the board	9.6
2.	Ensure long term water resource availability	9.0
3.	Invest in long term infrastructure	8.6
4.	Develop young leaders	8.6
5.	Continue building on our technology company base	8.6
6.	Attract high wage industries	8.4
7.	Focus on innovation in decade ahead	8.4
8.	Become a solar power leader	8.3
9.	Develop/promote a strong business friendly culture	7.9
10.	Expand focus on healthcare as an industry	7.8
11.	Focus on sustainability and green jobs	7.6
12.	Become well known as an inclusive state	7.4
13.	Expand global trade	6.8
14.	Attract/retain more senior business leaders	6.7
15.	Expand focus on tourism	6.6

"As technology continues to be recognized as a catalyst for economic growth in the U.S., Arizona has risen to become a center for innovation. Our state's leaders, lawmakers and economic development organizations have created the nation's prime business climate with relatively low corporate taxes and commercial real estate costs, affordable energy and huge swaths of available land. A lower cost of living, beautiful year-round weather and high quality of life compared with other U.S. technology hubs also makes attracting talent easier. Add to that our being home to some of the world's most prestigious technology and engineering schools such as The University of Arizona, Arizona State University and Embry-Riddle Aeronautical University, which keeps the talent pipeline full of top-notch graduates. Arizona's technology sector is growing at a rapid pace. In a decade, I expect us to be on top."

We also asked our Foresighters to narrow the list even further and identify the one most important area for Arizona to focus on in the decade ahead:

Question: *Congratulations. You have just been elected Governor of Arizona. As you reflect on the responses and our assessment of what Arizona should focus on in the decade ahead, and thinking about your own views/insights, what do you feel is the ONE MOST IMPORTANT area for Arizona to focus on in the decade ahead? Why this area? What would it allow us to do or do differently as a state?*

Here are some views about the ONE MOST IMPORTANT AREA for Arizona's future from our Foresighters. There was a *dominant theme*:

- "**Education**—we are consistently and embarrassingly ranked in the bottom 2-3 states nationally for pre-K and K-12 education quality. Unacceptable. The future depends on a well-educated and well rounded and informed population of citizens."
- "Drastically improve our actual **education** focus and development, and significantly change (improve) the external image of our state, which has been as an education laggard."
- "**Education**. The next generation is the future of our state. We need to invest in them at all levels: K-12 and through the universities and community colleges."
- "Develop a better K-12 **education** platform. Most people move from CA to AZ because of taxes and climate. They are reactively leaving. If we want to strategically attract larger corporations or

310

thought leaders from across the country, we need to make it attractive to their families and child development, or they won't come. Having a solid educational system is how we build and develop future leaders."

- "**Education**. This area needs our full effort. There are too many kids not meeting the minimum standards. There are too many kids who are not progressing because they can't read proficiently. Improving our education system is a long-term goal that has not been addressed by short-term politicians."

Look, I took a little editorial privilege here as there were other statements on other priorities, but if you are giving advice to Arizona leadership for the decade ahead, it's pretty simple: *It's the education, stupid.* Our thanks to James Carville for laying the groundwork on that one.

Adds one of our Foresighters on their optimism towards addressing the issue of education for Arizona: "We know what needs to be done, in large part. We just need the discipline and courage to do it. That can be done with the right leadership."

Why Leadership Matters

The need for leadership is not just a state-only need. Our Foresighters feel like there is a significant void across the country—state level, regional level and (seriously) at the national level. That may mean that Arizona's focus on leadership at the state level could make it look good by comparison. There is a large issue that needs to be addressed in America in the decade ahead: *where have all of our leaders gone?*

Question: *If you were handing out a report card on the state of leadership in America today and how we are performing, what grade do you give it?*

No.	Items	Times Selected
1.	I give it a 'D'	(36%)
2.	I give it a 'C'	(33%)
3.	I give it an 'F'	(17%)
4.	I give it a 'B'	(14%)
5.	I give it an 'A'	(0%)

Ouch. Is that really the best we can do? Here is some context by our Arizona Foresighters commenting on the larger issue of leadership in America:

- "There's a massive number of 'leaders' out there—so many Feudal lords of their own realms. But I'm going to say that we have very few real capable visionaries who summon together a national feeling of purpose and goodwill. We really need leaders who summon our 'better angels'."

- "Greed and self-interest have overtaken us systemically. Capitalism without virtue is just greed, according to Adam Smith. We have reached a level of self-interest that collective leadership is absent. The economic divide is beyond description—we have what will be our first "trillionaire" in Jeff Bezos. Think of what that means. The national deficit is so large that we simply just don't talk about it any longer, because why would you talk about that? And our political leadership is lacking in governance, it has become a game of thrones in our day and time."

- "It's at a crisis moment. The country has never been more divided. The change at the White House will be the first step to prevent it from sinking any lower. But our leaders at all levels of the federal government have to be willing to stop the divisiveness."

- "Antiquated. We are behind everywhere that is going to count in the coming years. Education, healthcare, social safety nets, environmental protection. Is what we have...seriously the best we can do? Seriously?"

- "I feel we have lost our compass heading for leadership. America needs to show innovation and true leadership on issues inclusive of political leaders, but more need in social leadership and innovation to be, and do, better for our people and our international partners."

- "We are seemingly afraid to 'let leaders lead'. When Teddy Roosevelt proposed his plan for National Parks he didn't have a groundswell of people who opposed or who lobbied against, giving him a political victory. Same was true for Eisenhower and his vision to build the interstate highway system or Kennedy's call to land a man on the moon. We just cannot seem to be able to let people have their victories for fear they will gain political power and will be harder to beat in the next election."

And where will the needed leadership come from in the future? Are we looking to Gen Z to step forward in the decade ahead, or one last hurrah from the Boomers?

Question: *As you think about the decade ahead in America, which generation will be MOST IMPORTANT in their leadership to move America forward?*

312

No.	Items	Times Selected
1.	**MILLENNIALS: Born 1977 to 1995 (ages today 25 to 43)**	**(60%)**
2.	GEN X: Born 1965 to 1976 (ages today to 44 to 55)	(26%)
3.	GEN Z: Born 1996 or later (24 or younger)	(11%)
4.	BOOMERS: Born 1946 to 1964 (ages today 56 to 74)	(3%)

Look, this is far from scientific, so we should watch this space. But I have to say that I agree with our Foresighters. It's time, for the most part, for our Boomers to grab some shade underneath those long-growing trees. *They have earned it.* And the Gen Z generation has great promise as the "problem solving generation" but, for the most part, it's not their time yet. I do think that Gen Z needs to collectively own and steward the issue of climate change for the next 25 years.

But for the decade ahead, it's time for the *millennials* to step forward. Sprinkle in some Gen Xers, but I think, *for the most part*, that we need the youth of ideas combined with a reasonable level of life experience and serious intolerance of the status quo. *It's time, millennials.*

Raising Arizona's Leadership Status

Raising Arizona. Now that was a weird movie back in 1987. Really helpful for the state brand image, you know? But what kind of leadership and focus will allow Arizona to emerge as one of bellwether states during the decade ahead? My friend John Little, a former city manager for the City of Scottsdale and past president of Scottsdale Leadership, likens Arizona's future as one that relies on their past and the rise of the mythical Phoenix:

Featured Foresights—John Little, Former City Manager for the City of Scottsdale:

"Arizonans will rely on muscle memory to re-emerge as a leader in the global economy. It has taken a full decade to recover from the pain of the 2007 Great Recession and the wounds we felt will long be remembered. Fortuitously, we will also recall the heroic effort that was required to lift ourselves out of the darkness. Scientists posit there are two types of memory. The first is declarative memory, which we use to remember the more tangible and empirical elements of the past. The second is episodic memory which we employ to remember stories and experiences. Arizonans will draw on both types of memories to rise again like the mythical Phoenix regenerating in new forms, bristling with accumulated potential energy."

John is a bit of a *cowboy philosopher* and indeed still rides a horse in the annual "Ride" as part of the Scottsdale Charros community leadership organization. The Charros help preserve Arizona's western heritage from the past, but they also focus on education and the future of Arizona. They were key to maintaining Spring training and the Cactus League in Arizona and recently coordinated an agreement with the City of Scottsdale and the San Francisco Giants to keep the Giants in the downtown Scottsdale Stadium through *at least* 2044. Now that is placing a bet on the future—well beyond even our focus on the decade ahead.

Below: The Scottsdale Charros Annual Ride

Above: The Charros Lodge at Scottsdale Stadium

And a note about the "Charros Lodge" that occupies right field at Scotts-dale Stadium. There is no better place to watch a Spring league game in Arizona than the Charros Lodge. They literally *own* right field as a return for their managing the revenues from the games (which they channel to a broad range of education programs in Scottsdale). On any game day in the Spring the Charros Lodge will be filled with Arizona community leaders, friends and families. It is an Arizona community happening. Notes Kevin Richard from Major League Baseball News: "The Charros Lodge is one of the hottest tickets in all of Spring training."

I can confirm this from personal experience. My thanks to Charros Executive Director (and Foresighter) Dennis Robbins for the tickets!

Future Influence Scenarios

Customary in our Foresight sessions, we bring a few ideas to the table about what kinds of scenarios might influence the future, and in this case, would *raise Arizona*:

Now, please assess each of the following future scenarios in two ways. First, the level of positive IMPACT to the future of Arizona in the decade ahead if the scenario was to occur (use a scale of 1-10 where a "1" means a very low level of positive impact and a "10" means a very high level of positive impact); Second, the LIKELIHOOD that this scenario will fully materialize in the decade ahead (use a scale of 1-10 where a "1" means a very low likelihood and "10" means a very high likelihood):

315

The scenarios are ordered by the *level of positive impact* but then contrasted with the likelihood of occurrence for a gap analysis rating...

#	Scenario Description	Impact	Likely	Gap
1	A COMPLETE EDUCATION TRANSFORMATION: From worst to first in a decade. Arizona stepped back and re-imagined education from advancement and equity in early childhood education to a new investment in traditional K-12, to new pathways into the workforce that blended college/university options with vocational options. No one in the country has better adult learning engagement as well. Teacher salaries are the highest in the country and so are graduation rates and overall educational levels.	9.3	5.7	(3.6)
2	THE ALTERNATIVE ENERGY ALTERNATIVE: Arizona has led the nation in the movement to solar technology. This is the global hub for research/development as well as advanced deployment. By the end of the decade 50 percent of all energy in Arizona is produced by solar.	8.9	7.3	(1.6)
3	THE SILICON DESERT: Arizona has continued to build on strong progress in the prior decade and is now one of the most preferred locations for software technology companies. They are now one of the big 5 along with Silicon Valley in California, the Wasatch Front in Utah, Austin, and the Northeast Corridor that covers NYC/Boston. Welcome to AZ Tech and the Silicon Desert. The new West in technology.	8.7	7.4	(1.3)
4	THE SUN CORRIDOR FOR ADVANCED MANUFACTURING: Arizona has utilized the I-10 corridor between Phoenix and Tucson to implement advanced manufacturing, research and design facilities. A constant skills pipeline is enabled via industry-oriented universities and community colleges. Arizona is on the map for manufacturing and can compete with any region in the country.	8.5	7.0	(1.5)

5	THE HEALTHIEST HEALTHCARE SECTOR IN THE COUNTRY: Bioscience and healthcare are thriving industries in Arizona providing advanced patient treatment and groundbreaking research. Supported by educational partners, Arizona's healthcare segment is making a difference in improving care and outcomes and has developed one of the most collaborative ecosystems in the industry.	8.5	7.1	(1.4)
6	A CASE STUDY IN ENVIRONMENTAL SUSTAINABILITY: We live in a desert. Supported by some of the best educational researchers and public/private partnerships, Arizona has become a model for sustainability with a zero carbon footprint, clean air and water, and has even re-established the Salt River through Maricopa County.	8.4	5.9	(2.5)
7	MULTI-MODAL TRANSPORATION LEADER: Arizona has implemented a regional transportation plan with high speed rail, smart freeway corridors supporting traditional and autonomous vehicles, regional airports and light rail. Considered to be a model for transportation planning in the country.	8.0	5.8	(2.2)
8	THE ARIZONA LIFESTYLE ENDURES: At the end of the decade, people still marvel at how Arizona does all that it does, but retains a simple and real lifestyle. The pioneer spirit. The welcoming and inclusive western hospitality. The preservation of open space. A balanced lifestyle that blends purposeful work with active recreation. The "Arizona Blue" sky against mountain backdrops. We prioritized our priorities.	7.8	7.3	(0.5)

9	SMART CITIES AND SMART GOVERNMENT: We value our towns and rural areas and the western heritage of Arizona, but our cities have followed Smart City approaches, integrating technology, urban planning and incredibly efficient operations. Electronic methods and sensors manage assets, resources and flow. State and local governments have found the right balance to strategic investment and local autonomy. It all works in Arizona.	7.7	6.3	(1.4)
10	GLOBAL TRADE: Arizona is viewed as one of the most progressive global trade partners on the planet. Providing a natural link to Mexico/Latin America to the south and Canada to the north, they have also established the needed business and transportation links to Europe and Asia Pacific. Smart and supportive trade regulations along with a welcoming culture, skilled workforce and educational support.	7.4	6.0	(1.4)
11	THE DESTINATION FOR TRAVEL/ENTERTAINMENT/TOURISM: Arizona is viewed as one of the premier travel destinations not only for U.S. travelers but for global travelers. And it is smart tourism leveraging open space, recreation, high-end events, business conferences and eco-friendly approaches. Experience Scottsdale has morphed into Experience Arizona.	7.4	7.6	+0.2
12	THE FOREFRONT OF AEROSPACE AND DEFENSE: We have come a long way since the titan missile silo on I-10. Arizona is a national leader anchored by companies such as Raytheon, Northrup Grumman, Honeywell, Boeing, General Dynamics, BAE Systems and MD Helicopter. It is complemented by a continued and valued presence of key military installations. Don't mess with us!	6.9	6.0	(0.9)

Pretty interesting. Overall, compared to some of our other influence scenarios, the gaps are more modest (with one highly notable exception):

Here is what Arizona must tackle. Look at the top four gaps between impact and likelihood:

1. A complete education transformation (3.5)
2. A case in environmental sustainability (2.5)
3. Multimodal transportation leader (2.2)
4. The alternative energy alternative (1.6)

The gaps suggest significant and long-term infrastructure development. The leadership group assembled at the Phoenix Country Club in 2005 would simply smile and say, *it's your turn.* Time to plant some trees. *Better get a truckload of the education variety.*

Five Reflections on the Future of Arizona as a National Leader for the Decade Ahead

1. KEEP THE HERITAGE: Arizona has a unique and distinctive heritage—that authentic mix of the Old West (the American cowboys and the American Indians) and the Mexican influence from the south. Independent, pioneer and maverick mindsets. As we advance, we don't want the quest for the economy to overshadow our value for the lifestyle.
2. A NEW SET OF THE FIVE Cs: Every Arizona kid growing up in my generation knew the five Cs: Copper, Cattle, Cotton, Citrus and Climate. There is a new set of five for Arizona's future. None start with a "C": Technology, Healthcare, Energy, Advanced Manufacturing and Tourism. Of all the Cs, I could argue that Copper is still a distinctive part of our past/future. If you live in Globe, Arizona, you are wrestling with that now.
3. LONG TERM LEADERS: We need leaders who see an Arizona not only in the decade ahead, but are thinking 25-50 years out. These will be the servant leaders today that will take our kids into the future. We have two relatively young Senators with name recognition, but they follow in big footsteps. We need leaders in all facets of Arizona's future—education, economic development, water/sustainability and eco-tourism.
4. FIND THE ENERGY: We don't need to drill wells for oil. Check the sky. Arizona should be the global leader in solar as well as other aspects of alternative energy. By the end of the decade we will all be driving electric cars—in Arizona, you won't even need to plug them in. That's not a ski rack on your roof, it's a solar receptor. Zoom/Zoom.
5. IT REALLY IS THE EDUCATION, STUPID: It's time to go from worst to first. Arizona must completely rethink its approach to education. Quality education will attract smart people and smart

companies. It will retain smart people in the state. The movie we want to watch at the end of the decade is *Educating Arizona* not *Raising Arizona.*

The Leadership Lessons From The Pandemic

As we conduct this session in December of 2020, the pandemic is far from over, but we are learning constantly and there may be light at the end of the tunnel. On December 10, the FDA Advisory Panel met and endorsed the Pfizer/BioNTech COVID vaccine. On the day of our session, December 17, the FDA Advisory panel endorses the second vaccine, Moderna. A mind-boggling timeline from the beginning of the pandemic in January 2020 to vaccine development, trial and approval in December. *Less than 12 months.*

So, what did we learn from a *leadership perspective* from the pandemic as we stand in December with some good news in hand but a long road ahead? Our Foresighters:

- "Shown who has real leadership chops. And also shown who can't find their way out of a paper sack."

- "I think that has yet to be determined. We'll know more once all the dust settles and we can see where leaders have landed. But overall, those who have the ability to change quickly and are flexible have had the most success—both are important traits for leaders."

- "You can't hesitate or you are lost. Leaders were not ready. At least we will have an example to follow for the future. We all knew that pandemics were a possibility/on the horizon. There was fair warning to be prepared."

- "COVID-19 has challenged leaders to become more flexible, innovative and resilient."

- "Our leaders have not offered the solution that was needed. This is challenging. COVID has come upon us with no real training or past experience to apply. This said, we need leaders that can see a balanced approach and common sense solutions."

For all that we have focused on in this chapter on long-term leadership, there will be times when the immediate becomes the urgent. This will be true for Arizona, for the country and for the world. The decade ahead will be influenced by the actions we take now, but also our ability to respond smartly in a time of crisis.

Meanwhile Back at The Ranch (Brown's Ranch)

It's the end of the day, *pardner*. In Arizona, the desert is finally cooling off. Some of my favorite critters are taking to the trails—jackrabbits, quail, gila monsters, rattlesnakes, mule deer, javelina, an occasional bobcat and a not-so-occasional pack of coyotes. I see all of them when I grab a few miles on my mountain bike in the Arizona Sonoran Preserve and Brown's Ranch Trailhead. Five minutes from my house, we all share the trails. My bike is my modern day horse, but I see a few horse riders out there as well. Lots of hikers: it's the best time to be out there.

Of all the sounds and sights at the end of an Arizona day in the desert, there is one that is the most peaceful and most calming sound I know. It comes from a mourning dove. The Cornell Lab "All About Birds" site tells us that, "The song (or "perch-coo") is given mainly by males from a conspicuous perch. It's a soft *coo-coo* follow by two or three louder coos." To the embarrassment of my children, I mastered the ability to mimic the call when I was a young Arizonan by clasping my hands together and using my thumbs as the whistle like blowing into a conch shell. *I am pretty damn good at it.*

Where I ride, mostly at Brown's Ranch, there is some educational information posted there that says there is evidence of nomadic bands of human hunters and gatherers dating back to 7000 B.C., right there in the Brown's Ranch vicinity. I imagine the mourning doves were abundant back then as well. I imagine that my *early Arizonans* enjoyed that same sound and it had the same effect. Be quiet, be still for a moment. We are not that different, then or now. And hopefully not in the future. That's our Arizona Heritage: *Timeless Land.*

The peaceful mourning dove

CHAPTER 10: The American Lifestyle and The American Dream

Don't you feel it growing day by day
People getting ready for the news
Some are happy, some are sad
Whoa, gotta let the music play

...
What the people need is a way to make 'em smile
It 'aint so hard if you know how...
Whoa, oh listen to the music
All the time

--The Doobie Brothers, <u>Listen to the Music</u> (1972)

January 14, 2021
Foresight 2030 Session

When we get out of this pandemic, we need to do exactly what The Doobie Brothers said in 1972*: We gotta let the music play*. We are not wired to be isolated. It is not who we are as Americans, it is not our *lifestyle*. I think on this point we can certainly agree.

But what is the *American Lifestyle?* How has the pandemic changed it and also *not* changed it, but simply reminded us what we really enjoy about that lifestyle? There are a series of forces lining up to impact our lifestyle in the decade ahead: the role of technology in our everyday lives, new approaches to work where the old norms of an 8-5 office environment may have changed forever, healthcare access and awareness that are leading to longer and more active lives, travel that focuses on delivering meaningful experiences, a new appreciation for all things outdoors, entertainment events that are more immersive and sports that get you closer to every play.

And what is the *American Dream?* Is the American Lifestyle the American Dream, or is the American Dream something far bigger. Bigger, but more basic. *The author has a confession: this chapter was supposed to be a lighter look at the American Lifestyle in 2030 but it morphed into a more serious look at the American Dream and why it still matters. No apologies.*

322

And if that doesn't get you intrigued about the decade ahead and how *your lifestyle* might change but *your dreams* still matter, you can just fire up the Winnebago, fire up The Doobie Brothers, and, well, *fire up a doobie*, since you can pull into a dispensary almost anywhere. There's a new level of *lifestyle freedom* in the decade ahead, but that lifestyle also needs to be aligned to your values and who you are authentically. You have some *choices* to make in the decade ahead.

The American Dream: Vintage 1930

The American Lifestyle is strongly influenced by the ideals of *The American Dream*. Wikipedia defines the American Dream as follows:

"The American Dream is a national ethos of the United States, the set of ideals (democracy, rights, liberty, opportunity and equality) in which freedom includes the opportunity for prosperity and success, as well as an upward social mobility for the family and children, achieved through hard work in a society with few barriers."

Wow. Welcome to the start of the decade where The American Dream is colliding with The American Divide.

Look, we can all have a different view of what *our* American Dream looks like, but we all just want the opportunity to pursue that American Dream: economic access, education access, social and racial justice, workplace inclusion, family support/structure and communities that matter. If we can solve some of the divides that are affecting us today, the opportunity for a *New American Dream* in the decade ahead is *limitless*.

This is not our first debate about the American Dream and how to pursue it. James Truslow Adams, a noted American author and writer, described the American Dream in 1931 as, "Life should be better and richer and fuller for everyone, with opportunity for each according to ability or achievement, regardless of social class or circumstances of birth." *True then and still true now.*

Still reflecting on the 1930s, the classic view of The American Dream for the American Family was based on three elements: *two children, a three bedroom house and a white picket fence.* That suggested a *material definition* of the American Dream. The housing industry in America still hangs onto that rather narrow definition of the American Dream...you have achieved the Dream when you get a 30-year mortgage. I think most Americans who have tried to pay that 30-year mortgage see it as the *American Nightmare*, but it beats living in a trailer park.

But still, this is the <u>*American*</u> Dream. That's almost a global brand. Nearly everyone on the planet has some vision of the American Dream. In reality it goes back to the Declaration of Independence and its preamble in 1776: *"We hold these truths to be self-evident, that all men are created equal, that they are endowed by their Creator with certain unalienable rights, that among these are Life, Liberty and the pursuit of Happiness."*

And Lady Liberty is the unequivocal symbol of that. It's the bumper sticker for the American Dream.

Liberty: The American Dream

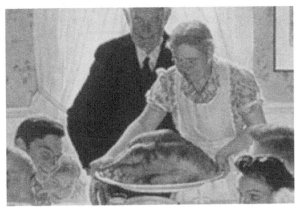

Simplicity: The American Thanksgiving (Norman Rockwell)

Over time, the perceived *American Lifestyle* and norms have influenced our perceptions of the Dream and the *attainability* of the Dream. The

324

1930s view was also influenced by the Great Depression, and getting back on your feet financially was a valid rallying cry to move America forward. So, financial prosperity was at the core. But affluence is a different goal than liberty and happiness. Somehow the definition and ideas of the Dream were narrowed over the last 90 years where the Dream is still desired, but the narrowed definition has become unattainable to many.

So, a *New Deal* in the 1930s sounded very promising then and, in fact, led to the idea of Social Security and some level of *social guarantee* for the financial part of the Dream. *I begin drawing mine next year, thank you very much FDR.*

But now America was ready to *export* the American Dream as a model for other countries to follow and specifically (according to Roosevelt in his 1941 State of the Union Address) *four freedoms:* freedom of speech and expression; freedom of every person to worship God in his own way; freedom from fear; and, freedom from want. Norman Rockwell took these four freedoms quite literally and *painted them* with perhaps the most famous being the *Freedom From Want*, the classic American Thanksgiving scene shown earlier.

Fast forward to the end of World War II and a *boatload* of young GIs coming back and, after saving the world, were ready for *their share* of the American Dream. That came in the form of the GI Bill to offer low-interest loans with no money down. The result: *American Suburbia.*

By 1950, American home ownership had increased to 55% from a remarkably steady state of around 40% from 1900 through 1940. In 1951, Levitt & Sons was America's biggest home builder. Famous for the building of Levittown in New York, the rather "cookie cutter homes" cost about $8,000 and had two bedrooms, one bath, a kitchen and an unfinished loft attic. According to historian Kenneth Jackson, "The family that had the greatest impact on postwar housing in the United States was Abraham Levitt and his sons, William and Alfred, who ultimately built more than 140,000 houses and turned a cottage industry into a major manufacturing process."

But that wasn't the only family that influenced the promise of the American Dream.

Let me introduce you to the Nelsons, the Andersons and the Cleavers. A few of my boomer aficionados will smile at those names. For those of you in the *younger generations,* the Nelsons were *Ozzie and Harriet,* the Andersons were *Father Knows Best* and the Cleavers...well, that was the classic *Leave it to Beaver* with Ward and June, their sons Wally and *the Beav,* and their friend Eddie Haskel. *Why hello, Mrs. Cleaver, you are looking lovely today!* Haskel was the teenage schmooze of his generation.

It was an iconic and idyllic representation of life in the late fifties and early sixties (the show was broadcast from 1957 to 1963). Ward Cleaver, the dad, was always on time for dinner at home. June Cleaver, the mom, had that dinner ready (dress and pearls every night). And man, *was that show ever white.* Because that was the media view of America and the American Dream then.

The American Dream Collides With the Sixties and Seventies
But then we added a little *color* to the American Dream. Martin Luther King Jr. had a different definition of the America Dream, one around social and civil rights for all Americans and especially for the opportunity for African Americans to have the same access to the American Dream. His "I Have a Dream" speech, delivered in the 1963 Washington, D.C., Civil Rights March, remains one of the most powerful speeches ever delivered.

Martin Luther King Jr., 1963

The iconic backdrop of the "I have a dream" speech

For me, the sitcom family that began to challenge the media view of the American Dream was *All in the Family*. It ran for nine seasons from 1971 to 1979 and was based on the perfect *American Bigot*—Archie Bunker.

326

He was White, Northeastern (set in Queens) and had Edith as his ditzy, faithful, but a little more open to changing ideas, wife. But the key to *All in the Family* was Sally Struthers who played Archie and Edith's college aged daughter (aka, Gloria Stivik), married to Michael Stivik (aka, "meathead"). The problem for Archie was Michael: the America Bigot meets the Polish-American Hippie.

Norman Lear used the sitcom to go after just about everything that was previously *off-limits* to the television and the media. Wikipedia notes: "The show broke ground in its depiction of issues previously considered unsuitable for a United States network television comedy, such as racism, antisemitism, infidelity, homosexuality, women's liberation, rape, religion, miscarriages, abortion, breast cancer, the Vietnam War, menopause and impotence."

At a time when there was no social media technology, *All in the Family* became America's social media *broadcast*. It simply suggested that maybe there was something wrong with our view of the American Dream and the limited number of people who could access it.

The American Family 1950s   The American Family 1970s

The American Dream Evolves

In 2006, Barack Obama came onto the main political stage in America with his book, *The Audacity of Hope: Thoughts on Reclaiming the American Dream*. This idea, espoused by many social and political leaders, was that the American Dream is the quintessential American Pursuit. A virtuous destiny that you can arrive at with hard work and equal opportunity.

Others are not so kind about the virtues of the American Dream. The 1949 play *Death of a Salesman* by Arthur Miller painted a darker picture

327

about capitalist pursuit and the toll it can take on a man's soul. Hunter S. Thompson wrote *Fear and Loathing in Las Vegas: A Savage Journey into the Heart of the American Dream* which again redefined the classic view of American success and American *excess*. The sixties comedian George Carlin (the seven words Carlin) joked that, "It's called the American Dream because you have to be asleep to believe it."

My good friend Will Marré, God rest his soul, was the founder of the *American Dream Project* and passionately argued that the *real* American Dream is about meaning and not about material accumulation. In his Emmy award winning 2009 PBS special titled *Reclaiming Your American Dream*, he had a very succinct message:

"I think the American Dream was really hijacked away from the Thomas Jefferson idea of life, liberty and the pursuit of happiness into just *the pursuit of stuff*."

Now George Carlin would have a few things to say about the concept of stuff. "That's what your house is, a place to keep your stuff, while you go out and get more...stuff!"

Chris Hedges went a step further in 2012 in his book *Days of Destruction, Days of Revolt* about the fallacy of the American Dream: "The vaunted American Dream, the idea that life will get better, that progress is inevitable if we obey the rules and work hard, that material prosperity is assured, has been replaced by a hard and bitter truth. The American Dream, as we know, is a *lie*. We will all be sacrificed."

Unless you escape in a Winnebago. Shit, these are dark thoughts about a bright idea.

But Marré made it very simple and perhaps attainable. He said that the new American Dream is simply going back to the Thomas Jefferson ideal of *pursuing happiness* not pursuing *stuff*. There are three things, he suggested, that have to come together for your *new American Dream:* your lifestyle, your relationships and your career. If you get those right, then life is *great*.

The American Dream and The American Lifestyle: 2030

Look, I side with the optimists about the notion of the American Dream. It's just that the definition of the dream has been evolving and, lately, evolving in a good way. Economic prosperity has its place, but the American Dream in the decade ahead is about a different way of living, a New American Lifestyle, that integrates our joy with our collective values. The millennials redirected the American Dream with a different view of the

328

values and desired lifestyle and that redirection will be continued by the Gen Z attitudes and values as they are shaped. The New American Dream is still about prosperity, but it's also about social equity and social responsibility. Achieve that, and our lifestyle can take advantage of new freedoms and opportunities in the decade ahead.

Let's see what our Foresighters have to say about the American Lifestyle in the decade ahead...

Foresight 2030 Session

First of all, we have made it to 2021. The combination of the continued COVID pandemic and the *insurrection on the Capitol of the United States of America* on January 6 had put a little doubt into our January 14 session, but our country and our Foresighters have persevered. We'll have more to say on the January events in the next chapter, so for now we will head to a little subject matter on the American Lifestyle and, later, a few thoughts on the enduring American Dream.

Thirty-seven Foresighters joined us for this session, let's introduce a few of them to you:

- "Retired CEO of global research firm. Married, two adult children and 2 adult grandchildren. Love reading and travel. Received my first Moderna vaccine shot yesterday!"
- "Grew up in a small town in Idaho. Served in the military. 4 awesome kids. Love the outdoors. Play golf. Avid reader."
- "A business consultant focused on teaching and utilizing effective communication/listening behaviors to develop leaders, build teams and solve complex business issues. Married 40 years, three adult children, two grandchildren. A passionate cyclist."
- "I am an artist, entrepreneur, clothing engineer and teacher."
- "Hi—I'm a professional woman, mother, grandmother and parent of 2 dogs. I live in the Pacific NW and try to get out every day (except for "atmospheric rivers") to walk, enjoy nature and watch the dogs run."
- Full stack software developer out of Scottsdale, AZ. Avid exercise seeker. Enjoy comedy and hot sauce."
- "My focus is to enjoy life and explore the mechanism of the mind."
- "I'm a materials chemist working in consumer electronics."

Hmmm. Those last 3: a hot sauce connoisseur, an explorer of the mind and a materials chemist working in consumer electronics. What could go wrong? Well, let's get into some lifestyle questions, shall we...

Reflecting on the American Lifestyle

We will develop some *foresights* about the American Dream at the end of this chapter, but we'll start with some *insights* about the American Lifestyle at the start of this decade:

Question: *Wind your thoughts back for a moment to January 2020 and the start of this new decade. Imagine you writing an article on "The American Lifestyle". What differentiates how Americans live their lives and what's important to them? How would you define "The American Lifestyle" at the start of the decade and how our lifestyle might be different than other countries/cultures?*

2020. Like the longest year ever. The year that felt like it was a decade. But our foresighters were up to the task:

- "The "Open Road"—freedom to pick everything up and move, not only for road trips but also professionally."
- "Americans live in the fast lane: profits are everything, time off is a luxury, not a necessity, the bigger the better, supersize it if you can, sports is a big part of the culture and heritage, freedom is everything."
- "Americans are voracious consumers of lifestyle and, consistent with our upwardly-mobile mythology, feel entitled to the most they can afford (or pretend to afford)—McMansions, pools, foreign travel, clothes, cars…"
- "Americans are more focused on continual working—culture is such that time off work is not valued as much as other countries. A consistent mindset of 'getting ahead' results in lower quality of life overall."
- "The American lifestyle is built upon acquisition and possession. It's a work for money, or work to live, cycle. Sadly, it leaves little room or time for enjoying life itself. It is possession, keeping-up-with-the-Joneses and keeping-my-job driven. Sadly, too materialistically driven."
- "Americans embrace and value freedom, experiences, innovation, family, material goods, entrepreneurship, free speech and the opportunity to pursue our dreams. We struggle with poverty and health care, civil unrest and other challenges, but are passionate about our beliefs and pursuit of the best life."
- "We are all about consumption. More is better. Also, individualism. We are not as community oriented as are other cultures. We like big—houses, cars, hair. We are very technology oriented, and not as science oriented as previous generations were. We are not sustainable. Many other cultures try to emulate our lifestyle, based on movies and TV, but none of that is sustainable."

- "Based upon my visits to Spain in the 1980s and 1990s, one of the biggest differences I've seen with the American lifestyle is a focus on work first, life second. They said, "Americans live to work, we work to live." However, I see that as having changed in the new millennium. Americans are getting better at life/work balance, and the folks in Spain seem to be working a bit more than I recall previously."
- "The 'American Lifestyle' is largely focused on the ideas of freedoms and personal rights, in addition to the work hard, play hard mentality. In many ways this can be a positive aspect of our lifestyle; however, since the beginning of 2020, it seems to be more negative than positive. Right now, for many Americans, individual 'rights' and the needs/wants of an individual are outweighing the needs of our society—namely our health."

Like I said, what could go wrong with this session with this group. Look, these are really profound opinions. Our lifestyle is based on personal freedom, but that personal freedom can lead to a sense of *entitlement*. It's the open road and life in the fast lane, but that constant speed leads to *burnout and disillusionment*. For many, the measure of success of our lifestyle is the *stuff we accumulate*. The good news is Americans can outwork anyone in the world. The bad news is that's all we do sometimes—just work. It can be a lifestyle of *exhaustion*. And finally, we embrace *our* individual pursuit of the American Dream, but ignore the lack of collective opportunity for others.

But, despite all of its flaws, the American Lifestyle still has a great aura around it. You can go anywhere you want, any time you want. Work hard (really hard) and you get all the *stuff* you want. You can be entertained by musicians, actors and the best athletes in the world. You can stay connected to everyone and everything with a 3x5 inch device in your purse or pocket. You can live your life the way you want, despite the fact that many around you *simply can't afford to live your life at all.*

The issue ahead is not so much about changing the American Lifestyle, it's about enabling more people to have an opportunity to have that lifestyle and to pursue their American Dream.

Some Major Influences to the American Lifestyle

There are certain things that occur in history that influence the American Lifestyle. Henry Ford came along and introduced the *Model T* mass-produced car on October 1, 1908, and sold 250,000 Ts by 1914, and by 1918 half of all cars in America were Model Ts. The Model T was *affordable freedom* at $825 for a *new car*. That changed the American Lifestyle in a big way.

The move to home ownership after World War II was another major event. More affordable home ownership with the GI bill, mass-produced homes and fast-produced suburban communities that led to a new American middle class. Work hard and you could have your own piece of the American Dream, complete with a backyard and barbecue grill. That changed the American lifestyle in a big way.

In the 1950s, the advent of commercial air travel and the jet engine changed the mobility of Americans. *And the speed of our lives.* While propeller driven planes had been providing passenger service in the 1930s and 1940s with the Pan Am Clipper and the TWA Stratoliner, the 1950s brought us the first jet airliner travel with the de Havilland DH 106 Comet in 1952. Then the big boys entered the game with the Boeing 707 and the Douglas DC-8. If you were lucky, you could be part of the *jet-set* of Americans. Now that was a *higher level* of the American Lifestyle, if you know what I mean. Eventually, carriers like Southwest and JetBlue helped to *democratize the skies* and now, as the Southwest *Ding!* so famously tells Americans: *"You are now free to move about the country."* That changed the American lifestyle in a big way.

United Airlines in the 1930s

Southwest Airlines today

But what was the next influencer in the American Lifestyle? In a single word it was *technology*. In fact, we asked our Foresighters what they felt had most impacted the American Lifestyle the prior decade and why:

Question: *Reflecting on the trends of the prior decade, what was the ONE TREND OR FACTOR that you feel most influenced "The American Lifestyle" in the prior decade? Why was this factor/trend so powerful?*

And while technology wasn't the only response, it was the *dominant* response:

- "Technology...gave instant access to information, made everything from shopping to restaurant reservations more convenient, created more of a global community. On the downside, it made it possible for disinformation to spread rapidly and for people to wall themselves off into information echo chambers. This was not one decade, it was two, bifurcated almost right at the midpoint."

- "I think technology has been the key driver for change of lifestyle. The impact on the number of hours people are tethered to it, and how it shapes thinking and the mind overall, has an impact on decisions people make and how they adjust their lifestyle and time."
- "I think that social media is the single most important factor. It gave rise to the world of 'influencers', who in turn created the perception of certain lifestyles that people need to follow in order to be perceived in a certain way."
- "Technology, without a doubt. It impacted so many other factors—access to information, access to entertainment, but also a decrease in personal connection/conversation."
- "Interconnectedness and rapid availability of information enabled through smartphone technology."
- "Social media platforms showed what was 'out there'—what was possible, what others were doing. Gave folks Fear Of Missing Out (FOMO)!"

FOMO: The Fear Of Missing Out. Just when I felt good about my lifestyle, I saw yours and *it looked better*! Welcome to social media and the Joneses.

But for our Foresighters, despite some potential downsides of technology and the changes to lifestyle in the prior decade, they felt good about the impact to *their* lifestyle:

Question: *Thinking about the prior decade—2010 through 2019—would you say that YOUR LIFESTYLE was more like you hoped it would be or less like you hoped it would be?*

No.	Items	Times Selected
1.	**MORE like I hoped it to be**	**(72%)**
2.	LESS like I hoped it to be	(28%)

- MORE: "Technology has enabled me to work from home or anywhere that I want to be for lifestyle interests. I can travel anywhere and do things I want and still stay connected to my responsibilities at work and at home."
- MORE: "Mostly due to retirement. With technology and a robust economy, I pretty much was able to do whatever I pleased,

333

whenever I pleased. While I never had a 'bucket list', I'm sure if I had one, I would have checked off all the boxes."

- MORE: "Success in both personal and professional life, living in a place where I can be outdoors as much as I wish and spending time with my loved ones. Working (from home), and the tech that allowed me to do that, gave me the ability to work at home/be at home and be the mom I wanted to be (present), so the best of both worlds."
- MORE: "Simple...there was more freedom of movement. I could pretty much do what I wanted, when I wanted it. Went to the theater, went into the city, went on vacation. Nothing extravagant, but enjoyable."
- MORE: "My lifestyle benefited from technological advances that I did not foresee impacting me to the extent that they ultimately have, and for the better."
- LESS: "Too much of people's lifestyle has moved online and revolves around perceptions rather than real life."
- LESS: "The prior decade was (still is) keeping up with the Joneses. Pressure and competition to keep up with what everyone else was doing and feeling left behind."

There is an old Spanish saying that bears on our own quest for the ideal American Lifestyle: *Salud, Amor y Pesetas—y tiempo para disfrutarlos.* Health, Love and Money—and the *time* to enjoy them. In many respects technology is the time factor—it creates time flexibility to help us achieve the lifestyle we want. Technology will continue to be an influencer of the New American Lifestyle in the decade ahead. But *how* you spend your time will influence your personal version of your American Lifestyle, and, for that matter, your personal American Dream.

Sports, Travel and Entertainment

So let's go further with the notion of how we might spend our time in the decade ahead and specifically how we might spend our *discretionary time.* We already know that we spend waaaaay too much available time on work, but we still like the great American motto of *work hard, play hard.* And Americans do like to play.

So we decided to spend some of our Foresight session *discretionary time* on three American favorites: Sports (Play Ball!), Travel (Welcome Aboard!) and Entertainment (Live Music!). Why are these elements so important to the American Lifestyle? Why do they consume so much of our discretionary time? Will they continue to be that influential in the decade ahead?

Our first question to our Foresighters was *which of the three* would be most important to them as part of their lifestyle in the decade ahead:

Question: *What our lifestyle is, and what influences it, is different for each of us. In this session we will look at three elements of the American Lifestyle to get your sense of the trends in each element and how that element might change. As you think about the decade ahead (ending in 2029), which of the following elements will be MOST IMPORTANT as an element of YOUR lifestyle?*

No.	Items	Times Selected
1.	**Travel**	**(81%)**
2.	Entertainment	(11%)
3.	Sports	(8%)

Now, to be clear, it's not that entertainment and sports are not interesting and compelling to Americans. But *travel* is deeply rooted in the definition of our American Lifestyle. The freedom to go where we want, to discover and learn to explore, to reconnect with family and friends, to renew our spirit. And, perhaps after being pretty much locked down for the last 9 months, having a *get-out-of-home/jail-free card* probably sounds pretty good in January of 2021. Our Foresighters agreed:

- TRAVEL: "The pandemic has shown the isolation and frustration being 'locked down' can produce."
- TRAVEL: "I am choosing freedom and opportunity to create my life independent of geographical location."
- TRAVEL: "Travel is really important to me. The ability to move around and explore new places, especially having been deprived of that during the current pandemic. I expect it to be a core part of my lifestyle again once things return to normal."
- TRAVEL: "Travel is a significant part of who I am. The places I visit enrich my life and broaden my view of life, allow me to be more grateful for what I have and to reach for new goals and areas of focus."
- TRAVEL: "Just love traveling, seeing different lifestyles, learning about other locations, other cultures, even within the U.S."
- TRAVEL: "I HAVE to get out of this house!"

Easy now! There is light at the end of the pandemic tunnel. No need to break a window in that house of yours, the doors will be opening later in 2021!

But seriously, whether it is by bike, car, train or that *big old jetliner,* we do love to travel. And part of that travel draw is the sheer size of the USA. Pull out the Rand McNally atlas and flip to a page and let's go. I first flew on a *jet airplane* in 1964 from Arizona to New York. I learned the joy of staring out of a window to the land below. *Mesmerizing.* Then I did a cross country drive with my family from Arizona to the East Coast and back by car in early 1970s. Drive until you reach the *Howard Johnson's* of your choice. But it really is the ultimate freedom. And if you run out of land, that just means you have made it to the beach.

But we Americans are fans as well as travelers. Baseball is the *great American pastime*, not standing in a TSA line. And there is a *great communal experience* about watching a big-screen movie, a show on Broadway or watching the Diamondbacks beat the Yankees in game 1 of the 2001 World Series (which I did). So let's explore all three of our American Lifestyle elements—Sports, Travel and Entertainment—in a little more detail for the decade ahead.

Sports for $100

If there was ever a perfect metaphor for life it would be sports. Fall down, get back up. Keep pressing to find your limits. As good as you are by yourself, you are better as a team. The unexpected moment when it all comes together.

Americans, by and large, are big sports fans. The stadiums we build in our cities are like modern coliseums. 100,000 people for a football game; 40,000 for a baseball game; 20,000 for basketball and hockey. Cities claim that they live and die for their teams—Chicago for their Cubbies, New York for their *damn* Yankees, Dallas for their Cowboys, Portland for their Trailblazers, Pittsburgh for *all of their teams* and Los Angeles for their Lakers (and other teams that seem to *migrate* their way like the Clippers and the Chargers).

When I was growing up I was a big fan of ABC Sports and their Saturday *Wide World of Sports.* Much of the country was. I can still see and hear the intro, hosted by Jim McKay:

"Spanning the globe (cue the cliff diver) to bring you the constant variety of sport (ice skater). The thrill of victory (boxer being carried by the crowd) and the agony of defeat (the ski jumper who eats it at the end and missed the jump), the human drama of athletic competition (soccer match with the Pele goal), this is ABC's Wide World of Sports."

The program aired from 1961 to 1998—over 35 years—and introduced about every young kid in America to the possibilities of sports. *The thrill of victory and the agony of defeat.* There's that life metaphor again. All of

336

us *dreamed* of that thrill of victory moment—in whatever sport we would pursue. And we all dreaded the idea of being *Vinko Bogataj*. Vinko was the dude doing cartwheels at the bottom of the ski jump instead of soaring off into the horizon. It actually became a term called 'agonosis' that Rich Hall in his 1984 book *Sniglets* defined as, "The syndrome of tuning in on *Wide World of Sports* every weekend just to watch the skier rack himself."

ABC also introduced us to the Olympics every four years, at least until NBC snagged the airing rights. The Olympics were not just about sport, they were about <u>politics and power</u>. Russia, East Germany, China, the U.S. and the UK. Throw in Australia in the summer and Finland in the winter, and *don't forget the Jamaican bobsled team*.

It was also about *national pride*. And for three weeks, *every American* became a sports fan. Beat the Russians. Beat the *cheating* East Germans. And, for the most part we did. Because the American Dream was also the American Athlete's Dream. Work hard, be dedicated, play by the rules and you had a chance to match yourself against the best in the country to represent *your country*. The American Dream was the perfect set up for the Olympic ideals. What young American kid has not dreamed the dream of being on the Olympic stage? *Why not me?*

And we all have our favorite Olympic moments. For me: *Franz Klammer* in the 1976 Innsbruck Men's Downhill ski race. *Completely out of control for 1 minute and 45.73 seconds* and was clearly looking to be the new feature for the Agony of Defeat video for ABC. But while he skied on what was referred to as being *on the edge of disaster*, he stayed upright and won by .33 seconds.

Franz Klammer, 1976 downhill

Bob Beamon, 1968 long jump

Here's another. Bob Beamon in the 1968 Mexico City Olympics. His jump would create a new term in the American language lexicon: *Beamonesque*. Why? On his first jump in Mexico City, he would jump 29 feet, 2 and ½ inches. It would break the world record by nearly *two feet*. He literally jumped out of the pit with his momentum once he had landed in the sand. In emotional shock he collapsed and could not get up. The distance was beyond what the Olympic measuring apparatus could measure...they had to bring in a *tape measure* and measure it like a high school meet. It was called the *Leap of the Century*. No other human would jump even *28 feet* for 12 more years and his 1968 Olympic record is *still* the Olympic record.

And this Bob Beamon guy was a young skinny Black kid who grew up in the New York Housing Authority's Jamaica Houses. And sports became his gateway to the ABC version of the American Dream. The American Dream was on stage in the Olympics for the world to see.

Another of my favorites was Dave Wottle in his 1972 800-meter final. This is the guy that wore a *golf cap* while everyone else was wearing spandex. In one of the most amazing comeback races ever run, he is at the back for the pack at 500 meters and then begins one of his patented kicks. *Seven* of the world's fastest runners are ahead of him including two Kenyans, an East German, a West German and, of course, a Russian, Yevgeny Arzhanov, who is *the favorite* and has not lost an 800-meter race in *four years*. And it's Jim McKay who is doing the announcing:

"The Kenyans are running like a mirror image of each other. There's Arzhanov taking the lead! Now Wottle is making his bid...stand by for the kick of Dave Wottle! Has he got it? Here he comes. He's got one Kenyan... he's got the other Kenyan...he's got to catch Arzhanov...can he make it? I think he did it! I think he got the gold medal!"

You really have to watch the race on YouTube. Arzhanov launches himself at the finish line in an act of desperation at the end but Wottle still edges him. Arzhonov surely knows that for a Russian track hero to lose to an American *wearing a golf hat* is going to get him a one way ticket to the Siberian Front.

Oh, and then finally, the ultimate good vs. evil drama, the David vs. Goliath classic: the 1980 winter Olympics and the hockey *Miracle on Ice*. The USA kids vs. the Russian giants. We had no chance. Even the jerseys were intimidating. We had the nice USA jerseys that looked like *cardigan sweaters*. They had the CCCP lettering that looked like it was *armor plated*. This time Al Michaels had the call and I remember the moment. *The longest minute ever recorded in human history*. Watch it yourself and you'll swear that we were in a time warp. But a beautiful time warp it was as the USA prevailed 4-3 with the now famous, *"Do you believe in miracles?"* call by Michaels. That put the cold war *on ice*. The American Dream defeats the Evil Empire.

And I watched all of those moments live on the television. Glued to the coverage like so many Americans at the time. It was the thrill of victory. But we also saw another side of the politics of sports come into play in Mexico City and then again in Munich. In Mexico City, after the men's 200 meter finals, most everyone remembers the "Black Power" raised fists and black gloves by the two black Americans, Tommie Smith and John Carlos. But there was much more to the scene as the silver medalist, Peter Norman, from Australia, was also involved. All three wore badges representing the Olympic Project for Human Rights (OPHR). Smith and Carlos were shoeless to represent black poverty. Smith had a black scarf on that represented black pride. Carlos had a set of beads on to symbolize individuals that have been lynched and killed, and his tracksuit top was unzipped to show solidarity with U.S. blue collar workers.

This was great symbolism and earned the two black American athletes expulsion from the Olympics and much negative feedback on the home front. America in 1968 was not ready for sports and social justice to collide.

I met John Carlos in 1982 in California. I had just run a regional track meet for the Corporate Cup where you could represent your company. I had run for IBM, and we had one of the better teams in the country. Largely because we had invented email and could coordinate a lot of runners. The meet was over and everyone had thrown their gear bags in a pile and (literally) were dancing to the track's loudspeaker playing some great music. Carlos was one of the organizers of the meet and was there. We all knew who Carlos was, but for that moment he was just enjoying the music with us. Cool dude. He went on to be part of the Organizing Committee for the 1984 Summer Olympics (which I was fortunate to see). I think he helped a lot of people reach their American Dream.

In Munich in 1972, in the Summer Olympics, global terrorism interrupted the purity of the Games. As we all watched live, a Palestinian terrorist group took nine members of the Israeli Olympic team hostage after killing two in their rooms. In the end, after a failed rescue attempt that we also all watched live, nine Israelis, one German and five of the hostage takers were killed. I remember Jim McKay, still with his ABC Wide World of Sports jacket on, simply saying about the hostages, "They're all gone." And sports again collided with politics and power and *terrorism*.

The thrill of victory and the agony of defeat.

So, sports is a big stage. And, for the most part, a great part of the American Lifestyle and the American Dream. Almost all of us see ourselves as athletes at some level—whether weekend warriors, ex-high school or college athletes, or just willing to put ourselves out there and try something *where you move* and, as Nike so famously said and gave us permission to, *Just Do It*. And as fans, oh do we love to cheer our teams—from soccer moms and dads with our five-year-olds to club sports, high school college and our beloved pro teams, they are part of our lifestyle.

And our Foresighters get the power of sports as well:

Question: *Let's be honest. America is pretty obsessed with sports. Whether as a participant or as a fan, sports is a part of the American Lifestyle. Why does sport matter? Why have we given it so much time and attention in our society?*

The themes were very clear:

- ✓ Great entertainment value
- ✓ A sense of escapism
- ✓ Brings families and communities together
- ✓ The real competition—*mano a mano*
- ✓ Two words: *Sports Bar*
- ✓ Cheer for the underdog
- ✓ How about a friendly wager?
- ✓ Americans *love to win*
- ✓ We can live vicariously through our favorite teams and players
- ✓ Most of the time, it's a fair playing field
- ✓ It's a social event (how about a beer and a hot dog)
- ✓ Life lessons through the games and events

Now, most of that was about *watching sports*. Many of our Foresighters talked about participation as well, but it's likely that most would say they are more active in *fitness* than in *sports*. And that's fair, but I think there is still a core athlete at the heart of just about everyone.

When I became really involved in running in the late 1970s/early 1980s, I was highly influenced (as were many at the time) by George Sheehan. He was the Medical Editor at Runner's World, a former college track athlete, a cardiologist and a *gifted writer*. He was our *running philosopher* and wrote two powerful books at that time: *Running & Being: The Total Experience* and *This Running Life*. His messages were about the integration of sport and fitness as an essential part of *your* American Lifestyle and that *anyone* could become a runner.

He had much to say about the pursuit of happiness as part of the American Dream: *"Happiness is different from pleasure. Happiness has something to do with struggling and enduring and accomplishing."* He believed that physical movement created clarity: *"The mind's first step to aware-*

ness must be through the body." And another favorite writing from Shee-han:

"Everyone is an athlete. The only difference is that some of us are in training and some of us are not." *And you already know where Nike went with that in their branding.*

He was way ahead of the curve on the fitness craze. The good doctor knew what endorphins could do, but also understood that a life of fitness, running and *active motion* was, in his view, a better life and one that could be part of a much larger set of American's lives. I have been running for over 40 years, not my only sport by any means, but the one that gives me great peace and mental clarity. Two-hundred-fifty road races, 50 marathons, another 25 ultras on the trail. Pretty fast at one point (a 2:33 marathon PR), but, *the older we get, the faster we were.* Or as the great Walt Stack used to espouse at the start of our races in San Francisco: *Just start slowly and then taper off.* Running and racing was really about the joy of motion and of being with your friends.

I ran a race with George Sheehan in Pennsylvania in the 1980s. Completely by chance, a little *serendipity*, I suppose. He had many years on me, but would not give an inch. But he was also the first to the keg after the race. After he *beat you.* Sport has been and always will be part of my own life. And sports will always be part of the American lifestyle.

Sheehan, after a run and hard at work

But, how will sports change in the decade ahead? Our Foresighters had some keen perceptions on the view for the future:

Question: *Thinking broadly about sports as an element of The American Lifestyle, what are some of the trends and changes that you forecast in sports for the decade ahead?*

In no particular order, here were some of the key trends that our Foresighters identified for the decade ahead (not prioritized):

No.	Idea
1.	Smaller venues
2.	More remote viewing options
3.	More racial/financial equality
4.	More focus on entertainment component
5.	Less focus on violent contact sports
6.	E sports gaining popularity
7.	Sports playing increased role in social issues
8.	Will participate more/watch less
9.	Less taxpayer support of large stadiums
10.	Sports teams becoming more philanthropic
11.	More automation of rules/regs
12.	New role for AI in analytics

Sports will continue to be a big player in the decade ahead. It will be a player on the economic scene, on the entertainment scene, but also on the issues of equality, inclusion and social justice. The NBA "Bubble" in Orlando in 2020 was a good bellwether of things to come. It's time for sports to flex its considerable muscle to help address some of the larger issues we face.

Outside!

Finally, on the *participation side* of sports, we saw a major change in the popularity of *outside* sports for average Americans. A general trend going into this decade was the advent and popularity of the *active lifestyle* that included fitness, travel and sports. But the pandemic pressed us all to get outside when we could and accelerated the popularity of these sports. I like to call them *life sports* because you can learn them early on and stay active with them throughout your life. Example: *skiing* is a life sport, however the *Olympic downhill* should remain a spectator event for most of us. Perhaps Franz excluded.

I dabbled in many sports growing up and enjoyed them all—basketball, baseball, wrestling, soccer and, proudly, I was high jump record holder in 4th grade. *Try jumping in a sawdust pit when it is 100 degrees in Arizona.* But I zeroed in on a series of *life sports* as I grew older as I knew that I could stay active with them long into the future (count me in through at least age 75 on all of them). And, you can teach and then do life sports with your kids and family. My core life sports have served me well: running, skiing, swimming, cycling, golf, tennis and hiking. They create seasons and events, memories, a few trips to the ER room, and your own version of the thrill of victory and the agony of defeat. But mostly, they keep you in motion and get you outside. *God help me, but I am seriously considering adding pickleball to my list.*

Above on right with brother Pete, 2007. We still ski.

Below on left with son Scott, 2019. A <u>Grand</u> hike!

343

Son Jack, 2006. Still beats me in golf.   *Brother Bruce, 2000. We still run.*

During the pandemic in 2020, outdoor sports exploded. In an article entitled, "Call of the Wild: Americans Find Escape in the Outdoors," the AP compiled research on the exodus to the outside and saw a 52.9% surge in outdoor participation. Another 8.1 million Americans went hiking in 2020 compared to 2019; 7.9 million more went camping; 3.4 million more went fishing; active, on-course golfers grew by 500,000 and the USTA reported that there were nearly three million new first time players on the tennis court and 21.6 million players overall. To be clear, I have not yet acknowledged *fishing* to be a life sport, but I acknowledge that it is best done outdoors.

Daughter Betsy, 2021. Sharks!

Son Sam, 2018. Tri Harder!

So, add the trend of *more active* to the American Lifestyle in the decade ahead. And add a new life sport to your own repertoire of activities: hit a mountain bike trail, try a little cross-country skiing, get back to swimming laps outdoors, hike the Grand Canyon, try kayaking or a SUP (Stand Up Paddleboard), *try a little pickleball* or do your first triathlon as a combo package of life sports. I think the good Dr. Sheehan would approve.

Our Traveling Lifestyle: Americans on the Move

A rolling stone gathers no moss. I don't want to take that one too far, but one thing is for sure: Americans feel like they have the God-given right to hit the open road any time they please. It is part of the American Lifestyle, a sense of mobility, a certain sense of status (we'll be at the *Cape* this summer) and just a sense of discovery—something new on the horizon.

And to have your travel credentials pretty much revoked in 2020, well, hit the gas in mid-to-late 2021 and tell Uncle Ed that we are on the way!

Our Foresighters were no different—anxious to be traveling again, but also providing some perspective on why travel matters:

Question: *On the road again. Travel is big business, whether it is a day trip in your state, a summer vacation to the beach/mountains or a global destination/experience. Why does travel matter? Why is it so important to Americans and their lifestyle?*

What was clear is there are a lot of forces at play in this travel imperative for Americans; you can pick and choose what seems to align with your views:

- ✓ An escape from reality
- ✓ Experiencing new cultures
- ✓ An ability to unplug/disconnect
- ✓ Go see friends and relatives
- ✓ *Get away from* friends and relatives
- ✓ Check off those bucket-list items
- ✓ We are all thirsty for new experiences
- ✓ Open our eyes to the outdoors
- ✓ Exercise a fundamental freedom to explore
- ✓ Sharing experiences with your family
- ✓ Change the temperature of your season
- ✓ It opens the mind
- ✓ It helps us grow, broadens our knowledge
- ✓ A change of scenery
- ✓ Recharges the batteries

- ✓ Can serve as a reward
- ✓ A better appreciation of history
- ✓ New food and beverage, the cuisine of another culture
- ✓ Creates memories to share for the future
- ✓ To scratch that itch left by the travel bug
- ✓ Well, simply because we can

Something happens when we travel. I think it puts our *soul* into motion. You go from a locked in (or locked down in 2020) daily routine, into a sense of a new adventure, that anything can happen, that your routine is set aside. New people, new places, new experiences. Reflections about what really matters to me.

Being Bit by the Travel Bug

To a certain degree, I think you either have the travel bug or you don't. I mean, we all like to see new things, go on a summer vacation, take a road trip. But, not everyone wanted to jump on the first wagon train and head west. *Count my ass in, Mr. Wagonmaster, you want me in the wagon or on a horse?*

I remember the first time I took a trip on my own. Sixteen years old, just got my license to drive, had my 1966 Ford Bronco, no top, windshield down (you could do that with a 1966 Bronco), sunglasses on and *The Who* on my Muntz 8-track playing *Teenage Wasteland.* I drove from my mom's house in Phoenix and was going to drive to Flagstaff. The first time ever on an interstate. I had some *belongings and some provisions.* My very own wagon train, just the four-wheel drive version. And I remember making the right turn from Glendale Avenue onto I-17 north. 20 miles an hour, now 35, the wind is really coming at me now as I hit 50 (well, Doug, that's because you don't have a wind*shield*), then 60 miles an hour. I am locked in and looking straight ahead, and I have no idea *what* is ahead, it's just that I am heading there. *What a rush to my soul.*

That's how a travel bug hits you.

I never really looked back. I still have that travel bug and I try and scratch it pretty frequently. I look at travel excursions as five different categories. Let's start with CAT1: *Day Trips.* In the car, out early in the morning, back sometime that night. In Arizona, day trips are plentiful, it's a big state and plenty to see and do. I can still do a day trip to Flagstaff for a ski day in the winter; Sedona for a hike; Tombstone for a little wild-west adventure; Tucson for a bike in Saguaro National Monument followed by Mexican food at *El Minuto.* Our cabin in Payson is less than two hours away, catch a fish or catch a hike. Probably 10 lakes I can hit for a kayak or a swim. When pressed, I can make the Grand Canyon as a day trip, including a hike to the bottom and back. My daughter referred to that particular day hike as a ride on the *Struggle Bus*.

Now CAT2 are *Road Trips*. My definition of a road trip is a venture by car that requires an overnight stay (or more), but you can reach within a 12 hour drive. I'm serious. And the great news is that Arizona is like the road trip headquarters of the country. From my house in Scottsdale I can hit the following in 12 hours: Rocky Point (Mexico), San Felipe (Baja Mexico), San Diego, Laguna Beach, Newport Beach, Dana Point, Moab (Utah), Park City, Las Vegas, Boulder City, Santa Fe, Telluride, Durango, Vail, San Francisco and Lake Tahoe. And there are plenty more that I haven't yet hit, but I still have the decade ahead to add them to my list.

CAT3 is *See The USA*. While you could do an extended road trip by car, these are generally a little more efficient when you hit *the friendly skies*. Damn, this is a big country. I have a map of the U.S. in my office of all the places I have done sessions for work. And, yes, I put *pushpins in the map* of all the places I have been. This is hereditary. My dad put up a map of the Tonto National Forest in our cabin when they first began building it in 1956 and carefully placed 24 pins in the map of places we hiked, camped, got stuck, etc. The map is still there. I was going to write a book one summer called *Twenty-Four Pins on My Father's Map* and go visit and chronicle all the places. Maybe I'll make that an article in the decade ahead. Nonetheless, back to my map in my office, I am pleased to say that I am up to 49 states. *Alaska remains the final frontier.*

CAT4 is *Spin The Globe*. I had a globe as a kid, maybe you did. A real globe, not a digital one. All those colors. All that ocean. No, I don't stick pins in a globe, but I must say that *traveling internationally* is pretty cool. I didn't need a passport for Mexico as a kid, not even for Guadalajara, but I remember getting my first passport when I was with IBM in San Jose at the Education Center in 1980. *A passport*. One goal: *fill up those pages*. And I have—Australia, New Zealand, Singapore and Thailand from the Education Center. Then with my own consulting work: UK, Spain, France, Russia, Germany, India, Brazil, Chile, Columbia, Venezuela, Guatemala, Costa Rica, South Africa, Morocco and the Dominican Republic. The Griff Squad (our family) has added Italy, Austria, Switzerland, St. John, Tortola and the pitons in St. Lucia. *Looking good, Mon.*

I think of one thing when I think of global travel: the 747. The Boeing 747 was the first *Jumbo-Jet* and was designed in the late 1960s with a test flight in 1969 and then was certified and entered service with Pan Am in January of 1970. It generally accommodates 366 passengers in three travel classes. You are *rich* (first class), You work for a *nice company* (business class), and you are *on your own* (economy class). I have been in all three classes, but the details by which I found my way onto business class and first class remain *classified*. Mostly, I am an *econo-traveler* and I enjoy that a great deal. It's where most of the real people sit.

Boeing has built some 1500 747s and they are still flying, though the manufacturing of the 747 is scheduled to end in 2022. If you have never experienced the take-off of a 747, well then, you must do this in the decade ahead. It's better than any Disney ride. You need a runway about the length of Arizona. There is great doubt in your mind that it will ever get off the ground. My 1966 Ford Bronco had far better acceleration. But when it does take off, it is *another rush to the soul.*

An early Pan Am 747. So wrong!   *A massive 747 in flight*

And CAT5. I must tell you that I have not reached CAT5 in my travel experiences. *But I have a dream*. Seriously, I have this dream about once a year. I am *strapped into a seat* on a NASA spacecraft. Sometimes it is an Apollo version and sometimes it is a Shuttle version. Incredibly vivid. And it is always a countdown to blastoff. And I thought the 747 was ultimate takeoff. In the decade ahead I plan on notching a CAT5. It won't be the Apollo or Shuttle version, I am sure that my best chance will be to tag along with *Sir Richard Branson* on one of the Virgin Galactic's spaceships. It looks like flights will be launching in 2022 at a cost of $250,000. I am waiting for *economy class* towards the end of the decade.

CAT5 travel: The Gallactic maiden voyage on July 11, 2021

The Future of Travel

So, if travel is already a mainstay of the American Lifestyle now, *and* we are coming off of a serious lockdown where the pent-up demand for travel in general will kick start this early part of the decade, then where are we headed for the *rest* of the decade?

Question: *Thinking broadly about travel as an element of The American Lifestyle, what are some of the trends and changes that you forecast in travel for the decade ahead?*

In this activity we not only brainstormed on the open question (some 100+ responses), but also summarized the responses and then assessed the themes in terms of the importance of the impact it might have on the decade ahead:

Now, please assess each of the following trends in terms of the impact you feel this trend will have on the future of travel in the decade ahead and the impact to the American Lifestyle. Use a scale of 1-10 where a "1" means not at all important and a "10" means extremely important. For this exercise assume that trend or change is valid—that it will likely materialize over the course of decade:

Rank	Idea	Avg.
1.	Less work-related travel	8.4
2.	Safety determining factor in how/when one travels	8.0

3.	Cheaper air fares	**7.6**
4.	Increased popularity of Airbnb type options	**7.5**
5.	More appreciation of local/regional destinations	**7.4**
6.	Combining longer term vacation/work stays	**7.3**
7.	More curated experiences	**7.0**
8.	More car travel	**6.5**
9.	Climate change may impact where people choose to travel	**6.2**
10.	Less reliance on flying	**5.9**
11.	Travel via virtual reality	**5.4**
12.	First opportunities for space travel	**5.2**

The top nine, in particular, seem to be well received by our group. Not only with our group, but just about all of the sessions I have been running with clients, and research I have been reading, consistently suggest that the less work-related travel the better. There will be times when it is appropriate, but the days of flying across the country, navigating two airports, some kind of local ground transport and working your way through a crowded hotel lobby for a two-hour morning meeting sounds archaic. And it also sounds really *expensive* for businesses. That doesn't mean travel overall will be less, other factors will combine to increase family and leisure travel.

Destinations are going to compete on *experiences*. Authentic, safe, unique and meaningful experiences. In my city in Arizona, it's no longer the "Scottsdale Convention and Visitors Bureau", but it is the "*Experience Scottsdale*" organization. They brand, advertise and help their destination partners deliver on a Scottsdale experience that their guests cannot get elsewhere. *Deliver the experience and they will tell their social media network, and they will come back personally.*

Air travel costs will likely rise as the pandemic wanes, but over time, it will become more competitive again. The destinations just want you to deliver their guests safely, and if you can make the airline fee a little more reasonable, then the guests will stay longer and spend more. Remember, I don't want to do pure business travel, but I might be more willing to do some virtual work in return for longer vacation stays. I actually saw a news item about an island that was offering a year stay with excellent internet and accommodations. *Paradise calls.*

And hotels and resorts will continue to be competing against the Airbnb and VRBO type options. *Because it feels less like a traditional hotel experience and more like an intimate family and local community experience.* The last VRBO that the *Griff Squad* stayed at was in Kauai in the Kukuui'ula community. OMG, great house, bike to the beach, golf at one of the all-time best golf courses we have ever played, still go completely local on long hikes and get the best shaved ice on the island. Easy dinners at night (especially easy as I wasn't doing the preparing).

On the local/regional front, shorter distances but authentic experiences are a good one-two punch. My brother, an attorney in Flagstaff, has bought land on lower Oak Creek south of Sedona in the Page Springs area where there are a series of good vineyards. They are redeveloping the land and will produce some 1000 bottles of *Echo Canyon* wine this Fall. But the real plans are for the wine tasting room and a series of *casitas* so you can stay on the property. I mean, it's a *crappy, rocky, long dirt road to even get to the property*. And no one even knows about it. And it's really isolated once you are there. *Perfect.* A unique and authentic experience, and an easy drive from the Valley, but light years away from the typical commercial destination.

You'll note that virtual travel is low on the list. *And it should be.* Travel should be the real thing. I will certainly use technology for a virtual preview, but travel is the analog experience to combat digital fatigue.

Our Foresighters weighed in on what they felt would be the one most significant trend:

- ✓ "Ability to work remotely will allow for more travel and longer stays. Personally, I'd love to go work on an island for a week." (*Consider the year option…*)
- ✓ "Less travel via plane, cruise and others where people are packed closely together. This could actually improve the travel experience, but for fewer people."
- ✓ "Adventure / Eco Travel—people today seek more 'experience' over visits."
- ✓ "Travel that will give people the opportunity to 'slow down' because everyone is over-committed in terms of time, effort, etc."
- ✓ "An increase in travel in conjunction with remote work flexibility. As people discover how to work remotely, they will explore the opportunities associated with working from anywhere. As a re-

sult, RVs and extended stay options are going to realize an economic boom." (RVs? Get ready *Quartzite...*)

✓ "Greater emphasis on 'globalization'. Traveling to gain knowledge of people, places, cultures, histories. The importance is travel will allow more people to become better 'global citizens', maybe making it less likely for major conflicts to occur."

✓ "A new appreciation for travel following COVID, and hopefully a renewed mindset for the working American about taking time to travel and go on vacations. I feel like many Americans feel pressure about taking time off to travel or taking days off from work, and I hope that once we are clear to travel again that this will change."

✓ "Access to outer space—this will completely reframe our thoughts about travel in a 'World is round, not flat' way. Once that becomes a real option, it will forever change the way we think of travel."

There! A vote for my CAT5 travel experience! And the world *is round*, isn't it? I'll confirm this when I use my iPhone 96 to send you a picture toward the end of the decade.

Look, all of this is good news for the travel industry if you are in the business of authentic experiences. It also reinforces that, for the decade ahead, America will be more on the move than ever. Locally/regionally first, then nationally, and then global travel will be back once there is a genuine sense of safety, health and vaccine protocols in the global destinations. In many respects, this could be the golden decade of travel.

And, at the end of the day, an authentic travel experience can just be driving an old VW bus up Highway 1 in California. Fire up the blender and the wi-fi hot spot. Simple is good.

Let Me Entertain You

Finally, as we look at three influences on American Lifestyle with Sports and Travel now in the proverbial rear view mirror, we arrive at *entertainment*, which we have not had much of in the last 12 months. Granted, we have had *guilt free streaming* which has been quite terrific. But I don't know about you, there have been some weeks that I have been a little *sleep deprived*.

Entertainment is a legitimate element of the American Lifestyle. Movies, theater (as in the Broadway/live performance kind), comedy and *especially* music. And I know you have a 1000-inch flat screen and an amazing speaker system at your house (the one with no neighbors anymore), but you and I have especially missed *live music*.

352

Every one of you can tell a story about the best concerts you ever attended. How the audience, whether an intimate setting with 25 or 30 by the beach, to a smaller music hall with 500 or so, to a megaconcert with 50,000 plus. I bet some of you who are reading this book right now actually went to *Woodstock*. Talk about an authentic experience. No wait—maybe it's better that you *not* talk about it. Your kids probably wouldn't believe you anyway.

The biggest concert I ever attended was the December 1981 Rolling Stones outdoor concert at the Arizona State University. George Thorogood and the Destroyers opened things up, but the crowd was restless for Mick Jagger and Keith Richards. But especially for *Jagger*. Iconic, and in amazing shape. One review said that he must have run five miles back and forth on stage. I remember two great parts of the concert. The first was when Jagger was full steam on a Stones classic and he ran to the front of the stage. They had put a cherry-picker crane there below the stage line and no one could see it. He ran off the stage and on to the cherry picker platform and suddenly they joy-sticked Jagger up in the air and straight into the audience, just hanging a few feet above the crowd. The place went nuts.

The second great scene was during *Honky Tonk Women* when the Stones had recruited 200 ASU co-eds to come out on stage dressed up like saloon girls. And these were very *well recruited*. And those were the scenes that I remember most because I can't remember much else about the concert. *Kind of like your Woodstock Festival.*

But the *best* concert I ever attended was completely different. I was in Moscow as part of the World Association of Newspapers conference in 2006. Talk about a travel experience overall, but let's get to the music. We were all sort of VIPs there as Moscow and Putin wanted to put on a show for the global media that they were supporting a free and open media (they weren't then and aren't now). We were invited to a special event by the mayor of Moscow. After a few welcoming speeches we got to the main event: *The Moscow Strings*. Look, I don't have *any* classical music performances on my play lists, but I got to hear 90 minutes of some of the most talented string musicians in the world. Masterful. Stirring. Timeless. We all just looked at each other afterwards: *wow!*

But that's what makes entertainment so special. It's live and you see it with a shared audience, so it's a communal and shared experience. And I include big screen movies in my definition of entertainment, as well as stand-up comedy. How about being in the audience for a Johnny Carson taping, David Letterman or Conan O'Brien? Saturday Night Live?

Well, we have sorely missed the entertainment options that take place outside of our living rooms. But why is entertainment so compelling as part of who we are as Americans?

Let's bring our Foresighters on Stage.

Question: *Let me entertain you. Whether it is a music concert, a stand-up comedy routine, a Broadway play or the release of a highly anticipated movie, we all like to be entertained. Why does entertainment matter? Why is it so important to Americans and their lifestyle?*

- ✓ It transports us into another reality
- ✓ A complete escape from stress
- ✓ To appreciate the talent of the performers
- ✓ It broadens our horizons
- ✓ It is a glimpse into our culture
- ✓ It can sharpen us mentally
- ✓ Just the joy of being there
- ✓ Creates empathy with people, cultures and causes
- ✓ It's a genuine social experience
- ✓ To experience someone else's freedom of expression
- ✓ A chance to see a better life, to live a dream
- ✓ In many cases, a transfer of learning
- ✓ Music can bring back great memories—or create new ones
- ✓ To be a loyal fan
- ✓ To experience a unique or unexpected moment
- ✓ To reflect on our lives and our unique journey

I should tell you that I am a movie-goer. When I am in Park City, I go to the Redstone theaters in Kimball Junction. Nice area, restaurants and night life, but really casual. Before the pandemic, and when I might be on a solo trip for a few weeks (because I can), I would usually hit the movies at least once a week. And, unless it was the latest release of *Mission Impossible*, I was there with maybe 5-10 other movie goers. It didn't bother me, I like the large screen and my small popcorn, *no butter*. And I get that some of the trends in the theaters are to upscale with the recliner and a cold beer and cheeseburger, but I like a movie for a movie, then I will head over to the pub for my beer and cheeseburger.

And just so you know that I am not an isolationist or something, I also am in Park City every year when the Sundance Film Festival is going on. My neighbor Vic (also a Foresighter) knows *everything and everyone* involved in Sundance, so I just wait for his recommendations. The last one I saw (pre-pandemic) was *Whirlygig* about the first news helicopter in LA. It's the guy that becomes famous for following O.J.'s Bronco on the LA freeways. The director always attends the showings, you get the inside scoop. A movie and an education.

Where was I? Oh yes, why entertainment matters. It's really simple. We love to be entertained, we dig being part of an *audience*. People are performing for us. They're working, we don't have to. We can just shut it down for a while, and while we do, we open up in an entirely different way. You can laugh out loud, scream, cheer, applaud and, perhaps, shed a tear.

The Future of Entertainment

So where are we headed in the decade ahead? Cocooning in state-of-the-art home theaters? Let's ask our Foresighters:

Question: *Thinking broadly about entertainment as an element of the American Lifestyle, what are some of the trends and changes that you forecast in entertainment for the decade ahead?*

Similar to our activity on travel, we did open brainstorming followed by a summary and assessment of themes. Here's the assessment:

Now, please assess each of the following trends in terms of the impact you feel this trend will have on the future of entertainment in the decade ahead and the impact to the American Lifestyle. Use a scale of 1-10 where a "1" means not at all important and a "10" means extremely important. For this exercise assume that trend or change is valid—that it will likely materialize over the course of decade:

Rank	Idea	Avg.
1.	More innovations across the board	8.8
2.	Trade movie theaters for home viewing	8.4
3.	More immersive entertainment -- AI and VR	8.2
4.	Faster content development via streaming	7.9
5.	More outdoor events	7.3
6.	Virtual concerts	7.3
7.	Smaller venues	6.9
8.	Increased use of computer graphics in movies	6.7
9.	More gamification of entertainment	6.5

10.	More thrill in entertainment choices	**6.3**
11.	Drive-ins make a comeback	**5.6**
12.	Traditional books rise in popularity	**5.3**

It's an interesting assessment. More innovations "across the board", sure. Technology, production, content, delivery, staging. All of that will continue to evolve. More immersive experiences? Definitely. I am already looking to suspend my reality to be entertained, so *have at it*. Smaller venues and more outdoors events—that's a good trend, and aligns with more intimate and authentic experiences and combines the outside ambiance. I am not sold, though, on virtual concerts and *all* movies in my living room. Some movies in my living room, yes. But Hollywood and the big studios are going to have to do some experimenting with content and the first release windows. If you do improve the theater environment, do you really want to spend $25 for a first release at home with HBO Max, or is it worth trading the living room for a Saturday night out.

And let's be real about the idea that drive-ins will make a come back. Outdoor theaters, maybe—showing a big screen movie at a park or the ski area in the summer with a blanket and a picnic basket. I like that. But going back to the *drive-in?* Don't tell your kids, but you weren't going to the drive-in to watch a movie anyway.

But, as we said at the start of this chapter, *let the music play*. The pandemic was a great awakening for what we really miss and really enjoy about the American Lifestyle. The home can only entertain us so long, real entertainment is the live kind.

The American Lifestyle: Future Influence Scenarios

As is our custom towards the end of a Foresight session, we offer up some potential scenarios for the future: submitted for your consideration and entertainment value:

Now, please assess each of the following future scenarios in two ways. First, the level of positive IMPACT to the future of the American Lifestyle in the decade ahead if the scenario was to occur (use a scale of 1-10 where a "1" means a very low level of positive impact and a "10" means a very high level of positive impact); Second, the LIKELIHOOD that this scenario will fully materialize in the decade ahead (use a scale of 1-10 where a "1" means a very low likelihood and "10" means a very high likelihood):

Here is how our Foresight session assessed the list. The scenarios are ordered by the *level of positive impact*, but then contrasted with the likelihood of occurrence for a gap analysis rating…

356

#	Scenario Description	Im-pact	Like-ly	Gap
1	LIFESTYLE IS LIFE BALANCE: In the decade ahead our lifestyle is a more deliberate design of our desired life balance. Technology gives us options that we simply did not have before, for work, school and staying connected. We tend to choose our lifestyle first, then choose our work that supports that lifestyle. Families do more activities together by design and it actually works. The level of geographic independence is unprecedented. You live where you want to live, everything else follows.	9.1	7.0	(2.1)
2	AIRLINES CHANGE THEIR GAME: Influenced by the COVID pandemic, but also based on clear/long term feedback themes from travelers, airlines based in the U.S. significantly change the travel experience for the better. Cabins are completely reconfigured with more space for each traveler (25-50 percent fewer seats), enhanced technology/entertainment support, better gate and boarding experience, less "death of a thousand cuts" fees, and a genuine commitment to a better passenger experience. A good sense of value for the dollar, it is easy and enjoyable to get to just about any location in the country.	8.8	5.1	(3.7)
3	WORKATIONS EXTEND THE JOURNEY: Americans are strongly influenced by remote/ virtual work capability and many book travel destinations that are one-to-three months in duration where the new location becomes a base of operation for vacation/leisure along with work connection. The hotels/resorts and private homes are geared to supporting a work/vacation combination, hotel rooms have guest offices integrated as part of the space or guest offices as part of their facility support. It's not where you are going for your summer vacation, it's where you are going for your summer.	8.6	7.7	(0.9)

4	LIFE SPORTS BECOME THE TREND: Health, fitness and wellness are drivers of the desired lifestyle in the decade ahead. Life sports become the trend and we work our travel, our family time, our friends, even the geographies in which we live, and the housing communities and amenities around them. Cycling (mountain bikes, road bikes, gravel bikes, e-bikes...) is a big winner; so are golf, hiking, tennis, swimming, stand-up paddling, kayaking and others. The goal is not to blow out a knee in tackle football, but to have a life-long affair with sport.	8.4	7.2	(1.2)
5	EVERYONE GOES GLOBAL: Global travel emerges as one of the most significant trends for the decade ahead. Better routes/non-stops from major American cities, technology that lets travelers feel connected, great options for planned tours and integrated experiences, and even advanced personal language translation apps that makes it easier to communicate and engage in any country. Part of the concept of travel with a purpose, cultural and global destination travel becomes more frequent for many Americans.	8.2	5.7	(2.5)
6	TRAVEL WITH A PURPOSE: Discretionary "impulse travel" takes a back seat to traveling with a purpose. Travel is well thought out, whether to retrace the steps of your ancestors, check off a real bucket-list item, initiate a family reunion or explore a certain region of the country. Often times this travel can be around an annual event but expanded to enhance the experience. Travel is more aligned with personal values than personal convenience.	8.1	7.3	(0.8)

7	SERVICE SABBATICALS: Another development that supports the importance of having a cause as part of your lifestyle is the emergence of service sabbaticals. It's like a paid mission for working professionals where an employee identifies an important issue/cause and then spends a month or so immersed in the cause. It could be in the U.S. or global. Broader, more Americans spend their discretionary time on a service-based mission or cause. Instead of a summer vacation it is a service vacation.	7.7	5.3	(2.4)
8	FIRE UP THE WINNEBAGO: Whether by car or travel trailer, extended road trips become a huge trend. No airports, no hassles. Tour a National Park, go along the Pacific Coast Highway, tour the South, check out New England in the Fall, dodge a fish at the Seattle fish market. Wi-Fi keeps you connected, the open road keeps you calm.	7.6	7.8	+0.2
9	CONCERTS ARE KING: Of all the live entertainment options that people missed most during the pandemic, live music was the one that stirred the soul. You can't reproduce the experience of a concert at home, no matter if it is rock or classical. Live music concerts almost single handedly rescue large venue facilities and remind us all of what a shared experience feels like. Woodstock II anyone?	6.9	6.8	(0.1)
10	MOVIE THEATERS BECOME EXPERIENTIAL: Americans enjoy their home theaters but still enjoy a night on the town and a great movie. Theaters create partnerships with restaurants, night clubs and ride-share services where the movie is just part of the evening experience. The seating, sounds and service inside the theater are amazing and all agree that it's an experience that cannot be reproduced at home.	6.9	6.9	(0.0)

11	STADIUMS ARE DOWNSIZED BUT THE EX-PERIENCE IS UPSIZED: There are very few 100,000 seat venues any more. Major league sports intentionally downsizes their venues to retain the big league sense but offer a more intimate experience. Entertainment, dining and technology are all more integrated into the venue. Better options for family attendance and business events. The big screen innovations are amazing; it's pretty mind-blowing how they can integrate you into the game. You don't have to go to every game, but when you do, it's a FANtastic experience.	7.4	5.9	(1.5)
12	THE CORPORATE YOUTH SPORTS LEAGUE: To expand youth sports participation, a new national sports league is formed. The league is a consortium of major corporations that all believe in social equality and the importance of sports in influencing young people and their families. There are no registration costs and no uniform fees. There are entry level, developmental and competitive leagues. It's like a new version of the AAU but built around a level playing field. Parents/families are more engaged and it also leads to a healthier lifestyle for young people.	6.5	4.7	(1.8)

Pretty interesting. Many of our core trends seem to be both influential and likely—more purposeful travel, lifesports, workations, the return of concerts, more experiential movie theaters and my personal favorite, *firing up the Winnebago.*

But there were some gaps on a few of our possible scenarios. Look at the top six gaps between impact and likelihood:

1. Airlines change their game (3.7)
2. Everyone goes global (2.5)
3. Service Sabbaticals (2.4)
4. Lifestyle is Life Balance (2.1)
5. The Corporate Youth Sports League (1.8)
6. Stadiums are downsized but the experienced is upsized (1.5)

The two on the bottom are easy—the Youth Sports League is an interesting and somewhat noble idea, but it's a swing and a miss (as we say in baseball language). On the stadiums, *some* of the stadiums will down-size and *all* will try and upsize the experience, but we like big venues in big cities. It's a badge of honor in America.

The others are a little more challenging—we all agree with the notion of life balance, but we know the realities of economics, work, and even the pressure we put on ourselves. But at least for the immediate 6-12 months post-pandemic, we will give it a whirl. Service sabbaticals can go in the drawer with the Corporate Youth Sports League, kind of a good idea, but unlikely to be realized at scale. Go global? It's a time and eco-nomic challenge, perhaps a safety issue for a while. But global travel overall will return.

Which leaves us with the elephant in the room. The 747-sized dilemma. For a brief moment, a 2020 release of *The Kinder and Gentler Airline Company* was on display. And for those of you who experienced it, it was a great view of a better future *that will never happen.* The space planners and revenue forecasters will rule, so that middle seat is coming back and the fares will be headed back up. *It is an unfortunate sardine future.* Wel-come aboard.

Five Reflections on the Future of the American Lifestyle for the Decade Ahead

1. THE OPEN ROAD IS STILL OPEN: We are not wired to be iso-lated. Americans have always been restless and on the move. As the pandemic recedes, we will get back on the road to travel and exploration *with a vengeance.* It will be more purposeful, a gen-uine desire for authentic experiences. Less tethered to a work office, our mobility increases.
2. FINDING A NEW BALANCE: 2020 was a major reawakening for many Americans about what really mattered and what they really valued. There is a glimmer of hope that Americans will see that life always driven in the fast lane is a dead end. Slow it down, work hard, but not exhaustively. It's the journey that matters.
3. THE ACTIVE AMERICAN LIFESTYLE: Health, wellness, fitness and life-sports will become more important in the decade ahead. It's not only a better level of enjoyment, it should lead to a *longer lifestyle.* Welcome to the great outdoors. Let the French sip their wine on the Avenue des Champs-Elysée's, we'll hike the trails first, then sip their wine.
4. THE LIFESTYLE DEPENDS ON THE DREAM: We need to make sure the American Dream burns bright for *all* Americans in the decade ahead. It can't be a lifestyle for just *the rich and fa-*

mous. Create access to the Dream, and then the American Lifestyle, your own version, will be the just reward.

5. LET THE MUSIC PLAY: We can't let this be the decade where technology becomes so dominant that we forget why live performances matter. Sports in person, theaters and shows, music on the patio and even catch a big-time concert. Save me a seat at the baseball game, and let Paul McCartney know I am in for a 2022 concert tour.

So, What About Your Lifestyle in the Decade Ahead?

As we wrapped up our Foresight session we asked a simple question and ended up with our most surprising result of the session:

Question: *How would you describe YOUR ideal lifestyle for the decade ahead? Think about the lifestyle that gives you the sense of balance, purpose and enjoyment that really aligns with you and your values:*

Now, the surprise is NOT in the description of the ideal lifestyles—you and I ponder this question frequently, I suspect. Here's what our Foresighters said:

- "I'd like to think I'd have a family to share my life with. More balanced life and work—mostly working remotely. Being financially stable and being able to travel with my family."
- "Lots of travel, stable health to enjoy activities and sports, sufficient income to comfortably meet obligations and still afford the cool extras."
- "More time to check-in with myself, my family and my loved ones. I hope America will slowly start to see that time to recharge is important to productivity."
- "Strong balance between enjoying time at home and travel/exploration with family and friends. It will be all about connections and giving back, less about wealth acquisition and career success. Significant time in nature, maintaining health and fitness. Focus on quality over quantity (simplification)."
- "I look forward to less pressure from work, more enjoyment of being with friends and family. I am eager to try working from other places. Enjoy each day as much as possible, and to not postpone joy."
- "I am working on being remote, free and flexible. Work from anywhere, when necessary. Travel and explore the people and places of this country and adequate time on the beach to recharge and regroup."
- "For me balance is an interesting place to live with lots of options for eating, cultural entertainment, ability to watch sport (some-

times) but combined with good exercise facilities—trails in a national park, a long walk along a river, and a good library nearby."
- "Working for a company that actually cares about me as an individual, and having a healthy work/life balance. Additionally, simply being happy with my personal life/relationships, being healthy, having a little less anxiety and being around dogs."

I love my dog-lovers. Health, fitness, *sufficient income*, better balance, recharge and explore. My favorite point from these views is the idea of enjoying every day and *to not postpone joy*.

Now the *surprising result* was not the description of the lifestyles above, it was the total level of optimism that they could achieve and sustain that lifestyle:

Question: *All things considered are you optimistic or pessimistic about your ability to achieve/sustain this lifestyle in the decade ahead?*

No.	Items	Times Selected
1.	**Optimistic**	**(100%)**
2.	Pessimistic	(0%)

2020 and the pandemic served as a powerful re-awakening about what matters in our lives and our lifestyle. Perhaps it has moved the desired American Lifestyle to a better place. Our Foresighters commented on the lessons learned from COVID on the American Lifestyle:

- "I spend a lot of time at home and it has made me realize how important staying connected to friends and family is."
- "It just emphasizes even more how grateful I am for my health and the health of those around me. It makes me more cautious about doing things that are detrimental to my health, but also has made me appreciate those I love even more."
- "It has definitely made me aware of some of the things that I took for granted before—even little things. It has shed light on what's important—family, friends, shared experiences."
- "It has allowed me time to think, reassess and retool my work/family/lifestyle balance. That is the silver lining for me, and for many of those I talk with as well."
- "COVID has reprioritized what to spend my time doing, with whom and where."

And here are the questions for *you* in the decade ahead: How will you adjust your desired lifestyle? Is it aligned with who you are authentically? Does the concept of The American Dream resonate for you? A few final thoughts on why the Dream is relevant for all of us.

They Have a Dream

Sports, travel and entertainment were just some examples and elements of the American Lifestyle. We can all have our own version of an "ideal lifestyle". But the American Lifestyle is just a subset of the American Dream. And make no mistake about it, the American Dream may have its naysayers out there, that it is a mirage and not a dream. But I say that the American Dream is real and as powerful today as it ever was. The decade ahead will be a test for the American Dream, and whether that dream can be accessed by more people, be they in America today or those who may want to pursue the Dream by migrating in the future.

What will create access to the American Dream in the decade ahead will be *access to opportunity*. Access to opportunity can then translate to the pursuit of prosperity, of a better life. Prosperity is not the mindless pursuit of *stuff*. The middle class in America, a dwindling group these days, have always understood the value of a little prosperity. It bought a home, it could send their kids to college, you could take a nice summer vacation, you could *see the USA in your Chevrolet*. For many, that was the American Dream. But it all hinged then and hinges now on *access to opportunity*. Your Dream might be bigger than mine, and that's OK. But we can all still enjoy our version of the American Dream.

The problem we face now is when we deny the opportunity to others. There are things happening in America today that deny the opportunity. Lack of access to early childhood education, lack of access to affordable healthcare. A minimum wage that means a minimum level of opportunity. And there are people who want to take away the opportunity of others— bullies in schools, workforces that are not inclusive, guns that are indiscriminately fired on others, gangs and racist groups that try to impose their will, partisan politicians that just don't get it and seem to want to turn back the clock.

The American Dream is not a free ride. It's a *quid pro quo*. If I give you access as an American to the Dream, you have to work hard, play by a reasonable set of rules and *give back* when you get a chance. If you don't do these things, or don't want to do them, then the Dream is *revocable*. I think most people who want access to the American Dream, that opportunity gateway, understand the deal and are willing to abide by it. The people who want to take the opportunity away from others are the

364

ones who should have their Dream revoked. Live your Dream and enjoy your lifestyle, but don't step on mine. *I worked too hard for it.*

Cue the Dreamers. In June of 2012, then President Barack Obama issued an Executive Order establishing the Deferred Action For Childhood Arrivals (DACA). It would allow certain individuals who were brought into the country illegally as children to receive a renewable two year period of *deferred action* on their deportation and would enable them to be eligible for a work permit. It did not include a pathway to citizenship. The DREAM Act (Development, Relief and Education for Alien Minors), on the other hand, is a legislative proposal to grant conditional residency to unauthorized immigrants who entered the country as minors *with a pathway to citizenship*. But, to attain that *American Dream* they would also have to abide by a set of rules regarding age, pursuit and completion of education, registration for the Selective Service and be of *good moral character* over a six-year conditional period to achieve permanent residency and, eventually, citizenship.

There are about 650,000 DACA recipients but the number of actual Dreamers is much higher, estimated to be around 3.5 *million*. Not all of the Dreamers applied for DACA coverage and many aged into the program after it stopped accepting applications. Many are college age students now and they are a *movement.* And they have a dream: that the U.S. will, someday, pass the DREAM Act that will allow them the opportunity to pursue the American Dream. And that will be a big test for the decade ahead. Do we build walls or do we enable Dreams?

The number of Dreamers in America today is estimated to be around 3.5 million.

CHAPTER 11: Clear the Mechanism—Reset the Decade

Now I've been happy lately
Thinking about the good things to come
And I believe it could be
Something good has begun

…

'Cause I'm on the edge of darkness
There ride the Peace Train
Oh Peace Train take this country
Come take me home again

--Cat Stevens (aka, Yusuf Islam), <u>Peace Train</u> (1971)

January 21, 2021
Foresight 2030 Session

Something good has begun. Well, we know that there is a bit of a split decision on that sentiment. The country voted in a new president in November, with both a popular vote majority and an electoral vote majority. 81,268,924 Americans voted for Biden, but 72,216,154 voted for the incumbent President Trump. Most incumbent presidents respect the voting process and the sanctity of an election. Trump says the election was *stolen*. Welcome to January 2021, one of the most historic months and mind-blurring months the country has ever seen.

Wednesday # 1: On January 6, the Congress meets to certify the Electoral College. Generally pretty mundane stuff, but Trump tries for a *Hail Mary* and incites his followers to head to the Capitol for a protest—to *stop the steal*. It turns into an *insurrection* where the United States Capitol is breached by a mob and even the vice president of the United States is running for his life. This is like a movie from a Tom Clancy novel. *Smoke billows from the U.S. Capitol. Insurrectionists have occupied the building.* I called my son Sam over to watch the live news feed. History in the making. *This is a really bad movie.*

366

And there it was. *The edge of darkness*. The fall of the Roman Empire. But it wasn't a military coup or a serious overthrow attempt. It was kind of Trump rally on steroids. One last hurrah. But really dangerous shit for everyone. I think we, as a country, dodged a bullet that day. There was real damage and death, but it could have been far, far worse. As the dust (and the smoke) cleared, there seemed to be a genuine *come to Jesus moment* for the Congress that we had all gotten way too close to that edge of darkness as a country.

Insurrection 2021	*Sen. Lindsay Graham: "Count me out!"*

Even the Majority leader Mitch McConnell and Republican Senator Lindsay Graham made impassioned comments about the moment when Congress reconvened that evening. Said Graham (it still feels you are watching a Young Frankenstein movie when he speaks): "But today, all I can say is to count me out, enough is enough." Further in his comments regarding Trump: "If you're a conservative, this is the most offensive concept in the world—that a single person could disenfranchise 155 million people." And finally, "It is *over*...Joe Biden and Kamala Harris are lawfully elected and will become the president and vice president of the United States on January 20." *Time to move on. There ride the Peace Train.*

Wednesday # 2: On January 13, the U.S. House of Representatives votes to impeach sitting President Trump on a single count of impeachment for "incitement of insurrection". Look, Trump is actually leading in the impeachment race among all previous presidents as this is his second impeachment; no one else has made it beyond one. That would be his only successful *second term* as a president. The House votes to impeach 232-197. Lots of procedural maneuvers by Pence and the Senate, the impeachment papers would not reach the Senate chamber until January 25, and Trump, now a *past* president, would be acquitted by the Senate 57-43, falling short of the 67 votes needed. Of course, removing him from the presidency was not the issue (America did that in November), it was about preventing him from running again in the decade ahead. *Let's keep a little drama aboard the Peace Train, shall we?*

Wednesday # 3: And, as we progress through our weekly Wednesday highlights in January of 2021, we reach January 20 and the Inauguration of the 46th President of the United States, Joseph R. Biden. *The Conductor-in-Chief of our Peace Train.*

There are times in American history when a single event can signal the beginning of a needed reset. Sometimes it is a speech, sometimes it is a battle victory, sometimes it is a Supreme Court decision. In this case, it was the January 20, 2021, inauguration of a new president. So much noise and controversy over the last four years. So close to the *edge of darkness.* Like Kevin Costner who plays an aging pitcher in *For the Love of the Game*, it's time to *clear the noise and reset the mechanism.* This was an opportunity for a fundamental reset for the country for the decade ahead.

And look, if you are writing a book about the decade ahead, a reset sounds like a pivotal moment, and you better catch it with your final *Foresight* session. That was the bet we placed in June of 2020...that Biden would win and that our final session should take place on January 21, the day after the inauguration. And that the inauguration would signal a reset for the country that badly needed a new direction after battling a global pandemic for a year and a divisive president for four years. *All Aboard!*

Previous Resets in America
Despite the political speeches and promises, we don't hit the reset button that often in America. Looking at the current century, I think it's fair to argue that 9/11 was a reset for the country, a wakeup call about the danger of global terrorism and that we are not immune to attack on our own shores. It was an event that unified nearly all of us. It quieted the skies for nearly a week, it created a new wave of patriotism and military sign-up, it created the Transportation and Security Administration (TSA) and also created the Department of Homeland Security (DHS), formed as a result of the Homeland Security Act and began operations in 2003. *If you see something, say something.* It also created some tension around personal freedom, border security policy, surveillance tactics and technology, profiling and how Americans viewed the Muslim religion and the followers of Islam. In some respects, it has taken us 20 years to bring that view back to a more moderate stance.

But it was a powerful reset. Whether you were a fan of President George W. Bush or not, you listened to his words in the aftermath of the attack

368

and arguably the most powerful image of his presidency was when he took the bullhorn in the rubble of the World Trade Center in New York City. He had started his speech on September 14 when a rescue worker in the crowd yelled out, "I can't hear you!" Bush responded:

"I can hear you! I can hear you! The rest of the world hears you! And the people—and the people who knocked these buildings down will hear all of us soon!"

President Bush in 2001: the bullhorn heard around the world

And, whether or not we went about it the right way, someone was going to get hit back for the attacks, and it largely thrust us into a long series of Middle East conflicts. It took a powerful event to reset America at the start of the century, but it influenced a decade and a young generation.

If that was the reset *before* the Biden Inauguration, then what might be the reset *after* the Biden Inauguration and decade ahead? I would argue it will be the long-term reset of climate change and the impact it has on everything we do, but also how America and the globe will come together to fundamentally save the planet. That's a pretty good rationale for a re-set, but, sadly, I don't see that reset really happening until the end of the decade ahead. The reset that we are about to begin, symbolically start-ing with the January 20 inauguration, may take us the decade to get *oth-er things* done. But it has the prospect of being one of the most important decades ever.

Let's check in with our Foresighters…

Foresight 2030 Session—Reset the Decade

For our final Foresight session we rounded up a top notch set of 50 Foresighters. Their homework assignment had been to watch some of the inauguration coverage and consider the symbolic impact of the event as a reset to the country for the decade ahead. Allow me to introduce a sampling of our January 21 participants:

- "Hello, I am a professional serving the public sector through local, federal, tribal and special districts providing emergency response services. My career has focused on leadership and improving our craft and service to the public. I work in Tucson, Arizona, and hold a primary residence in Paradise Valley, Arizona."
- "Happy to join you all today and discuss the decade ahead. Yesterday I recalled a distant conversation where I discussed whether Elizabeth Dole could run as a vice-presidential candidate. Only two decades we later we actually have a female VP!"
- "Retired marketing research consultant in the Midwest, enjoying time for hobbies & grandchildren. In a very good mood today!"
- "I'm from Chicago, I love cooking, drawing and I teach fitness classes part time, in addition to my full time job in marketing & PR."
- "Fitness-loving marketing specialist in agriculture who loves her little chihuahua."
- "Wife, mom, Christian, in the market research industry currently living in Texas."
- "A dad of three adult children, married 41 years, a proud former Wolverine and Detroiter, love to ride my bike." *(I have a good story about another Wolverine later…)*
- "Young professional, mother, dog owner, hiker, yogi, social butterfly."
- "Recently retired, doing volunteer work, hiking and now optimistic (as of yesterday!)"

Consultants, retirees, chihuahua owners and social butterflies. You can't say that we don't encourage diversity and inclusion in our Foresight sessions.

I only know one Chihuahua joke, so before we get into the session, here it goes. Two guys are walking their dogs on a Sunday afternoon in the city. It's a little warm out and they happened to see a bar and thought it looked pretty inviting. But what to do with the dogs? One was a German Shepherd and the other was a Chihuahua. One guy says to the other, "Put on sun glasses and we'll tell them we are blind and these are our

370

seeing-eye dogs!" The bouncer, after hearing their story, passes the first guy with the German Shepherd but stops the second guy, and says, "Hey, you can't come in here...that's a Chihuahua you have there!" The second guy appears perplexed and throws his hands up in in the air and says,"What! They gave me a Chihuahua?"

Personal Reflections on 2020

Part of our premise about the reset of America in January of 2021 was that the combined experience of the Trump presidency leading into 2020 and the COVID pandemic itself had pushed the country to a tipping point —a sense that change was essential, that the level of political, economic, and social divide was unsustainable. Our participants shared their very personal reflections about 2020 that seemed to validate our premise:

Question: *Our Foresight 2030 Project has focused on the decade ahead from the lens/experience of 2020. But perhaps a good place to start our session is by reflecting back on 2020 (Hindsight 2020) as an unexpected way to start this decade. How did 2020 affect you personally and your way of thinking? How has it affected your outlook on the future?*

These are powerful and emotional statements, and we are sharing a larger number of them as they really set the tone for why the reset was on the horizon:

- "Reminded me of how little I really have control over. I learned to relax, focus, readjust. It brought a great deal of clarity to my pur-pose and my passions, and helped ground me in the true values of what was most important. It was a very difficult, challenging season, not easy to navigate, but extremely productive and transformational."
- "I became disenchanted with my fellow American citizen, suspi-cious of my neighbors and felt hopeless about our politics."
- "2020 was not a good year for anyone. In some ways it made me learn that some people are selfish beyond words and cannot come together to put aside differences in a time of need. On the other hand, it re-affirmed to me that life is short and precious and that we should take time to do the things that matter and spend time with those we love."
- "Work slowed and we ran into some non-COVID related health problems. Lifestyle was significantly altered...no vacation, bundling up to go out to eat at the restaurants we trusted with good heating systems. There were times I was really depressed and worried about the state of the country, but was hopeful for positive change with the election."

- "2020 was a bit of a splash of cold water. It made me much more aware of the divisions and problems in our society—and the level to which people were willing to pull together. More so, that there were A LOT of people who think very differently than I do."
- "I'm typically optimistic, but from 2016 on, felt angry and hopeless. The Trump administration wreaked havoc with what this nation was, what we stood for globally and our ability to make wise decisions based on truth and science. As of yesterday, I'm feeling optimistic again."
- "2020 exposed the fragility of life and society. The ripple effects of the pandemic on work, social life, community and government have been profound and have caused most to think about and reevaluate priorities and aspirations."
- "2020 was terrible for so many people and our society. I felt it was the perfect storm, having feared what would happen if a disaster hit this country with the prior leadership, that it would be bungled, and it was, and then the falling economy, hardships for so many. It provides a chance now to learn and grow and improve as a society, if we all rise to the challenge."
- "This past year demonstrated how we are socially at a crossroads, i.e., do we embrace growth/evolution/enhanced knowledge (e.g., the vaccines) or do we deteriorate into irrational tribes with manifestly negative behaviors (the unwillingness to wear masks in a health crisis). Being an optimist, I believe over time we are likely to embrace progress if we can find leaders who have real vision for the future…a vision people can understand and embrace. In the interim, I just stay focused on what I can control and do."
- "In all of its relative absurdity, I believe 2020 was a sign of things to come. As a young person, it almost felt validating to see such a mess unfold and encompass everything and everyone. I lost my job, had school devolve into an online joke, got a dog and found ways to make myself happy. I don't anticipate the future being less ridiculous."
- "COVID highlighted the importance of family and reduced, in my mind, the importance of work, although I was moving toward semi-retirement at the same time. The BLM protests raised my consciousness about the prevalence of police brutality. The counter-protests indicated an emboldened white nationalist thread that had been abetted by Trump. The authoritarian nature of this segment, and the support that Trump got in the election, makes me very concerned about the future of democracy in the U.S."
- "It was crushing. As an introvert, I probably fared better than others but it was very challenging not to be able to be with loved ones during this time. I missed hugs and being able to be affec-

tionate with family living outside of my home. I was devastated by the displays of white supremacy and sickened by the impact COVID has had on people of color. I feel that goodness prevailed in many situations, which made the year survivable. I am struck by the fragility of our society and the economy and how quickly things fell apart."

- "Incredible disappointment in our leadership, Trump was a disaster. Every day waking up to dread. Virus changed travel plans and family visits, conflicts with friends about mask wearing and politics. So much division in personal friendships. So looking forward to this new administration and resolving the pandemic."

- "A long hard look at what I am most afraid of, a total reset of how I show up in the world, both revolving around where I am best fit to be of service. As distressing, frightening and painful as 2020 was, on all kinds of levels, it was my best year yet in coming closer to what I really value and what is important, versus what I need to let go of. I am hopeful for a 2021 where we all seem to be getting to put our "reset" buttons into action!"

2020 was many things for each of us personally. But for the country, it was the *pre-set to a re-set*. On the personal level, it was a re-awakening, due to COVID, about what was important in our lives, what really mattered. On the national level, there was a growing dismay about the direction of our country and the retreat of social equity, opportunity and *decency*. Civic leadership was being displaced by a complete lack of civility, emboldened by the Trump presidency and the ability to yell *fire* in a crowded theater on the internet with no responsibility for facts or accountability for impact. On January 6, what has been playing out on the internet simply played out in reality at the Capitol.

A reset happens when the status quo, for a majority, is simply no longer sustainable.

If you are driving at fast speed and headed for a cliff, you hit a reset or you go over the cliff. *Ask Thelma and Louise*. For many, as they reflected on 2020, the sense was that America was headed for a cliff. The answer was a reset, a new driver. Biden would become the new driver.

Years ago, I read the book *The Art of Racing in the Rain*, by Gareth Stein. A terrific and fun read, especially for my dog lovers out there (it's about a race car driver and his dog). A memorable quote comes to mind as you think about the perspective and impact of the driver:

"In racing, they say that your car goes where your eyes go. The driver who cannot tear his eyes away from the wall as he spins out of control will meet

the wall; the driver who looks down the track as he feels his tires break free will regain control of his vehicle."

Trump hit the wall in 2020. Biden was the new driver and would look at the future and see a different path. And, for many, the inauguration was a time to cheer that new path, a reset of direction for the country, that maybe we had avoided a spin-out and crash of democracy and what the country stood for. A battle for the *soul of America* according to Biden. And, of course, we must still be mindful that just because you came out of the spin and missed the wall on this turn, the political race track is just like the real race track, it is an oval, and that turn will come back around again. Which is why the driver matters. *The car goes where the driver's eyes go.*

The Impact of 2020 on the Country

To be sure, 2020 was a *shared experience* for the country. The last time we had a deep and emotional shared experience as a country was really 9/11 in 2001. Vietnam was a shared experience in the Sixties. World War II was a shared experience in the 1940s. The Great Depression was a shared experience in the 1930s. They are all historical points in American history and how they impacted social change, political direction and even the *American Dream.*

And, for my younger readers, this may have been your first *American shared experience.* It won't be your last. To live history, to see it rather than read about it in a text book, is a powerful experience that shapes values and viewpoints. And a *sustained shared experience*, like 2020 and the combination of a global pandemic and divisive politics, sets the stage for a reset. But does it make us better for the decade ahead?

We asked our Foresighters in the next activity that very question:

Question: *Thinking about America as a country in the decade ahead, do you think the shared experience of all that occurred in 2020 will make America better for the decade ahead or worse?*

No.	Items	Times Selected
1.	**It will make America BETTER for the decade ahead**	(88%)
2.	It will make America WORSE for the decade ahead	(12%)

Really? Nearly 90% indicated that 2020 was a *good thing* for America for the decade ahead. Not because there is anything inherently good about a global pandemic or social unrest, but that it would serve as the trigger for a great American reset. We asked our Foresighters to explain their selection about the impact of the 2020 shared experience—for better or for worse:

- BETTER: "I think (or hope) with new leadership, that if we can get the pandemic under control and continue with social justice reform, we will make life in America better in the next decade."
- BETTER: "2020 really highlighted the importance of good leadership and the need to work together as a nation. It's an object lesson I think we're going to learn, and it sets up the Biden administration well."
- BETTER: "I hope that people feel more inclined to consider how their decisions affect others. I am not sure that is being shown with the previous president, but I hope that the new presidency will spotlight kindness, which will affect people's decisions."
- BETTER: "COVID will be eradicated, a lot of the people who damaged our society will be marginalized, and the majority of us have hope with a new political administration addressing real, pertinent issues in our lives."
- BETTER: "We saw much more clearly some critical inequities in our society. We experienced how interconnected we are. We got a slap-in-the-face reminder about democracy."
- BETTER: "The holes in our political systems, social systems, and economic systems have been brought to full light. As a young woman, I am optimistic that my generation and others will now spend the next years addressing them for the better."
- BETTER: "This is tough, as I think it will make us slightly better in some ways and worse in others. I think the polarization of the country is something that will not heal quickly, if ever, even with Biden and Harris in office. I think we will be better prepared when the next pandemic hits."
- BETTER: "I hope we all learn and grow from what we have experienced. Focusing our energy and efforts on what truly matters to us as a society and individuals. Taking more time to check-in with ourselves and loved ones, to outline a path for the future that is inclusive and prosperous."
- BETTER: "I think yesterday will go down in history as a watershed event. There will be those who remain stuck in following the divisive talk of Trump, but I think there will be many, many Americans and many in the world who see hope and see America and our society being able to lead and improve, be better. We had tears in our eyes yesterday, and, with Celebrate America, we were watching much of the best of this country's potential."
- BETTER: "There are inflection points in our history when we look into the abyss and collectively decide to re-up on our country

375

when we might have allowed it to fall apart. April 1865 was one, and the 2020 election was another."

- BETTER: "We need to get past the political and social conflict so America as a country will be better. I expect we'll be in a better place by the end of the decade, but it could take a while to get there."
- WORSE: "The 'COVID Year' had strong influences on American life, most of them not for the better. COVID created a microscope on the government response, and that was negative and carried over to the political season, which made things all the worse. We were not "neighbors" to our fellow Americans. We will need to re-establish relations with our American neighbors."
- WORSE: "Too much division in our country and it appears to just be getting worse."

For many, the 2020 shared experience did feel like we were spinning into the wall, headed for the proverbial cliff. *This is not where we wanted to be; it is not who we are.* So, we vow to drive differently, to get back on the American track in terms of our values, our freedoms, of what we stand for. But there is a yellow flag on the track: the caution flag of division. It's as if one set of Americans is driving one direction on the track and another set of Americans is driving the other direction. *A race director's nightmare, wouldn't you say?*

How January 20 was a Reset
Well, let's move to 2021 and specifically the *inauguration* and why January 20 was such a powerful moment for many Americans, and as we argue in the book, why it was so important as a reset for the decade.

Question: *In what ways was yesterday's inauguration and start of a new administration an opportunity for America to "clear the mechanism", to reset who we are and what we are about?*

Our themes seemed to focus on the *art of the possible*:

- ✓ A sense of a new beginning
- ✓ That America is not broken, just *unfinished*
- ✓ That we can be unified in the decade ahead
- ✓ It was a tone of civility, a contrast to what we have been used to
- ✓ That we can re-establish our relationship with our allies
- ✓ The beauty of poetry and art
- ✓ A path towards reconciliation
- ✓ A core message of democracy
- ✓ A sense of shared community
- ✓ A first step towards bipartisanship

- ✓ Pence was there, and Trump was not
- ✓ The message was of inclusiveness not divisiveness
- ✓ A focus on what we can achieve, not what is wrong
- ✓ Calm and experienced leadership
- ✓ A call to work for the collective greater good
- ✓ To reawaken the positive aspects of America
- ✓ That our democratic guardrails prevailed
- ✓ The power of three former presidents sitting together
- ✓ That our diversity was on display in a positive fashion
- ✓ An effort to address all Americans as one
- ✓ A reverence for the value of our traditions
- ✓ For a moment, a quieting of division

It really did feel like a reset, that we had turned the clock back, not in a sense of avoiding the challenge of the future, but in a way to make ourselves *more prepared* for the future. Some of our Foresighters noted its importance in terms of the great American *experiment*:

- "Return to kindness, respect, decorum and reminder of the symbols of this great experiment in democratic republic government. It was like taking a really deep breath and feeling a collective hug that we can be OK."
- "The adherence to, and reverence for, the 200 year-old traditions we have to mark the peaceful transition of power. Biden's line: "We'll lead, not merely by the example of our power, but by the power of our example." A call to arms to be the best versions of ourselves instead of the worst. We are often the worst, but the grit and resilience to keep trying to be better (not best, just better) is my favorite American quality."

There were also certain moments within the inauguration that resonated with people—images and performances that seemed to exemplify the reset themes and what's possible for the decade ahead with a more unified America:

Question: *If you watched or listened to the inauguration events/media coverage yesterday, what was the one most powerful moment, image or language that resonated with you personally? Why was that so powerful?*

- "Joe Biden being normal, being honest, being genuine and speaking to "all Americans". But, there wasn't really just one point, it was the entire day, and evening, the tone, the vibe, like we were reborn as a country, with a long way to go, but things are different."
- "When Lady Gaga turned toward the flag, '*still waves*'."

377

- "So many, it's tough to pick one. Perhaps Kamala Harris being sworn in as first black female in VP spot. Second would be the airplane with Trump flying away!"
- "There was a message of hope. The theme seemed to be about rebuilding as though something was broken (it was) and our responsibilities and opportunity to engage in the rebuilding process."
- "Past presidents/first ladies chatting pre-ceremony. It was easy to think that approach to transition had passed. It was very powerful to see leaders on both sides committed to the process of transition and to see them do it with genuine friendship and care for each other."
- "Jennifer Lopez connecting the diversity of our country."
- "Garth Brooks, a Republican, singing "Amazing Grace" with all."

Honest to God, when Garth Brooks walked out on stage with a belt buckle the size of Texas and sang with a heart the size of America, if that didn't stir you as an American I don't know what would.

Garth Brooks and Amazing Grace   *Three ex-presidents were in attendance*

Except that none of those were really the highlight. Not the ex-presidents, not Biden's quiet honesty, not Kamala breaking several barriers at once, not Lady Gaga, JLo or Garth. Something entirely unexpected stole the inauguration and sent the exact right message for the decade ahead:

Amanda Gorman.

A 22-year-old young black woman, a *national youth poet laureate*, who delivered poetry and a message in her poem *A Hill to Climb*:

And yes, we are far from polished, far from pristine, but that
doesn't mean we are striving to form a union that is perfect.
We are striving to form our union with purpose.
To compose a country committed to all cultures, colors,
characters and conditions of man.

378

And so we lift our gaze, not to what stands between us,
but what stands before us.
...

And it wasn't just the eloquence of her words and themes, it was her delivery, her joyfulness. She was the very definition of why diversity is so essential and so much a promise for the decade ahead.

Amanda Gorman at the inauguration

I was mesmerized by the poem and the delivery. *And those fingers!* But I wasn't the only one. Here are some comments from our Foresighters:

- "Amanda Gorman's recital of her poem. Powerful. The cadence, the words, the emotion. I heard it on the radio while in the car, and now look forward to watching the video."
- "The poem by Amanda Gorman. Everything about her poem and her delivery resonated with me. I keep watching it on repeat."
- "The presentation by the poet laureate, by far. She was young, powerful, articulate...and her message was sensational. She should run for Congress!"
- "Amanda Gorman. It was powerful not only because of her message, but because of her age, gender, racial background, family social status...and because she was amazingly eloquent after four years of a president who constantly misused language in a hateful way."
- "Amanda Gorman's poem. It captured hope without political jargon, told in beautiful verse, delivered by an individual symbolic of a strong and positive future by her age, sex and race."
- "Amanda Gorman. She is smart, young, poised and fierce."

Fierce. That's it, wasn't it?. *This is who I am and I don't need to apologize.* This is who our country is and we don't need to apologize. *"A nation that isn't broken, but simply unfinished."*

Look, a lot of things have to happen for a genuine reset to take place. A poem, despite its eloquence and delivery is not a reset. Garth Brooks crossing the aisle and singing *Amazing Grace* is a damn good performance but is not a reset. A well-produced overall inauguration is not a reset. This has to be a genuine reset of American values, direction and inclusion in the decade ahead; that what we all saw and experienced in 2020 was an undesirable and unacceptable way forward. If that reset holds, we have the potential for an *Amazing Decade*.

Presidential Reflections

So, including the incoming Joe Biden, there have been 46 *presidencies* in our country's history. An interesting factoid that I stumbled on in researching this book is that there have only been 45 different people who have served as president. History records that Grover Cleveland was elected to two terms but they were *non-consecutive terms* and he is therefore considered to be the 22nd as well as the 24th president. *The entire Trump nation sees a glimmer of hope!*

As it turns out, I have had the good fortune of meeting two of the 45 different people who have been president, indeed while they were in office. I define "meeting" as either shaking hands in person or being elbowed in person. Both of these have occurred.

Let's start with shaking hands in person. In August of 1999, I conducted a set of sessions for the Wirthlin Worldwide team in Chicago around the theme of *Welfare to Work*. It was to support the Clinton Administration's focus on strategies and success stories of activating welfare recipients to move back into the workforce. The sessions were quite cool—welfare recipients were shoulder to shoulder with business executives at our laptop lab commenting on the power of the transition, what it meant for them and what it meant for America. After the sessions, we were invited to the main event, where President Bill Clinton would address the entire conference.

The Wirthlin team had some pretty good connections and my colleague Maury Giles (see chapter 12) was able to get me on the main stage as part of the background audience while Clinton addressed the main audience. Probably 50 of us on stage, but I was literally in the first row behind Clinton watching him and taking the whole event in. *Breathe deep, relax, don't trip or fall out of your chair.* Ninety minutes and I must say that Clinton had the audience spell-bound. He really is exceptionally *empathic*. It was towards the end of his second term, I think he was pretty loose and just enjoying the events like this. Domestic legacy for his programs.

He stayed after the speech and we all got a chance to meet/greet. Shake hands and say hello. *Really enjoyed the speech, Mr. President! What a terrific subject!* I am quite sure he remembers me to this day. But I remember flying home that evening, still in my business suit. Normal chit-chat with the fellow passengers. *"How was your day?"*, someone asked me. I could only smile. You don't get many days like that in your professional work.

Oh, and the second president must be the *elbowing incident*. It was actually much earlier and I was still in college at the time. I can say with confidence that the day was January 1, 1977, Vail, Colorado. It was a super-cold day. The temperature was -8 and the wind chill was purported to be about -20. We skied a couple of runs to see if our gear would hold up and what a wind chill of minus 20 felt like. *It felt really cold.* It was still and quiet, we moved but did not talk. I don't bail very often on a ski day with friends, but we called it at 10:00am.

Things happened for a reason. Back then, many of you will recall, January 1 was college bowl day. The big games were on back to back—Rose, Cotton, Peach and Fiesta. The Rose Bowl was the *big daddy* of all of the games. We found our way to a local Mexican Food café/cantina in Vail and settled in for the duration. I think there were six of us in our group; we were at the bar on traditional bar stools, a big screen TV behind the bartender. My girlfriend (and now wife of 40 years) Janet was sitting to my right. We had ordered up a first round of cold cervezas, the perfect antidote to the cold day outside.

The first elbowing occurs. This one is from Janet. A sharp one to the right ribs with her left elbow. I turn to my right...*what the heck?* Janet is staring straight ahead and begins to speak like a ventriloquist with her teeth clenched.

JANET: *Don't look to your left. I think you are sitting next to the president.*

DOUG: *Have another beer, Janet! (OK, I keep my head straight and look to the left with all of my eyeball power...)*

JANET (teeth still clenched): *Seriously. It's Ford, isn't it?*

DOUG (teeth now clenched): *Yes, I think it's the president. What do I do?*

Well, you do what you do when you are sitting next to anyone on a row of barstools at the counter watching sports. You babble about the game. Besides the secret service are beginning to talk into their lapels about the two people talking oddly with clenched teeth sitting next to the president. *I swung my barstool to the left.*

GRIFFEN: "Helluva game, isn't it?"

FORD: "Helluva game!"

GRIFFEN: "Too damn cold to be skiing!"

FORD: "Way too cold!"

Now, I haven't been elbowed yet, but I am counting this as a compelling conversation and interaction with the current *President of The United States of America.*

A few things you should know about President Ford. He was the 38th president of the United States which means, of course, that this was the 39th presidency. In December of 1973 he was appointed to the vice-presidency after the resignation of Spiro Agnew. In fact, he was appointed under the provisions of the 25th amendment, that handy amendment that was being considered by some for the removal of Trump. And, as many of you history buffs know, Ford assumed the presidency in August of 1974 when Richard Nixon famously resigned: *I am not a crook!*

Ford served as president until January of 1977, as he was defeated by Jimmy Carter in the 1976 election. God, what a track record: appointed to the vice-presidency, assumed the presidency, so you make it to the top without ever getting elected on the ticket. Then you lose to a peanut farmer. According to Wikipedia, "Surveys of historians and political scientists have ranked Ford as a below-average president."

Well, none of that matters to me. The president is the president. It also turns out that he is a skier, so my admiration is already on the rise. The International Skiing History Association (yes, that's a legit organization—see skiinghistory.org) notes: "Ford had many friends in the Vail community and the ski industry. During his presidency he was often photographed with his Vermont-built Rossignol skis, accompanied by Vail execs, patrollers and Secret Service agents."

Count me in as a friend of the president's. And note that I am skiing at the time on a pair of Rossignol ST Comps.

Back to the game. Ford was really glued to the screen. That's because the University of Michigan Wolverines were playing, and, as some of you know, Ford played football for the school and was a center, linebacker and long snapper. Those Wolverines were *undefeated* and took *national titles* in 1932 and 1933 while Ford was there. Man, this guy is the *people's president.*

As we watched the game, something very interesting happened. Janet and I noticed that no one was coming up to the president. We looked around and realized (and I swear this is the truth) that all of us at the bar had been cordoned off by the Secret Service. *We were in for the duration*. Not only that, but things were loosening up. The bar staff had brought out, on the Secret Service's request, bowls of *Secret Sauce*. A special recipe for the president. *Clearly not the first time he had visited this establishment.*

So, why am I so sure that this was January 1, 1977? Well, his Wolverines were playing USC in the Rose Bowl and this one was a nail biter. Now, I can't recall what quarter it was or what the score was at the time (remember, we had been there a while...), but there was a play near the end zone where the Michigan ball player appeared to have fumbled the ball.

FORD: (*elbows Griffen in the left ribs to get my attention...*) "That's not a damn fumble!"

GRIFFEN: "Hell no! That's not a damn fumble!"

I mean, this conversation is getting *next level*. And besides, you think I am going to argue with the president? Sadly, his Wolverines lost the game to USC 14-6. But we walked away with a *helluva* story.

Ford as a young skier in Vail

Ford as the President, 1974

A 2010 View of the World

Now, to round out my *Presidential Reflections*, I saw President Clinton one more time. But, of my three presidential interactions, this one has the most genuine bearing on Foresight 2030. His *Foresights* that were delivered in May of 2010 at the start of that decade are equally as relevant for 2020 and the start of this decade.

My son Scott graduated in the Yale class of 2010. Everyone gets a graduation speaker, but *Yale* commands some of the best. Bill Clinton got the nod for 2010. *Hillary would get the nod in 2018, I figure it was a package deal.* But the whole scene was really cool—I had *met* Clinton before and still admired his views.

We had the whole *Griff Squad* in the outdoor grassy area for the graduation festivities. Scott was wearing my Arizona cowboy hat with the graduates (a tradition at Yale to wear something that signifies your heritage/home). Things are about to get underway when someone in my family saw that they were serving complimentary coffee at the adjacent building behind us. *Would I go get some coffees? Now? Are you serious?* I mean we had pretty good seats up front.

So I relented. I am grabbing coffee and things were *getting underway.* So I break into a sprint, turn a corner and run right into Denzel Washington (his daughter was also a Yale 2010 graduate). *He had a coffee in his hand as well.* He looks at me and smiles, "You late too?" I smiled, looked at the two coffees in my hand, and said, "Yeah!" He does that funky *chin-tuck-thing* and says. "Well let's go!"

Sonofabitch. I am headed for Clinton's speech being escorted by the Equalizer.

And Clinton was sharp that day. Masterful. I seriously took notes. He did not mince words as he told the graduates that, "the world you are entering is far different and far more challenging" than it has ever been. He made three key points:

- The world is *more unequal.*
- The world is *more unstable.*
- The world is *more unsustainable.*

That was the start of the prior decade in 2010. Just play repeat for the start of 2020. And maybe these are some of the real fundamental global challenges we must truly engage on in this *most consequential decade of our lives.* Or we may not get to the next one.

384

My escort back to the ceremonies!

Dad and Grad at the 2010 Yale graduation

Back to the American Reset and Our Foresighters

But make no mistake about it, a reset needs a *born-on* date. And this American reset was born on January 20, 2021. Let's see what our Foresighters said:

Question: *All things considered, do you think that January 20 was a "reset" for the decade ahead, an inflection point for America?*

No.	Items	Times Selected
1.	**Yes**	**(68%)**
2.	Not sure yet	(26%)

3.	No	(6%)

Hey, a two-thirds majority in this country is kind of the *Holy Grail* if you know what I mean. Here are some explanations from our Foresighters:

- YES: "Deep down, I believe most people are ready to move beyond the bitterness and polarity, and work towards healing from both the past four years, and also the pandemic."
- YES: "I think everyone breathed a sigh of relief yesterday. We can only hope that this was the turning point."
- YES: "More inclusive, more diverse, more logical (hopefully more willing to come across the aisle) viewpoints leading the country."
- YES: "To be candid, 'there are more of us than there are of them'. More of us are good people, not afraid to be vulnerable, helpful to others over ourselves, and convicted to returning truth and honor to our politics."
- YES: "We just experienced a very negative and tumultuous four years of pitting Americans against one another. The areas that need improvement are exposed and raw, and I think we have some leaders that will try to improve. I also think, by the responses of leaders around the world, that they will too."
- YES: "It felt a little easier to breathe. It's hard to explain. The whole process leading up to this day was filled with a lot of misinformation, a lack of peaceful transition and tradition. But inauguration day was like the pieces of the puzzle came together for the first time..."
- NOT SURE: "We are better focused (issues and unity) but we still need a clear future vision that enfranchises across our current lines...a vision that builds off our shared values and aspirations."
- NOT SURE: "My desire is to say yes. Politics is a game of multiple players though. It is a reset in the sense of restoration of expertise where needed."
- NOT SURE: "It's very hard to pinpoint specific events or dates in historical shifts. I think Trump's election and subsequent defeat weren't hard points of transition, but rather long-building fallout from other factors. This could be a reset, but it could also be a continuation of the anger and extremism we see across the nation—all depends on what the administration and Congress does next."
- NOT SURE: "There's simply too much work to do to be sure. And, no administration in a couple of generations has faced more."

386

And there is *much work to be done* to validate the reset, that it wasn't just a political change but a sustainable directional change for the country. Let's give it a *decade*, shall we?

The Priorities of the New Administration

A decade sounds too long, you say? Then let's get our Foresighters after it right now. With a *reasonable validation* that the inauguration signaled a reset for the country, we asked our Foresighters to lend a hand and identify what they felt should be some of the key priorities for the country that would give that decade a serious *kick start*:

Question: *The next four years will take us to the mid-point of the decade and will largely influence the direction and impact of the decade ahead. What do you feel should be the focus/priorities for the next four years in America?*

With over 200 open responses, we whittled the list down to 20 key themes as follows:

No.	Idea
1.	Climate change
2.	Successful rollout of vaccine
3.	Strong/sustained economic growth
4.	Return of bipartisan politics
5.	Sustainable energy
6.	Social justice for all
7.	Preparedness for future global pandemics
8.	Addressing infrastructure
9.	Restoring our nation's place in the world
10.	Education reform
11.	Improving healthcare access/equity
12.	Raising impact/influence of science
13.	Addressing domestic terrorism

14.	Helping those in poverty
15.	Gender equality
16.	Addressing gun violence
17.	Advancing civil discourse
18.	Uniting the nation
19.	Improving public transit
20.	Monitoring global political threats

One of our Foresighters had commented previously that no administration "in generations" had faced more work to be done...and the list would substantiate that. We then asked the group to prioritize the list in terms of impacting the decade ahead:

Now, please assess each of the following in terms of how important that priority will be in impacting the success and trajectory of the decade ahead. Use a scale of 1-10 where a "1" means not at all important and a "10" means extremely important. Assume that significant progress could be made for each priority over the next 4 years:

Rank	Idea	Avg.
1.	Successful rollout of vaccine	**9.3**
2.	Uniting the nation	**8.8**
3.	Strong/sustained economic growth	**8.8**
4.	Advancing civil discourse	**8.6**
5.	Raising impact/influence of science	**8.4**
6.	Preparedness for future global pandemics	**8.4**
7.	Social justice for all	**8.3**
8.	Improving healthcare access/equity	**8.3**
9.	Return of bipartisan politics	**8.1**
10.	Addressing gun violence	**8.1**
11.	Climate change	**8.1**

388

12.	Education reform	**8.0**
13.	Sustainable energy	**7.9**
14.	Gender equality	**7.9**
15.	Addressing domestic terrorism	**7.8**
16.	Helping those in poverty	**7.7**
17.	Addressing infrastructure	**7.6**
18.	Restoring our nation's place in the world	**7.6**
19.	Monitoring global political threats	**7.4**
20.	Improving public transit	**6.4**

The top three seem like a good start: a successful COVID vaccine roll-out, a strong economic recovery and unite the United States. By the way, the first two *really help* with the third.

But it is a long list indeed. You can likely do the first two in 2021. The problem is that the economic recovery is simply not sustainable without addressing so many of the underlying issues—education reform, health-care access, social justice, infrastructure, addressing gun violence, bi-partisan politics and, *dare we say,* climate change.

Our Foresighters had their favorites when asked what they felt was the one most important priority that would influence the success of the decade ahead:

- "Reaffirming our shared values and aspirations (particularly at the community level) is essential. With that, all those other is-sues will be tractable and solvable; without this, any one issue will be undermined by disagreement and tribalism."
- "Reestablishing civil discourse debate. If half the country thinks the other half is morally bankrupt and evil, any progress we make will be instantly undone when power switches. It's also not a sustainable way to live together."
- "Healing the divisions of the nation, creating the vision and reality that everyone counts and is being heard and their needs are be-ing addressed."
- "Economic justice because of Maslow's hierarchy. People need a roof over their heads and food on the table before they can even begin to think about being kind to their neighbor or showing up to

learn or work. Economic justice is table stakes for everything else."

- "Uniting the country, particularly promoting bipartisanism in politics so that we can best address the challenges facing us."
- "Effectively solving the COVID crisis. Countries which do that will see economic prosperity return more quickly. Simultaneously building unity in the U.S. so we don't split into two countries!"
- "Equal Justice—if the law protects everyone equally and there is a level playing field, then the foundation is there to address all other inequalities. It will lessen the fuel of division and resentment."
- "Improved social discourse. We cannot solve our complex problems with partisan politics, ignorance or simple answers. Until we learn to engage in listening, learning and understanding, our issues will never be addressed and we will remain on this pathetic hamster wheel."

So you can be on the hamster wheel or the peace train. Options for the decade ahead. I mean, seriously: if we don't figure out a way to get America on the same page, to get to a level of meaningful social discourse and civility, of bipartisan political efforts, of fundamental *unity* — then we are going to go around in proverbial circles.

The Incoming Administration and The Challenges Ahead

Our Foresighters have been most generous in providing the new administration with a jump start on their strategic plan. A new administration is always an opportunity to reset the table and, perhaps, be the strategic reset that America needed for the decade ahead. It was certainly a powerful visual reset as the very image of Biden along with the first woman vice-president in Kamala Harris was one of the lasting images from the January 20 inauguration.

Incoming President Biden with the First Lady

Kamala Harris takes the Oath

Biden would follow our script well in the first 100 days of his Administration. A heavy emphasis on the rollout of the COVID vaccine for all Americans with a goal of reaching 100 million vaccine shots by his 100th day (he reached that target by day 58); economic focus with the $1.9 trillion coronavirus relief package signed in March and a bold effort to go after a strategic infrastructure investment with some level of bipartisan support. *Maybe a tad too bold, Joe.*

NPR reported that in his first 100 days Biden signed 11 bills into law, issued 42 executive orders, *rescinded* 62 of Trump's executive orders and enjoyed a 53% job approval rating. Which sounds pretty good except that it was a little unbalanced—93% of Democrats approved of his job in the first 100 days while only 12% of Republicans approved. The number two priority on our Foresight New Administration Priorities was to unite the nation. *We'll give Joe a little more time on this one.*

So the first 100 days looked pretty good on the reset meter, but it does not guarantee smooth sailing for the future. Biden ran into the *perfect storm* at about the six-month point: the surge of the Delta variant, the controversial exit from Afghanistan (probably the right decision but terrible communications and implementation) and a batch of natural disasters with the wildfires in the western United States (causing an evacuation of my own subdivision in Park City) and Hurricane Ida, that ripped through Louisiana and then strafed about the entire East Coast. Drag out the sump pumps for the New York subways.

Look, I think Biden is a very able captain. But the reality is that he will need to grow into the presidency just as all of us will need to grow into this decade. 2020 launched us into rough water and we have a lot of work ahead to find smoother water. Remember what former President Clinton advised in 2010:

- The world is *more unequal.*
- The world is *more unstable.*
- The world is *more unsustainable.*

That's the environment which this new administration is acquiring. I am not sure we can fix the *world* over this decade, but I would take an America that is more equal, more stable and more sustainable. And, for the record, I think we'll see this captain in place for two terms. A chance for a little stability. Let the White House know I would look forward to meeting the captain sometime during the decade to round out a trio of presidential acquaintances.

The Most Consequential Decade of Our Lives

If the inauguration signaled the reset of America, then we might as well get a little *bold* in our thinking about the decade ahead. What if we could close that level of division? What if we could move to the level of social equity, economic equity and racial equity that we have long desired? What if we could create and sustain one of the largest and most inclusive economic recoveries that any of us have ever experienced? What if I finally reach *CAT5* in my travel experiences and grab an orbit around the globe?

Well, maybe this could be the most consequential decade of our lives.

Why not? Technology that continues to connect us and provides time and flexibility in our lives. A new work model that is more of a hybrid model between home/office and *on the road*. Education reform that creates new learning models and career pathways and gives everyone the best start possible in life with early childhood education. Some level of universal healthcare where affordable and accessible health care, including more focus on health education and preventative care. A better lifestyle, with more focus on fitness, wellness and life sports. A willingness to address the really hard things ahead like infrastructure, climate change and re-ducing global conflicts. And maybe, *just maybe*, genuine bipartisan poli-tics.

So we asked our Foresighters to consider this idea of the *most conse-quential decade* of our lives and what it might take from their perspective:

Question: *Imagine it is December 2029 and the Time Magazine cover story is: "The Most Consequential Decade of Our Lives." What needs to happen (outcomes, accomplishments, advances, agreements, discover-ies, etc.) for this decade ahead to be considered as the "The Most Con-sequential Decade of Our Lives?"*

We received over 100 responses and created a real-time summary of the ideas. In no particular order (the list was not prioritized) here are the 20 themes that were developed:

No.	Idea
1.	The world collaborated on key problems
2.	We successfully reversed climate change
3.	We defeated COVID
4.	Nuclear disarmament
5.	Developed a cure for cancer
6.	Advanced educational reform
7.	Restored truth
8.	Implemented universal healthcare
9.	A great sense of a unified country
10.	Bipartisan cooperation
11.	Addressed global terrorism
12.	Significant medical advances that result in healthier and longer lives
13.	America's role in the world has been restored
14.	We finally balanced gun rights and gun control
15.	We successfully moved from fossil fuels to renewables
16.	Science has been de-politicized and fully valued for its positive/ vital impact
17.	Racial/gender/immigrant inequality is behind us, all are valued and all have opportunity
18.	Successful rollout/adoption of electric vehicles as the norm
19.	We discovered and verified life beyond the Earth—we are not alone
20.	America truly came together—it was the decade of unity

Look, you don't have to agree with all of these from a political or personal perspective. But surely you would go along with longer/healthier lives, nuclear disarmament and a cure for cancer. I mean, that would make it a *reasonable decade ahead*, would it not? For you, what would the list need to be for it truly to be the most consequential decade of *your* life? And, at the end of the day, the most consequential decade for *this country*?

Outlook for the Decade Ahead

But a decade is a long time. *Mucho trabajo mañana.* And no doubt there are reasons for optimism for the decade ahead, and reasons for pessimism as well. So we asked our Foresighters to step back again and consider both sides of the 2030 coin:

Reasons for Optimism	Reasons for Pessimism
Fresh leadership—a new administration	The growing divide in America
The role of a new generation and their values	That we can't get to racial equity
A willingness to restore civility and discourse	Intolerance for opposite views
An economy set for sustained growth	The evolution of the cancel culture
Our personal reawakening to what matters	Partisan politics
The resilience of the American spirit	Inability to control gun violence
The impact and rollout of the COVID vaccine	The inequality gap and lack of access
America ready to rejoin the global community	The potential for the next pandemic
Advances in ending racism	The power of mis-information
New flexibility in work	The rise of tribalism
The shared experienced of 2020	The blurring of social media/mainstream media
The promise of further technology change	Inability or unwillingness to address climate change

And, without a doubt, there are many other themes/subplots on both sides. So do we just "flip the coin" and see where it lands for the decade ahead? Heads we go optimistic, tails we go pessimistic? It would certainly save a lot of time and *nasty arguments*. The reality is that we are going to have to *work things out* in the decade ahead. There has to be a sense of the *greater good* that rises above the individual *"what's in it for me"* fallback. When the greater good wins, we all win. You know, the *rising tide* theory.

So how do our Foresighters see the optimism vs. pessimism narrative?

Question: *All things considered, reflecting back on 2020 as the start of the decade but reflecting forward on 2021-2029 for the remainder of the decade, are you optimistic or pessimistic about the decade ahead?*

No.	Items	Times Selected
1.	**Optimistic**	**(88%)**
2.	Pessimistic	(12%)

That's a pretty heavy dose of optimism. A double-headed coin?

Our Foresighters had strong views about that level of optimism, thinking about how it might play out over the course of a full decade:

- OPTIMISTIC: "I think we're ready to turn the page and work to regain what we've lost as a country."
- OPTIMISTIC: "Between a new administration and a pandemic, I learned a lot about myself and society, and would like to think that we are on an upswing."
- OPTIMISTIC: "2020 provided the opportunity to prove hard things can be done. There is nothing left to be afraid of—only work to do."
- OPTIMISTIC: "Technology improving lives globally. Relatively stable/peaceful world."
- OPTIMISTIC: "The forces of good have won the day, and the opportunity to repair and envision a future of decency."
- OPTIMISTIC: "The U.S. will resume productive discourse with the rest of the world, we'll get past the pandemic, we will be better prepared for future pandemics (technology/distribution/remote work)."

- OPTIMISTIC: "More optimistic, we have seen the bottom, and I think it is hitting people. We have got to change."
- OPTIMISTIC: "New leadership will foster unity and begin to solve real problems—gun violence, social injustice, climate change, etc."
- OPTIMISTIC: "The systemic issues that have been exposed by the pandemic are too great to continue to ignore/sweep under the rug. We have to deal with them if we are to remain a viable nation and society. I sincerely hope that American ingenuity has been reset by hardship and will be turned to building for the future instead of tearing down and destroying for momentary, fleeting gain."
- OPTIMISTIC: "It can only get better, no?"

I say "yes". And I really liked the sentiment from our Foresighter above that said, "2020 provided the opportunity to prove hard things can be done. There is nothing left to be afraid of—only hard work to do." And Americans are built on a platform of *hard work*. We've never been afraid of that. We really do believe that we can outwork anyone. *American ingenuity.*

And, remarkably, our Foresighters are *more optimistic* about the decade ahead now (January 2021) than they were in January 2020 when we had not yet entered the pandemic:

Question: *We are also interested in how the events since January 2020 may have changed your level of optimism about the decade ahead. Would you say you are more optimistic now than at the start of 2020 or less optimistic?*

No.	Items	Times Selected
1.	**More optimistic now than I was on January 1, 2020**	**(67%)**
2.	About the same	(19%)
3.	Less optimistic now than I was on January 1, 2020	(14%)

There's that elusive two thirds majority again! Seriously, think about this finding: we feel better about things after a global pandemic and one of the most divisive political elections in our history. *We should have thrown in an asteroid crash and a few 9.0 earthquakes.* 2020 reawakened us personally and, we hope, as a country as well.

And, by the way, it's not just our Foresighters that feel this way. In the next chapter we will share the analysis of quantitative polling that was done throughout 2020 on Americans and their values and how 2020 shaped a new future. We'll also share a final poll conducted in February 2021 with 1000 Americans about their view of optimism and pessimism in the decade ahead. Our Foresighters were *spot on*.

The Decade Ahead: Future Influence Scenarios

And our Foresighters, for this—their *final session*—are not done yet. Still thinking about the decade ahead, we provided a dozen themes that suggested a key focus/emphasis for the decade ahead. We are *optimistic* that it won't be Time Magazine's *A Decade From Hell* as they pronounced in December, 2009, about the preceding decade. But what might this be the decade *of*? Consider the following themes:

No.	Idea
1.	THE DECADE OF INCLUSION/EQUALITY: The decade saw a fundamental change in the country for racial equality and genuine inclusion of Americans of all backgrounds. We moved past some long and difficult history to a new era.
2.	THE DECADE OF AI AS THE PROBLEM SOLVER: Technology in all of its best aspects was released to address some of our most challenging issues. Artificial Intelligence (AI) along with the use of advanced analytics, big data, virtual reality and the Internet of Things were combined to help with astonishing advances in healthcare, transportation, energy, security and other fields.
3.	THE DECADE OF HEALTH: Americans raised the bar on their health, fitness and wellness across the board. Better policies on healthcare access, preventive measures, new treatments and medicines, wearable technologies, supportive programs for drug abuse/mental wellness and better patient acceptance of health accountability created a healthier population and future.
4.	THE DECADE OF EDUCATION REFORM: America completely rethought education from early childhood education, traditional K-12 and new pathways for workforce training via vocational, college/university programs and certificate programs where education gaps/inequalities were closed and more Americans could pursue a purposeful future.

5. THE DECADE OF BIPARTISANSHIP: Stung by the political and social divide that was evident at the start of the decade, a genuine level of bipartisan politics emerged. America became the model for an effective government that really addressed the issues that mattered. You could still have party allegiance and views, but the aisle was a busy crosswalk in the legislative bodies.

6. THE DECADE OF SHARED ECONOMIC GROWTH: It was hard to imagine a stronger sustained level of economic growth for any decade. The middle class re-emerged, large organizations had strong growth and sustained hiring, entrepreneurs flourished, the minimum wage was raised and improved the lifestyle for many. Americans saved more and lived better.

7. THE DECADE OF SCIENCE: Advanced by the unprecedented impact of science to solve the COVID crisis, our investment in science allowed us to better predict and address many issues in the country. Already a strong focus, STEM education and careers became even more popular and attracted young talent. Generation Z, in particular, became a driving force for science in the country.

8. THE CLIMATE DECADE: Not unlike the bold goal of putting a man on the moon at end of the 60s decade, America and the world put the issue of climate change forward as the global imperative. By the end of the decade the data showed that we had reversed the course of global warming and had the metrics, regulations and technologies in place to sustain that reverse.

9. THE DECADE OF YOUNG LEADERSHIP: This decade marked the hand-off from the Boomer generation for leadership to the millennial generation. Sure, there were Gen-Xers and Gen Zs that stepped up, but it was the millennial generation that had the experience, foresight and passion to take the leadership mantle for the country.

10. THE DECADE OF MOBILITY: Virtual workplaces changed the game for Americans in the decade. More Americans simply chose where they wanted to live and then connected to their workplace from that location. More second homes/locations where Americans migrated for "seasons of choice". Hotels/resorts became "extended stays" where work/vacation could be blended. Mobility and technology support a new American Lifestyle. Catch me if you can!

11. THE SPACE DECADE: We should have seen this coming. Private investment in space travel accelerated the exploration of space. An active colony on the moon and on Mars. You could book a space orbit around the earth as easily as you used to book a flight to Europe. Beam me aboard, Scotty!

12. THE DECADE OF AMERICA: America's global standing was completely refreshed and renewed in the decade. America returned to traditional allies but forged new/unexpected relationships as well. There was an unprecedented sharing of knowledge, technology, leadership, resources and democratic principles. Our borders were strong, but our commitment to world issues and global collaboration was stronger. We were once again that 'Shining City Upon a Hill'.

Here is how our Foresight session assessed the list. The scenarios are ordered by the *level of positive impact* but then contrasted with the likelihood of occurrence for a gap analysis rating.

Now, please assess each of the following future scenarios in two ways. First, the level of positive IMPACT to the future in the decade ahead if the scenario was to occur (use a scale of 1-10 where a "1" means a very low level of positive impact and a "10" means a very high level of positive impact); Second, the LIKELIHOOD that this scenario will fully materialize in the decade ahead (use a scale of 1-10 where a "1" means a very low likelihood and "10" means a very high likelihood):

#	Scenario Description	Im-pat	Like-ly	Gap
1	THE DECADE OF BIPARTISANSHIP: Stung by the political and social divide that was evident at the start of the decade, a genuine level of bipartisan politics emerged. America became the model for an effective government that really addressed the issues that mattered. You could still have party allegiance and views, but the aisle was busy crosswalk in the legislative bodies.	9.2	4.4	(4.8)

2	THE DECADE OF SHARED ECONOMIC GROWTH: It was hard to imagine a stronger sustained level of economic growth for any decade. The middle class re-emerged, large organizations had strong growth and sustained hiring, entrepreneurs flourished, the minimum wage was raised and improved the lifestyle for many. Americans saved more and lived better.	9.1	6.0	(3.1)
3	THE DECADE OF SCIENCE: Advanced by the unprecedented impact of science to solve the COVID crisis, our investment in science allowed us to better predict and address many issues in the country. Already a strong focus, STEM education and careers became even more popular and attracted young talent. Generation Z, in particular, became a driving force for science in the country.	9.0	7.1	(1.9)
4	THE DECADE OF EDUCATION REFORM: America completely rethought education from early childhood education, traditional K-12 and new pathways for workforce training via vocational, college/university programs and certificate programs where education gaps/inequalities were closed and more Americans could pursue a purposeful future.	9.0	5.4	(3.6)
5	THE DECADE OF INCLUSION/EQUALITY: The decade saw a fundamental change in the country for racial equality and genuine inclusion of Americans of all backgrounds. We moved past some long and difficult history to a new era.	8.9	6.0	(2.9)
6	THE DECADE OF HEALTH: Americans raised the bar on their health, fitness and wellness across the board. Better policies on healthcare access, preventive measures, new treatments and medicines, wearable technologies, supportive programs for drug abuse/mental wellness and better patient acceptance of health accountability created a healthier population and future.	8.8	6.2	(2.6)

7	THE CLIMATE DECADE: Not unlike the bold goal of putting a man on the moon at end of the '60s decade, America and the world put the issue of climate change forward as the global imperative. By the end of the decade the data showed that we had reversed the course of global warming and had the metrics, regulations and technologies in place to sustain that reverse.	8.8	5.9	(2.9)
8	THE DECADE OF AMERICA: America's global standing was completely refreshed and renewed in the decade. America returned to traditional allies but forged new/unexpected relationships as well. There was an unprecedented sharing of knowledge, technology, leadership, resources and democratic principles. Our borders were strong, but our commitment to world issues and global collaboration was stronger. We were once again that "Shining City Upon a Hill."	8.4	6.5	(1.9)
9	THE DECADE OF YOUNG LEADERSHIP: This decade marked the hand-off from the Boomer generation for leadership to the Millennial generation. Sure, there were Gen-Xers and Gen Zs that stepped up but it was the millennial generation that had the experience, foresight and passion to take the leadership mantle for the country.	8.0	7.3	(0.7)
10	THE DECADE OF MOBILITY: Virtual workplaces changed the game for Americans in the decade. More Americans simply chose where they wanted to live and then connected to their workplace from that location. More second homes/locations where Americans migrated for "seasons of choice". Hotels/resorts became "extended stays" where work/vacation could be blended. Mobility and technology support a new American Lifestyle. Catch me if you can!	7.4	7.8	+0.4

11	THE DECADE OF AI AS THE PROBLEM SOLVER: Technology in all of its best aspects was released to address some of our most challenging issues. Artificial Intelligence (AI) along with the use of advanced analytics, big data, virtual reality and the Internet of Things were combined to help with astonishing advances in healthcare, transportation, energy, security and other fields.	7.3	7.0	(0.3)
12	THE SPACE DECADE: We should have seen this coming. Private investment in space travel accelerated the exploration of space. An active colony on the moon and on Mars. You could book a space orbit around the earth as easily as you used to book a flight to Europe. Beam me aboard, Scotty!	6.1	5.4	(0.7)

Beyond interesting. We've never had a set of influence scenarios that show such a collective level of positive impact on the decade ahead, yet such a large collective gap in the likelihood of achieving the potential impact. Half of our scenarios had gaps of 2.0 or higher. So, the good news is that we are on the right track with the scenarios, but even for our *optimistic Foresighters,* there is a heavy sigh about the work to be done to stay on track.

Here are the top six gaps between impact and likelihood:

1. The Decade of Bipartisanship (4.8)
2. The Decade of Education Reform (3.6)
3. The Decade of Shared Economic Growth (3.1)
4. The Decade of Inclusion/Equality (2.9)
5. The Climate Decade (2.9)
6. The Decade of Health (2.4)

Where is Amanda Gorman when I need her? There is an old adage in business that "there is a difference between selling apples and eating apples." *I have no idea where that came from.* In fact I googled it and could not find it, though I learned a lot about apples in the process. I think it was from one of my clever IBM mentors. *Anyway,* the point is the apples on display look pretty damn good, pretty tasty, just like these ideas look. We need to bring them home while they are fresh.

Can bipartisanship really be that elusive in the decade ahead? Thinking back to January 6 and our now infamous *insurrection,* that certainly seemed like a genuine bipartisan moment when Congress came back in session *after* the insurrection and storming of the Capitol. The power of a *shared experience*, I suppose. I suspect what we really need for the decade ahead is a *shared vision* for America and what we can and should be. Ideologies can blur any vision. If we can genuinely close the political gap between the parties, then maybe—*just maybe*—we can begin to close the Great American Divide in the decade ahead.

Five Reflections on the Reset of America and the Decade Ahead

1. THE POWER OF SHARED EXPERIENCE: 2020 was a powerful prelude to the reset of America that occurred in 2021. It was a shared experience on two fronts—a global pandemic and a contentious election. But, for many, the sense is we came out stronger with important lessons about what America can do and the opportunity ahead.
2. MIND THE GAP: We need to align to work on a compelling set of issues that can create opportunity and access for everyone. If we maintain the level of division in America that we saw at the end of 2020, we can only make slight and incremental progress on the issues that matter. That is insufficient for the decade ahead.
3. EDUCATION SETS THE TABLE: The ability to sustain success in the decade ahead and *beyond* is highly dependent on rethinking our approach to education, from pre-school to adult learning. We need to accelerate problem solvers across multiple disciplines for advancing healthcare, transportation, food production and climate change.
4. A FACT-FILLED FUTURE: We can agree to disagree, that's surely in our Bill of Rights somewhere. But we have to be able to agree on what constitutes the set of facts we are looking at. We need a shared reality, not an alternate universe. Civil discourse can let us argue the merits and the political platforms, then make a decision and move forward.
5. A DECADE OF CONSEQUENCE: We can't afford to whiff on this decade. The stakes are too high and we have so much wind at our back. Hoist the mainsail and let's make this a decade of massive consequence, where we reset the course of America and create a *decade of shared experience and prosperity*.

A decade of consequence. That this decade ahead, which sounds so long but will pass by so quickly, will make a difference. That the reset, regardless of why it occurred, actually worked and helped us navigate some difficult, and in many cases, *lingering* challenges. You either believe that we will be better working together in the decade ahead, or face

403

a different consequence: an America divided will lead to an America dissolved.

The Critical Lessons of the COVID Pandemic

As we wrap up our 10th and final Foresight session, we are reminded that as of January 21, 2021, we are still in the pandemic. But there is a sense that we are entering the exit lane. The U.S. is ramping up the distribution of two effective vaccines with a third (J&J) likely to be approved in February. It's likely that by the end of June of 2021, a majority of Americans will be fully vaccinated and states will be opening up with a degree of return to normalcy. Sports, travel and entertainment will be ready for a serious uptick in the summer.

But what are the most critical lessons learned from the pandemic? We asked our Foresighters this final question:

Question: *We have asked a question about COVID-19 in all of our sessions and how it has influenced a wide range of topics during the course of 2020. Assuming we have COVID largely behind us by the end of 2022, what's the one lasting impact it will have on the decade ahead from a leadership POV?*

History will review 2020/2021 and how we handled the pandemic for years to come; where we made the right moves and where we stalled. We have to learn from the experience—we could face another pandemic in the future—or simply learn how we need to circle the wagons when faced with a crisis in America. Here are a few of our Foresighter views:

- "Once the dust clears on the pandemic, people will be able to realize how important science and facts were."
- "Closely monitoring pandemic possibilities and also possibly looking at infrastructure, as well as quicker response to locate patient zero and how it happened in the first place."
- "I think it will define even more the leaders who see the good of the people, and those who are selfish. Trump had the chance to stop COVID by being aggressive and he failed to do so. We can only hope that Biden is going to put the health of his people first."
- "That a global perspective and response to global issues is required, and in the U.S. a national response to a national issue is required."
- "I think it shows how fragile our current infrastructure is in its current state. Aspects such as healthcare, small businesses, workplaces and schools were so immensely negatively affected."
- "A lasting economic impact, but it has also highlighted the racial injustices in this country and so many more are now aware of

this new wave of civil rights (symbolized by BLM). I'm hopeful that lasting impact will be positive."
- "Leadership will make plans with mobility and portability in mind as a means for operational activities to respond to large scale crises. From a work perspective, less focus on centralized offices. Greater investment in infrastructure (digital and physical). Better planning for contingencies of this nature."
- "There is no going back. We will engage in a perpetual form of social responsibility as it relates to virus hazards and spread mitigation.
- "The need to make response to a global pandemic or other disaster *nonpartisan*".

Variants as the Variable: For most of us, Thanksgiving 2021 felt more normal. A lot of America was traveling (albeit with higher gas prices), but there was a sense of reconnection occurring. The problem was, *the day after* Thanksgiving, the WHO formally named the 13th variant of the COVID pandemic as *Omicron*. Which sounds a lot like *ominous* or *omigod*. The media went into hyperdrive and seemed to rename it *armageddon*. But it is a stark reminder that we cannot let down our guard. That this is a *global pandemic* and until we marshal the resources to vaccinate the world, then no single country is truly safe. We have already learned the fallacy of closing airports and borders to stop the spread, but we'll try it again by quarantining the entire country of South Africa. Variants are the variable as we head into 2022.

So, as we reflect on these pandemic leadership lessons from our session earlier in the year, they send a message of vigilance. And that our respective governments must be more prepared in the future and more *agile*. We can't expect governments to solve the pandemic by themselves. They need great academic researchers, innovative private sector companies and an ability to collaborate globally real-time. But make no mistake, we need our governments. *Now more than ever.*

You know, I am a pretty big fan of limited government. I don't need a lot of it to go about my everyday life, but I also try to abide by what I think are shared American values and reasonable laws. I drive the speed limit (my family reminds me that this is partially because my car has 290,000 miles and can't *exceed* the speed limit). But I also value *good government*. And I think that was a crucial lesson in 2020/2021. A good government is one that can get on the same page, especially during a time of critical need or crisis. You need it at the federal level and you need it at the state level. And it has to take care of its people. *Of the people, by the people and for the people.* It's really a pretty simple, but essential, model for the decade ahead.

And remember, this is *my decade* ahead. It's why I wrote the book. I am optimistic about the decade, realistic about the work to be done and the divides to be narrowed. But, at the end of the day, I roll the dice with the American Dream. I have my *version* of the American Dream, but I know I couldn't pursue my version without it being America. And, as we get *seriously into the decade ahead*, that's really what everyone wants. The opportunity to pursue their version of the American Dream. *Welcome Aboard.*

...
Get your bags together,
Go bring your good friends, too
'Cause it's getting nearer,
It will soon be with you

--Cat Stevens (aka, Yusuf Islam), <u>Peace Train</u> (1971)

CHAPTER 12: Surveyin' USA: How American Optimism and Values Changed in 2020/2021

If everybody had an ocean
Across the USA
Then everybody'd be surfin'
Like Californi-a
...
We'll all be gone for the summer
We're on surfari to stay
Tell the teacher we're surfin'
Surfin' USA

--The Beach Boys, Surfin' USA (1963)

Hey Doug—I thought this chapter was supposed to be about *Surveyin' USA*, not *Surfin' USA*. Yeah, well you try and find some lyrics about surveys. Just not on the Billboard 100 list. But I promise to make a connection here.

One element we wanted to add for the *Foresight 2030* book was to conduct a quantitative survey of Americans about some of the key questions we had posed to our Foresighters and see if a much broader cross-section of America was seeing some of the same trends that we were seeing in our Foresight sessions. We just needed 1000 Americans to be willing to be surveyed and be part of our book.

Well, as luck would have it, our friends at Heart+Mind Strategies, a Virginia-based research consultancy, had launched an initiative, not long after the COVID pandemic had hit in early 2020, to survey Americans in a regular set of *pulse surveys* to look at how the pandemic and the politics were shaping attitudes, emotions and even the values that Americans use to make decisions. The surveys began in March, 2020, and then were reported out in a weekly *Business Roundtable* held each Friday afternoon for an hour. Zoom format, an open session for Heart+Mind Strategies' clients, business partners and an invitation to fellow business and thought leaders.

To be honest, back when everything and everybody had shut down, we all just needed a safe place to check in with each other and see if the world was hanging together. The reality was that organizations and their leaders were really feeling their way in the dark. Setting up WFH (Work From Home) infrastructure and policies, communicating messages of support, thinking about how we might conduct business in this strange environment and wondering what the long-term consequences might be. I don't know if we were genuinely hanging together at that time; I think we were *hanging by a thread*.

What's the mood of America? What are the dominant emotions? How are fundamental values like peace of mind, freedom, tolerance, personal satisfaction and concern for others being impacted by a pandemic and social/health crisis that most Americans had never faced in their lifetimes? What is impacting your optimism now and your outlook for the decade ahead?

Surfin' USA

So, back in the early 1960s, the mood of America was pretty joyous. Young Americans had a young president, Vietnam was still (for the most part) in the future and music could set the tone for how a young generation felt. And this young generation was feeling *freedom*. Load up the *Woodie* and head to the beach. Strap on some surfboards to the top of the car and you are in for an endless summer.

The Beach Boys were a classic American rock group and started as a garage band in 1961, but capitalized on a unique social phenomenon and cultural happening. Wikipedia notes that the Beach Boys, "Reflected a southern California youth culture of surfing, cars and romance, dubbed the 'California Sound'." And Surfin' USA, released in 1963, was their first national hit and the *California Sound* was suddenly heard across the USA.

I was seven years old when Surfin' USA was released. But I had two older brothers, so the music made it into the house. *On vinyl.* And while it wasn't quite my generation, I could see and hear the appeal. Surf all day, bonfire on the beach at night. Muscle beach for the guys and bikinis for the gals. Not particularly inclusive, but it was all part of an American youth culture that was big on freedom, enjoyment, fulfillment, personal satisfaction and belonging.

Surfin' USA Capitol Records
album 1963

The iconic surfing car—the Woodie

The Beach Boys helped launch surfing music to become a national phenomenon. It created a national *trend* that was based on underlying American emotions and values. Biographer Luis Sanchez followed the cultural impact of the band: "Their music gave voice to a Southern California mythos and compelled an audience across the nation and beyond to live out their own versions of the fantasy." Sanchez singled out *Surfin' USA* in "creating a direct passage to California life for a wider teenage audience...and a distinct California sensibility that exceeded its conception as such to advance right to the front of the American consciousness."

So, if you were *Surveyin' USA* in 1963, you could have tracked core American emotions and values and seen how they were affecting *that decade*. And by surveying core American emotions and values in 2020/2021, you can see how they are affecting *this decade.*

Cowabunga, Bro.

Research on American Values

The team at Heart+Mind Strategies has been researching American values for decades, monitoring the impact of values on decision-making since the origin of the Wirthlin Worldwide consultancy that was established by Richard Wirthlin in 1969. Wirthlin was a brilliant pollster and political strategist, and was Ronald Reagan's chief strategist from 1968 to 1988. His research on how values influence presidential campaigns and how Americans make decisions for specific candidates based on values was groundbreaking. It was also highly effective in guiding the election of Reagan to the presidency.

Many of the Heart+Mind leaders today were part of the Wirthlin Worldwide organization then and they continue the work of Wirthlin and the values research. The Heart+Mind Strategies' Center for Applied Values

Research honors the Wirthlin legacy and continues to explore the impact of values on our decisions today.

The Center defines values and their impact as follows:

"Values are the criteria people use in assessing their daily lives, arranging their priorities and choosing between alternative courses of action."

Heavy stuff. Alternative courses of action in 2020/2021 included what president to elect, whether to shelter at home, whether to wear masks in a pandemic and, in 2021, whether to get a COVID vaccine shot. You and I make decisions on countless issues in our daily lives, the question is what *influences* our decision-making progress. If leaders understand the values that influence our decision-making, they can communicate at that values level to influence our decisions. Wirthlin chronicles this communication influence intimately in his 2004 book *The Greatest Communicator* that highlights the communication skills of Ronald Reagan.

19 Values That Influence Our Decisions/Priorities (alpha order)

Accomplishment	Happiness	Self Esteem
Belonging	Inclusiveness	Social Order
Concern for Others	Peace of Mind	Success
Dependability	Personal Satisfaction	Tolerance
Enjoyment	Pride	Well-Being
Freedom	Productivity	
Fulfillment	Security	

VALUES EXAMPLE: Let's apply values research to our 1960s surfers in Southern California. *Means End Theory Values Laddering* is the approach that researchers, like the Heart+Mind team, use to uncover the end value that is derived in our decisions and activities. It's an iterative set of questions that starts at the simple attribute level, but moves into a very personal and emotional level:

1. What are some of the things (attributes) you like about surfing? (Being in the water, being in the sun, spending an afternoon with friends, catching an unexpected wave, getting myself into good physical shape, finding some quiet time...)

410

2. What's the ONE ATTRIBUTE that is most important to you personally and what's the BENEFIT of that attribute—what does it allow you to do or do differently in your life? (For me, it's the quiet time, being out on the water alone. The benefit is that it lets me reflect on what is important to me in my life—not only for that day but for what's ahead of me as a young person.)
3. When you experience that benefit, when it is present for you, how does it make you FEEL? (I feel like I have so many things ahead of me, that I can make decisions in my life that are based on what's important for me. That I am really in control of my life.)
4. And when you feel those emotions, it gives you SENSE of what? (It gives me a great sense of freedom, that I can catch any wave in life that I want.)

Cowabunga again. So in our example above, the terminal or decision value was *freedom.* That's why I surf. And for other surfers, it may have been *fulfillment* (always wanted to try something that was a great challenge); or it may have been *well-being* (a sense of balance in my life, of mental sharpness along with physical development). The point is this: if you understand how products, sports, cars, geographies or even presidential candidates affect the decision values and the very sense of what matters to *me*, then you can communicate to and *persuade* me.

I met Wirthlin in 1997 in Washington, D.C., along with several of his leadership team members including Dee Allsop, Jim Granger, Dave Richardson, Jim Hoskins *and this young researcher Maury Giles.* They had heard about our use of collaboration technology from an Arizona based Wirthlin Worldwide consultant, Cathy Chamberlain (also in attendance), with whom I had facilitated a Women's Leadership Conference for John McCain. I still remember the meeting in Washington: I was six months into the launch of my consulting practice and pitching our *Advanced Strategy Lab* approach to some of the smartest opinion researchers in the country. *I was so over my skis.*

But Wirthlin and his team were gracious, and *very forward looking.* They understood the power of anonymous and simultaneous brainstorming and how it could help understand how people see attributes, benefits and emotions of their decisions. My first paid engagement with the Wirthlin Worldwide team was in March of 1997 for General Motors, where we did consumer sessions on GM taglines and messaging using our mobile laptop lab. 1000+ sessions later, now mostly online, I am still working with many of those same core leaders. In fact, while Richard Wirthlin and Cathy Chamberlain have passed on, I am pleased to say Allsop, Granger, Richardson, Hoskins and Giles are card-carrying *Foresighters* and provided immense thought leadership on our Foresight sessions in 2020/2021. Dee Allsop is one of the co-founders of Heart+Mind Strategies. Others are retired (Granger) or, in the case of Richardson, have started their own consultancies.

So, I am deeply grateful to the Heart+Mind Strategies team for their work in tracking American attitudes, values and emotions since the start of the pandemic and sharing their insights in this chapter as part of our book. Their "Pulse" surveys (each survey was an online survey conducted with 1000 Americans) reveal powerful emotions and attitudes that are shaping the future of the decade ahead and illuminating some of the conflicts and divides that America is experiencing.

I am especially appreciative for them allowing us to ask a specific set of questions in the February Pulse conducted on February 18-23, 2021. These questions were very relevant for Foresight 2030 as they were fundamental questions about optimism towards the decade ahead, the impact of the presidential election and the January 2021 inauguration, and a key set of Foresight 2030 influences that we had developed as a result of our Foresight sessions.

We'll start with the February 2021 pulse survey questions, which I will cover; then my *esteemed colleague* Maury Giles, Chief Growth Officer at Heart+Mind Strategies, will provide his analysis and insights on how American values/emotions were impacted through mid-2021 by the COVID pandemic, and how this impact may influence the decade ahead.

More on Giles later. We have a long history that began with the 1997 meeting in Washington.

Author Griffen (left) and Giles (right) on assignment in Morocco, 2011

412

February 2021 Pulse Survey: The Decade Ahead

The February 18-23, 2021, Pulse surveyed 1001 Americans. *Far larger than our normal Foresight sessions!* I am not sure I even know 1001 Americans. But I am grateful to them for sharing their assessments on the following questions:

This next set of questions will focus on the decade ahead—now through the end of 2029:

1. All things considered, would you say you are optimistic or pessimistic about the decade ahead?
2. Would you say that you are more optimistic or less optimistic about the decade ahead now than you were in January, 2020, at the start of the decade?
3. To what extent do you agree with the following statement: "The inauguration on January 20 and the transition to a new administration was a fundamental reset for America for the decade ahead."

These questions would serve as a baseline for optimism and the impact of the presidential election. We would also ask about their assessment of 15 influences that we had identified in our Foresight sessions—both the level of impact on their optimism for the decade ahead if they occurred and then how likely each might be to occur in the decade ahead:

No.	Idea
1.	Meaningful progress on climate change
2.	A successful rollout of the COVID-19 vaccine and preparedness for future pandemics
3.	A strong and sustained economic recovery
4.	A return to bipartisan politics
5.	A significant advancement in social equality (racial, economic, diversity)
6.	Addressing domestic terrorism
7.	Restoring America's leadership in the world
8.	Investing in America's infrastructure (roads, bridges, utilities, digital connections)
9.	Significantly reducing gun violence

413

10. Education reform to address access, cost and new employment pathways

11. Raising the impact and influence of science

12. Uniting the nation, creating more common ground

13. Improving healthcare access and affordability

14. Monitoring global political and military threats

15. A transition to younger leadership

Lastly, we added one open text question just to see where 1001 Americans might take us:

1. If you were to make ONE PREDICTION about the decade ahead —now through the end of 2029—what would that prediction be?

Here is your ever-so-brief analysis of 1001 open statements: *some light and some darkness. Highly divided.*

Before we dive into the results of our *Surveyin' USA* findings, a note on the survey methodology:

> **Audience: General Population, n=1001. Respondents were selected from among those who have volunteered to participate in online surveys and were then screened in the survey based on quotas and survey audience definition. The data (approximately 1,000 respondents) were gathered across multiple, large online survey panels that included a cross-section of the US population. To ensure representation of a wide variety of demographic groups, we established quotas by age, gender, region, race/ethnicity and education based on US Census data for people aged 18 and older. In a hypothetical case of probability of sample size of 1,000, the margin of error would be +/- 3.1% at the 99% confidence level.**

Interpretation: A serious survey covering Americans of all backgrounds/beliefs.

Optimism About the Decade Ahead

Our Foresighters were exceptionally optimistic in our final Foresight session about the decade ahead. That session was held on January 21, 2021, the day after the Biden Inauguration. For many, it felt like a turning point, that we were headed in a new direction. But to be fair, a majority of our Foresighters were highly educated, successful in their careers, com-

414

fortable with their bank accounts. They were looking for less drama in politics, an economic rebound, a victory over the disruptive COVID pandemic and a return to a well-earned normalcy of lifestyle.

Our pulse survey showed a slightly more divided America on the issue of optimism.

> *Question Q211*: All things considered would you say you are optimistic or pessimistic about the decade ahead? (NOTE--response options were: very optimistic, somewhat optimistic, somewhat pessimistic, very pessimistic. *Net Optimistic* combines very optimistic and somewhat optimistic responses; *Net Pessimistic* combines very pessimistic and somewhat pessimistic responses.)

Demographic/Group	Net Optimistic	Net Pessimistic
All respondents	*60%*	*40%*
Male	60%	40%
Female	60%	40%
Boomer	62%	38%
Gen X	60%	40%
Millennial	62%	38%
Gen Z	55%	45%
White	58%	42%
Black	64%	36%
Hispanic	63%	37%
Asian	72%	28%
< $50K income	59%	41%

$50K - $100K income	62%	38%
> $100K income	63%	37%
Urban	64%	36%
Suburban	60%	40%
Rural	56%	44%
High School or less education	59%	41%
College Degree or higher	60%	40%
Republican	55%	45%
Democratic	68%	32%
Independent	51%	49%
Voted for Trump	*48%*	*52%*
Voted for Biden	*71%*	*29%*

Look, you think this is a lot of data? This overall pulse survey has 1,925 pages of data. Technology gone wild. Excel spreadsheets on steroids. There are 100+ categories of demographics…but the above table gives us some of the baseline looks at gender, generation, race, education, income, geographic region and *most interestingly* whom you voted for in the 2020 Presidential election. *Talk about sore losers!*

Analysis: Americans are optimistic about the decade ahead by a margin of 60% net optimistic to 40% net pessimistic. This is in February of 2021 after one of the most divisive presidential elections we have ever seen, a nearly year-long COVID pandemic, a major economic downturn and massive social protests in the summer of 2020. That's remarkable. And it backs up our Foresighters and their sense that despite the raw disruption of 2020, we may have reset America onto a more positive path for the future. Dare I say, what could be the *most consequential decade of our lives.* But, 40% net pessimistic says we have a long journey ahead to provide access and opportunity to those who may not yet see or feel that optimism ahead.

Some interesting points in the data:

- ✓ There is no gender difference in that net optimism. Perhaps on this we have found a level of gender equality.
- ✓ From a generational view, Boomers and Millennials lean slightly more optimistic at 62%, while our younger Gen Zers lean more pessimistic at 55% net pessimistic. I am not surprised at this—this is a generation that is being handed over some massive issues: gun violence, climate change, tired old politics, racial/economic divide and (in my opinion) early digital exhaustion. I think the Gen Zers will make progress in this decade, and then will help take America to an entirely new level in the subsequent decade.
- ✓ White Americans are not far off the baseline at 58% net optimistic, but *less optimistic* than their Black, Hispanic and Asian counterparts. Initially that was counterintuitive for me. But I think the summer of 2020 raised the bar on social/racial inequality and created a sense that perhaps in this decade we will turn the corner. If history is a lesson, we will likely need every year available in the decade to turn that corner.
- ✓ Here's a shocker: if you make more money you are more optimistic. But not wildly so—those in less than $50K segment are still 59% net optimistic, so only slightly below the 63% net optimistic of the $100K+ segment. We actually have the data on the $300K+ segment: they come in at only 62% net optimistic. They probably just found out that a seat on the Virgin Galactica will cost them a year's salary.
- ✓ Rural is interesting, but not surprising. Our rural participants face some difficult challenges in their economies, job availability, technology access and a sense that their voice has not been heard well politically, at least pre-Trump. Suburban is right at the baseline (the classic American lifestyle), while urban is up at 64% net optimistic and rural is down at 56% net optimistic.
- ✓ Another expected result was education, with our college graduates a bit more optimistic at 60% than high school graduates or less at 59%. But that's not a huge divide and may suggest that more vocational pathways are becoming available to the non-college graduate segment. Not to mention bypassing massive student debt.
- ✓ And then we finish on the political front. If you are Republican you are not quite feeling that baseline optimism; if you are Democratic you feel like the ship has been righted and the decade ahead could be eight years of your party; if you are Independent

417

you are shaking your head at the two party partisan system and calling it a coin-flip at this point.

✓ And only *one group* in our highlighted segments that falls below the optimism equator line: the Trump voters lean pessimistic about the decade ahead at 52% net pessimism (48% net optimism). Biden voters are 71% *net optimistic*. That is a 23 point gap and just reminds us that the divide in America is very real.

More Optimistic in 2021 than 2020?

One of our more interesting findings in our January 21, 2021, Foresight session was a majority of our Foresighters (67%) were *more optimistic* about the decade ahead in January 2021 than they were at the start of the decade in January 2020. For them, the change in political leadership, the personal reawakening as a result of the COVID pandemic and the focus on social justice and broader economic opportunity were all factors.

In the February 2021 pulse survey we posed the same question:

> **Question Q211A**: *Would you say that you are more optimistic or less optimistic about the decade ahead now (February 2021) than you were in January 2020 at the start of the decade. (NOTE: response options were more optimistic now, about the same, less optimistic now.)*

Demographic/Group	More Optimistic	About Same	Less Optimistic
All respondents	28%	43%	29%
Male	28%	44%	28%
Female	29%	42%	30%
Boomer	28%	36%	36%
Gen X	26%	47%	27%
Millennial	33%	44%	23%
Gen Z	23%	54%	23%

White	25%	40%	35%
Black	33%	55%	13%
Hispanic	36%	42%	22%
Asian	34%	46%	20%
< $50K income	25%	46%	29%
$50K - $100K income	32%	36%	33%
> $100K income	35%	41%	24%
Urban	36%	43%	21%
Suburban	28%	42%	30%
Rural	20%	44%	37%
High School or less educa-	24%	47%	29%
College Degree or higher	34%	36%	30%
Republican	19%	41%	40%
Democratic	40%	41%	19%
Independent	20%	46%	34%
Voted for Trump	*16%*	*39%*	*45%*
Voted for Biden	*41%*	*40%*	*19%*

Something's happening here. What it is ain't exactly clear. Well, that's not entirely true. What is clear is that 2020 (inclusive of January 2021) impacted certain demographic groups in either a net positive fashion (causing them to feel more optimistic about the decade ahead) or a net negative fashion (causing them to feel less optimistic about the decade ahead).

Analysis: 13 months into the decade and a majority of Americans (57%) had changed their outlook on the decade ahead. And, in keeping with the theme of a divided America, 28% were more optimistic and 29% were less optimistic. But the very fact that this 13 months had that level of impact simply says that we are in for a wild ride. That this decade indeed may be the most consequential decade of our lives.

And what does it say about some of our selected demographic groups?

- ✓ If you use the baseline that 28% of Americans were *more optimistic* about the decade ahead in February of 2021, compared to their view in January of 2020, then certain groups were actually above that line (by at least 2%). The glass is half full in the decade ahead for: millennials, minorities (Black, Hispanic and Asian), those who make more money (>$50K), urban dwellers, college graduates, Democrats and *if you voted for Biden that beer mug is overflowing.*
- ✓ Similarly, if you use the baseline that 29% of Americans were *less optimistic* about the decade ahead in February of 2021 compared to their view in January of 2020, certain groups were also above that line (by at least 2%). The glass is half empty in the decade ahead for: boomers, middle income Americans ($50K-$100K), White Americans, rural Americans, Republicans, Independents and *if you voted for Trump that glass is bone dry.*

Most of these variances are aligned with our previous analysis on groups that were more optimistic in general about the decade ahead. But there were a couple of anomalies. Boomers, slightly more optimistic in our initial question about the decade ahead than the base response (62% vs. 60%), were a segment that had become significantly *less optimistic* by February 2021 than the base response (36% vs. 29%). As a spokesperson of that demographic, I would offer a couple of views: 1) The negative health impact of the pandemic was heavy on our seniors. That was a hell of a way to start the decade; 2) The level of division in America that we saw heightened in 2020 was disheartening to that generation. Not exactly what they wanted to see in their golden years. And then I suppose there is a third issue: you are asking me about my optimism for the decade ahead when I am a year older and there was some doubt in my mind about getting to 2030 when you asked me at the start of the decade…

And we might as well speak about that same uncomfortable finding that we saw in our initial question as it relates to ethnic views. It's very positive that historical minorities in America including Blacks, Hispanics and Asians have a higher net optimistic outlook for the decade ahead and that the outlook after the first 13 months of the decade became *even*

420

more optimistic than the baseline of our respondents. But why are White Americans decidedly *less optimistic* than their minority counterparts. A sense that the social justice fabric is changing for real? A more uncomfortable change than first imagined? For this decade to have the positive consequence for America, it has to be viewed as a decade forward for *all* Americans. We're not there yet. We need to watch this issue carefully, and to talk about it more openly.

Was January 2021 a Reset for America?

This was yet another finding in our January 21 Foresight session that some 68% of our Foresighters felt that January 20, 2021—the inauguration of Biden and the symbolic transition to a new administration—was a fundamental reset for America. An inflection point. The question, of course, was whether a broader set of Americans saw it the same way:

> **Question Q223:** *To what extent do you agree with the following statement: "The inauguration on January 20 and the transition to a new administration was a fundamental reset for America for the decade ahead." (NOTE: response options were strongly agree, somewhat agree, neither agree nor disagree, somewhat disagree, strongly disagree. Net Agree combines strongly agree and somewhat agree; Net Disagree combines somewhat disagree and strongly disagree.)*

Demographic/Group	Net Agree	Neither	Net Disagree
All respondents	*51%*	*25%*	*24%*
Male	54%	22%	24%
Female	48%	29%	24%
Boomer	54%	20%	26%
Gen X	49%	27%	24%
Millennial	50%	30%	20%
Gen Z	48%	31%	21%

White	48%	25%	27%
Black	57%	30%	13%
Hispanic	54%	24%	22%
Asian	65%	18%	17%
< $50K income	47%	29%	24%
$50K - $100K income	55%	19%	26%
> $100K income	63%	16%	22%
Urban	62%	23%	15%
Suburban	50%	26%	24%
Rural	40%	27%	32%
High School or less education	44%	32%	24%
College Degree or higher	60%	16%	23%
Republican	35%	24%	41%
Democratic	73%	17%	9%
Independent	38%	34%	28%
Voted for Trump	*32%*	*22%*	*46%*
Voted for Biden	*76%*	*16%*	*8%*

This is powerful language in the question. *Was the inauguration on January 20 and the transition to a new administration a <u>fundamental reset</u> for America for the decade ahead?* For the record, the days leading up to January 20, 2021, were rather impactful for the country as well—an insurrection on January 6 following by a *second* impeachment of the sitting president (Trump) by the House on January 13. So the fact that *we even* *got to January 20* certainly set the stage for the symbolic impact of the Inauguration.

Analysis: A majority of Americans agreed that the inauguration on January 20 and the transition to a new administration was indeed a fundamental reset for the country. Full stop. That qualifies as *breaking news*. But it also comes with some qualifications: 24% disagreed and 25% neither agreed nor disagreed (we'll see how this goes...). But the sheer finding that 51% agreed is powerful. It also sets an *enormous expectation* for the Biden Administration to deliver upon. And for those who disagreed, then it becomes a rallying cry. Closing this gap of division will be perhaps our most significant challenge of the decade ahead.

And, once again, the details of the demographics matter:

- ✓ For the first time, our generations see it the same. Boomers (with a little more life experience and historical perspective) come in higher at 54%, but Millennials, Gen X and Gen Z are also of the mind that it was a reset. Millennials are at a net agreement of 50%, Gen X at 49% and Gen Z at 48%. We may not be unified politically, but to have a level of alignment across generations is a powerful—and positive—statement.
- ✓ Urban, suburban and rural follow the same trend lines that we have been seeing in our prior survey questions. Urban above the baseline, suburban on the baseline and rural below the baseline. Rural America matters; they are kind of *the heart of America*. In the decade ahead there has to be the economic, healthcare, education and technology access and opportunity for that segment to prosper. Call it *rural equity.*
- ✓ Income is interesting. At the < $50K level still good support of the reset at 47% net agreement; higher for $50K - $100K at 55% and the "*Looking good, Louis"* segment of you > $100K income are at 63%. I think the prospect of *prosperity for the country* is well received by this group.
- ✓ At the education level, it's interesting to see that the net disagreement level is about the same—24% for high school or less, and 23% for college or more. The difference is that the high school or less segment is still in a more wait-and-see attitude as to whether this transition will translate to a better decade ahead. The college educated or more has already made their conclusion—60% are in net agreement.
- ✓ On the gender side, I was a little puzzled by this one. It's kind of a similar finding as we see in education: for male and female, the net disagreement is the same at 24%. But there is a 6 point swing on net agreement (54% male, 48% female). I need to be *really careful* in anything I say about this. My wife and my daugh-

423

ter have promised to read my book. *Maybe check this finding in the 2028 presidential election.*

✓ On ethnicity, we see our same pattern as in previous questions, a bigger reset (in terms of net agreement) for Black, Hispanic and Asian Americans (the promise of inclusion and social justice and more economic opportunity), but White Americans still see this as a fundamental reset, and, in fact, see it the same way (48% net agreement) as the female demographic and the Gen Z demographic. *But note a higher net disagreement than their female and Gen Z segment counterparts.* More of that uncomfortable conversation.

✓ And, on the political party and *how you voted side*, I believe that the numbers speak quite clearly for themselves.

So, the real question for the decade ahead is this: was January 20 and the transition to a new administration a fundamental reset that signals a new direction that can be sustained for America, or will it simply be a shift in the swing of the pendulum? I am not sure this country can handle too many pendulum shifts in the decade ahead.

The Issues That Will Influence The Decade Ahead

And finally, in terms of our special *Foresight 2030* questions that were part of the February 2021 pulse survey with 1001 Americans, we asked them about 15 "influences on the decade ahead" and the level of impact they might have on the decade as well as the likelihood of that influence actually happening. This is similar to what we did within each of our Foresight sessions where the influences were specific to the Foresight chapter topic (work, education, media, lifestyle, etc.). In this case we just took 15 higher level influences forward for the survey.

Question Q224: Please assess each of the following in terms of how INFLUENTIAL each of the following would be on your level of optimism on the decade ahead. (NOTE: response options were 1-10 where a "1" is a very low level of influence and a "10" is a very high level of influence. Net High Level of Influence combines assessments that were 6-10, Net Influential is the mid-point where the area was rated a '5', and Net Low Level of Influence combines assessments that were 1-4.)

NOTE: This table will list the 15 areas based on the percentage of Americans in the survey that assessed the area in the 6-10 range and indicate a Net High Level of Influence:

Influence Area	Net High Level of Influence
Improving healthcare access and affordability	74%
Investing in America's infrastructure (roads, bridges, utilities, digital connections)	70%
Monitoring global political and military threats	69%
A strong and sustained economic recovery	69%
Uniting the nation, creating more common ground	69%
Restoring America's leadership in the world	68%
Addressing domestic terrorism	68%
A successful rollout of the COVID-19 vaccine and preparedness for future pandemics	67%
Education reform to address access, cost and new employment pathways	64%
Raising the impact and influence of science	64%
A significant advancement in social equality (racial, economic, diversity)	63%
Significantly reducing gun violence	61%
A transition to younger leadership	59%
Meaningful progress on climate change	55%
A return to bipartisan politics	52%

Analysis: First, the very high level view. Over half of our survey participants agreed that all 15 factors were a Net High Level of Influence (50% or higher). So, we are on a pretty serious set of topics in terms of impact for the decade ahead.

I saw the 15 falling into three groups in the preceding table. The first group was the set of topics where two thirds (66% or higher) of our participants agreed that these were Net High Influential areas. Not surprisingly, on the heels of a global pandemic, healthcare access and affordability was at the top of the list. But to be fair, healthcare is always one of the top influential issues on Americans' minds. On that we agree. On how to *deliver* affordable and accessible healthcare—on that we have a very difficult time agreeing. *But the decade is still young.*

Rounding out that first group are pretty fundamental topics that are within 4% of each other—infrastructure, global threats, the economy, a unified America, an America that leads globally, that we address and diminish domestic terrorism and, of course, that we rollout the COVID-19 vaccine and prepare for future pandemics. *Oh, that vaccine rollout sounded so simple and straight-forward in February 2021, didn't it?*

Group Two: Core influencers, still at 60% or higher Net High Level of Influence. An interesting set with education reform, advancing science, social equity and addressing gun violence. None of them easy (as we will see in the assessment of likelihood) but all influential.

Group Three: Still 50% or higher Net High Level of Influence, but we clearly lack consensus on these three. Younger leadership is the strongest of the three at 59%—I think this is the market permission for our Millennials to step forward. You'll need to prove your leadership, but I remain convinced that this decade is where the mantle of leadership is passed from our beloved boomers to our millennials to guide the latter half of the decade.

Next in Group Three is climate change. At least it's not last on the overall list. But the level of urgency is still not there, especially in competing with COVID, the economy and *world peace*. And just to be clear, this cuts across just about all of the demographics (with a couple of notable exceptions that you will see). While we have the demographic data for all 15 of the areas, we'll just a share a snapshot of climate change so you can see some of the variances:

Climate Change—Percentage of Net High Level of Influence (selected demographics)

Demographic	Net High Level of Influence
All respondents	*55%*
Male	56%

426

Female	54%
Boomer	55%
Gen X	49%
Millennial	60%
Gen Z	60%
White	51%
Black	63%
Hispanic	61%
Asian	77%
< $50K income	51%
$50K - $100K income	64%
> $100K income	60%
Urban	56%
Suburban	53%
Rural	45%
High School or Less Education	49%
College or Higher Education	65%
Republican	39%
Democratic	76%
Independent	45%

Voted for Trump	**35%**
Voted for Biden	**77%**

Lastly, in our Group Three, is a return to bipartisan politics. Our Fore-sighters had this at the top of their list in many of our sessions, especially in addressing the American Divide and what will create optimism for the decade ahead. But I'm afraid that for many Americans they see the promise of *bipartisan politics* as carrying two suitcases full of baggage: 1) any politician is a bad politician and, 2) a high level of distrust for government as an entity. *Maury will comment on that in Side B.*

To avoid going down a *complete rabbit hole* by looking at any other demographics on any of these, we will press on to the likelihood assessment of these 15 areas. *Otherwise you will need to go to Amazon for the Volume 2 Foresight Series.*

> *Question Q224A: Please assess each of the following in terms of how LIKELY each of the following would be to occur in the decade ahead. (NOTE: response options were 1-10 where a "1" is a very low level of likelihood and a "10" is a very high level of likelihood. Net Likely combines assessments that were 6-10, Neither is the mid-point where the area was rated a "5", and Net Not Likely combines assessments that were 1-4.)*

NOTE: This table will list the 15 areas based on the percentage of Americans in the survey that assessed the area in the 6-10 range and indicate a Net Likely:

Influence Area	Net Likely
A successful rollout of the COVID-19 vaccine and preparedness for future pandemics	69%
A strong and sustained economic recovery	62%
Monitoring global political and military threats	62%
Improving healthcare access and affordability	61%
Raising the impact and influence of science	61%

428

Investing in America's infrastructure (roads, bridges, utilities, digital connections)	60%
Restoring America's leadership in the world	60%
Education reform to address access, cost and new employment pathways	59%
Addressing domestic terrorism	59%
A significant advancement in social equality (racial, economic, diversity)	55%
Uniting the nation, creating more common ground	54%
Meaningful progress on climate change	53%
A transition to younger leadership	53%
Significantly reducing gun violence	49%
A return to bipartisan politics	45%

Analysis: I have some good news, and I have some bad news. Which would you like first?

Let's start from the bottom and get the bad news out of the way. This time I see four groups so we will reverse our start with *Group Four.* Two members of this group, where a majority of our Americans surveyed see *less than a 50% chance of the influence occurring in the decade ahead.* Just like our Foresighters, this survey gives low odds of a return to bipartisan politics. But this survey also put bipartisan politics at the bottom of the list for its possible influence for the decade ahead. So, according to the survey, it was kind of a lost cause anyway.

The second topic in this group is distressing to say the least, but is also consistent with the last ten years of reality. Only 49% of our Americans surveyed rate the likelihood of reducing gun violence at a six or higher. *And that is why we are where we are.* I don't think that *any* American doesn't want to see gun violence reduced, it's just that so many have given up hope that we will take meaningful action as a country. My only hope is to turn to the Gen Z cohort and ask, knowing it is completely unfair and an admission of your older generation's failure, to please change this for the future. We could accomplish all of the other 14 areas on this list in the decade ahead but if we don't address this one, then you cannot call it a successful decade for this country. *You either stand for something or you stand for nothing at all.*

OK, let's move to G*roup Three.* Four members of this club; harder to accomplish, but we have not written them off yet. Look, I know why three of the four are so hard—social equality, unite the country and climate change. But I don't know why a *transition to younger leadership* is so hard. Does it scare you? Do you not understand how exciting it was when John F. Kennedy was president and *everything was possible*? Two things must happen for the young leadership transition to happen in this decade: 1) many of our older/incumbent leaders need to *step aside,* and 2) many of our younger potential leaders must be willing to *step forward*.

Let's get to the good news. *Group Two* are core enablers of the decade ahead. High Net Level of Influence as all eight are assessed at 64% or above on *influence* and all eight look like they have a shot in terms of *likelihood*. They create a safer, stronger and more enduring America. In fact, if you do all eight of those in my G*roup Two,* you just might make some nice progress on Groups Three and Four. *It's kind of a Trojan Horse strategy.*

And this leaves us with *Group One*. A single, but essential, member to this club: the rollout of the COVID-19 vaccine and the preparedness for any future pandemics. We did not ask for this nor anticipate this, but it is now clear: the gateway to the decade ahead is moving past this destructive and divisive pandemic. *Now*, or it will linger the duration of the decade.

The Most Impactful and the Most Likely

Finally, before I hand the reigns of this *Surveyin' USA* chapter over to my anxiously awaiting colleague Maury Giles, we'll conclude the view of our 15 influences by looking at the ones that are *most influential* (were assessed a 9 or 10 by our participants in terms of their potential influence to the decade) and that are *most likely* (were assessed a 9 or 10 by our participants in terms of the likelihood to occur). In the vernacular of quantitative survey research this is called a top two box assessment. *This is really exciting stuff for researchers*. And, it is actually quite meaningful for all of you as readers:

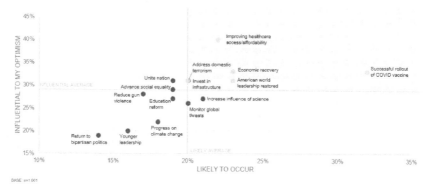

Actions Most Influential to Optimism AND Most Likely to Occur in Next 10 Years

The top right quadrant is the set of six areas that, based on high influence and high likelihood, where our survey participants have placed their initial bets for the decade ahead: successful rollout of COVID vaccine, improving healthcare access/affordability, economic recovery, address domestic terrorism, American world leadership restored and investing in infrastructure. And that's a good list, essential for the decade ahead, *but insufficient* if we want this to be the most consequential decade of our lives. You cannot move that much forward, and at the same time, leave that much behind. This is the challenge we face in the decade ahead.

Surveyin' USA—Side B

Back in the vinyl days (as in albums), you had a Side A and a Side B. We've just concluded Side A of *Surveying' USA* with my look at a key set of questions and topics that we posed to 1001 Americans to check some of our insights for Foresight 2030. The survey questions that we just shared were part of a larger series of Pulse Surveys that have been and, as of the writing of this book, are still being conducted by the Heart+Mind Strategies Team.

So, I am pleased to turn over the writing of Side B of this chapter to my good friend and colleague, Maury Giles, who is the Chief Growth Officer at Heart+Mind. It is appropriate that Maury and I are collaborating on this chapter. *We have been collaborating for more than 20 years.* Let me introduce you to Maury Giles:

I first met Maury in 1997 when he was part of the Wirthlin Worldwide team (which I referenced towards the start of the chapter). He was a *young* project director and progressed to become a VP and senior research executive. I was introducing our *Advanced Strategy Lab* platform and process to the Wirthlin team, and, well, Maury invited himself into the meeting. *Maury has a habit of dealing himself into just about everything*

431

interesting that might be happening in his professional place of employment.

There are some people who, when you introduce the notion of *collaboration,* look up and it's like a whole new world has opened up. *They get it.* They see implications and consequences, things that could never have been done before suddenly become possible. It's not a trend, it's a life-long journey. And as soon as Maury saw what we were imagining in terms of a technology-based collaboration approach, he was in. He volunteered to lead the project for Wirthlin. Twenty-five years later we are still collaborating together on the art and science of collaboration. We are both *heavyweight facilitators*, so we compare notes often. I am a little more linear in my approach and sessions. One thing at a time. Maury is a little more *out on the edge*. Let's try this. In the Olympic context, he often adds a new *degree of difficulty* to his events.

But that's what makes him world class as a facilitator and a colleague. He has changed the game at many organizations—from Wirthlin World-wide, to Harris Interactive, to ad agency GSD&M, to the Ipsos Global consultancy to launch a new consultancy, Strategy 3 (the impetus to our Morocco sessions previously pictured) and then regrouped with a core set of the original Wirthlin Worldwide team members who reformed as Heart+Mind. *The band is back together.* A journalist before he was a consultant, he is a skilled writer and interviewer. He speaks better Spanish than I do, but we can carry a good conversation and facilitate *en Español* in a pinch. Call it cultural collaboration.

He is particularly skilled on the issue of *values research* and how values impact decision-making in everything from politics to products. Part B of our *Surveyin' USA* chapter will look at the tracking of American values and emotions in 2020 and early 2021, and how these values—and American's perceptions and attitudes towards these values—may impact the decade ahead. I introduce you to Maury Giles, who will be driving the rest of the chapter. I will be along for the ride, and will weigh in at the end.

Ay que curvas, y yo sin frenos! Let the rollercoaster begin…

Personal Reflections: Heading Into the Pandemic (Maury Giles)

It was a few minutes before 6:00pm Mountain Time on March 11, 2020. My wife and I were in town for Spring break gathering with several of our children for dinner at Tony's Tacos in Heber City, Utah. We drove up from Arizona and had been enjoying family time in the area all week.

I noticed a bizarre developing news story playing out on the TV at the restaurant. The Utah Jazz game against the Oklahoma City Thunder was being canceled after center Rudy Gobert tested positive for the novel coronavirus COVID-19. We had been talking about COVID amongst ourselves over the few days prior, but we had absolutely no idea what was coming.

Within hours, most of life as we knew it would shut down. It would be far more serious and last much longer than any of us had imagined at the time.

We called family back in Arizona and asked them to please get us some basic staples from the store, given all we were hearing. The drive back home to Arizona felt like we were passing through a war zone—making eye contact at the gas stations and open stores along the way felt like a shared, "Good luck, but stay away." We even wondered if we'd be allowed back in the state given how fast things were being locked down everywhere!

We made it back home and, like everyone across the country, embarked on the *emotional roller coaster* of uncertainty, concern, confusion and isolation that was 2020. My parents, in their 70s, had moved in with us after selling their home of 40+ years in New Mexico and were building a home near family in Arizona. Little did they know the slight "delay" in the construction of their home would end up, 18 months later, still dragging on toward completion.

Emotions ran high as expectations had to shift in almost every facet of life. One after another, things we took for granted in daily living either disappeared altogether or were dramatically altered. The idea this would be a weird few months became the reality that this will never fully end.

For my immediate family, the chaos was just enough to trigger the decision to sell our home in Arizona and move. We figured we would go to Utah to be closer to our kids and, hopefully, find some financial security. We wanted to manufacture a bit more control over our circumstances.

433

Our place of security was Utah. Both my wife and I were born in Provo 50 years earlier. She lived most of her life in Utah County. Our youngest kids were still living at home, my stepchildren had grown up there as well. Most of our kids were in Utah going to school or working. We were in *familiar territory*. We were in control. Sort of...we thought.

One bizarre thing about moving during a pandemic is the covert lifestyle of moving in quietly and living among strangers while purposefully never getting to know anyone. School, church, activities, etc., were all cancelled or seriously altered, so we simply did not get to know other people in this new "home" for our family. It has been harder to feel connected to our new community.

Getting Personal With COVID

Between Christmas and New Year's Eve 2020, it was our turn to get COVID-19. Each of us in the household, within 24 hours of each other, was sick with the virus in our new home. Quarantine. Movies. Rest. More movies. More attempts to rest.

At the tail end of our household quarantine another shock and a new "division" entered with a force on January 6, 2021. I've always been engaged in politics, but on that day everyone in our home was seeing the events at the U.S. Capitol unfold together. My reaction was disbelief, sadness and anger. One of our teenage sons, however, reacted with laughter at social media memes mocking the chaos. I was indignant. He was humored by the intensity of my response. What was going on? Insanity.

Spring 2021 brought hope. By now we were all used to the COVID chaos. The novel coronavirus was anything but novel and we were all done with it—at least we wanted to be done with it. The news of the vaccine was exciting. My wife got a temporary job helping distribute the vaccine at a large outdoor venue in Salt Lake. Things were going to change and the light at the end of the tunnel was getting brighter. Or was it?

But even something as seemingly simple and obvious as the good news of the COVID-19 vaccine has brought arguments to the dinner table and division with our young adult kids. This time, as the COVID Delta variant of 2021 brought back high numbers of infection and deaths, we seem to be more "used to" this news and have found our routines to deal with it. But the debates now focus on the "politics" of the pandemic: masks and the vaccines. At Sunday dinners, when everyone is gathered, we either take on the topic for another round or agree to disagree and leave it alone to eliminate conflict. *Sound familiar?*

434

This is just my story, and only part of it at that. Everyone reading this has their own version. Such is the manner in which this new decade has been introduced. COVID-19 has shaped personal and societal expectations for life in the decade ahead. It has influenced the optimism or pessimism we feel about what comes next. And that's why this book, this research, this personal and collective reflection, matters so much. We are all placing certain bets about the decade ahead. Those bets are influenced by our life experiences, our values and our emotions.

Organizational Reactions: Tracking the Mood of America

At Heart+Mind Strategies, as our updated financial projections quickly became increasingly dire at the beginning of the pandemic, we took action to lower senior leadership salaries and cut everything we could. Everything was *unclear*. Nobody, really, could project what might happen next. These were not scenarios we had rehearsed for.

In that moment, Spring 2020, we decided, at Heart+Mind, to gather with other clients and partners to share ideas. Mostly, looking back, I believe we wanted to connect with other people and get to the raw human emotions of what everyone was feeling. We wanted security in helping each other. There was very little security to be found elsewhere. *We would circle the organizational wagons.*

So we launched the online Heart+Mind Roundtable series every Friday along with our national tracking survey, Pulse, to inform how Americans were responding. We expected 10-15 clients to gather. Our first session was over 40 people. It grew rapidly to sometimes reach 100-120 live (but virtual) participants. As of Fall 2021, these sessions have become part of our corporate DNA and over 1,000 people from nearly every industry sector have joined to "hit the pause button" and share ideas (more to come later on what we've learned from these two vehicles).

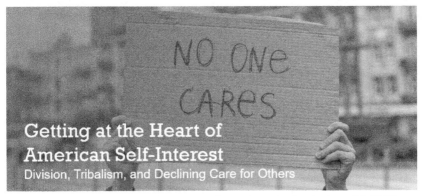

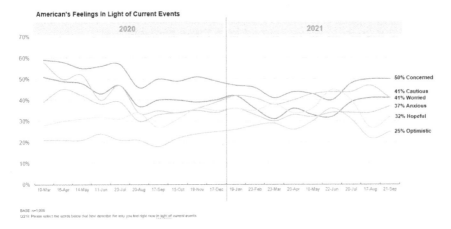

Getting at the Heart of American Self-Interest
Division, Tribalism, and Declining Care for Others

August 2021 Roundtable—The 33rd edition since the beginning of COVID

Reflection on the National Mood

I shared my personal story to offer a relatable account of our collective experience. But our Pulse national survey tracking data since April 2020 has shown a very similar pattern of the national mood in great detail and similar ups and downs (we talk with over 1,000 U.S. adults at least monthly via an online survey asking the same set of questions each wave). You have been on this shared rollercoaster with us.

Major Change in the Mood of the Nation

American's Feelings In Light of Current Events

50% Concerned
41% Cautious
41% Worried
37% Anxious
32% Hopeful
25% Optimistic

BASE: n=1,000
Q210: Please select the words below that best describe the way you feel right now in light of current events

Initially, the shock of the pandemic resulted in Americans expressing *concern, caution and worry* as the top three emotions felt in Spring 2020. These same three top emotions are expressed, nationally, in Fall 2021, having dropped only by 10 points (from roughly 60% to 50% for concern and 50% to 41% for worry—but caution has dropped from 60% to 41% as many have adapted to this new reality). Only 21% of Americans felt optimistic in March 2020, and only 25% feel optimistic today, at the time of this writing.

But by September 2020 things were starting to change for the better. We started tracking a steady uptick in the optimism Americans felt. This sentiment peaked when news of the effectiveness of the vaccine hit and numbers of cases and deaths were in decline as a result. In fact, our June 2021 survey showed the top emotion across the country was, in fact, *hopeful* at 45%, the highest measured since the outset of the pandemic.

Then news of the COVID Delta variant spread and impact, division over vaccine and mask mandates and public reaction to the conflicting reality of the U.S. departure from Afghanistan all converged to create an abrupt and significant change in public sentiment. *Hopefulness* dropped to the lowest in 18 months at 27% by August. *Optimism* dipped back down to only 22%, the same level expressed at the outset of the pandemic.

Even more concerning: as optimism declined we also noticed a reversal in the impact the pandemic was having on the genuine concern people had for one another during this crisis.

Concern for Others

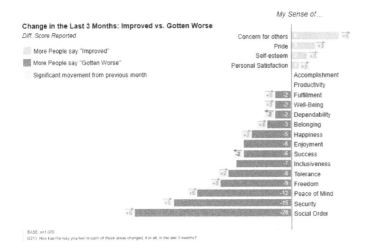

My Sense of...

Change in the Last 3 Months: Improved vs. Gotten Worse
Diff. Score Reported

More People say "Improved"
More People say "Gotten Worse"
Significant movement from previous month

Concern for others	
Pride	
Self-esteem	
Personal Satisfaction	
Accomplishment	
Productivity	
Fulfillment	
Well-Being	
Dependability	
Belonging	
Happiness	
Enjoyment	
Success	
Inclusiveness	
Tolerance	
Freedom	
Peace of Mind	
Security	
Social Order	

D213: How has the way you feel in each of these areas changed, if at all, in the last 3 months?

A particularly bright note, in an otherwise bleak outlook in our early tracking data in Spring 2020, was that one in five Americans were saying the pandemic was improving *their personal sense of concern for others*. This mirrored the good news we saw in a majority (54%) of Americans telling us the pandemic was bringing us closer together. The feeling was similar, for a few months at least, to how we, as a country, came together post 9/11. There was a sense we were in this together and we'd find our way out together.

The feeling of unity was short lived at best. By July 2020, as governors began to announce different policy responses to COVID, most Americans were clear this pandemic was seriously dividing us.

However, while concern for others dropped slightly, we noticed a consistent silver lining of between 10% and 20% of Americans feeling they had *an improved focus on the needs of other people*. This was true up through July 2021. It seemed like the underlying goodness in this country was seeking to lift us past the divide.

Suddenly, just as we saw hope and optimism fall dramatically in one month, from July to August 2021, the percentage of Americans feeling an increase in concern for others also dropped *by nearly 20 points* nationally. The stable sentiment of focusing on the needs of others was being replaced by a growing frustration fueling a decision to "take care of me" and forget about other people.

438

Thankfully, it appears at the time of this writing there is a directional return to becoming more concerned about others beyond self. How will it continue ahead? This dynamic offers the ultimate decision we face as Americans that will determine the outcome of the decade ahead.

An Erosion of Trust Gives Rise to Self Interest

The massive disruption to social order through this past year has caused *anxiety and worry*. Perhaps more lasting in its impact, however, is the erosion of *trust* in our institutions as we have faced what seemingly should have been a crisis that united the American spirit. Clearly it has not.

At the outset of the pandemic, trust in government was already at a near all-time low. We measured that only 34-38% of Americans said they had a great deal or complete trust in federal, state and local governments in March 2020. This has steadily declined to only 18%, at the time of this writing, who trust the federal government (only 11% for Congress), 24% trust state government and 21% trust local government.

Continued Decline in Trust in Government

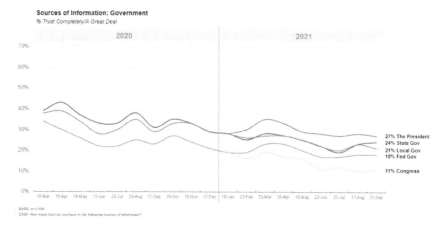

Sources of Information: Government
% Trust Completely/A Great Deal

Trust in the news media has fallen from nearly 40% to 15% over the same time period. *I believe my colleague Mr. Griffen wisely devoted a chapter to the issue of the future of the media.*

Trust in the CDC has dropped from 60% to 39%. Trust in the WHO has dropped from 55% to 32%. Even trust in our local health department has dropped from 48% to 36%.

These are dramatic declines in a very short period of time that cannot avoid reshaping societal constructs. Social order is a casualty when our institutions are no longer relied upon by the majority of Americans. New constructs for trust will be needed to chart a path ahead.

In a recent roundtable session (Fall 2021) we discussed this dynamic in detail with 60+ business leaders across many different sectors. Most (63%) told us they believe what we are experiencing is a fundamental shift in our society similar to something that has happened multiple times before in our history. More than a third (37%), however, believe this is a more catastrophic event, almost *pre-revolutionary* in tone, tenor and direction. Either way this is a big deal.

Beyond trust issues, what else might be the cause of this rapid decline in optimism and increase in self-interest? Our group of business leaders brainstormed and voted 10 root causes at the top that can be summarized into five buckets:

1. Information sources/knowledge
2. Inequality
3. Lost anchors
4. Profiteering polarization
5. Fear from loss of control

Information Sources/Knowledge: During the pandemic we have been inundated with conflicting information, guidelines and perspective about what is going on, and what we should do about it. We heard from the White House new terms such as "alternative facts" and "fake news" so many times they now codify the chaos of mis- or self-serving information. Social media, 15 years after hitting mainstream in 2005, has been around long enough that its advanced algorithms now fuel the echo chamber and special interest tribes.

Can we be surprised that we don't trust each other or the information we hear that doesn't align with our view?

Inequality: The pandemic has accelerated the gap between the haves and have-nots in ways previously impossible to note within a lifetime. In just 18 months, as so many have lost so much, we have collectively watched a trio of billionaires ride their rockets into space only to come back and thank us for having "paid for it" for them.

Can we be shocked that people are losing trust that anyone is out to give them a voice?

Lost Anchors: The pandemic isolated us in many ways from many social connections in education, religious practice, activities and even core Americana ideals. This trend has been documented prior to the pandemic as a major contributing factor to the ardent and passionate support for Trump. During the pandemic it became more tangible and widespread as we literally lost physical and emotional connection with others in the age of social distancing.

Can we wonder why we have lost trust in each other or why we crave the familiar more than ever?

Profiteering Polarization: The 2020 election, held in the heat of the pandemic between two octogenarians in a political climate of extreme partisan divide and vitriol, was evidence that practically brought "fight club" to mainstream culture. Trump's failure to concede, the uprising on January 6 and the continued efforts to demean the other side have become the hallmark of party politics in the U.S. But it's not an accident. The system, political parties and the new media that relies on their ad spend, is producing exactly what it is designed to yield…a lot of money, power and control to those running the parties and media outlets. The incentive is to keep us polarized in order to profit on the intensity of the chaos…on both sides.

Can we truly not see why the average American voter sees little reason to participate in the process? Are we surprised that family and friends censor topics to save relationships?

Fear From Loss of Control: Fear is this COVID-19's middle name. Loss of money, home, connections, opportunity and hope have characterized the dynamics that individuals and families have come to terms with during this pandemic. For some, the fear is paralyzing. For others, the fear is a catalyst for acting out pent-up aggressions. Each of us, in our own way, is seeking to find a little more control.

Can we honestly be caught unaware that people who are afraid will have a hard time extending trust?

Together, these factors—misinformation, inequality, lost anchors, polarization and fear/loss of control—are fueling a shift toward self-interest at a time when our country longs for unity and direction.

What the Data are Telling Us
We also have looked at this phenomena through our tracking data. Dr. Carlos Elordi, our resident statistician and magician with *all things big data* at Heart+Mind, looked at what was most correlated with Americans

feeling optimistic, or not, in recent months. Carlos also analyzed what is driving the feeling of division and a personal concern for others. The results are very clear and compelling.

First, we know that Americans feel optimistic when their daily life is improving with a sense of *happiness, enjoyment, security and belonging*. We also know optimism increases the more trust one has in government.

Second, we know that the more Americans feel divided as a country, the more their personal sense of *social order, enjoyment, security and tolerance* drops. Our perception of the strength of social structures and institutions, our own tolerance for others and our own enjoyment in life, predict whether we feel unified or divided. Stronger institutions, more tolerance for those different from us and more joy we find in daily life all contribute to a greater sense of national unity.

Today, those who feel the most worried about the pandemic, those with higher education and more money, and those with the least trust in the federal government, see a highly divided country. Each of these groups is turning to their "tribe" to fight "the other side" and look out more for themselves.

Third, the data unquestioningly show that tolerance for and the dependability of those around you are the two greatest contributors to improving your personal sense of concern for others. In contrast, a rapid decline in social order and one's personal sense of security are the two greater drivers of becoming less concerned about others.

- As a country, we have to bring stability to the social constructs that bind us. We need to be focused on the factors that help all people feel more secure, not only certain groups.

- As individuals, we need to be focused on what we can do to be more tolerant of people who are different from us. We also need to find ways to be the dependable person we seek in others around us.

In short, the COVID pandemic has demonstrated the need for systemic changes to shore up the fabric of our social structures to rebuild trust in the decade ahead and bring increased security for all. We must directly and meaningfully address misinformation, inequality, lost anchors, polarization and fear/loss of control. We can and must increase tolerance and promote and provide dependability.

The optimism needed to catalyze growth and change in the coming decade depends on our commitment to take these steps. Can business,

442

the private sector, fill the leadership vacuum we face right now? We think it can. We think it will. Leadership matters. Always. But especially in times of crisis and fundamental change. It defines the character, intent and direction of societal change.

Business Leader Recommendations: August 2021

Our group of business leaders who gathered in August 2021, at our most recent roundtable, expressed a number of ways in which the division in society today is directly impacting their organizations.

Some of the impact is actually positive as business leaders are filling the void that institutional leadership has been leaving behind. Organizations are stepping up with a higher expectation for meaningful purpose and values. This is facilitating deeper conversations about what brands stand for and how their actions align or do not. It is also driving a power shift from the employer to the employee. There is a new focus on mental health as more people are seeking the peace in personal and professional life balance. There also seems to be a rapid increase in attention to diversity and inclusion.

But in other ways the impact is more significant and clearly negative:

- Many told us they are facing higher turnover and new job candidates coming in with a very different self-interest profile.
- Some say a new divisiveness has emerged between management and staff with a lower acceptance of consensus-building and willingness to collaborate on tough issues.
- Others are seeing increased mental health claims and confrontational interaction with customers.
- Many see skepticism, distrust and cynicism on the rise, even being treated as a "virtue".
- Most feel the pressure of being caught in the middle of political extremes as the general public more loudly expresses their view directly at companies.
- Many are having to address the difficulty of discussing current events at work, with division among their staff on political beliefs, driving highly emotional narratives.

These issues in the workplace are but a microcosm of the reality we all experience in our families and communities today in different ways. What can we do about it?

Our group of business leaders came up with a few specific recommendations for the opportunity in front of businesses today and into the decade ahead in this time of division:

- Be a leader in what you stand for AND how you act.
- Embrace diversity and inclusion.
- Influence public officials and institutions for positive change.
- Find authentic ways to make a difference in the communities where you operate.
- Provide a vision of hope and emphasize the good in society.
- Be a purpose-driven/purpose-based organization by choice.
- Lead with unifying products, services and solutions.

The trust afforded business today means this is possible. Our Pulse national survey showed 33% of Americans trust their employer and that has only dipped slightly to 28% over the last 18 months. A foundation exists, but it is not strong (for comparison, 27% trust the U.S. President today).

Directly within the political sphere, is it possible to unite around some common ground issues and build momentum for bringing change?

Again, exploring this question with our business leader group we struggled to find the silver bullet issue today around which we can unite. The dilemma is interesting because the issues we generated as possible ways into the unity are also the most complex and fraught with political extremes:

- Poverty
- Terrorism
- Infrastructure
- Climate Change/Catastrophic Weather Events
- Mental/Emotional Health
- Community Health/Impact—Localized Connections
- Cyber Security
- Importance of Family
- Future of Our Children/Protecting Children

It would seem this list actually represents some of the most compelling issues that we must address in the decade ahead. I believe our business leader group optimistically hoped that the gravity of these issues alone will be sufficient enough to drive us to collaborative solutions.

Optimism Now vs. The Decade Ahead

In February 2021, only 28% of Americans told us they felt optimistic given recent events—36% told us they felt worried. At the time, the most improved value in the country was a concern for others at 29%—this was especially true among Gen Z (40%) and younger Millennials (36%). This value improved to 49% of those who were optimistic about the decade ahead, the highest group with such a reading in the survey results.

Looking ahead, twice as many Americans (60%) in February said they were optimistic *about the decade ahead*. This measure came shortly after President Joe Biden's inauguration as the country took a collective sigh of relief after the events of January 6. It's not surprising, then, that those most optimistic about the decade ahead at that time were people most supportive of Biden:

- Democrats 69% vs. Republicans 56%
- Liberals 66% vs. Conservatives 52%
- Urban 64% vs. Rural 56%
- Minorities 64-72% vs. Whites 58%

Even so, this optimism for the decade ahead still was expressed by a majority of all people surveyed at the time. The 2020 COVID reality had caused 28% of Americans to feel more optimistic about the decade ahead and 29% to feel less optimistic. But for a plurality (43%) their sentiment for the future was not changed by their 2020 COVID experience.

The more deeply-seated sentiment today, however, appears to be pessimism over optimism. Half of those who expressed optimism for the coming decade offered both positive and negative emotions about current events. In sharp contrast, 77% of the super pessimistic could only think of negative emotions about current events, offering no positive emotion felt at all. They have a strong negative filter through which they are seeing daily life today.

Wrapping up late summer 2021, as of September, we find half of the country are only able to express negative emotions (48%) about current events and very few (14%) experiencing only positive emotions. This negativity remains highest with Trump voters and Whites. Where they go from here will sharply influence the national sentiment in the coming decade.

The central theme of our collective COVID-19 story and how it will shape the decade ahead centers on its impact upon *familiarity and security*. The sudden and extended disruption of everything familiar to us has threatened security on all fronts: personal, familial, financial, physical, communal, societal, etc. At times this has caused us to reach out and help others. But at other moments we have felt and experienced the opposite, choosing to "control" our own destiny by shutting out and even belittling other people, other views or other ideas.

I believe the desire to lift another, however, will prevail over the debilitating division that results from the tribal individualism in response to threats on our security. But we must choose this path as a people, collectively and individually. To succeed, it must flow beyond security to directly

445

address the happiness, enjoyment, and belonging that Americans feel in daily life.

This is the recipe for optimism to achieve our potential in the decade ahead:

1. Individual focus on improving tolerance of others and personal dependability for those around us.
2. Collective focus on happiness, enjoyment and belonging.
3. Practical and meaningful efforts to address systemic solutions for misinformation, inequality, lost anchors, polarization and fear/loss of control.

And, I now turn the turntable back to your primary author, my long time colleague, Douglas Griffen, after playing the Side B track: *The values and emotions of Americans at the beginning of the decade.*

Adds Author Griffen

Deep tracks there, Maury. I mean, I was looking for a couple of paragraphs on the future of joy in the decade ahead. Lost anchors and profiteering polarization? But I get it. The reason why this may be the *most consequential decade of our lives* is that it has become the *most complex decade of our lives*.

As an optimist at heart, I endorse your recipe for optimism in the decade ahead, but that recipe will need to confront many of our fundamental challenges identified in the Foresight 2030 project: addressing the American Divide and returning to civil dialogue (a better way of showing respectful tolerance for others); reminding ourselves what really matters in our lives that creates a genuine sense of joy (the reawakening we felt during the pandemic); and being willing to address many of the tough issues ahead including disequity, disinformation and destabilization (a return to a sense of control and an American Dream that matters).

We went down a dangerous path of American self interest over the past four years that was inconsistent with the need to recognize the collaboration needed for a *global* future. The rise of personal/self interest draws the same parallel. This is a decade where we must balance personal interest with the value of a collective societal interest. This is the core societal rebuilding that Maury alludes to. We can still have pride in the *American Tribe* but we need to support and respect everyone that is part of the tribe. Otherwise we head down the 1954 path that William Goulding described in *Lord of the Flies*: the choice between living together in a civil manner or decaying to individualism at all costs. *I actually read the book in high school.* Gave me a headache trying to understand it then. I understand it better now.

Maury graciously invited me to speak on the issue of self interest for a minute at his Heart+Mind Business Roundtable on August 26. *Give me a minute and I'll stretch it to five.* I outlined five fundamental causes of self interest:

1. DISINFORMATION: Massive disinformation means I can back up my view. I am right and I can show you the evidence. And I will *shout* it out without regard to you/others.
2. DECLINE IN CIVICS AND CIVILITY: We have not only devalued Civics Education in America, but we no longer even know how to engage in civil discourse.
3. AMERICA FIRST SO WHY NOT ME FIRST: It was a bad message that set the wrong tone. I will lead with *me* in the future without regard to *you.*
4. THE DUMBING DOWN OF AMERICA: Seriously, everyone has a responsibility to be informed. Take the time to be *accurately* informed on the issues that matter.
5. LACK OF A SERVICE ETHIC: Too few people are stepping up to serve the greater good. It's like a national NIMBY movement. John Kennedy would roll over in his grave.

I have often thought of a concept of *an invisible guardrail* that is built on American values and the role of civility. It keeps people from doing stupid things. When I go up to the top of a tall building, or stand at the edge of a canyon, I stay back a little. I sense an invisible guardrail. Otherwise, bad things might happen. When we no longer abide by shared values—in our families, in our organizations, in our communities and in our country, bad things will happen. You remove those values, and the role of civil discourse, and respect for the laws, then you remove that guardrail. People don't care about the consequences. *It's all about me, and you're in my way.* And that's the real problem with self interest.

Maybe it's just been too long since we genuinely felt united. There was a period of time when we rallied around COVID in 2020. Then we let politics and feigned *personal freedom* seep in. As we wrap up this chapter and our overall content for Foresight 2030, we reached the 20th anniversary of 9/11. *Twenty years.* That was a reflection on what *genuine freedom* means for a country. I remember the first anniversary in 2002. I was flying into Washington, DC, on an evening business flight. You know how many other people were on that flight? *Zero.* That's how palpable the memory and genuine concern was. *Scared the shit out me.*

Reflecting on Unity

I was in San Francisco this September 11. My daughter Betsy and I (see picture in chapter 10) were swimming an open water race in the Bay. Like every other event and gathering that day, it began with a prayer and remembrance of 9/11. One of the local firemen spoke on stage. 100 wet-suit clad swimmers sang *America the Beautiful*. Not corny. Just quiet and meaningful. Helpful to remember why the country and why being togeth-er matters. It felt good to be doing something hard that day.

I met my friend David Calef and his wife Violeta along the waterfront in San Francisco after the race at the Buena Vista Café. *Perhaps you know the place.* We were talking about 9/11, quietly. They were in New York City on the morning of the attack. *Wow.* What would that have been like? After our discussion they said they were going to do the same thing they do every September 11. Go sit on a bench in the sun, pause and reflect. I decided to do the same. It felt good to do something quiet that day.

In the decade ahead I don't think we need a catastrophe to create a sense of unity to bridge the American Divide. No one genuinely wants that. But perhaps some genuine reflection and historical context would help the cause. I wonder what my parents—that *greatest generation* that chose to serve—would think of the political and social discourse of the present day.

Our purpose in this chapter—*Surveyin' USA*—was to step back and see how the values and emotions of Americans were being affected by the global pandemic and politics of the early part of this *roller-coaster* of a decade. We have to ride out this roller-coaster together. I think if we hang on together it will prove to be a hell of a good ride in the long run. We are a little upside down now, which is part of the thrill, I suppose, but I'm with my friend Maury that a smoother ride ahead and a little more control over the track will be the ride we enjoy more. Together.

Giles (left) and Griffen collaborating on Chapter 12, Summer 2021 in Utah

AFTERWORD: Reflecting on 2020 and the Start of the Decade

Stand up in a clear blue morning
Until you see
What can be
Alone in a cold day dawning
Are you still free?
Can you be?
...
When some sad old dream reminds you
How the endless road unwinds you
While you see a chance
Take it

--Steve Winwood, While You See a Chance (1980)

Let's be honest. 2020 was not the year any of us had anticipated. Not you. Not me. Not anyone. Reflecting back again on January 1, 2020, on the beach in Tortola, I was certain it was the start of the *best decade of my life*. A plan for a book about the future, *Foresight 2030*, would help me launch the decade. On the island, the sun was hot, the cerveza was cold and the vibe was ideal. Then, it all changed in 2020. The wind shifted our course. But I still think it is going to be the best decade of my life. And I hope it will be the same for you.

But I finally get to say it: *Hindsight is 2020.* It's in our rear view mirror. The year that we did not anticipate at the start of the decade may have changed the entire trajectory of the decade. In a single word, it was *disruptive.* In fact, it was the *perfect storm* of disruption.

It was disruptive *politically*. We endured one of the most divisive presidential elections of our time and, while there was a winner, it's still not clear what direction our country will take in the decade ahead. Will we unite to close the gaps that have been persistent for so long, open up a new era of opportunity and move past historical inequities? Or do we fortify the lines of division, use disinformation to disagree on everything, let civility decay in every aspect of our daily lives?

It was disruptive *economically*. Shelter in place. Shut it down. Close the doors. We literally had to print money to save the economy. Payroll Protection, SBA Disaster Loans, Unemployment Payments, Stimulus Checks. Remarkably, we got through the year and now many businesses can't find the people they need to keep their operations going. A neon sign is flashing *inflation ahead*. And, we know we need to invest in our infrastructure for the decade, but the same government that moved quickly to react to a crisis in 2020 has shifted into *slow motion* in 2021.

It was disruptive *socially*. A global pandemic that shook our lifestyles to the core. A summer of protests that shook our country to the core. For many students it was a lost year of education, for many parents it was a loss of a work routine. It's just weird when you get up to go to work but then you stay home to go to work.

2020 was like a giant snow globe. So clear and peaceful at the start of the year, and then we just shook it all year long—so by the end of the year you couldn't see a thing. But that's the great thing about disruption. It shakes *everything and everybody* up. It's an equal opportunity snow globe. We were all swirling around in 2020 and into 2021. But now it's time to see where we want to land as we turn the corner into 2022. *Perhaps it will be a restart of the decade.*

While you see a chance, take it. That's what's at stake now for this decade ahead. Like the swirling flakes in the snow globe, everything is up in the air right now. We all have to decide where we want the decade to go and what we want to change. And, unlike the store-bought globe that you shake and it looks the same when the flakes settle down, our globe could look entirely different. That's the great consequence of disruption—everything can look different.

So, *in hindsight*, 2020 was an accelerator. Disruptive, but an accelerator. But it sets the stage for a very different decade ahead *if we take the chance*. And who needs to take the chance? Just about everybody:

- ✓ OUR EDUCATORS: Education needs to look very different in the decade ahead. It isn't about K-12 anymore. We need to start with *Pre-K* and understand that if we don't set the environment correctly for learning early, we will have lost a learning window we cannot recover. We need to draw more talented people into the education profession and compensate them as if the success of future generations depends on it. Because it does. And we need to rethink the pathways into careers so more people can find the work and purposeful impact they want to make. And we all need to be life-long learners.

451

- ✓ OUR WORKFORCES: Our Foresighters were very clear on this. The dignity, the value, the sense of accomplishment and the idea of being something larger than yourself will always draw us to meaningful work. But we can't have the workplace itself be what diminishes our workforce. Don't say the words *Diversity, Equity and Inclusion* like they are an HR initiative, live them as values and ideas as leaders and as organizations. We need great organizations to do great things in this country, and globally as well. In the decade ahead, these great organizations can be the catalysts for needed social change.
- ✓ OUR INFORMERS: We cannot operate in the decade ahead on multiple versions of the same facts. Traditional media and social media need to be stewards of the truth. I can't have CNN on in one room and Fox on in another room and hear two entirely different realities. The media need to be relentless watchdogs and investigators to uncover the truth and uphold the virtue of transparency. When governments, politicians and special interest groups interfere with a free media by distorting reality, we will distort our decade.
- ✓ THE NEXT POLITICAL GENERATION: The decade ahead needs a new political generation to step forward. A problem-solving generation. A bipartisan generation. One that is guided by American values and ideals, and not sidetracked by lobbyists, political ego/ambition and political-party gamesmanship. One of the remarkable outcomes of the 2020 pandemic and level of disruption is the realization that a government really matters. Let the decade ahead usher in a set of new politicians that inspire us, not embarrass us.
- ✓ OUR GLOBAL COMMUNITY: Part of our human diversity is that we can have a globe full of different countries, cultures, languages and people. This is likely to change a bit in the decade ahead, but the United Nations tells us that there are 195 sovereign states at the end of 2020—and if you include the two UN observer states of Vatican City and Palestine—you are at 197. The U.S. *cannot* be an isolationist entity in the decade ahead. There is too much as stake with climate change, terrorism, human rights abuse and avoiding the *next global pandemic.* Or getting out of this one, for that matter.

While you see a chance, take it. And for the decade ahead, that also means for all of us as individuals and our families. Where do you want to land after this disruptive 2020? What did 2020 tell you about what matters personally? Look, I actually wrote down in January 2020 (see chapter 1) what I intended to focus on for the decade ahead...in *hindsight,* I am looking back at my plan to see how 2020 affected what matters to me so I can still make this my best decade ever. So, the window is open for all of us, the chance to reconsider the direction of your journey:

- ✓ YOU CAN LIVE ANYWHERE: Within reason, of course. But the reality is, that for many people/families, there is a new level of geographic independence. Technology enables virtual work (that doesn't mean you have to work from your kitchen, hall closet or garage), so you can have a professional work environment in a location, community and region of the country that fits your family and your lifestyle.
- ✓ WORK WITH A PURPOSE: If the economy rebounds the way we think it will post-2020/2021 and post-pandemic, then there will be a lot of organizations looking for talent. Looking for *you*. Who do you want to work with *for the rest of the decade*? What kind of organization? What size? What industry? Remember, the snow globe is still in full shake mode, that disruption will settle in at some point.
- ✓ RETHINK YOUR LIFESTYLE: 2020 was a great *reawakening* for many people about what really mattered. Health, fitness and wellness. Open space. Re-engaging with family and friends. Purposeful travel. Finding the lifestyle that creates the life balance. Remembering why social interaction has an upside. We are really not wired to be isolated in the decade ahead. Rediscover the joy of discovery.
- ✓ TAKE A STAND ON WHAT MATTERS: Don't be the silent majority in the decade ahead. Be informed, take a stand on the issues that matter. Be engaged in your community, in your school, in your home-owners association. Be more civically aware. Volunteer for something, *anything*. Being engaged creates a level of ownership for the future, for the decade ahead. Be an owner in this decade, not a victim.
- ✓ BE FUELED BY OPTIMISM: It's been a theme throughout the book. I am not talking about cheerleading, a Pollyanna view, but to approach the decade with a sense of what can be done, what the opportunities are, not why the road is so difficult. The car goes where the driver's eyes go. Optimism is a decision. You see different doors, optimism becomes the pass-key. Besides, It's a hell of a lot less stressful.

While you see a chance take it. Despite the disruptive 2020/2021, I believe it sets the stage for the most consequential decade of our lives. Well, at least for mine. We could have come out of 2020 in far worse shape—further devastated by a pandemic with no vaccine; an economy that had moved into a genuine depression; a political outcome that was heading us into further isolation, closing down social reform and opportunity.

2020 was a reminder of how quickly things can change, how fragile we are as a democracy, how important normalcy and simplicity can be in our lives. But also that choices matter. The ones we make individually, the ones we make as a country, the ones we make as a globe. Life is a journey, choose your destination well.

And it's time you should be going
While you see a chance
Take it

Best of the decade ahead to all. See you in 2030.

Douglas S. Griffen

The Griff Squad, aging nicely, and looking forward to the decade ahead!

454

I'm handing over the Foresight book today to Amazon for publishing. *That's exciting.* It's been a long journey over the course of 2020/2021. We are all a little exhausted, I suspect, reflecting on the last two years.

December 7, 2021. Wow. It's the 80th anniversary of the attack on Pearl Harbor. Did you take a moment to reflect on the day and the event? We did in Arizona. We have a rather powerful and emotional connection with Pearl Harbor. On that morning, 80 years ago, 1,777 died when the USS Arizona battleship was sunk. I know most of you have visited Hawaii on a vacation. Have you visited the USS Arizona Memorial? You should. It's somber and powerful. It reminds us that we are all Americans. Almost on cue this morning there was a glorious orange Arizona sunrise here in the desert. I am quite sure that John McCain flipped the light switch. Even from above, I knew he would remember.

It's a little uneasy in the country and world today, isn't it? And I mean *today*, on December 7, 2021. The new omicron variant has us a little spooked. Russia is massing troops on the Ukraine border and Biden and Putin are testing each other's nerves on a call this morning. China has its eyes on Taiwan and we just had our diplomats boycott the upcoming Winter Olympic Games in Beijing. *I don't think any of the diplomats were actually competing.* Bob Dole passed away two days ago and will lie in state this week. A symbol of bipartisanship and selfless service. A young congresswoman jokes about another congresswoman being a terrorist because of her Islamic faith. A symbol of self interest and hate. The Supreme Court is considering taking up Roe v. Wade. And no matter what the outcome, it is sure to divide us even further as a country.

The stakes are high as we head into 2022. It's still a little unclear what direction we will take in the decade ahead. December 7 reminds us of what it means to be united. Tomorrow may remind us of what it means to be divided. It's all why this decade is so important. The decade is in play now. *The most consequential decade of our lives.*

> *The Foresight 2030 project will be providing an analysis/ update at the end of each calendar year from 2022 through 2029 to reflect on the events of the year and how they influenced and impacted the decade. Please visit www.foresight2030.info for further information on updates.*

EPILOGUE

I like Fridays. I suppose we all do. But a Friday in Park City when the ski season is on *and it's your birthday?* Well, now you're talking. And it's not just any birthday, it's number 65. The U.S. Government says I am eligible for Medicare. My Epic ski pass says I am eligible for an afternoon of skiing. Both are valuable, I just choose to focus on the skiing.

I've had a house in Park City since 2008, but I have been coming up to Park City since I was in college. It's always been a great vibe. A mining town turned into a ski town. A great Main Street that turns back the clock. Perfect after a good snowstorm in the winter with strings of lights overhead and a vibrant restaurant/bar scene. A totally different scene in the summer with everyone walking the streets with their dogs and heading up to the end of Main Street for *Park Silly* on a Sunday, arts and crafts, food and entertainment, slow down and kick back.

If I had not been an *Arizonan* originally, I am quite sure I would have been a *Parkite.* How cool it would have been to grow up here, learn to ski when you are five years old, hike and bike all summer long with your family and friends, play sports and go to the Park City High School, enjoy the seasons. *But no! The Griffens are third generation Arizonans and we love the summers when it hits 118 degrees.* I remember driving north to Payson, Arizona, in my parents' 1957 Chevy station wagon when we were building the cabin. *Could have just pointed the Chevy a little further north, padre.*

So I have settled for a balance, splitting time between Arizona and Park City. But when I am in Park City, I just pretend that I have been placed in the *witness protection program* and that I am a local Parkite. I read the *Park Record* newspaper, I have an old 2002 GMC Suburban (Big Red) that I keep at the house that has Utah license plates (the plates that say *greatest snow on earth),* I drop into the No Name Saloon occasionally on a Saturday night, and I'll eat breakfast at the counter at Squatter's on a Sunday morning on my way into skiing. As a long time Parkite, I know that Squatters was originally the Mt. Aire Cafe and was the best local breakfast 50 years ago.

457

So, I smile as I drive past Squatters (aka, Mt. Aire) and head to the ski area on this, my 65th birthday. Big Red is transporting me; it's an authentic ski-mobile, it just looks like it belongs in Park City. Ski rack on top, plenty of well deserved dings on the body and just a little rust on the bumper. I have the window down, it's overcast and cold, but feels good out. I've got a good Bob Seger tune on the FM radio. Left the house about noon after a little work in the morning. I emphasize *little*. Kind of jazzed for a good afternoon of skiing; after all it only takes me 10 minutes to get from my house to the Park City ski area.

I look to my left and there is a sports car. I feel like I am driving a semi compared to the little Fiat. But I love what this guy has done with the spoiler on the back of his car. He has taken his snowboard and *a pair of bungie cords* and attached the snowboard to the spoiler. I swear the snowboard is wider than the car. I looked back at the driver, he has this great handlebar mustache, a pair of aviator sun glasses and a *shit-eating grin* on his face. I smiled back, we are both headed for a traditional Park City Friday afternoon on the slopes. *A kindred Parkite.*

I've been looking forward to this birthday and this afternoon. It's been 15 years since my 50th birthday in Vail when I decided to write a book about the future. It's been 15 years since I had the realization that I was just beginning the second half of my life journey and that I was sure I could stay as active for the next 25 years as I was for the previous 25. *So far so good.* No guarantees after age 75, but that will be *after* the current decade. We'll deal with that in 2031. Maybe I'll write a sequel: *Foresight 2040: Still Crazy After All These Years.* Big Red and I will still be hanging in there. Hopefully on our way to the ski area.

But for now, in January 2021, I am pretty *stoked.* I have completed the 10 Foresight sessions with the wrap up session on January 21. Biden won the election and, in my very humble opinion, reset the country and my decade ahead. We are beginning to emerge out of a *global pandemic* which may fundamentally alter the rest of the decade and how we think about everything from work, to technology, to our lifestyle and to what matters to us. What a paradox: such a bright opportunity for the decade ahead after such a strange start in 2020, but yet so divided as a country when we should be so united after the shared experience. *Get it together.*

I've got some writing to do in the next few months to reflect on 2020/2021 and incorporate all of these *Foresights* together for the book. *Mucho trabajo mañana.* But for right now, there is only one task at hand. Some light flakes are beginning to fall as I pull into the ski area base parking lot. You have to know the local timing rules in Park City. Either be in the lot by 8:15am or wait until noon when the morning skiers are bail-ing out. Today was a nooner. I grab a front row parking spot. I consider it a small birthday gift.

Now some more local knowledge for you. There are two ways up the mountain in Park City. You can pull into the *Canyons* side of the mountain, park and take the *cabriolet* lift, which is like standing in a soup can, to get to the mountain base, then take either the Red Pine Gondola or the Orange Bubble Express up to the runs. Interesting, but almost always crowded and a lot of work to get to your first run. A better option, known to us local Parkites, is the Eagle lift at the *Park City* side (the other half of the mountain). Grab your *front row* parking spot, walk 50 yards, jump on without the crowds and you will be on *Temptation,* which is a tasty first run in a matter of minutes.

But wait! There is one more thing that I always look forward to on my birthday when I am skiing in Park City. One you kind of have to know about on how ski passes and scanning systems work, but I have always admired the IT dude that put in this little *Easter Egg.* On the first lift in Park City they scan your pass with a hand-held scanner. It just brings up your picture (heaven forbid you are using your friend's pass!) and logs you in for marketing purposes. *But on your birthday:* it blasts out the Beatle's song *Today is Your Birthday!* I raise my voice and I call to my fellow skiers in the lift line to lean in: *Scan Me!* And it does not disappoint. "*Dude!*" somebody nearby barks out, "*Have a great birthday!*" I am ecstatic. I am 65 and I can still pass in Park City as a *dude.*

Up the Eagle lift. The liftie at the top gives me a glance as I am about to get off the lift. I lower my goggles off the top of my helmet and turn to him and say: "*The Eagle has landed.*" I get nothing in return on this. The liftie is probably 17 years old. No historical context. No hindsight, no *foresight.* No worries, I may be a little over-amped anyway. *It's my birthday.*

When I ski a half day on the mountain I have a pretty good routine. Eagle up to my favorite first run which is *Temptation.* Aptly named, a nice cruiser that you can push a little if you want, it feels like you are on your own ridge line heading into a valley. That takes you to the King Con lift (short for Consolidated, one of the old mining companies in Park City). There are about ten parallel runs that feed off of King Con—Sitka, Shamus, Climax, Seldom Seen and even a return loop to Temptation are a few of my favorites. Like eating an ear of corn on skis. 45 minutes into your afternoon and you have a half dozen runs in.

Then work your way up the mountain. A few runs off of Silverlode lift to Mel's Alley, Hidden Splendor, Newport and Assessment. When it gets a little crowded on Silverlode lift, I just drop off the other side to Motherlode and ski two of my favorite runs—Parley's Park to Carbide Cut and Sunnyside, which keeps you on the Mother *Toad* and is like its own ski area. I swear half the people on the mountain have never skied over there, which is great, never a line on the lift and plenty of open space on the runs.

Snowing a little harder now. It's about 3:00pm and you really have to want to be out here to still be on the mountain. I want to be out here. *It's my birthday*. But it's more than that. I missed the entire season in 2020 with a combination of knee surgery in late 2019 and the shutdown of the ski season in March due to the pandemic. It's just good to be back on the mountain, quiet runs, remembering the rhythm, enjoying the vibe. It's good to be a 65-year-old *dude*.

I know where I have to head now. It's a run off the beaten path that leads to the lift most people don't even know about. Let's start with the run. *Keystone*. It's not long, but when you drop into it, it just feels a little timeless. It's your own private roller-coaster. Winds its way through the trees, narrow but comfortable. Opens up a little at the end. Stay up high left and it's always great snow. It drops you past some of the old mining structures into the Thaynes lift. On Clown Day in Park City (April 1), Keystone is also the secret access to the trail that leads to the locals' party on the mountain. I cannot reveal the access to you, but I can reveal that there are plentiful PBRs and you have to be a local to be admitted. And if you don't know what a PBR is, then you definitely wouldn't be admitted.

Now, there are a couple of things about the Thaynes lift that make it a birthday must for me. It's kind of like a real miner's camp with all of the old mining structures around. Like some miners just built it for their use in the winter. The lift is right next to the actual Thaynes Shaft which was sunk down in 1937 as part of mining operations by the Silver King Coalition. The shaft goes down 1700 feet to hit the Spiro tunnel. *And this has what to do with skiing?* Well, in 1965 you could board an ore car some four miles away where the Spiro tunnel begins (now in the Silver Star development) and go *underground* with your skis to the Thaynes shaft and ride the shaft elevator 1700 feet up to the surface and—voila!—you were at the Thaynes lift. It was called the *Skier's Subway* and actually operated for four seasons.

'Skiers Subway' in 1965 at the entrance to Spiro Tunnel (mining cars to the left)

Sounds like it would have taken all afternoon just to get to the lift. So, my route of dropping in from Keystone seemed like a better way of getting to the Thaynes lift. Aside from the mining nostalgia, the other reason that the Thaynes lift was a must today is that it is a classic *two-seater*. Around the fly-wheel and no matter how capable or well-meaning the lift operator is, it still *hits you in the ass* and you just hang on and settle in. It's a bit of a relic, which I guess just matches up perfectly with me on this fine January day for my 65th birthday.

Keystone run, Park City Ski Area (1/29/2021)

Thaynes chair—All Aboard!

461

The snow is really coming down now. It's getting close to 4:00pm. Just about everyone is off the mountain now. A few of us heading up the Thaynes two seater for a last run. I drop back into the Keystone run, quiet, surreal. Up high left as it opens up at the end I catch fresh powder, and then back to the Thaynes lift. I am the last one on the lift as they rope it off—closing time. I look ahead at the chairs and realize I am the *only one* on the lift. *It's right where I want to be.*

This decade ahead is going to be a wild ride. I think it's going to be my best decade ever. And I hope it will be for you as well. When it gets a little too wild out there, a little too noisy, a little too connected and a little too unclear, just take a Friday afternoon and find your own Keystone run and Thaynes lift. Clear the noise, reset the mechanism. But then get back out there.

…
Against the wind
I'm still running against the wind
I'm older now but still runnin'
Against the wind.

--Bob Seger and the Silver Bullet Band Against the Wind

Author Griffen, January 29, 2021

APPENDICES

APPENDIX 1: *A Summary of the Foresight Influences on the Decade Ahead*

In each of our 10 Foresight sessions we developed a set of *influences* on the decade ahead. In most cases our Foresighters assessed the influences in terms of the *level of impact* they might have if they occurred, and, secondly, the *likelihood of occurring*. We thought it would be interesting to provide the list of influences (by topic) in the appendix. They are presented in their original order before any assessments; you can refer back to that actual chapter in the book to see our assessments and key insights.

How do *you* see these influences in the decade ahead? Which are the most impactful, the most likely? What influences did we miss at the start of the decade and what *new influences* are emerging as we move through the decade?

We hope that you will consider these influences personally, and we would be honored if these become the subject of a classroom or workplace debate. Not likely that they will make it to the Thanksgiving dinner table discussion, *but perhaps they should*. Enjoy!

FORESIGHT SESSION 1: *Setting The Baseline* **(conducted March 19, 2020). A set of 20 overall decade influences that could positively impact the decade ahead if they occurred. (Assessment of these influences and our analysis is covered in Chapter 2.)**

No.	Idea
1.	CLIMATE CHANGE: We addressed climate change in a meaningful and measurable way on a global basis. Corporations and governments were fully aligned on long-term strategies. At the end of the decade, the scientists agree we had turned the corner.
2.	GEN Z INFLUENCE: The impact of Gen Z into the workforce and society, a new set of values that will help solve problems and address social issues. (Gen Z are generally considered to have been born between 1995 and 2015, now 5-25 years old. There are 74 million in the U.S. alone.)
3.	GUN VIOLENCE: A change in attitude, regulation and behaviors regarding gun violence, active shooter situations and mass shootings, that significantly reduces gun violence in the U.S./ globally. Schools, especially, feel safe again.

4. OPIOID CRISIS: We have addressed the opioid crisis in a significant way and provided treatment to those addicted, and reversed the trend of oversubscribing by the medical community. (Currently, some 130 people a day die in the U.S. alone.)

5. RACIAL INEQUALITY: The decade has created a new and widespread level of understanding about racial inequality as a fundamental divide in our society. It feels like it is in "the rear view mirror" and we feel like one people at work, at school, at our communities and in our neighborhoods.

6. TECHNOLOGY BALANCE: We seemed to have found the right balance with the role of technology in our lives and the value of personal interaction and emotional connection. There is a genuine analog balance to digital world.

7. 4th INDUSTRIAL REVOLUTION: The revolution arrived in the decade, but we managed it effectively. We took advantage of artificial intelligence, voice activation, the internet of things and autonomous vehicles in a way that was productive and enhanced our workplace and society. Jobs/tasks that were replaced simply allowed people to be retrained and activate their skills in a new way.

8. GLOBAL CONFLICT: Governments and leaders leveraged negotiation and long-term interests to defuse many long-standing global/regional conflicts. Bodies like the UN were re-tooled to help mediate and resolve conflict. Conflicts that arose were quickly addressed by global interests.

9. MIDDLE CLASS: The divide between the haves and the have-nots changed during the decade where a new middle class arose. They were the drivers of the new economy, hard working but well compensated. The new middle class was easy to get into and a great place to stay. You were welcome to go further and move on to a different wealth category, but many found the middle as the right place to be.

10. RETOOLING EDUCATION: Education was completely re-invented. Early childhood education (ECE) became highly valued and publicly funded, and gave children (birth through age eight) the best start possible. All young people had access to quality higher education with no-cost alternatives for community and state colleges, to reasonably priced private universities. Education was far more aligned with the workforce needs, graduates were workforce ready. The majority of graduates entered the workplace debt-free.

11. HEALTH CARE ACCESS: We finally figured it out. How to provide healthcare to everyone in an efficient and low cost way. No one was denied healthcare and there were still options/providers that people could escalate based on their preferences. A more multi-dimensional healthcare model emerged (body/mind/soul) that dealt with the whole person and emphasized preventive and long-term care.

12. GLOBAL PANDEMICS: The world learned from recent pandemics such as SARS, MERS, H1N1, Ebola, Zika and COVID-19 on how to better monitor, prepare for and respond to potential pandemics. While new strains emerged post coronavirus, there were no global pandemics at scale during the decade.

13. COMPASSION: A new level of genuine compassion emerged during the decade. People were more compassionate to each other; families were more united; workplaces were respectful and fully supported diversity and inclusion; communities were more civil. We just treated each other a little better in the decade, fewer people felt lonely or isolated.

14. MENTAL HEALTH: Mental health was completely repositioned in society. Mental health check-ups were as commonplace as the traditional physical. Treatments and therapies were advanced and well beyond drug therapy. PTSD (post traumatic stress disorder) could be diagnosed and managed in effective ways with those individuals fully integrated back into family, workplace and society.

15. POLITICAL UNITY: Remarkably, in the U.S.—as a model for the world—our political divides had been largely bridged. While there was still room for different approaches and ideologies, there was more common ground and effective legislation and policy in the areas that mattered. The U.S. Congress drew in some of the best and brightest in the decade and became one of the most admired institutions in the country.

16. ELEGANT AGING: Our boomer populations were well cared for and respected. Long-term health care was affordable and available, and the general level of wellness and active lifestyles of those in their 60s, 70s and 80s was the envy of many who were 20 years younger.

17. PRESS FREEDOM: No more "fake news", no more journalists jailed or killed. Journalism experiences a rebirth, the press becomes highly admired and respected across the globe. The news and information that are reported are accurate and consistent, we are a more informed society.

18. NEW BOUNDARIES: We have returned to space in a big way. Countries and consortiums have pushed new boundaries of exploration. We have landed people on Mars and established an ongoing base of operations, like the International Space Station, but this one is on the Red Planet. If you want, by the end of the decade, you can go on supersonic craft and orbit the earth and return. It's like a party in the sky.

19. SUSTAINED ECONOMIC GROWTH: While there may be some ups and downs, we were able to sustain measurable economic growth over the decade. Nearly every country participated in the growth and it had a measurable impact on community development and quality of life.

20. INNOVATION AT SCALE: We take a page from the Tesla playbook and apply innovation at scale to a broad set of issues, products, processes and services. We change the way we do things in a modern and forward thinking way. We have really reinvented the way to do just about everything.

FORESIGHT SESSION 2: *The Role of Technology in the Future* (conducted April 30, 2020). A set of 12 technology influences that could be in play by the end of the decade. (Assessment of these influences and our analysis is covered in Chapter 3.)

No.	Idea
1.	UNLIMITED BANDWIDTH: Bandwidth is like air...it is everywhere and everyone has access. You have unlimited bandwidth at home, at work, while you are traveling. We have moved to a smart infrastructure at the regional level where we can adjust the bandwidth thermostat up and down as needed (all automated, of course). There is no more digital divide.
2.	ALONG FOR THE RIDE: Autonomous vehicles are the norm. We are used to them and we all value them. Enter a freeway and the autopilot takes over and slots you into a speed lane. A voice command moves you to your desired off-ramp. Need a ride in a new city? Reserve an autonomous rental, dispatch your Uber ride with a quick voice request on your iPhone 1000. All trucking is handled by autonomous rigs. Autonomous travel is completely safe and incredibly efficient.
3.	CONSTANTLY CONNECTED: Mobile connectivity is an entirely different level. A micro device can be implanted in your ear for crystal clear sound and communications--you can connect with anyone, anywhere with a simple voice command. No need for a video chat, just activate your holographic display for super clear video (with your friends, research a new vacation destination, catch the news...). Another micro implant allows you to transmit what you see. Share a view, share a ski run, share a moment in time.
4.	A NEW LEVEL OF ENERGY: Solar, wind, thermal and hydro technologies have progressed where nearly all residences and many cities are powered by these alternative energies. Home solar/wind units are compact and include adequate storage capacity for any peaks. Devices come with lifetime batteries (micro-generators) so that replacing batteries or worrying about laptop/ phone battery time is no longer an issue. Ninety percent of all cars/trucks are electric and efficient, a combination of rooftop solar and ultra-fast drive-by recharging panels have eliminated the need for electric plug in stations. Oh, by the way, the air is MUCH cleaner.

5. HEALTHCARE IS SELFCARE: Home and wearable diagnostics have replaced the need for most doctor visits. Everything is constantly monitored—O_2 level, temperature, heart rate, a monthly scan for diseases, nutrition index and overall health/fitness level. If you do need to see a doctor, it is by tele-med with an ability to run advanced remote diagnostics. Nearly all surgeries, if needed, are outpatient and mostly automated or augmented by robotics and micro-surgery devices. Nearly any joint can be replaced and the replacement joint is superior to the natural joint. There has been a measurable and sustainable increase in life expectancy.

6. WAR GAMES ARE THE REAL GAMES: Most military conflicts are resolved with technology—unmanned aircraft, virtual fences/borders, weapons that are largely controlled by joystick. Advanced cyber approaches allow us to disarm enemies and prevent many conflicts. Stealth advances are amazing: we pretty much know when anyone will make a move before they make it. Shields up, we can avert a strike on any city/location as needed. Our most powerful weapon is technology itself.

7. AGRI-TECH IS THE NEW TECH: Agriculture technology allows us to optimize the nutrition and yield of nearly any crop while eliminating nearly all of the diseases and threats real-time. Pesticides are no longer needed. All watering systems are automated and highly efficient to provide the ideal growing conditions. Fruit has a longer window for retaining ripeness, which minimizes food spoilage and loss. Home gardens with rapid-yield technology supplement the food needs of many families.

8. THE NEW DIGITAL UNIVERSITY: After the pandemic in the early part of the decade, we never really went back to traditional education. Most education was delivered digitally with virtual reality classrooms that allowed us to interact with multiple cultures and learners. Our learning modules were customized and aligned to our career/professional interests and enabled us to be job ready on day one. Educational content could be streamed and stored with a micro-implant and recalled as needed.

470

9. THE 4TH INDUSTRIAL REVOLUTION WAS A PEACEFUL TRANSITION: It did not happen overnight, but it did happen. By the end of the decade the way work was done had been fundamentally changed. Artificial Intelligence, robotics, big data, nanotechnology, ubiquitous 3-D printing and limitless computational power were working in harmony in development, design and manufacturing. Products were better, people were coordinating and applying new knowledge and many previously unsolvable problems had been addressed. The new age created new opportunities. There were still plenty of traditional trades and crafts that people could pursue, but many in Gen Z had become the leaders in the implementation of the revolution, and guided it with purpose and value. The economic divide has been narrowed.

10. SPACE IS THE COOL FRONTIER: Technology advances and private sector investment ushered in a new travel boom—space tourism replaced eco-tourism. A joy ride was now a quick earth orbit or a sling shot around the moon. Multiple planets had destination colonies that you could book for a week, a month or even a year. Nearly every major city on the globe had a space port to transport you to an outlying destination. While not affordable for everyone, it was within reach of many. Our horizons had been expanded.

11. INTELLIGENT RECREATION: Weekend warrior? Would you like to ski better, learn to sail, ride a surfboard, cycle on the road (not on your Peloton at home)? Imagine the micro-intelligence that could be built into a pair of skis. Autosense the slope, the condition of the snow, see the moguls, set a perfect line. Click on the auto-pilot on your ski pole, record the run with your Google goggle-cam. It auto-corrects if you catch an edge. And you can apply this to nearly any sport. Gotta catch that one last ride? Surf's up.

12. VIRTUAL STADIUM: Look, a hot dog and a beer sounds great, but nearly everything else about getting to the ballpark (sport of your choice) is a hassle. Why go to the game when you can be PART OF the game from home. Want to feel what it is like to be the center fielder climbing the wall to rob a home run? Be an NFL running back and accelerate through a narrow gap? Strap in at home and watch the game from any angle, listen to any voice. Everyone on the team has micro cameras you can display, everyone has a mic. Are you a wannabe coach...well, here's what is really going on in that time out!

FORESIGHT SESSION 3: *The Future of Work* **(conducted June 25, 2020). A set of 12 influences that could influence the future of work by the end of the decade. (Assessment of these influences and our analysis is covered in Chapter 4.)**

No.	Idea
1.	PURPOSE BASED ORGANIZATIONS: More organizations/brands will adopt a powerful and compelling "Core Purpose" about the difference they want to make in the world. While they will still want/need to be financially successful, they will be guided in all they do by their fundamental purpose and aligned with values that matter. The core purpose and aligned values will be highly attractive to people who want to be part of that cause and purpose. People will feel like they matter and are making a difference.
2.	GENUINE INCLUSION/DIVERSITY IN THE WORKPLACE: The new decade will create a new openness and acceptance in the workplace for all backgrounds. Diversity becomes a cultural strength and you are encouraged to bring "your best self" to work. The old stereotypes fade away (the "Good Ol' Boys" club, loyalty buys you advancement, personal/sexual favors, wait your turn, etc.) You are welcome and included, respected for your talent and work ethic, encouraged to challenge the status quo and your individuality is appreciated.
3.	VIRTUAL WORKPLACE: The cubicle is dead. The technology, in some ways accelerated by COVID-19, fully enables high-impact, virtual workplaces. Home offices are productive and secure, collaboration tools are amazing and workers have learned to thrive in the virtual space. Life balance is better, travel is reduced (commute and air) and people feel more in control of their schedule and work flow. It doesn't mean we don't get together, it just means that when we do, it really matters and advances our work or sense of workplace community.
4.	COMPENSATION EQUITY: If you do the work, you are compensated at the right level. Pay disequity based on gender, age, race or geography is simply not tolerated any more. Professions that have been constrained in the past by being undervalued by society, even when their contributions have been high (teachers, for example), have seen their compensation realigned to reflect that value.

472

5. MORE ENTREPRENEURIAL OPPORTUNITY: Just about anyone can take their shot on "Shark Tank". More educational institutions and communities are encouraging entrepreneurial activity. Start-up capital is plentiful, the new and small businesses are recognized and supported for their impact to sustaining a growing economy. Innovations are happening at a fast pace and these new start-ups attract passionate people and provide terrific working environments and rewards. Welcome to You, Inc.

6. REALIGNING EDUCATION: The educational environments will fundamentally change to be more aligned with work/career interests. High schools adopt more vocational alignment, you can graduate with a set of skills that you can immediately put into use. Colleges and universities have strong industry partnerships for advanced training where the students are workplace ready and there is a regular return to the campus for experienced workers to further develop their skills. Education and training become more integrated to support lifelong learning.

7. UNIVERSAL HEALTHCARE: While workplaces and employers can enhance healthcare plans, benefits and options, the decade ahead sees an implementation of universal healthcare where all citizens have baseline, quality healthcare. Changing a job does not result in the loss of your base healthcare plan—you are free to move about the market and the geography you desire.

8. LONGER TERM CAREER PATHING: More organizations plan and hire for the long term. Their advanced financial planning and support infrastructure (supported by AI and predictive analytics) insulates them from some of the economic waves that might require reactive downsizing. Longer term career planning is in place with an alignment of the company needs and the individual interests. Pace of advancement can be dialed up or down as required, but the idea of long-term stability and career growth within a single organization has returned for those who have found the right home.

9. NEW GREEN ECONOMIC DRIVERS: An entire new set of jobs, companies and opportunities come into play with a shift to addressing climate change and environmental sustainability. It's not a trend; it's a global commitment that requires a huge investment in talent, process and infrastructure. It's like the WPA (the depression era Works Progress Administration) for the Plant Earth.

10. NATIONAL MINIMUM WAGE: Everyone can get a good start in the workplace with a standardized and fair national minimum wage. If you are willing to work hard, you can earn a good salary and, for many, avoid the need to work multiple jobs just to make ends meet. It's up to you if you want to stay at that minimum wage. Most will want to advance their work and careers and earning capacity, and find that "dream job", but an entry level hourly job brings a good return and feels like meaningful and appreciated work.

11. THE ROBOTS DID NOT TAKE OVER: The 4th Industrial Revolution (a fusion of the digital and physical worlds characterized by artificial intelligence, robotics, 3D printing, cloud computing, The Internet Of Things, advanced wireless, etc.) turned out to be more of an evolution that improved the workplace and made it easier to get things done. Repetitive/menial tasks were further automated just as data entry and the switchboard operator went away in the past. Workers simply had better information support, tools and infrastructure. No Danger, Will Robinson!

12. JOB HARMONY: The job matchers (Indeed, ZipRecruiter, Monster, SquarePeg, Glassdoor, etc.) really ramp up their game in the decade ahead. Their technology and ability to match you to an ideal situation is amazing. They can assess and understand what you are all about and what will let you thrive in a work environment. Companies have huge confidence in them, the employees that are placed match the culture and result in high performance and low turnover.

FORESIGHT SESSION 4: *Division in America* **(conducted August 20, 2020). A set of 15 influences that could impact the level of unity in America by the end of the decade. (Assessment of these influences and our analysis is covered in Chapter 5.)**

No.	Idea
1.	PROLONGED ECONOMIC RECOVERY: Starting in 2021, and influenced by a post-pandemic level of consumer demand and confidence, we experienced a prolonged economic recovery and level of growth that was one of the strongest on record. It was a recovery that nearly every sector and every demographic participated in. A rising tide lifts all boats.
2.	THE PANDEMIC IS BEHIND US: In the 1Q2021 an effective vaccine was validated by phase 3 trials and made available to any American who wished to be vaccinated. The country finally moved to a national set of measures on masks and protocols that helped to achieve a significant reduction in COVID cases. There was an element of herd immunity that occurred and, even after the availability of the vaccine, Americans were careful to adhere to published protocols. By the Summer of 2021 the COVID pandemic was largely behind us. Schools, sports and social activities were fully normalized by the Fall.
3.	WE UNITED ON THE CLIMATE: The U.S. rejoined the Paris Climate Agreement and served as a catalyst to move the world to aggressively address the challenge of climate change. Countries and companies committed resources and set strong goals for carbon reduction, and also to meet the scientific goals of limiting global warming. While it will take decades of continued work, there was agreement that we had reversed the course of climate change and our globe looked positive again for future generations.
4.	RACIAL INEQUALITY WAS FINALLY ADDRESSED: Buoyed by the activism and outcry from events in 2020, including the street protests, sports activism, political change, corporate cultural changes, police policy changes and strong leadership from Black and other minority groups, the decade saw a fundamental reversal of racial inequality in the country. Our leadership looked like our communities. While we might still value and appreciate our racial heritages, we valued being equally treated Americans above anything else.

5. THE REBIRTH OF THE MIDDLE CLASS: The highest growth of any economic segment in the decade was the new middle class. Strong economic growth and new opportunities enabled nearly every American family willing to work hard to have a strong level of earning power and financial security. In many respects, the new middle class was the place to be—financially comfortable, a balanced work/life environment, career growth and a terrific environment to raise a family. The Gen Z crowd fully endorsed the lifestyle.

6. A NEW UNITED NATIONS: Strengthened by global collaboration and success in addressing two of the most significant issues facing mankind—climate change and the COVID-19 pandemic—the world moved to a new level of cooperation. The United Nations and other global organizations such as the WHO enjoyed a new level of attention and investment. You could still flex your nationalistic muscle and protect your borders, but the world realized that a peaceful and more united globe allowed leaders to focus more on their people, economic strategies and social agendas. Conflicts, when they occurred, were short and were quickly addressed by global leaders.

7. A WOMAN AT THE HELM: The decade finally saw the election of a woman to the U.S. presidency. It was an election that was supported by nearly every demographic, and the new president ushered in a new respect for women's leadership and equal footing. For younger girls/women it was a sign of great hope for their futures; for the world it was a sign that the U.S. had finally caught up. It created pride for all Americans that we had moved past one of the last gender biases.

8. HOW ABOUT THAT MARS LANDING: The bold goal of reaching Mars with a manned mission was achieved with spectacular success. A combination of NASA, private firms such as SpaceX and a global collaboration pulled it off, with the landing being one of the most watched moments of the decade. It was not going to be a one shot deal; it was determined from the landing and exploration that Mars was suitable for a colonization effort in the next decade (2030-2039) and there was a sense that we had reopened the universe. Adding to the national pride, it was an American who was first to walk out of the landing vehicle. In an odd twist, a small, previously-farmed potato field was found in a valley near the landing vehicle.

9. BIPARTISAN POLITICS: While the decade did not see an end to the traditional two-party system in the U.S., it did see an end to damaging partisan politics. New leadership on both sides of the aisle focused on common ground for Americans—the economy, education, healthcare, racial equality and the environment. There was a new level of responsiveness to issues when they arose where the U.S. government could take decisive and bipartisan action. The respect for government as an institution was one of the most remarkable turn-arounds of the decade.

10. A NEW RESPECT FOR MEDIA AND JOURNALISM: The "sensationalized" news and journalism trend (infotainment) came to an end in the decade where a new level of journalism and media excellence emerged. Mainstream media became a trusted source of news and information, and there was minimal political bias in the reporting. Americans were more informed in the decade through a combination of mainstream media and a more accountable social media. Oh, you could still fire away your opinions, but you were more like the corner speaker at Hyde Park in the UK. Loud and tolerated, but unlikely to sway significant public opinion when the facts were not present.

11. UNIVERSAL HEALTHCARE: After decades of effort we finally moved to a well-designed healthcare system for all Americans that guaranteed basic/affordable healthcare for every American. It was not only a relief to many lower/middle income families but it seemed to spark a stronger interest and commitment to wellness and preventive measures. There was still room for enhanced company health care benefit programs and private insurance, but for many, the basic universal healthcare program provided the care needed for themselves and their families. It removed one of the fundamental divides that Americans had been dealing with for more generations.

12. EXTENDED PUBLIC EDUCATION ACCESS: Another long-simmering debate was addressed in the decade where free public education was extended through the state college level and community college structure. Any student who was willing to work hard could attend a public two-year or four-year program at no cost, to earn their basic degree. In the process of having a higher volume of students (and more consistent volume) the colleges became more aligned with career-ready programs for these students to align specific curriculums with the job requirements of the students. Private colleges and universities never skipped a beat, their market was still strong.

13. COMMON SENSE GUN SAFETY: Led by a bipartisan Congress, an engaged president and supported by the NRA, responsible gun owners and young voices/activists, a common-sense set of gun safety measures were adopted, including universal background checks, a ban on assault weapons and a new level of support to better understand and deal with mental health issues in the country. Mass shootings were reduced significantly and, overall, guns were in the right hands of responsible people. The right to bear arms was better balanced with the right people to have those arms.

14. IMMIGRATION REFORM MOVED FORWARD: Long standing issues on DACA (aka, "dreamers"), pathways to citizenship and immigration policies were resolved. Border security was strong and appropriate, but a new message emerged that America valued the diversity and the commitment of a new wave of immigrants to our country. The welcome mat was out for those who shared our values and wanted to be part of the American Dream. New immigrants were a strong part of the economic growth during the decade.

15. A CHANGING OF THE GUARD: A new wave of young leaders, diverse as America itself, stepped forward in America with new ideas and a new vision for the future. They were welcomed and mentored by existing leaders, and a new level of civic engagement and commitment to service seemed to develop in the country. Millennials and Gen Zers accepted a new mantle of leadership and also helped engage a broader set of Americans in the democratic process.

478

FORESIGHT SESSION 5: *The Future of News, Media and Information* **(conducted September 24, 2020). A set of 12 influences that could impact how we perceive news, media and information by the end of the decade. (Assessment of these influences and our analysis is covered in Chapter 6.)**

No.	Idea
1.	JOURNALISM EXPERIENCES A REBIRTH: The importance of quality journalism to inform our society experiences a rebirth as a profession. More influential schools and universities emphasize journalism as a vital profession and role for the future. Business leaders and their companies advocate and support journalism, and existing media companies provide more funding and support for future journalists.
2.	A NEW WALTER CRONKITE EMERGES: In the 1960s during his time as CBS News anchor, Cronkite was often cited as "the most trusted man in America". During our new decade, a new Cronkite emerges that a majority of Americans believe is informed, accurate, relevant and unbiased. Likely using a combination of traditional media and social media platforms, their voice is an essential part of us staying informed.
3.	YOUR OWN PERSONAL CHANNEL: Technology in the decade ahead comes to our rescue. We are able to customize the information topics, sources, level of detail and essential integrity of the news and information we receive. A daily summary, specific alerts, scenario forecasts, detailed research insights. It's an aggregation of global sources, filtered by interests and guided by artificial intelligence.
4.	GLOBAL PRESS FREEDOM USHERS IN A NEW POLITICAL REALITY: Oppressive leaders and oppressive governments are simply no longer a match for the people and their fundamental right to be informed and for the free press to be supported. New global organizations—think of them as the UN for the press—emerge to protect journalists and their methods. The pen (or keyboard) is truly mightier than the sword.
5.	SOCIAL MEDIA CLEANS UP ITS ACT: The major social media companies take important steps to safeguard the accuracy, security and intent of information on their platforms. New leaders emerge in the companies with stronger values on privacy, misuse of robotics/trolls, unlawful intent and influence. The dark side of social media retreats.

6. MAINSTREAM MEDIA REGAINS TRUST: You simply can't make it in this decade if you can't be trusted. Mainstream media re-prioritizes accuracy, source validation, fair visibility to both sides of an issue, less focus on sensationalism and more focus on balanced reporting. Mainstream media returns to watchdog journalism, getting ahead of issues and helping to shine the light on truth. Breaking news is REALLY breaking news.

7. GENERATION Z COMES TO THE RESCUE: A new generation of information consumers takes hold with Generation Z (those born in 1997 and later). They become known as the "Informed Generation". They tackle critical issues such as climate change, education reform, healthcare access and even global conflict with fact-based and research-based approaches. They are problem solvers but they use information, fact and science along with a refreshing dash of optimism.

8. NEGATIVE POLITICS DISPLACED BY ISSUE-BASED CAMPAIGNING: Politics undergoes a fundamental change. Americans no longer tolerate negative campaigning, dis-information approaches and fear-based communications. You campaign on, and are elected on, your knowledge and position on issues that are important for the future. You are measured on your commitments. You can still be very persuasive on your issues and their impact, but a more informed and discerning electorate will determine whether you are on the right track for the future.

9. INFORMATION FITNESS IS THE NEW TREND: It just matters more in the decade ahead to be informed. Education at all levels refocuses on the importance of informed and engaged students, people actually work out their minds and knowledge at least an hour a day just like they were at the gym, technology provides alert information on a real time basis. Informed Singles—no joke—becomes one of the most successful new online dating sites.

10. NEURALINK ADVANCES THE BRAIN IMPLANT INDUSTRY: Elon Musk was right. The Neuralink concept of a micro implant in the brain to work with neuroscience principles becomes an affordable reality. Imagine programmed chips that transmit information and expertise to your brain in way that enables you to perform tasks you never thought possible.

480

11. THE TRUTH NETWORK: A new digital news/information network emerges as a brand that differentiates itself by being completely objective, non-biased, fact based and respected for its research and journalistic integrity. They deliver on a consistent basis, and have a broad base of viewers/followers who simply value their programming and dial into 'The Truth'. And here you can handle it.

12. A NATIONAL REINVESTMENT IN PUBLIC MEDIA: There is a new recognition that the principles embodied within our public media system (The Corporation for Public Broadcasting that supports PBS and NPR) have long been aligned with fairness, truth in broadcasting and supporting local community engage-ment. New federal funding is added to strengthen the public me-dia role and voice as a trusted source of news and information, and its audience grows substantially.

481

FORESIGHT SESSION 6: *48 Hours—The Whole World is Watching* **(conducted November 5, 2020). A set of 10 influences that could impact the way we perceive politics and elections in the decade ahead. (Assessment of these influences and our analysis is covered in Chapter 7.)**

No.	Idea
1.	ONLINE VOTING FINALLY ARRIVES: While in-person and mail-in voting are still options, we have implemented online voting for all state and national elections. It's simple, secure and it has measurably increased voting turnout. Clear processes are in place (i.e., voting begins 30 days prior to the election and stops on election evening). You are given a clear confirmation that your vote has been received and validated.
2.	CIVICS RETURNS TO THE CLASSROOM: Government and education leaders realized that too many young people were not taught the fundamentals of civics in the classroom nor that the vital role of exercising civic responsibilities matters for everyone. Civics became a required educational component in middle school/high school and it influenced more young people to be engaged in community/government issues, thereby increasing young voter turnout.
3.	SPORTS REALLY LEARNED TO PLAY: The 2020 election showed the power of sports in engaging in social and political issues that mattered to the players and their leagues. Sports became a powerful influencer on issues in America (and globally) and candidates and their parties sought out their support and endorsements. It's what we play for and what we stand for.
4.	A NEW AMERICAN PARTY EMERGES: Frustrated by the lack of bipartisanship and disillusionment with the traditional two-party system, a new party/movement emerged in the decade ahead called the "American Party". It developed a set of values, principles and platform issues that drew in many independents but also attracted forward thinking Democrats and Republicans. It was not a fad, and a New American Agenda emerged and was largely enacted upon as result.

5. YOUNGER LEADERSHIP STEPS FORWARD: While it's OK to have some elder statesmen in the picture, it was clear that we had gone too far. A fresh set of younger leaders stepped forward, many in their late twenties and early thirties, to provide new energy and ideas for America's future. It was like entrepreneurism meets politics. It was disruptive but effective. These young leaders will be influencing the future for an entire new generation.

6. BIPARTISANSHIP COMES BACK IN STYLE: 2020 showed that we had put the needs of Americans at risk while we gridlocked many key issues. The decade ahead showed a slow but steady return to a level of bipartisanship, where crossing the aisle meant you were willing to put American issues above party issues.

7. MEDIA RETURNED TO A ROLE OF INFORMING: Mainstream media and, in many cases, social media recognized that an informed electorate moves America in the right direction. The media understood the danger of mis-information and dis-information to the values and security of the country and doubled down on informing rather than influencing. A level of trust returned to the media.

8. WE STOPPED TALKING ABOUT GENDER/RACE/DIVERSITY: Not that we didn't care and value diversity, it's just that diversity was simply accepted. Leaders were leaders, lives were lives. We turned an important corner in American history in the decade ahead and fully embraced all that a diverse people can provide.

9. SCHOOL'S OUT FOR THE ELECTORAL COLLEGE: It was a spirited debate, but the country left the electoral college behind in the decade ahead and the popular vote was used for presidential elections. It served to increase the perceived value of the individual vote (my vote matters) and helped support strong and consistent voter turnout.

10. AMERICA'S STATURE ON THE GLOBAL STAGE RETURNED: The balance was struck between our important self interests as a country and the importance of American leadership and influence in world issues and events. Not everyone likes us, but we are respected in our leadership role. Our allies (new and old) value this role and a renewed commitment to partnerships.

FORESIGHT SESSION 7: *The Future of Learning and Education* **(conducted December 10, 2020). A set of 12 influences that could impact learning and education in the decade ahead. (Assessment of these influences and our analysis is covered in Chapter 8.)**

No.	Idea
1.	EQUALITY IN EARLY CHILDHOOD EDUCATION: Government, policy-makers and public/private partnerships collaborate to create a new level of access and equality for early childhood education. EVERY young child experiences a supportive and qualified learning environment regardless of who they are and where they live.
2.	AMERICA RE-INVESTS IN ITS PUBLIC EDUCATION INFRASTRUCTURE: The number one infrastructure project for the decade ahead is a massive investment in our K-12 infrastructure. Facilities, classroom space, technology support and learning methods all go through one of the most significant upgrades imaginable. It is a partnership at the Federal/State and Local government level that really works.
3.	WE RE-IMAGINE LEARNING TECHNOLOGY: The great technology companies that have led so many advances in core technology, communications and social media turn their attention to re-imagining learning technology. The components of the 4th Industrial Revolution are harnessed to create a learning revolution. Strap on a set of learning goggles my friends!
4.	TEACHER COMPENSATION ACHIEVES WORKPLACE EQUALITY: Teaching becomes one of the most sought after professions in the decade ahead. In addition to creating compensation equality to other professions, their own professional development is enhanced/supported, their level of administrative support is expanded to enable more time on core teaching and new career pathways are developed to retain them in the profession.
5.	PUBLIC COLLEGE IS FUNDED AS A BASIC RIGHT: The burden of a base two-to-four year public college expense is removed by a nationally funded program. It's not a free-for-all approach, it's a free-for-those-who-need approach and those-who-want-to-work-hard approach.

6. EDUCATION AND INDUSTRY CREATE A NEW ALIGNMENT: New partnerships and alliances are created between industry and education. Curriculums are aligned with the skills and entry level positions that are in demand. There is an unprecedented level of resource exchange between schools and industry.

7. THE WORKPLACE IS THE NEW CENTER OF LEARNING: In the decade ahead, a new level of investment in continual education emerges within companies/organizations. It is recognized that a career is not fueled by politics or seniority, but by continual skills and career shifts that are supported by the organization. It becomes one of the key factors for why a young person will choose a certain company to work for. The education journey is part of the workforce journey.

8. THE VALUE OF VOCATIONAL: The stereotype of a traditional college experience changes in the decade ahead. Technician skills become highly valued as many campuses create partnerships with industry for construction, automotive, mechanical and industrial positions where the compensation, training and benefits help drive the new middle class in America.

9. TRADING DEBT FOR SERVICE: The heavy debt of advanced degrees (law, medicine, technology, education doctorates, etc.) can be off-set by students or the hiring organization via a new Federal program that will waive or significantly reduce degree debt by applying that skill for a specified duration in a service environment. The environment could be military service, government service, foreign service or critical public service roles. It creates a new transition for young people between the education and their industry placement.

10. EARLIER ALIGNMENT TO EDUCATION/CAREER PATHING: Less of a roll of the dice on where to go to school and how you end up in a job/career. A new focus at the high school level upscales traditional counseling with AI, industry expertise and skills assessment to develop and define a combination education and career pathway that greatly increases the likelihood of success for a young person. There is often early funding from industry and state/local government to support the educational pathway.

11. THE UNIVERSITY OF V: That would be the University of Virtual. Accelerated by the COVID pandemic in 2020, virtual access and learning changed the game. Students anywhere can now access education everywhere. It broadened the reach of education and created new equity in education and learning.

12. ADVANCES IN NEURAL PATHWAYS TO ACCELERATE LEARNING: At a very core scientific level we progressed the understanding of how the brain learns and retains information via neural pathways. It led to a better understanding of behavioral learning and methods that significantly improved the capacity to learn.

FORESIGHT SESSION 8: *Arizona as a Leader in the Decade Ahead* (conducted December 17, 2020). A set of 12 influences that could impact Arizona's leadership in the decade ahead. (Assessment of these influences and our analysis is covered in Chapter 9.)

No.	Idea
1.	MULTI-MODAL TRANSPORATION LEADER: Arizona has implemented a regional transportation plan with high speed rail, smart freeway corridors supporting traditional and autonomous vehicles, regional airports and light rail. Considered to be a model for transportation planning in the country.
2.	THE SUN CORRIDOR FOR ADVANCED MANUFACTURING: Arizona has utilized the I-10 corridor between Phoenix and Tucson to implement advanced manufacturing, research and design facilities. A constant skills pipeline is enabled via industry-oriented universities and community colleges. Arizona is on the map for manufacturing and can compete with any region in the country.
3.	THE SILICON DESERT: Arizona has continued to build on strong progress in the prior decade and is now one of the most preferred locations for software technology companies. They are now one of the "big five" along with Silicon Valley in California, the Wasatch Front in Utah, Austin and the Northeast Corridor that covers NYC/Boston. Welcome to AZ Tech and the Silicon Desert. The new West in technology.
4.	GLOBAL TRADE: Arizona is viewed as one of the most progressive global trade partners on the planet. Providing a natural link to Mexico/Latin America to the south and Canada to the north, they have also established the needed business and transportation links to Europe and Asia Pacific. Smart and supportive trade regulations along with a welcoming culture, skilled workforce and educational support.
5.	THE ALTERNATIVE ENERGY ALTERNATIVE: Arizona has led the nation in the movement to solar technology. This is the global hub for research/development as well as advanced deployment. By the end of the decade 50 percent of all energy in Arizona is produced by solar.

6. THE DESTINATION FOR TRAVEL/ENTERTAINMENT/ TOURISM: Arizona is viewed as one of the premier travel destinations not only for U.S. travelers but for global travelers. And it is smart tourism, leveraging open space, recreation, high-end events, business conferences and eco-friendly approaches. Experience Scottsdale has morphed into Experience Arizona.

7. A CASE STUDY IN ENVIRONMENTAL SUSTAINABILITY: We live in a desert. Supported by some of the best educational researchers and public-private partnerships, Arizona has become a model for sustainability with a zero carbon footprint, clean air and water, and has even re-established the Salt River through Maricopa County.

8. A COMPLETE EDUCATION TRANSFORMATION: From worst to first in a decade. Arizona stepped back and re-imagined education from advancement and equity in early childhood education to a new investment in traditional K-12, to new pathways into the workforce that blended college/university options with vocational options. No one in the country has better adult learning engagement. Teacher salaries are the highest in the country, and so are graduation rates and overall educational levels.

9. THE FOREFRONT OF AEROSPACE AND DEFENSE: We have come a long way since the titan missile silo on I-10. Arizona is a national leader anchored by companies such as Raytheon, Northrup Grumman, Honeywell, Boeing, General Dynamics, BAE Systems and MD Helicopter. It is complemented by a continued and valued presence of key military installations. Don't mess with us!

10. THE HEALTHIEST HEALTHCARE SECTOR IN THE COUNTRY: Bioscience and healthcare are thriving industries in Arizona, providing advanced patient treatment and groundbreaking research. Supported by educational partners, Arizona's healthcare segment is making a difference in improving care and outcomes and has developed one of the most collaborative ecosystems in the industry.

11. THE ARIZONA LIFESTYLE ENDURES: At the end of the decade, people still marvel at how Arizona does all that it does, but retains a simple and real lifestyle: the pioneer spirit; the welcoming and inclusive western hospitality; the preservation of open space; a balanced lifestyle that blends purposeful work with active recreation; the "Arizona Blue" sky against mountain backdrops. We prioritized our priorities.

488

12. SMART CITIES AND SMART GOVERNMENT: We value our towns and rural areas and the Western Heritage of Arizona, but our cities have followed Smart City approaches integrating technology, urban planning and incredibly efficient operations. Electronic methods and sensors manage assets, resources and flow. State and local governments have found the right balance to strategic investment and local autonomy. It all works in Arizona.

FORESIGHT SESSION 9: *The American Lifestyle and The American Dream* (conducted January 14, 2021). A set of 12 influences that could impact the American Lifestyle, how we spend our time in the decade ahead, and our pursuit of the American Dream. (Assessment of these influences and our analysis is covered in Chapter 10.)

No.	Idea
1.	AIRLINES CHANGE THEIR GAME: Influenced by the COVID pandemic, but also based on clear/long term feedback themes from travelers, airlines based in the U.S. significantly change the travel experience for the better. Cabins are completely reconfigured with more space for each traveler (25-50 percent fewer seats), enhanced technology/entertainment support, better gate and boarding experience, less "death of a thousand cuts" fees and a genuine commitment to a better passenger experience. A good sense of value for the dollar, it is easy and enjoyable to get to just about any location in the country.
2.	EVERYONE GOES GLOBAL: Global travel emerges as one of the most significant trends for the decade ahead. Better routes/non-stops from major American cities, technology that lets travelers feel connected, great options for planned tours and integrated experiences, and even advanced personal language translation apps that makes it easier to communicate and engage in any country. Part of the concept of travel with a purpose, cultural and global destination travel becomes more frequent for many Americans.
3.	WORKATIONS EXTEND THE JOURNEY: Americans are strongly influenced by remote/virtual work capability, and many book travel destinations that are 1-3 months in duration where the new location becomes a base of operation for vacation/leisure along with work connection. The hotels/resorts and private homes are geared to supporting a work/vacation combination, hotel rooms have guest offices integrated as part of the space or guest offices as part of their facility support. It's not where you are going for your summer vacation, it's where you are going for your summer.
4.	MOVIE THEATERS BECOME EXPERIENTIAL: Americans enjoy their home theaters but still enjoy a night on the town and a great movie. Theaters create partnerships with restaurants, night clubs and ride-share services where the movie is just part of the evening experience. The seating, sounds and service inside the theater are amazing and all agree that it's an experience that cannot be reproduced at home.

490

5. FIRE UP THE WINNEBAGO: Whether by car or travel trailer, extended road trips become a huge trend. No airports, no hassles. Tour a National Park, go along the Pacific Coast Highway, tour the South, check out New England in the Fall, dodge a fish at the Seattle fish market. Wi-Fi keeps you connected, the open road keeps you calm.

6. CONCERTS ARE KING: Of all the live entertainment options people missed most during the pandemic, live music was the one that stirred the soul. You can't reproduce the experience of a concert at home, no matter if it is rock or classical. Live music concerts almost single handedly rescue large venue facilities and remind us all of what a shared experience feels like. Woodstock II anyone?

7. TRAVEL WITH A PURPOSE: Discretionary "impulse travel" takes a back seat to traveling with a purpose. Travel is well thought out, whether to retrace the steps of your ancestors, check off a real bucket-list item, initiate a family reunion or explore a certain region of the country. Often times this travel can be around an annual event, but expanded to enhance the experience. Travel is more aligned with personal values than personal convenience.

8. THE CORPORATE YOUTH SPORTS LEAGUE: To expand youth sports participation, a new national sports league is formed. The league is a consortium of major corporations that all believe in social equality and the importance of sports in influencing young people and their families. There are no registration costs and no uniform fees. There are entry level, developmental and competitive leagues. It's like a new version of the AAU but built around a level playing field. Parents/families are more engaged and it also leads to a healthier lifestyle for young people.

9. SERVICE SABBATICALS: Another development that supports the importance of having a cause as part of your lifestyle is the emergence of service sabbaticals. It's like a paid mission for working professionals where an employee identifies an important issue/cause and then spends a month or so immersed in the cause. It could be in the U.S. or global. Broader, more Americans spend their discretionary time on a service-based mission or cause. Instead of a summer vacation it is a service vacation.

10. STADIUMS ARE DOWNSIZED BUT THE EXPERIENCE IS UP-SIZED: There are very few 100,000 seat venues any more. Major league sports intentionally downsize their venues to retain the big league sense, but offer a more intimate experience. Entertainment, dining and technology are all more integrated into the venue. Better options for family attendance and business events. The big screen innovations are amazing; it's pretty mind-blowing how they can integrate you into the game. You don't have to go to every game, but when you do, it's a FANtastic experience.

11. LIFESTYLE IS LIFE BALANCE: In the decade ahead our lifestyle is a more deliberate design of our desired life balance. Technology gives us options that we simply did not have before for work, school and staying connected. We tend to choose our lifestyle first, then choose our work that supports that lifestyle. Families do more activities together by design and it actually works. The level of geographic independence is unprecedented. You live where you want to live, everything else follows.

12. LIFE SPORTS BECOME THE TREND: Health, fitness and wellness are drivers of the desired lifestyle in the decade ahead. Life sports become the trend, and we work our travel, our family time, our friends, even the geographies in which we live and the housing communities and their amenities around them. Cycling (mountain bikes, road bikes, gravel bikes, e-bikes...) is a big winner; so are golf, hiking, tennis, swimming, stand-up paddling, kayaking and others. The goal is not to blow out a knee in tackle football, but to have a life-long affair with sport.

FORESIGHT SESSION 10: *The Reset of America—The January 20th Inauguration of President Biden* **(conducted January 21, 2021). A set of 12 different themes that could become the dominant influence on the decade ahead. (Assessment of these themes and our analysis is covered in Chapter 11.)**

No.	Idea
1.	THE DECADE OF INCLUSION/EQUALITY: The decade saw a fundamental change in the country for racial equality and genuine inclusion of Americans of all backgrounds. We moved past some long and difficult history to a new era.
2.	THE DECADE OF AI AS THE PROBLEM SOLVER: Technology in all of its best aspects was released to address some of our most challenging issues. Artificial Intelligence (AI), along with the use of advanced analytics, big data, virtual reality and the Internet of Things were combined to help with astonishing advances in healthcare, transportation, energy, security and other fields.
3.	THE DECADE OF HEALTH: Americans raised the bar on their health, fitness and wellness across the board. Better policies on healthcare access, preventive measures, new treatments and medicines, wearable technologies, supportive programs for drug abuse/mental wellness and better patient acceptance of health accountability created a healthier population and future.
4.	THE DECADE OF EDUCATION REFORM: America completely rethought education from early childhood education, traditional K-12 and new pathways for workforce training via vocational, college/university programs and certificate programs where education gaps/inequalities were closed and more Americans could pursue a purposeful future.
5.	THE DECADE OF BIPARTISANSHIP: Stung by the political and social divide that was evident at the start of the decade, a genuine level of bipartisan politics emerged. America became the model for an effective government that really addressed the issues that mattered. You could still have party allegiance and views, but the aisle was a busy crosswalk in the legislative bodies.

6. THE DECADE OF SHARED ECONOMIC GROWTH: It was hard to imagine a stronger sustained level of economic growth for any decade. The middle class re-emerged, large organizations had strong growth and sustained hiring, entrepreneurs flourished, the minimum wage was raised and improved the lifestyle for many. Americans saved more and lived better.

7. THE DECADE OF SCIENCE: Advanced by the unprecedented impact of science to solve the COVID crisis, our investment in science allowed us to better predict and address many issues in the country. Already a strong focus, STEM education and careers became even more popular and attracted young talent. Generation Z, in particular, became a driving force for science in the country.

8. THE CLIMATE DECADE: Not unlike the bold goal of putting a man on the moon at the end of the '60s decade, America and the world put the issue of climate change forward as the global imperative. By the end of the decade the data showed that we had reversed the course of global warming and had the metrics, regulations and technologies in place to sustain that reverse.

9. THE DECADE OF YOUNG LEADERSHIP: This decade marked the hand-off from the Boomer generation for leadership to the Millennial generation. Sure, there were Gen Xers and Gen Zs that stepped up, but it was the millennial generation that had the experience, foresight and passion to take the leadership mantle for the country.

10. THE DECADE OF MOBILITY: Virtual workplaces changed the game for Americans in the decade. More Americans simply chose where they wanted to live and then connected to their workplace from that location. More second homes/locations where Americans migrated for "seasons of choice". Hotels/resorts became "extended stays" where work/vacation could be blended. Mobility and technology support a new American lifestyle. Catch me if you can!

11. THE SPACE DECADE: We should have seen this coming. Private investment in space travel accelerated the exploration of space. An active colony on the moon and on Mars. You could book a space orbit around the earth as easily as you used to book a flight to Europe. Beam me aboard, Scotty!

12. THE DECADE OF AMERICA: America's global standing was completely refreshed and renewed in the decade. America returned to traditional allies but forged new/unexpected relationships as well. There was an unprecedented sharing of knowledge, technology, leadership, resources and democratic principles. Our borders were strong, but our commitment to world issues and global collaboration was stronger. We were once again that "Shining City Upon a Hill".

Author's Note: All told, there are 129 influences across our 10 Foresight topics. They won't all happen. Some will fade away, either entirely or move to a subsequent decade. Some will be replaced by new influences, driven by innovation and scientific breakthrough or, sadly, by social decay, global conflict or unforeseen health impacts.

Considering the decade ahead is a dicey proposition. But if you don't consider the influences and implications, then you are just *winging it* individually, as a family, as a community, a state, a country and a globe. Personally, I'd rather have a map. It can serve as a guide, how things look at a point in time. But in the journey ahead, especially this *exceptionally important* decade ahead, recognize that our map is a model based on real-time variables. There may be some detours ahead. Be an alert driver on this journey ahead to arrive at your destination safely.

APPENDIX 2: *Acknowledgement of our Foresighters*

Initially, they were *participants* in a set of interactive sessions. It did not take long, though, to see that they were more than participants, they were our *Foresighters*. A set of friends, colleagues, friends of friends, even *innocent bystanders* that jumped into a session or two to share their own experiences, emotions and views about the decade ahead. I owe each and every one of them a debt of gratitude for their time and their willingness to be part of the Foresight 2030 project.

There was no payment for their time. This was an all-volunteer set of Foresighters who each had something to say about a set of issues that mattered. Some of our Foresighters were on a single session, others jumped into several of the topics, and I had a few that made the *platinum level* by participating in all 10 sessions. I will say this: I valued every Foresighter, every session and every insight and assessment they had about the decade ahead.

I also valued that they did not agree on many topics. Some were optimistic about a topic or trend, others profoundly pessimistic. But they had ideologies and life experiences to back up these views and that led to the richness of their comments and insights. And to be sure, they will not agree with some of my assessments and conclusions. But, in 2020/2021, to have a civil dialogue and debate about these profound issues for the decade ahead is worth its weight in gold. I suspect that all of our Foresighters would agree on that point.

So, *thank you* to each and every one of you for taking the time to reflect on the future as part of the Foresight project. You are all thought leaders and influencers. I look forward to continuing our discussions in this collective journey to 2030.

Introducing the *Foresighters*: A global set of influencers and thought leaders

#	Name (listed in alpha sequence by first name)	Location
1	Aaron Bare	Phoenix, Arizona
	Allison Powell	Aubrey, Texas
	Amalia Parry	Austin, Texas

	Ari Bruening	Salt Lake City, Utah
	Austin Kennedy	Washington, DC
	Beth Overton	Scottsdale, Arizona
	Betsy Griffen	San Francisco, California
	Bill Heckman	Scottsdale, Arizona
	Brian Elkins	Denver, Colorado
10	Brian Middleton	Mesa, Arizona
	Bruce Griffen	Flagstaff, Arizona
	Candace Thomas	Scottsdale, Arizona
	Carl Lundblad	Prescott, Arizona
	Carol D'Amico	Indianapolis, Indiana
	Carol Gstalder	Toledo, Ohio
	Carol Stevens	Tempe, Arizona
	Charlie Garbowski	Webster, New York
	Christina Tieri	Sturbridge, Massachusetts
	Clay Dethloff	Dallas, Texas
20	Dale Fingerish	Scottsdale, Arizona
	Dan Flynn	Davis, California
	Dana Markow	New York, New York
	Dana Newton	Warrenton, Virginia
	Dave Clayton	McLean, Virginia
	Dave Cooke	Scottsdale, Arizona
	Dave Richardson	Fairfax, Virginia
	David Baltaxe	Arlington, Virginia
	David Calef	Larkspur, California
	Dee Allsop	Fairfax, Virginia

498

30	Deepti Patel	Detroit, Michigan
	Dennis Robbins	Scottsdale, Arizona
	Don Henninger	Scottsdale, Arizona
	Donna Jacobsen	Wheeling, Illinois
	Dorothy Peterson	Chicago, Illinois
	Doug Kline	San Luis Obispo, California
	Eduardo Tessler	Porto Allegre, Brazil
	Erin Norman	Oakton, Virginia
	Francisco Melero	Tucson, Arizona
	Gabi Enriquez	Scottsdale, Arizona
40	Gage Griffen	Tucson, Arizona
	Gayle Fluster	Southlake, Texas
	Geoffrey Dick	New York, New York
	Greg Giczi	South Bend, Indiana
	Haley Rushing	Austin, Texas
	Hasan Dajani	Ossing, New York
	Jack Griffen	Las Vegas, Nevada
	Janet Griffen	Scottsdale, Arizona
	Janet Salm	Seattle, Washington
	Janna Crittendon	Scituate, Massachusetts
50	Jason Edwards	Phoenix, Arizona
	Jenna Kohl	Scottsdale, Arizona
	Jerome Norris	St. Andrews, Scotland
	Jim Granger	Washington, DC
	Jim Hoskins	Reston, Virginia
	Jim Meyers	Chandler, Arizona

	Joan Sinopoli	Newton, Pennsylvania
	John Little	Scottsdale, Arizona
	Jon DeWitt	Middletown, Maryland
	Jona Davis	Scottsdale, Arizona
60	Josh Kurzman	San Francisco, California
	Julie Paasche	Austin, Texas
	Juliemar Rosado	Winter Park, Florida
	Karin Patterson	Detroit Michigan
	Ken Lethbridge	Rochester, New York
	Lani Lott	Phoenix, Arizona
	Larry Chandler	Glenview, Illinois
	Laura Tanzer	Tucson, Arizona
	Lauren Brown	Tempe, Arizona
	Lee Ann Witt	Scottsdale, Arizona
70	Lesli Griffen	Cornville, Arizona
	Linda Sanpei	San Luis Obispo, California
	Marie Case	Austin, Texas
	Marilyn Gottsch	Clermont, Florida
	Mark Arney	Orlando, Florida
	Mark Aspey	Flagstaff, Arizona
	Mark Smither	Sioux Falls, South Dakota
	Mark Stanton	Scottsdale, Arizona
	Mark Wirthlin	Sandy, Utah
	Martina Wagner	Oakland, California
80	Mary Granger	Barcelona, Spain
	Matt Lerhman	Scottsdale, Arizona

500

	Maury Giles	Herriman, Utah
	Megan McKenna	Winter Springs, Florida
	Mike Hillegass	Washington, DC
	Mike Ryan	Fountain Hills, Arizona
	Mike Simons	Tucson, Arizona
	Monty Becton	Scottsdale, Arizona
	Nate Currey	Toronto, Canada
	Olivier Viel	Washington, DC
90	Pat Kidd	Lumberton, New Jersey
	Paula Stratton	Portland, Oregon
	Pete Griffen	Sandy, Utah
	Rachel Pearson	Scottsdale, Arizona
	Rachel Schumm	San Luis Obispo, California
	Rebekah Dossett	Winter Springs, Florida
	Rhonda Blatti	Chanhassen, Minnesota
	Richard Getzen	Scottsdale, Arizona
	Richard Tollefson	Phoenix, Arizona
	Robin Shaeffer	Tempe, Arizona
100	Robyn Letters	San Luis Obispo, California
	Rod Lenniger	Scottsdale, Arizona
	Roz Boxer	Tucson, Arizona
	Ryan Freeburg	Scottsdale, Arizona
	Sam Griffen	Scottsdale, Arizona
	Sammy Papert	Arroyo Grande, California
	Scott Griffen	Vienna, Austria
	Shireen Olsen	Queen Creek, Arizona

	Stephane Vidry	Washington, DC
	Stephanie Barlow	Orlando, Florida
110	Steve Helm	Scottsdale, Arizona
	Steve Peters	Tucson, Arizona
	Steve Zylstra	Phoenix, Arizona
	Susan Baier	Chandler, Arizona
	Taylor Reak	Washington, DC
	Terry Williams	Keene, New Hampshire
	Todd Peterson	Scottsdale, Arizona
	Tom Granger	Redmond, Washington
	Tom Knapp	Tucson, Arizona
	Tom Nagle	Gaithersburg, Maryland
120	Vic Method	Park City, Utah
121	Virginia Korte	Scottsdale, Arizona

ABOUT THE AUTHORS

Douglas S. Griffen is a third-generation native Arizonan and attended Phoenix Central High School. He earned an undergraduate degree in 1977 in Business at Northern Arizona University in Flagstaff, Arizona, with a dual major in Marketing and Management, and a teaching minor in Spanish (hence the Spanish language references in the book). He was recruited by, and joined, the IBM Corporation upon graduation and spent 19 years at IBM in a variety of assignments.

In 1996 Griffen left IBM to form his own consulting company (DS Griffen & Associates) and then launched the Advanced Strategy Center in Scottsdale in 2000 to focus specifically on facilitation and collaborative software. He has facilitated *somewhere in the range of* 10,000 group sessions on strategic planning, culture, purpose, leadership and brand with CEO audiences, employee groups, industry thought leaders and direct consumers. He has conducted in-person sessions in just about every state in the U.S. along with global sessions in nearly 20 countries.

Over the past 10 years he has focused on the facilitation of *online sessions* with groups of 25-100 participants that would respond simultaneously to real-time questions and assessments using the *Advanced Strategy Lab* technique.

Griffen is married (40+ years) and has four children (ages 27 through 33). At age 65 himself at the time of the Fall 2021 first edition of Foresight 2030, he shows little sign of slowing down and vows to hit 2030 in full stride from both a work and sports standpoint. He is also launching a new collaboration platform called *Converge* in 2022 (startconverge.com) to take real-time session engagement to the next level. Griffen can be reached at the Center at dgriffen@advancedstrategycenter.com.

Maury Giles was our co-author on Chapter 12 and provided the support for our quantitative "Pulse" survey used in the chapter and contributed to our Foresight sessions. Maury is the Chief Growth Officer at Heart+Mind Strategies and has been involved in conducting market and social research and consulting for more than 25 years. He is a skilled facilitator with specific expertise in human decision journey mapping, messaging and communication strategy. He has been a catalyst and collaborator in multiple organizations including Media News Group, Wirthlin Worldwide, GSD&M and Ipsos. Maury founded Ipsos' global consultancy, Strategy3. He is a graduate of New Mexico State University and currently lives in Herriman, Utah. Maury is married and has a blended family with 10 children and three grandchildren. Mr. Giles can be contacted at mgiles@heartandmindstrategies.com.

Made in the USA
Monee, IL
04 July 2023

38405361R00282